ORGANIZATIONAL BEHAVIOR FOR THE HOSPITALITY INDUSTRY

Florence Berger

Professor Emeritus

Cornell University School of Hotel Administration

Judi Brownell

Professor

Cornell University School of Hotel Administration

PEARSON

Prentice Hall

Upper Saddle River, New Jersey 07458

Library of Congress Cataloging-in-Publication Data

Berger, Florence
  Organizational behavior for the hospitality industry / Florence Berger,
Judi Brownell.—1st ed.
    p.   cm.
  Includes bibliographical references and index.
  ISBN-13: 978-0-13-244737-9 (alk. paper)
  ISBN-10: 0-13-244737-1 (alk. paper)
  1. Hospitality industry—Management.   2. Organizational behavior.   I. Brownell, Judi, 1949–
II. Title.
  TX911.3.M27B475 2009
  647.94068—dc22

                                                                2008011360

Vice President and Executive Publisher: Vernon R. Anthony
Executive Editor: William Lawrensen
Editorial Assistant: Lara Dimmick
Production Manager: Wanda Rockwell
Art Director: Jayne Conte
Cover Designer: Bruce Kenselaar
Cover Image: Getty Images, Inc.
Director of Marketing: David Gesell
Senior Marketing Manager: Leigh Ann Sims
Marketing Assistant: Les Roberts
Manager, Visual Research: Beth Brenzel
Manager, Cover Visual Research & Permissions: Karen Sanatar
Image Permission Coordinator: Nancy Seise
Photo Researcher: Richard Rodrigues

This book was set in 10/12, Times by Integra Software Services. It was printed and bound by Courier Companies.
The cover was printed by Phoenix Color Corp.

Pearson Education Ltd.
Pearson Education Singapore Pte. Ltd.
Pearson Education Canada, Ltd.
Pearson Education—Japan

Pearson Education Australia Pty. Limited
Pearson Education North Asia Ltd.
Pearson Educación de Mexico, S.A. de C.V.
Pearson Education Malaysia Pte. Ltd.

10 9 8 7 6 5 4 3 2 1
ISBN 13: 978-0-13-244737-9
ISBN 10:   0-13-244737-1

To our husbands, Toby and Gary

CONTENTS

PREFACE

Organizational Behavior for the Hospitality Industry is designed specifically for those interested in launching or advancing their careers in hospitality management. Success in this arena requires not only traditional knowledge of how organizations work but also a strong skill set to effectively address the range of people-related challenges that arise daily in hospitality organizations.

Our goal is to provide a complete package: current theory, Power Point presentations for faculty use and exercises intended to make the theory come alive. The exercises are designed to be embodiments of the following celebrated dictum of Confucius:

I hear and I forget,
I see and I remember,
I do and I understand

This book is designed for use by colleges and universities with hospitality programs. The text is organized into three sections:

- Organizational Behavior Essentials—which covers customer care, communicating in organizations, customer service, understanding the diverse workforce, and the power of teams in hospitality.
- The Individual and the Organization—which covers managing time and stress, promoting creativity, and setting goals.
- Key Management Tasks—which covers managing conflict, motivating employees, counseling employees, understanding power and politics in organizations, and leading hospitality organizations.

The detailed exercises that accompany each of these topics help provide students with hands-on experience that is necessary for success in this industry.

Organizational Behavior for the Hospitality Industry can be adapted to meet both the educator's instructional preferences and the participants' backgrounds and needs. This tailored text therefore serves as a valuable resource for four distinct learner groups—undergraduates at the freshman/sophomore or community college level, upper level undergraduates, graduate students, and practicing hospitality managers.

When using the text in a course designed for first-year and second-year undergraduates, who have little hands-on industry experience, the instructor may elect to focus on the rich array of experiential exercises provided at the end of each chapter. Students may benefit most from chapters that facilitate their self-awareness and enable them to identify personal strengths and set developmental goals that will prepare them for work in today's dynamic hospitality industry. Such topics include managing time and setting personal and professional goals. The skills required in working as a team participant are also valuable to first and second-year students who will likely be called upon to work in groups in both academia and the hospitality industry. The chapters on understanding teams and making decisions in organizations present these materials.

Upper level undergraduates will find the theoretical principles in each chapter to have value that continues to last after they have entered the hospitality workforce. These students may soon be moving to positions which require that they not only assess their own behavior but also coach and counsel other service employees. This requires consistent and informed application of the theory provided in each chapter. Discussion of the examples and real hospitality cases provided in the body of the text ensure that underlying principles are understood and that students will become equipped for addressing and resolving the many organizational behavior challenges they are soon to confront in the workplace.

At the graduate level, students are likely to have work experience and will appreciate opportunities to share their ideas with classmates as they focus on chapters that help them accomplish key management tasks. This group will benefit from the principles that will enhance their success in the workplace—managing conflict, motivating and counseling employees, and leading hospitality organizations. These adult learners are likely to have an experiential base that allows them to put course content into a real-world perspective. Their insights, stories, and frustrations gathered from experience can become a valuable component of the learning process. Such background also allows them to recognize how knowledge of the contents of this book will help them better analyze workplace situations and increase their flexibility as they bring organizational behavior theory to bear on management situations.

The text also is a valuable resource for those facilitating programs with practicing hospitality managers. Experienced adults may be most engaged by starting each topic with an activity that illustrates a problem to be resolved or a skill to be mastered. Experimenting with a range of behaviors and discussing theory as it applies to these illustrative situations can enhance one's ability to address real-world challenges. Facilitators may need to select a limited number of topics to cover because of the desirability of deeper discussions and a student-centered approach. A single chapter may serve as the basis of a one-topic seminar, such as communicating in organizations, promoting creativity, or motivating employees, or several chapters may be combined into broader hospitality management themes.

The following chart shows where material appropriate to the aforementioned four learner groups may be found. The authors have developed this chart in conjunction with their teaching organizational behavior to students in the Cornell University School of Hotel Administration and in hospitality industry seminars worldwide. Nonetheless, the chart is only advisory in nature. Every instructor has a unique set of preferences and goals.

Adapting Organizational Behavior in the Hospitality Industry to Instructor Preferences and Participant Needs

TOPICS	Fresh/Sophomore		Junior/Senior		Graduate		Industry	
	Theory	Application	Theory	Application	Theory	Application	Theory	Application
Ch 1	X	X	X	X	X	X	X	X
Ch 2	X	X	X	X	X	X	X	X
Ch 3	X	X	X	X	X	X	X	X
Ch 4	X	X	X	X	X	X	X	X
Ch 5		X	X	X	X		X	
Ch 6		X		X	X		X	X
Ch 7		X		X	X	X	X	
Ch 8					X	X	X	X
Ch 9		X	X	X	X	X	X	
Ch 10					X		X	X
Ch 11			X	X	X		X	
Ch 12			X	X	X	X	X	
Ch 13			X	X	X	X	X	
Ch 14			X	X	X	X	X	X

FB and JB,
March 2008

ACKNOWLEDGMENTS

We want to thank our colleagues who shared valuable ideas and insights regarding organizational behavior: Ed Merritt, associate professor at Cal State University, Pomona; Hannah Messerli, clinical associate professor at NYU Center for Hospitality and Tourism; Joe Perdue, professor at UNLV; Peter Rainsford, Vice President for Academic Affairs, Culinary Institute of America; Dennis Reynolds, professor at Washington State University; Tony Simons and Kate Walsh, faculty at Cornell University School of Hotel Administration; Masako Taylor, University of Tsukuba, Japan; Carl Winston, Director of School of Hospitality and Tourism Management, San Diego State University; and Robert H. Woods, professor at UNLV.

Our industry-leader friends provided practical insights regarding organizational behavior in the hospitality industry. Ken Blanchard, Chief Spiritual Officer, The Ken Blanchard Companies (San Diego, CA) who is always at least one step ahead regarding leadership and OB; Richard Born and Ira Drukier, owners of BD Construction (New York City); Stan Bromley, previously of the Four Seasons, currently in private consulting (San Francisco, CA); Michael Bonadies, Co-owner, President and CEO, 21c Museum Hotels; Robert Cima, Regional Vice President for the Four Seasons (Carlsbad, CA); Stephen Brandman, Co-owner and COO, Thompson Hotels (New York City); Shari Claymann-Kerr, Director of Human Resources, Le Parker Meridien (New York City); David Colella, Vice President and Managing Director, The Colonnade Hotel (Boston); Michael Chiu, President and owner of Prima Donna Development Corporation (Los Altos, CA); Bill Eberhardt, President of Dining Associates (Skaneateles, NY); Steve Eckler, Lever House GM and Red-Cat co-operator (New York City); Ed Evans, Executive Vice President of Human Resources and Organizational Development, Allied Waste Industries, Inc. (Phoenix, AZ); Valerie Ferguson, Regional Vice President and Managing Director, Loews' Hotels (Philadelphia, PA); Ajay Ghei, Senior Management Consultant, The World Bank Group; Mark Giangiulio, GM of The Grand Summit Hotel (Summit, NJ); Thomas Gurtner, Regional Vice President and GM of Four Seasons (Westlake Village, CA); Erika Gwilt, Vice President of Training Development, Kohl's Department Stores (Menomonee Falls, WI); Jenny Herman, Training Director of Loew's Hotels (New York City); Mitchell Heymann, Director of Marketing Strategy for Marriott Hotels (New York City); Judith Kalfon, GM of Radisson Plaza Hotel (Minneapolis, MN); Arthur Keith, Senior Vice President and GM of Gaylord Opryland Resort & Convention Center (Nashville, TN); Phil Kiester, GM of Farmington Country Club (Charlottesville, VA); Toni Knorr, GM of the W (San Francisco, CA); John Longstreet, Senior Vice President of Human Resources, ClubCorp Inc. (Dallas, TX); Alan Momeyer, Vice President of Human Resources, Loews' Hotels (New York City); Chiaki Tanuma, President and CEO of Green House Co., Ltd (Tokyo, Japan); Phillip Truelove, GM of Hotel (THE MERCER) (New York City); Brian Young, Vice President, Rosewood Hotels (Dallas, TX).

We would also like to thank our superb editors, Cate Dodson, Bill Lawrensen, and Wanda Rockwell, who were generous with their time and their efforts on our behalf. We are also grateful to our copyeditors, Shiny Rajesh and Daniel Trudden, for their efficiency and thoroughness. Prentice Hall, our publisher, is the best.

We were fortunate to have intelligent, creative, and resourceful research assistants who had access to the libraries at Cornell University and at the University of Virginia. They are: Rachael Alberico, Mia Brennan, Cheryl Ciszek, Jessika Dollins, Jennifer Drukier, Holly Donahue, Amy Greenhouse, Ned Groves, C. Walker Holmes, Melissa Moschella,

Kate Naunheim, Justin Newman, Bethany Thomas, and Nicole Thompson. Mihoko Hosoi, reference librarian at the Nestle Library at the Cornell School of Hotel Administration, repeatedly tracked down elusive data and journal articles for us. Moreover, we want to acknowledge the excellent work of our administrative assistants Rebecca Daniel, Jennifer Macera, Marion Stallings and Agnes Tagliavento. Rebecca's attention to detail and excellent proofreading were particularly appreciated, and Marion's library searching, book and journal acquisitions, scanning, copying, and mailing were most valuable.

Finally, we would like to thank the reviewers who provided insightful comments. They are:

Paul R. Timm—Brigham Young University

Dennis Reynolds—Washington State University

Bonnie Canziani—University of North Carolina–Greensboro

Kenneth P. Morlino—Nashville State Community College

Ona Ashley—Johnson County Community College

John Courtney—Johnson County Community College

Michael Owen—Lewis Clark State College

Ed Evans—Executive Vice President, Human Resources and Organizational Development, Allied Waste Industries, Inc.

ABOUT THE AUTHORS

Florence Berger, Ph.D.
Professor Emeritus, Cornell University School of Hotel Administration

Dr. Florence Berger is a professor in the Cornell University School of Hotel Administration, where she has taught courses in human resources management, human relations skills, hospitality industry training, creative management, and organizational behavior. She has a master's degree from Harvard University and a Ph.D. from Cornell University. She was a research associate at Harvard University and the Massachusetts Institute of Technology, and was Assistant Dean and Associate Dean of Students at Cornell University.

Professor Berger is a management consultant in the areas of human resources, training, and organizational behavior; her clients include Marriott, Four Seasons Hotels, Hilton International, Loews' Hotels, ARAMARK, Club Med, Le Parker Meridien, and Bronx-Lebanon Hospital. She has lectured in the United States, Europe, the Middle East, Asia, and Australia on team building, creative management, human relations skills, creativity, and organizational change. Professor Berger has taught in a number of Hotel School Executive Education Programs, and has been faculty coordinator for the Club Managers Association of America (CMAA) Business Management Institutes 4 and 5 on-campus programs. Professor Berger has authored many articles in *Lodging Hospitality*, *International Journal of Hospitality Management*, *Cornell Hotel and Restaurant Administration Quarterly*, *Briefings*, and *Hospitality Research Journal*. She has also written two management books for the hospitality industry: *INNovation: Creativity Techniques for Hospitality Managers* (with Dennis Ferguson), and *The On-Track Trainer: A Training Handbook for Hospitality Managers* (with Bonnie Farber). She developed, with Ed Merritt, the CMAA On-Line Team Building Course.

Dr. Berger was selected The Teacher of the Year for 1996 and 1998 by the freshman and sophomore classes of the Hotel School. In 1999 Dr. Berger received Cornell University's premier teaching award, the Stephen H. Weiss Presidential Fellow Award for Distinguished Teaching. After becoming professor emeritus on July 1, 2004, Professor Berger has focused on executive education and the development of eCornell online courses for hospitality managers.

Judi Brownell
Professor, Cornell University School of Hotel Administration

Judi Brownell is a professor of organizational communication and Dean of Students at the School of Hotel Administration, Cornell University. She has also served as the Associate Dean for Academic Affairs and as the Richard J. and Monene P. Bradley Director for Graduate Studies at the Hotel School. Professor Brownell teaches graduate and undergraduate courses in organizational behavior, human resources, and management communication and has been the Academic Area Director for these fields. She participates regularly in the School's executive education program and has designed and conducted training seminars for a wide range of hospitality and other work organizations. Professor Brownell has international teaching experience and her online eCornell executive courses, co-authored with Professor Florence Berger, are used worldwide.

Her current research projects include studies related to identifying key competencies for global hospitality leaders, the communication of service quality, and the career challenges women hospitality managers confront. Professor Brownell has identified six components of managerial listening behavior and has completed a comprehensive survey exploring the specific communication practices of middle- and upper-level hospitality managers. Her current research also focuses on listening as it relates to communicating and maintaining service quality standards in the highly international cruise industry. Dr. Brownell is author of several textbooks and has published over eighty articles in professional journals. She is a past president of the International Listening Association, and has been inducted into the International Listening Association's Hall of Fame.

INTRODUCTION

Hospitality managers confront unique challenges. Focused on providing customer care, and equally interested in serving their staff, they must lead with clarity of purpose and an eye on the bottom line. How does one lead to serve? What are the tools of managing? When the product you must market is so person-oriented and seemingly intangible, how do you make noticeable or measurable improvements? The human interactions that can make or break a hospitality organization must be understood in all their variety and carefully managed by competent staff and executives schooled in business, leadership, service, and human behavior. These areas of expertise can be grouped into the following categories:

- Customer care
- Communicating in organizations
- Understanding the diverse workforce
- Harnessing the power of teams in hospitality
- Group problem solving and decision making
- Managing time
- Managing stress
- Promoting creativity
- Setting personal and professional goals
- Managing conflict
- Motivating employees
- Counseling employees
- Understanding power and politics in organizations
- Leading hospitality organizations

This book provides the knowledge, skills, and attitudes that hospitality managers can use to enhance employee productivity and guest satisfaction.

1

CUSTOMER CARE

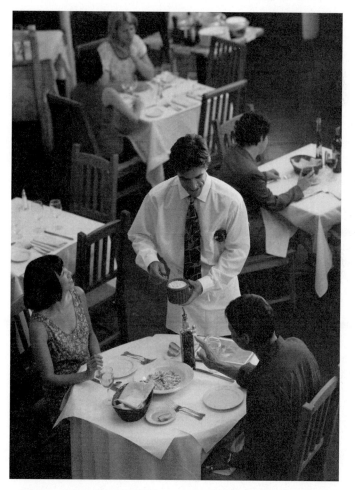

When you have a true passion for excellence, and when you act on it, you will stand straighter. You will look people in the eye. You will see things happen. You will see heroes created, watch ideas unfold and take shape.

—Tom Peters

CHAPTER OUTLINE

Introduction

Service Defined
   Components of Service
   Define Your Target Customer
   The Unique Nature of Service

Creating and Managing Service
   Importance of Quality Service
   Assessing Service Quality

Two Perspectives on Service
   The Customer's Perspective
   The Service Provider's Perspective

Service Recovery
   Effectiveness of Recovery Strategies
   Consequences of Service Failure
   Role of the Service Employee in the Recovery Process

Select and Train for Service Excellence
   Selecting Service Employees
   Training and Developing Service Employees

Internal Service
   Emotional Labor and Contact Overload Syndrome
      Emotional labor
      Contact overload syndrome
   Integration of Successful Internal Service
   Costs and Benefits of Internal Service
   Internal Service Initiatives

Creating a Service Culture

Technology and Customer Service
   Prevalence of Technology in Hospitality Organizations
   Customer Feedback Through Technology
   The Challenges of Technology in the Hospitality Workplace
   Customer Service and the Telephone

Summary

LEARNING OBJECTIVES

After reading this chapter, you will be able to do the following:

1. Discuss the three components of service.
2. Describe four differences between a service and a product.
3. Explain how managers assess the quality of their service.
4. Identify, from a consumer's perspective, why service is important.
5. Discuss the theory of service within.

6. Describe how to implement internal service within a hospitality organization.
7. Define emotional labor and contact overload syndrome.
8. Understand how to create and maintain a service-oriented culture.

Scenarios: How Do You Care for Your Customers?

Incident 1: When you made your hotel reservations, you asked for connecting rooms so that you could keep a close eye on your two children, ages 7 and 11. You arrive at the hotel and find there are no connecting rooms available. The front desk associate reminds you, "Oh, well, that was only a request. We try our best to accommodate requests but unfortunately that is not always possible. Ok, where were we? Oh, yeah . . . I'll just need to make an imprint of your credit card."

Incident 2: As you wait to pay for your purchases at the hotel's cafe, you observe the cashier talking loudly on the telephone. "And, like, I told him that I wasn't going to take that from him anymore. You know? It's been a, like, awful. Ok, whatever. I gotta go. There's someone here that needs help." The cashier flips the phone closed as she yells "NEXT!" You look over your shoulder to find no one else in line. Apparently she's talking to *you*.

INTRODUCTION

Do the above scenarios sound familiar? Whether it was a case of inadvertent rudeness or blatant incompetence, you can probably recall at least one poor service experience in the past week that left a bitter taste in your mouth. Perhaps it was severe enough for you to reconsider whether or not you will ever visit the offending business again. Isn't it fortunate that *your* guests or customers never have to tolerate such poor service experiences?

Regardless of how long they have been working in the industry, all service providers benefit from continuous improvement and retraining. Just as a star athlete's performance will quickly decline without regular practice, so will the service habits of employees who fail to fine-tune their performance.

Service is the foundation of many competitive companies. In the twenty-first century, customers have become more savvy and demanding and, as a result of globalization, they have more alternatives from which to choose. More consumers travel around the world, have a good handle on what various hotels and restaurants offer, and are demanding quality services and goods wherever they go. Hospitality organizations need to have policies, processes, and procedures that will serve these discriminating travelers well. They must rely on intangibles, such as the quality of service, to establish and sustain a competitive advantage.

Quality service does not just happen by chance. It is not the result of an extraordinary employee who goes out of the way to please a particular customer. Quality service needs to be planned and managed, from the design of the service delivery system to maintaining efficient operations that ensure quality is both high and consistent. The goal of a service organization is to attract and retain a loyal customer base. To achieve this goal, hospitality organizations must deliver a level of quality that not only satisfies customers but exceeds their expectations.

In this chapter we begin by exploring the big picture of what services are and their impact on the economy. Next, we discuss the importance of improving quality in the design of services. We then explore both consumers' and service providers' perceptions of service, which draws our attention to the effectiveness of the service staff and internal services. Finally, we present various strategies which can help you manage and implement an effective internal service program.

SERVICE DEFINED

Services can be defined as economic activities that produce time, place, form, or psychological utilities. A stay at a hotel provides a comfortable experience away from home. Department stores and grocery stores provide many commodities for sale in one convenient place. A database service puts information together in a form more usable for managers. A "night out" at a restaurant provides psychological refreshment in the middle of a busy workweek.

Components of Service

A service can be broken down into three components: technical, functional, and image. The technical aspect of service is tangible; it includes the organization's facilities. The lobby, guest rooms, and restaurant in a hotel would all fall under the technical component of service. The functional aspect of service is intangible; it includes the speed at which an employee attends to guest inquiries, the degree to which an employee is willing to help a customer, and the manner in which an employee speaks to a guest. Finally, the image aspect of service includes a company's reputation. An organization's reputation is built through advertising, price, performance and customer expectations, perceptions, and experiences.

The quality of a service is dependent on these three components. Together they should provide customers with a value-added service that exceeds expectations. The underlying assumption is that by delivering quality that satisfies customers, organizations can attract, retain, and grow a solid customer base. Customer satisfaction can help protect the existing customer base against competitors. It can also be a powerful tool for customer acquisition. When customers are satisfied with an organization's delivery of service, not only will they remain loyal, but they will also help to attract new customers through positive word of mouth.

> Describe in detail an organization with regard to the three components of service. How did each affect you as a guest?

Define Your Target Customer

Increasing market segmentation as well as globalization has drawn attention to the need for understanding your customer well. Before you can provide quality service, you must know exactly what is important to your guests. While the business traveler may value efficiency at check-in and ready access to exercise equipment, the young family on vacation will undoubtedly want attention to their special needs and a staff that is willing to spend a little extra time interacting with the children. When companies have a highly international customer base, it is even more important that employees understand their specific requirements and how to meet their expectations with regard to customer service.

It is the guest profile that determines how the organization's culture is best shaped and what employee behaviors will be reinforced and rewarded. Defining target customers is not a task for individual employees. Rather, each company requires a shared organizational understanding of those behaviors and activities most likely to impact guest satisfaction. A common vision can then be created that will guide the details of service delivery.

> Name two service organizations that attract very different markets. What are some of the features that vary significantly from one organization to the other?

The Unique Nature of Service

Managing the delivery of high quality service is different from managing the manufacturing of a product. For example, managing a guest's stay in a hotel is clearly different from managing the assembly of a computer. To manage service effectively, one must first understand the unique characteristics of a service and how it differs from a product.

The major difference between a service and a product is that a service is **intangible,** while a product is tangible. The outcome of a service is intangible because it cannot be seen, felt, touched, smelled, or heard before it is purchased by a consumer. In contrast, a consumer can see and test a product before purchase. Since a service is intangible, it needs no shelf space, has no shelf life, and cannot be easily inventoried. Another key difference between a service and a product is that a service does not exist until after it is purchased by the consumer; the production and consumption of the service occur simultaneously. A product, on the other hand, is produced first, then purchased and consumed by the customer.

Services have become an integral part of the new global economy. In many countries, the consumption of services generates more capital than the production and sale of products. New markets in Asia, in particular, have created an increasing demand for U.S. hospitality organizations to better understand the needs of new target markets. Tourism continues to grow in all parts of the world, and sophisticated, world-travelers are demanding services in increasing numbers.

Customer service delivery can have a significant impact on the success of an organization. Companies that deliver a consistently high level of customer service can both charge more for their services and see the impact of service in the expansion of their market share. Providing quality service to consumers should be a primary goal for managers. They should maintain efficient operations and ensure that employees are consistently providing quality service.

While most people are aware of the importance of services in the economy, few seem to realize the scale of that dominance. It is essential that the service sector be properly managed. In the following section, we will discuss how managers should create and manage distinctive services.

CREATING AND MANAGING SERVICE

Importance of Quality Service

A manager should strive to satisfy all of the customer's needs. Satisfied customers not only continue to conduct business with the company, but they also tell their friends and colleagues about their positive experiences. Dissatisfied and disgruntled customers take their business elsewhere and also tell others about their negative experiences.

While companies cannot sacrifice their financial health to the demands of customer service, they must take a long-term view of this dynamic. Over a ten-year period, how much revenue would the company lose if that one customer started doing business with a competitor? Over the same ten years, what might the financial impact of either positive or negative word of mouth be on the company? On average, it costs businesses five to six times more money to attract new customers than to retain current customers.

With global competition and increasing geographical dispersion of company operations, providing service that exceeds consumers' expectations is one of the most important tasks for a service-oriented organization. In order to do this, several factors that managers should remember are as follows:

1. Excellent service is the key to global success in the service industry.
2. Service is the outcome of three factors (the technical aspect, the functional aspect, and the image aspect).
3. Customers judge the quality of a service based on a comparison of their expectations *before* the service and their perceptions *after* the service.
4. Employees can affect the service encounter through personality, displayed emotions, and communication.

Assessing Service Quality

As the global market becomes more competitive and the tastes of consumers become more sophisticated and demanding, organizations have greater incentives to focus on managing and improving the quality of customer service. However, a manager cannot improve the quality of a service until that quality has accurately been measured. Managers often have a difficult time assessing the quality of the services they provide. Measuring service quality requires that managers observe the process as it unfolds and evaluate outcomes against the consumer's expectations. By comparison, quality control of a product is simpler; it entails weighing, measuring, and comparing the finished good against the industry standard. For a service, the manager can only base his or her assessment of quality on the customer's level of satisfaction. What makes this difficult is that customers are likely to have different perceptions. The customer's prior expectations of the service experience are integral to his or her satisfaction with the outcome. Thus, a portion of service quality is subjective.

Service firms use a different set of criteria than manufacturing firms to measure the effectiveness of service generated within the organization. Technology is creating a radical new business model that alters the dynamic of customer service. For the first time, companies can measure exactly what services cost at an individual level and assess the return on each dollar. They now know exactly how much business one person generates, what a particular customer is likely to buy, and how much it costs to answer the phone. Advances in technology are also allowing organizations to monitor the effectiveness of particular means of delivering customer service, whether by phone, email, online chat, or in-person interaction.

As a customer or guest, how do you assess service quality? What are some of the factors that make the most difference to you when you stay at a hotel or dine at a restaurant? Do you think you are typical of the market each organization is targeting?

TWO PERSPECTIVES ON SERVICE

To improve service quality, managers must view the service encounter from two different perspectives: the consumer's and the service provider's. Managers in service-oriented organizations need to explore the differences between these two perspectives and identify how to better integrate the customer experience into the design of services. Once a manager takes the time to recognize and understand the consumer's perspective, he or she will be better able to improve the service.

The Customer's Perspective

We went to dinner at a restaurant in New York City with friends from New Jersey. One of our friends was suffering from cancer. We were seated next to a table where everyone was smoking. Our friend was coughing from the smoke. When I complained to the manager, his response was, "We let our 'good' customers smoke. I cannot move your table–we are very busy." The four of us had a very uncomfortable dinner.

Understanding how consumers decide, purchase, and evaluate hospitality services is important for the improvement of service delivery. The consumer may be concerned with satisfying basic physiological needs, such as hunger and thirst. In most cases, these are accompanied by more complex psychological needs, such as identity, status, and security. Psychological needs may be determined by expectations derived from the consumer's lifestyle and prior experience.

It is important to understand the consumer's perceptions and expectations because the service rendered is ultimately only as good as the customer perceives it to be. Customer needs can be very specific or very vague. Customer perceptions of service quality often result from comparing expectations prior to receiving the service to the actual experience. Keep in mind that assessments of quality are derived from the service process as well as the service outcome.

Customers most often require an immediate response from the service provider. If they are not satisfied, complaint behavior may be triggered. The consistency and quality of service delivery is important because the customer has little or no control over the environment in which consumption takes place.

Hospitality service interactions are typically short and extremely variable in nature. Every guest has a slightly different expectation of staff during service delivery. If these expectations are not met, the individual is likely to feel dissatisfied. The delivery of service—and the customer's satisfaction with that service—is more difficult to evaluate over a long period of time since it is based on the accumulation of many service data points. The evaluative procedure must account for this complexity and provide an overall measure of satisfaction.

Understanding the customer proves essential for organizations that strive to deliver quality service. Evaluating the delivery of service from the customer's perspective is necessary for the successful management of customer relationships. For many customers, good relationships are the most important part of a service experience. Consequently, managers need to learn about their customers and pay attention to all details of their experience. In an increasingly technological age, this might include the speed at which customers navigate the organization's website or the average number of rings it takes for an employee to answer telephone service calls. When it comes to customer service, little things often mean everything.

Would you say that you have a "relationship" with a service organization? What would that mean to you?

The Service Provider's Perspective

Our first priority is to accommodate our regular customers. The folks at that table have been our guests every week for 20 years. They enjoyed smoking after their dinner long before the no smoking rules went into effect, and managers above me have decreed that they will be permitted to continue to do so. Their table is near an open window to provide ventilation and I don't see how the other table would have been bothered by it. I would have been happy to move the out-of-town group to another table, but there really were no other tables. It was Saturday night when we are always fully booked. I know the old adage, "The customer is always right," but what do you do when customers have opposing needs?

As hospitality services are consumed at the point of production, the customer becomes personally involved in the production process. The guest arrives with a set of needs and expectations about the service and the environment in which the service will be delivered. The service provider's ability to control and regulate service delivery depends on the use of sensitive feedback mechanisms and corrective measures.

That's why it is essential to focus considerable energy on collecting customer satisfaction data and feedback. When you read about service recovery, you will become even more convinced that service organizations not only need to carefully design their services but they also need to know exactly how these services are perceived. Accomplishing this goal is no small task. Managers and quality control officers have implemented such methods as satisfaction surveys in hotel rooms or at tables, online questionnaires, and focus groups of past customers. The shared belief is that the more information that can be generated and the more past guests involved, the better able the organization will be to continuously improve its service quality. When service delivery occurs over a long period of time, as in a hotel, continuous performance monitoring must be used to minimize service variability.

Under all circumstances, improvements in the quality of service must be a continuous improvement process of implementation, feedback, and enhancements rather than one quick fix. This process of ongoing improvement needs to become part of the organization's culture. Service assessment must become an integral part of the way members of an organization go about their daily tasks, and the redesigned processes should be passed on to new employees. You will learn more about this process when service training is discussed.

SERVICE RECOVERY

You might think of service as the gap between what the customer expects and what he or she receives. There's an industry belief that slipping up on service delivery may not be a bad thing—*if* you can take the opportunity to recover with such enthusiasm that the guest will never be able to forget the positive experience. What is needed is a bonus for the customer to make up for the poor service; this is called a **service recovery.** The question becomes, "What does that take?"

In the case of the dissatisfied restaurant customers above, what would it take to make up for their uncomfortable dining experience? Bear in mind that the discomfort was physical as well as psychological. They were physically uncomfortable because of the smoke. They were concerned for their friend who, because of ill health, was particularly sensitive to the smoke, and they were relegated to a lower status by the manager who referred to the others as his "good" customers.

Effectiveness of Recovery Strategies

The methods of service recovery and the effectiveness of each type of effort are of high interest to service professionals. Among the most common strategies are (a) apology, (b) correction, (c) empathy, (d) compensation, (e) follow-up, (f) acknowledgment and explanation, and (g) exceptional treatment. The sobering fact is, very seldom do these efforts produce the desired results.

Experiments conducted to determine the effectiveness of various recovery strategies have reached the same conclusion; when service providers fail to satisfy their customers, effective recovery requires a great deal of effort and often cannot manage to overcome the customer's negative view of the organization. While factors such as the type of hospitality service and the purpose for purchasing the service have an impact, more than one recent study concluded that none of the typical recovery strategies could turn around the negative perceptions. Common recovery strategies include apology only, immediate assistance, compensation, and assistance combined with compensation.

Other researchers have found that customer perceptions of justice or fairness in service recovery have a significant impact on the success of service recovery efforts. These perceptions influenced the customer's attitudes toward the organization as well as his or her intentions of continuing doing business. The degree of previous customer loyalty experienced by the individual also has a bearing on the individual's willingness to mend the relationship.

Describe a situation where you had particularly poor service. Was there any attempt at service recovery? If so, was it effective? If not, what do you think should have or could have been done?

Consequences of Service Failure

Consequences of service failure have been listed in a variety of contexts and most often include the following:

1. dissatisfaction;
2. a decline in customer confidence;
3. negative word of mouth;
4. loss of revenue;
5. increased costs; and
6. a decrease in employee morale and subsequent performance.

As you know from earlier discussions, to improve their service and avoid the outcomes listed above, managers need to know exactly what problems customers have encountered. Research has demonstrated that, unfortunately, very few customers present their complaints to the company. Of the customers who report complaints, approximately 50 to 70 percent will do business again with the organization if their complaint is resolved. Several studies have addressed employee behaviors when service failure occurs and have distinguished poor service as it relates to (a) the core service, (b) requests for customized service, and (c) unexpected employee actions. While this topic is easy to avoid, high performing companies spend a great deal of effort collecting information from dissatisfied customers to better understand just where their service missed the target.

Role of the Service Employee in the Recovery Process

All agree that service recovery is dependent on the customer contact employee and his or her responsiveness. It is important to keep in mind that employees cannot effectively engage in service recovery unless they are satisfied. Therefore, the notion of service within is perhaps one of the most powerful when organizations look to increase their effectiveness and profitability. The traditional ingredients of response, information, action, and compensation that have repeatedly been applied to external customers might well be translated to address the needs of internal service providers who require intervention for service recovery.

It seems clear that the highest performing organizations improve the service delivery process through (1) excellent methods of selection, training, and empowerment; (2) establishing both internal and external service recovery guidelines and standards; and (3) responding to customer complaints through call centers and other means that facilitate a timely and meaningful response to problems.

SELECT AND TRAIN FOR SERVICE EXCELLENCE

Effective hospitality managers understand the important implications of staff recruitment, selection, and training for the service experience. Skilled personnel have a major impact not only on daily service interactions, but also on the organization's planning and strategic direction. Service firms will need to respond to future challenges with appropriate programs for recruitment, personnel development, and training at all organizational levels, from frontline to executive.

Employees who render service are responsible for its quality. Organizations must ensure that the employee who waits on the customer will provide excellent service. Since services are primarily experiential, requiring customer contact, the conduct of service employees is crucial in providing a consistent level of quality to the customer.

The customer deals with a frontline employee, rather than with supervisors, managers, or executives. The customer receiving poor service gets little comfort or satisfaction from being told that the poor quality is due not to the employee but to management who is absent or inaccessible. Consequently, in service, the employee has a great deal of responsibility for quality.

Selecting Service Employees

Management is to blame for poor-quality performance if it hires unqualified persons. As you will learn in the following chapter, service employees require basic attitudes and skills to perform effectively. Often, these competencies are more a matter of having the right personal characteristics than of demonstrating a specific behavior. Selection methods must assess such characteristics as an individual's ability to empathize, show respect for others, and have patience with all types of guests.

What do you think is the most important characteristic of an effective service employee from the guest's perspective? Why?

Training and Developing Service Employees

There are at least two major advantages gained from a systematic and comprehensive approach to improving service quality. First, a competitive advantage develops if the quality of a service is clearly perceived by the consumer. Second, the motivation to improve standards and achieve consistency becomes integrated in the organizational culture. Thus, by understanding both the consumer's and service provider's perspective of service, the organization can deliver a more effective and satisfactory service.

Starting as well as maintaining a quality improvement program is a key human relations endeavor. In most organizations, the frontline employees receive the lowest pay, get the least training and development, and have the most turnover.

INTERNAL SERVICE

"Service within" is a term for the concept of **internal service.** This philosophy holds that employees, supervisors, and managers must be treated well and given good service in the same way that customers are provided with excellent care. The **moments of truth** that take place when the customer has contact with the service personnel must be effective for customer satisfaction. Employees who feel valued and appreciated will, in turn, provide service excellence to the guest. It takes teamwork and cooperation across the organization to make sure service quality standards are achieved. Given the concept of service within, every employee has a direct or indirect responsibility for service quality and customer satisfaction.

The service staff in hospitality organizations can be divided into three categories:

1. primary service employees;
2. secondary service employees; and
3. service support employees.

Every employee's activities, no matter what position they hold, affect the customer. The **primary service employees** have direct contact with the customers. The **secondary service employees** serve customers without directly interacting with them. The **service support staff** consists of everyone else within the organization. In a hotel, the primary service staff includes front desk associates, bell persons, door persons, and restaurant servers. The secondary service staff consists of housekeepers, chefs, and cooks. The maintenance and laundry departments in a hotel would fall under the service support staff category. Maintenance does not directly serve customers, but if they do their job improperly, they could still affect the customer's stay.

Without help from the people who work at the internal levels of the organization, the frontline employees cannot do their jobs properly. The frontline employees can help the support people do their jobs as well. There must be an effective partnership between the people out front and those in the back for the whole service organization to function effectively.

In a truly service-driven organization, everybody and every unit has a customer. Your customers are the people who depend on you, wholly or in part, to get their jobs done. All of the functions and departments of a service business are linked, and each one depends on others to various degrees in accomplishing its mission. In fact, we can argue that the main purpose of the organization is to support the efforts of the frontline employees to do their jobs.

Employees are the key to success at the "moments of truth" when the service provider and the customer meet and interact. Behind this moment, however, is a team of service employees responsible for all aspects of the operation. Employees are every manager's first customer as they influence the overall organization and the specific guest experience in every on-the-job encounter.

> Give an example of three "service within" relationships; for example, who does the dishwasher or the maintenance technician serve? And who do those employees serve?

Emotional Labor and Contact Overload Syndrome

Given the critical role service employees play, it is important for managers to recognize two distinctive aspects of service positions that make them especially difficult and stressful. One is emotional labor, the other is called contact overload syndrome.

EMOTIONAL LABOR   Service jobs require more than just physical labor, which is commonly called for in other types of organizations. When a server brings an entrée for a guest, physical labor is being done. However, when the server handles a drunken guest or a dissatisfied customer, mental work is being done. According to Hochschild (1983), service personnel do something more, something that she calls **emotional labor.**

> This labor requires one to induce or suppress feeling in order to sustain the outward countenance that produces the proper state of mind in others. This kind of labor calls for coordination of mind and feeling, and it sometimes draws on a source of self that we honor as deep and integral to our individuality.

Emotional labor occurs when the employee's emotions are a part of the work itself. That is, the employee's psychological and emotional reactions become involved as a consequence of some aspect of the job. As you can imagine, service jobs involve a relatively high degree of emotional labor. For example, a person who handles lost baggage claims all day deals with a lot of angry people. Seldom does a traveler stop by the lost luggage counter to wish the person behind it a pleasant day.

> Do you think that everyone is equally suited to a job that requires emotional labor? How well suited are you for this type of work? What makes you reach that conclusion?

CONTACT OVERLOAD SYNDROME   The second distinctive characteristic of service work is **contact overload syndrome.** Karl Albrecht and Zemke (1985) identify this as a distinctive reaction in human beings. It is experienced when individuals are in jobs that require one-on-one contact with many people on a repeated basis. A person can handle only so many of these emotional events in a given period before he or she begins to feel overloaded, tired, and stressed. Some people can tolerate high frequency contact much better than others. Employees vary in their ability to handle emotional labor as they do on other dimensions. Managers need to be aware of the negative reactions of contact overload. The following list suggests a few of the warning signs:

- physical fatigue, tension, elevated stress levels, moodiness, and irritability;
- indifference toward the job and the customer;
- loss of interest in the work quality—lack of personal pride or sense of achievement; and
- detachment from the situation—an emotional reaction that becomes robotic and programmed.

These reactions to emotional labor have two primary consequences. First, psychological stress can carry over into the employee's personal life. Second, the negative emotional reactions experienced by the employee often spill over onto the customer. An employee who is apathetic, withdrawn, emotionally flat or hostile, and uninterested in his or her job will transfer those feelings to the customer. This individual experience results in a negative customer impression of the organization. Competitive organizations, therefore, must consider their employees as an internal market and strive to create a strong service culture within.

Integration of Successful Internal Service

As we have suggested, internal service must be integrated with other management factors and considered an integral part of the strategic management plan. Second, top management must constantly demonstrate an active involvement in and support for internal service initiatives.

Internal marketing starts with top management and moves outward to middle management and supervisors. Everyone in the organization must accept and live up to their role in an internal service process. Only then can internal service activities directed toward customer contact employees be successful, as the contact employees' ability to perform high quality service depends on the support they receive from their managers and peers. The large number of support persons who do not come in contact with customers themselves must recognize that the contact employees are their internal customers.

Costs and Benefits of Internal Service

Effective internal service requires total commitment to be successful. There are a number of indicators that signal poor internal service. These include the following:

- customer dissatisfaction about their interactions with the company;
- tension between functional areas;
- low employee awareness about the company's mission as well as their own role in the organization; and
- low employee morale.

Internal service is not without costs. It requires a major commitment of resources, including time demands, plus significant changes in thinking and behaving at all levels of the organization. Effective internal service demands a team approach to developing and implementing a meaningful program. The major benefit of a successful initiative is happy and satisfied customers who ensure the development of long-term relationships. Positive internal service and customer satisfaction also have a synergistic impact on the contributions from the individual units of the organization and this optimizes the return on the company's investment in its employees.

Internal Service Initiatives

Employees need your help in getting their jobs done. If you are service oriented, your employees are far more likely to be service oriented toward their customers. Thus, the concept of internal service works most effectively from the top down as employees appreciate and respond to their manager's attitudes and behaviors.

Albrecht (1985) was among the first to propose the idea of an internal service triangle whereby the employees are the customers of management. The topmost point of the internal service triangle is the organization's culture. The bottom-right point of the triangle is service leadership, which provides personal, caring attention to employees' needs. The bottom-left point of the triangle is the organization itself, which gives employees the resources they need to serve customers. As we can see in Figure 1.1, the culture, the service leadership, and the organization combine synergistically to make frontline employees maximally effective. The concept of internal service, while sounding like a good philosophy to most managers, is challenging to put into place. Specific steps must be taken to effectively implement this type of approach (see Box 1.1). Think

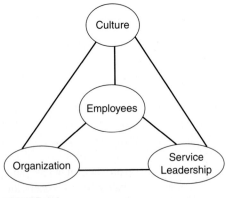

FIGURE 1.1

BOX 1.1

Implementing Internal Service Practices

- Define your customers. First identify a list of people who rely on you and others like you to get their work done. Then prioritize the names on that list, with the people or departments that rely on you the most at the top.
- Identify your contribution. For each customer on your list, specify the primary need you think they have to which you can contribute.
- Define service quality. Try to recognize a specific quality factor, or criterion that you believe the customer considers critical to the successful performance of the service involved.
- Validate your criterion. Talk to your customers and find out if their perceptions of quality coincide with your criterion.
- Develop a mission statement.

of an internship or job you have had in the hospitality industry and use that as you proceed with the following steps that help managers align their internal service program with their organization's overall mission:

CREATING A SERVICE CULTURE

A service culture is created when the customer—either external or internal—is the most important focus of the organization. Nearly a quarter century ago researchers (Grönroos, 1984) identified four areas that they believed had to be developed for a strong service culture. This framework is even more relevant in today's service economy.

First, there are organizational requirements for good service. Second, there are strategic requirements for good service. Good service and the development of human resources must be recognized as high priority strategic variables. Third, managers must believe that these variables can position the organization for a competitive advantage. They must actively support a service orientation and develop customer-focused employees. Finally, there are attitudinal requirements for good service. Every employee has to understand and accept the importance of providing excellent service.

While internal service programs operating in a vacuum cannot establish a service culture, they are a powerful means for developing such a culture in connection with other managerial activities. The internal service goals that help to achieve a service culture include the following:

- Enable all employees to understand and accept the business mission, the strategies, and tactics.
- Develop a service-oriented management style.
- Teach all employees service-oriented communications and interaction skills.

Once a service culture has been created, it has to be maintained. Otherwise, service-oriented attitudes and behaviors may be reduced or may disappear altogether. The internal service goals that help to maintain a service culture include the following (Congram, 1991):

- Ensure that your methods are supportive and enhance the service-mindedness and customer orientation of employees.
- Ensure that the employees receive continuous information and feedback.
- Treat your employees in the same manner that you expect them to treat the customers.

The most important theme is the essential support of every single manager. When you encourage your subordinates, when you open channels of communication, and when you make sure that feedback regularly reaches members of your staff, you directly impact and improve your organization's service culture. Your goal is to develop and maintain a culture that supports and rewards attention to customer needs and sustains consistent quality service.

Think about two jobs you've held. How were you treated by your supervisor in each case? What impact did his or her behavior have on your job satisfaction?

TECHNOLOGY AND CUSTOMER SERVICE

Research has documented the importance and multiple uses of technology in today's organizations. Although companies grapple with issues of security, potential lost productivity, intercultural misunderstandings, and message retention and discoverability, hospitality organizations are increasingly dependent on electronic communication to provide effective customer service.

Perhaps the most central issue with regard to technology is the impact it has on relationships with guests and perceptions of "customer care." It is difficult to imagine a computer monitor communicating, "It's been wonderful having you stay with us, please come again" in a sincere and warm manner. Are guests really opting for efficiency and accuracy over the "high touch" that was once an organization's main competitive advantage? The answer, as always, is—it depends! What we do know is that technology is here to stay. It makes many services possible that were not imagined a decade ago, and for hospitality employees it is becoming a way of life.

Prevalence of Technology in Hospitality Organizations

As today's young people enter the workforce and as more companies become multinational, we can expect the use of technology to increase substantially for both internal and external communication. Computer-mediated communication (CMC) is how employees communicate via computers through synchronous, asynchronous, and real-time interactions. Email, instant messaging (IM), text messaging, bulletin boards, distance learning—and even online shopping—fall into this definition.

Instant messaging is becoming increasingly prevalent in the workplace, joining email as among the most frequently used business communication channels. The increasing workplace applications of these technologies have profound implications for hospitality organizations seeking to gain a competitive advantage in tomorrow's business environment.

Although adoption of information technology in hospitality companies relative to other industries has been slow, this situation—particularly in larger organizations—is changing rapidly. Global interests have made electronic communication even more vital. The use of email for marketing purposes is particularly powerful. With 63 percent of American adults using the Internet to make travel reservations (Fox and Madden, 2005), hospitality companies are reaching increasingly large audiences through email marketing. Permission marketing, which targets customers who have registered to receive emails, allows companies to personalize messages and address the customer's specific needs.

Customer Feedback Through Technology

In addition, hospitality companies find email an effective feedback mechanism. Many executives from luxury brand hotels use email surveys extensively. In one case, a top executive explained that she uses email as part of an extensive total quality management (TQM) process. In other cases, surveys are sent to individuals who book online. Then, 24 hours after they check out of the hotel, guests receive an automatically generated email form, with just two fields for reporting the best and worst part of their experience. Responses immediately appear in the GM's inbox, and a call is made to guests within minutes. With high survey response rates, hotels undoubtedly benefit from the service recovery made possible by the use of electronic communication.

Hotel companies are also connecting their guests with these new technologies. The BlackBerry, which now boasts over 12 million subscribers, makes possible the convergence of communication technologies and expands the reach of a company's server. Starwood, for example, offers guests in some hotels a device similar to a BlackBerry. Stay InTouch allows guests to access their room voice mail from outside the hotel, contact the concierge and their buddy list from home through IM, obtain local restaurant listings and attractions, and complete other similar services (DeNise, 2005).

Employees generally view email as preferable to a phone call, citing advantages such as providing a paper trail (e.g., for disputing a charge), being less intrusive, and increasing the likelihood of getting a fast response. Like email through BlackBerries, IM is used for quick communication within hospitality companies, with employees in supplier organizations, and—in a growing number of instances—with guests or prospective customers.

There is no question that this new technology is pervasive and burgeoning, bringing with it individual-, unit-, and corporate-level challenges never before encountered in the hospitality workplace. Few recent developments have so clearly distinguished the Net Generation from their more senior counterparts.

> In what ways do you think technology enhances a guest's service experience? What are the possible dangers of technology's impact on a guest's perceptions of service quality?

The Challenges of Technology in the Hospitality Workplace

While technology is fast becoming the channel of choice among young professionals, it is not always the most effective means for accomplishing workplace goals or increasing customer satisfaction. Too often, communicators rely on channels with which they are familiar or which are the most efficient rather than those that best accomplish their purposes. A hospitality employee accustomed to contacting friends and family online may find it difficult to determine when a telephone call or a face-to-face meeting may be the most effective means of accomplishing the task.

Some critics worry—and with good reason—that the casual nature with which technology is used tempts individuals to communicate what is on their minds at the moment without the self-reflection that has been the hallmark of effective communication practices. Young people using email or IM, in particular, are writing more, translating every thought and feeling—whatever comes into their minds—into words. This may not always be a good thing when the goal is to create a specific perception of service quality. The immediacy of technology also contributes to rude or angry email, what researchers have called flaming. Service employees who respond without consideration for the particular reader characteristics risk sending inappropriate and unprofessional communications.

Failure to implement policies on the proper use of electronic communication also leaves corporations vulnerable to security issues. Companies can protect themselves by implementing enterprise systems, which include security features, and by educating employees on the risks involved and how to defend against them.

It would seem that employees require special training in the effective and appropriate application of technologies to ensure that they enhance the service experience. The consequences of misuse are substantial, and future hospitality managers must be prepared for the challenges ahead.

While the topic of employee training is beyond the scope of this chapter, it may be helpful to closely examine one important way in which almost all customer contact employees use technology to provide service—the telephone.

Customer Service and the Telephone

Mary needed a simple question answered by Graham Telephone. Her call was immediately answered by a computer expressing concern for her call and appreciation for her value as a customer. The machine kept repeating "Your call is important to us. We are experiencing unusually heavy call traffic at this time" while she waited on the line for 35 minutes with the same message being repeated. The same thing was repeated the week before and the week before that. She wondered why, if they were experiencing "unusually heavy traffic" every day, they hadn't hired more service employees. They stated they cared about their customers, and maintaining an inadequate staff was a sign that they did not care about her.

Increasingly, businesses are relying on computer answering services. In the above anecdote, the stated goal of valuing customers conflicts with the actual lack of service. We in the hospitality industry must be especially cognizant of this kind of pitfall when incorporating technology into our organizations. In this case, a service recovery will need to be made as soon as the customer ever speaks to an actual service representative. So you are starting off at a loss in customer service simply because of poor use of technology. For this reason, some hospitality organizations still require an actual person to answer each telephone call. In either case, it is important to keep in mind that *the service encounter begins the moment the telephone is answered.* While the details of effective telephone communication might seem obvious, it is important to establish guidelines that will enable you to provide consistent and quality service. Telephone courtesy must become a habit. The following principles should be employed to ensure quality service when no computerized answering method is used.

1. *Answer the phone by the second ring.* Immediate attention to the phone communicates your interest in serving the customer.
2. *The best greetings usually include your name, your department, and the name of the organization.* Callers like to be reassured that they have reached the right number. You can eliminate unnecessary conversations if the caller knows right away what person and department he or she has reached.
3. *Never answer a call by saying "please hold" before the caller has a chance to speak.* When someone makes a call, he or she is ready to make a request or deliver a message of some sort. To block the speaker before he or she is able to say anything at all is likely to appear rude and overly abrupt.
4. *When callers must be put on hold, wait no more than a minute or two before reassuring the person that he or she hasn't been forgotten.* When was the last time you were put on hold—perhaps with a repetitious recording—and were sure that no one would ever pick up the phone again?
5. *Listen carefully to the caller.* It's easy to scramble telephone messages, especially where there are a lot of other activities going on around you. Don't hesitate to ask the caller to repeat something if you haven't heard it correctly or completely. Be prepared to take a message. Write down messages as they are delivered. Repeat the important information to make sure you have it right.
6. *Take the time to be helpful.* It's easy to treat the caller as if he or she were what they sometimes are—an interruption! Remember that the caller's impression is important. Personalize the call if you can; use the caller's name if appropriate. Do everything you can to make the customer experience a positive one.
7. *Speak directly and clearly.* Make sure that you are easy to understand and provide the caller with the necessary information.
8. *Be tactful and treat the call as important to you.* Always use the same courtesy and tact that you would if the caller was standing in front of you. Let the caller know that you take his or her needs seriously, regardless of what they may be. It's easier to be abrupt with someone you can't see, but the impression you make lingers just as long.
9. *Keep promises made over the phone.* Because the caller isn't in front of you, it's often easy to make promises. Remember, never make a promise you can't keep.
10. *Always thank the caller.* Any call is an opportunity to make a good impression and provide exceptional service. Thank the caller for making contact with your organization.

One instance where it is appropriate to defer a call is if you are currently assisting another customer in person. Do not interrupt service to a customer to answer a telephone call. If circumstances require that you do use a computerized answering service, keep the following points in mind.

1. Answer calls as quickly as possible, using the computer as a last resort.
2. Create an excellent first impression by making your message brief, friendly, and easy to understand.
3. When listing voicemail options, include each person's job title with their name so that callers unfamiliar with your employees can still reach the appropriate person.

What are the limitations of service delivered on the telephone—or through any distance technology? Do you think technology will increase in the future, or do you believe that we have reached the final stage of its use? Explain.

Summary

In this chapter, we discuss the process of creating and managing services. We define services as economic activities that produce time, place, form, or psychological utilities. Globalization has enriched the hospitality industry and we emphasize that providing quality service that exceeds a customer's expectations is the source of a valuable competitive advantage.

Offering customers quality service is important for many reasons. Companies that deliver a consistently high level of customer service can both charge more for their services and see the impact of service in the expansion of their market share. It costs companies five to six times more money to attract new customers than to retain current customers.

We discuss the importance of selecting service-oriented employees. Customers primarily deal with frontline employees; these employees have a large impact on the quality of service a customer receives and shape the perception the customer holds of the organization. When hiring an employee, managers should assess such characteristics as an individual's ability to empathize, show respect for others, and have patience with all types of guests.

We also discuss the importance of taking care of employees the same way an organization cares for its customers (internal service). If the employees within an organization are unhappy and neglected, they are more likely to neglect customers and provide poor service.

Key Words

services *4*	moments of truth *11*	service support staff *12*
intangible *5*	primary service employees *12*	emotional labor *12*
service recovery *8*	secondary service	contact overload syndrome *13*
internal service *11*	employees *12*	

Exercises

Exercise 1   Assertive Role Plays

Objectives:

- To practice assertive skills
- To identify situations where an assertive response is appropriate and helpful
- To handle situations involving internal service and external service

Number of Participants: 10–25
Time Frame: 60 minutes
Materials: "Assertive Role Plays" worksheet
Procedure:

1. Review the elements of assertive communication and distinguish it from nonassertive and aggressive behavior. Discuss the potential problems created by lack of assertive skills.
2. Distribute "Assertive Role Plays" sheet.
3. Arrange participants in groups of five, evenly spaced throughout the room. Assign each group a different role play, or allow participants to choose role plays.
4. Give participants the instructions at the top of the "Assertive Role Plays" sheet.
5. Tell participants they have approximately ten minutes to create and practice their role play before presenting it to the entire group.
6. After ten minutes, check to make sure all groups are ready for their presentations. Ask the first group to move to a place where everyone can easily see them and then to perform their "problem" role play. A member of the group will facilitate discussion of the problem, after which the group will again perform the role-play situation, this time demonstrating what would have happened if one of the characters had been assertive.
7. A member of the group again leads a discussion regarding the effectiveness of the assertive response in their particular situation. Group members are given feedback regarding the effectiveness of their assertive skills.

ALTERNATE ASSIGNMENT

Participants can create original role plays using troublesome situations of their own.

***

ASSERTIVE ROLE PLAYS

As a member of a small group, you will be asked to role-play one of the situations below. The first time you perform the role play, members of your group are to demonstrate *ineffective handling* of a difficult customer.

After some discussion of the problem that was role-played, your group will perform the role play once again. This time, the principles of *assertive communication* are demonstrated by at least one of the participants to resolve the interpersonal problem.

The two responses to the problem will be discussed and their impact on customer–employee relationship will be emphasized.

Situation 1

One customer comes to your desk and she's exceptionally upset. You are talking on the phone and have motioned to her that you will be right with her when you finish, but she persists, almost talking over your telephone conversation. You have just hung up, and turn to find her staring at you.

Situation 2

The hotel occupancy is 100 percent for tonight. A potential customer comes in and states that he has a reservation for this evening. You look and see that he is not on your list of customers. He becomes outraged, stating that he made his reservation three weeks ago.

(continued)

(continued)

Situation 3

Although you never considered yourself a high stress type, lately you've been experiencing a great deal of stress when employees ignore you or won't do what you ask. Whenever you want to get cooperation, you feel as if you're ignored. You know you have to do something because your stress level is increasing daily because you feel totally powerless.

Situation 4

You have three children and, although you love your work, you also look forward to seeing your family in the evenings. A colleague who works the evening shift has asked you to fill in for him on several occasions when he has had an evening engagement. Each time you have agreed, but regretted it later as you watched the hours pass, knowing you were missing out on family time. Now it has happened again. Dan has just told you about a wonderful date he has set up for the next evening, and knows you won't let him down. What do you say?

***

Exercise 2   Be Sure to Remember

Objectives:

- To demonstrate the importance of memory for providing excellent customer service
- To provide an opportunity for participants to practice their memory skills

Group Size: 12–25 participants

Time Frame: 30 minutes

Materials: "Be Sure to Remember" participant handouts (Option 1 or Option 2 handouts, to be given to senders only.) Your instructor will provide these handouts.

Procedure:

1. Emphasize the importance of listening to effective service. Restate that part of being an effective listener is remembering what you have heard.
2. Introduce the activity by asking participants to find partners.
3. Ask each pair to determine who will be person A and who will be person B. Person A is the sender, and person B is the receiver.
4. The instructor will distribute the list only to the senders.
5. Tell participants that the sender will read a list to the receiver in the following manner:
   - Sender will first read line one, then the receiver will repeat it.
   - Sender will then read lines one and two, and the receiver will repeat both in order.
   - This procedure should be repeated until the receiver memorizes the entire passage. Each time the entire passage must be repeated from the beginning.
6. Allow ten minutes for senders to teach their partners the passage. All participants reconvene at the end of the ten minutes. Receivers volunteer to demonstrate what they have learned!
7. Discuss the questions on participant handouts.
8. If possible, a prize should be given to any pairs who successfully memorized the passage within the allotted time.

Exercise 3   Hotel Celebration

Category: Customer Service

Objective: To formulate criteria for the selection and hiring of new employees for a new hotel

Group Size: Works best with several groups of 4–5 people

Time Frame: 25 minutes

Materials: Pen and newsprint for each group

Procedure:

1. Divide the participants into groups, with 4–5 people in each group.
2. Read the following passage to the participants:

   You and your teammates are developing a new boutique hotel with 89 rooms: Hotel Celebration. You want your hotel to be distinctive in its attention to customer service—service will receive even more attention than the rooms, the food, and the décor. It is now time to choose an executive team that will support and execute your vision.

3. Have the groups select five celebrities who have characteristics of the executive team they would like to hire. Next to each celebrity, state what characteristic each one represents. Of course, the group will not be hiring celebrities; they will be hiring applicants for the management positions.

4. Provide the teams with 10–15 minutes to write on newsprint their list of five celebrities.

5. Discuss each group's list and look for similarities among the various lists.

6. Make a group list of the managerial characteristics the class as a whole is looking for.

Exercise 4   Customer Service Debate

Category: Customer Service

Objective: To allow participants to evaluate a customer complaint-handling situation

Group Size: 3–5 participants

Time Frame: 1 hour

Materials: Handout for each participant, LCD projectors and SmartBoards of the handout, flipchart papers with statements

Procedure:

1. Divide the participants into small groups of three to five, and distribute the handout "Handling a Customer Complaint."

2. Ask each group to go through the exercise. Allow them 20 minutes to complete the exercise. Ask them to choose a spokesperson.

3. Ask each group's spokesperson to list the five principles that they have on their flipchart. Ask them why they thought each principle they listed was important.

4. Post all the flipchart papers around the room and open the class for discussion. The facilitator should wind up the discussion by consolidating the opinions and get the class to agree on the principles that must be upheld when responding to angry customers.

***

HANDLING A CUSTOMER COMPLAINT

In your managerial career, you will have the opportunity to serve unhappy or disgruntled customers. This is a chance to make a service recovery; that is, to turn the unhappy customer into a devotee of your organization.

You, a hotel manager, get a call that there is a problem at the front desk. You must react to the following situation:

A customer comes to the front desk for the double queen room that she requested. All you have is a single queen. She is angry as she says that her girlfriend was going to stay with her tonight.

Write on your flipchart five principles that must be upheld when responding to this angry customer.

***

Exercise 5   Practice Basic Telephone Skills

Objectives:

- To provide an opportunity for participants to practice some of the telephone courtesy skills presented in the text
- To provide an opportunity for participants to hear each other handle a telephone service situation
- To provide an opportunity for participants to receive feedback on their telephone courtesy

Group Size: 12–25 participants

Time Frame: 1 hour

Materials: "Let's See Those Telephone Courtesy Skills" handout

Procedure:

1. Review the telephone guidelines. Present them as a visual, if possible.
2. Break participants into small groups. Assign one role-play situation to each group. Not all members of the group will be involved in the role play.

Option: Participants can be encouraged to create their own role-play situations from experiences they have had in the past.

3. Inform participants that they will be demonstrating telephone courtesy to other groups.
4. Allow approximately ten minutes for participants to create their role play.
5. Ask each group to present their role play in turn.
6. Facilitate a discussion of the role play immediately after it is presented.

***

LET'S SEE THOSE TELEPHONE COURTESY SKILLS

Below is a list of situations that might arise in handling telephone calls. Using the guidelines presented in your text, determine the most appropriate way to respond to the caller.

You will be assigned, or you will be asked to create, one example to demonstrate your telephone courtesy to other groups. Do not rehearse the role play!

Situation 1

An older woman calls the front desk for a restaurant recommendation. You have one for her, but sense she will have trouble understanding directions because of her hearing deficit.

Situation 2

A guest calls from her room, saying, "What kind of hotel is this? I have been trying for 20 minutes to get an outside telephone line!"

Situation 3

A customer who comes to the restaurant regularly calls to chat. You have a line at the reservation desk and do not have the time to spend on the telephone with this customer, but she is obviously determined to "get your ear."

***

Exercise 6   Quiz Yourself—No Grades!

Objectives:

- To encourage participants to think about their own listening behaviors
- To identify listening concerns common to the entire group
- To help participants begin to identify weak listening areas that need to be addressed

Group Size: 12–25 participants

Time Frame: 30 minutes

Materials: "Quiz Yourself—No Grades!" worksheet

Procedure:

1. Discuss the fact that most people have bad listening habits—the first step in overcoming them is to identify specific behaviors you want to modify.
2. Distribute the "Quiz Yourself—No Grades!" worksheet and allow approximately five minutes for participants to complete the questions.
3. Emphasize that no one exhibits poor listening habits all of the time; the point of the quiz is to identify tendencies that may create listening problems.
4. Ask participants to circle one or two of the questions that hit on behaviors they would like to improve.
5. Determine whether there is any consensus among participants—Are there one or two listening tendencies that are potential problems for several participants? If so, which ones?

***

QUIZ YOURSELF—NO GRADES!

This is a simple quiz that should give you some useful information about yourself as a listener. Respond to each question with either "yes" or "no."

- You think about three times faster than a customer talks. Do you use this time to think about other things while you're keeping general track of the conversation?
- Do you listen primarily for facts when customers are speaking, or do you try to understand how they are feeling as well?
- Do you make judgments about a customer from his or her appearance before the person has had an opportunity to speak?
- Do certain words or phrases elicit an emotional response, making it difficult for you to listen?
- Do you turn your thoughts to other subjects when you realize that a customer doesn't have anything interesting or helpful to say?
- When you're listening to a customer, are you easily distracted by other things going on around you?
- If you are annoyed by what a customer says, do you try to get things straightened out immediately?
- If you are confused by something a customer says, do you ask for clarification right away?

***

Exercise 7   Voice Analysis

Objectives:

- To emphasize the importance of voice in telephone courtesy
- To provide an opportunity for participants to analyze their voices

Group Size: 12–25 participants

Time Frame: 45–60 minutes

Materials: Flipchart, "Conversation Starters Sheet," "Voice Self-Assessment" worksheet, tape recorders for each group of four

Procedure:

1. Discuss the qualities of voice so that all participants are clear on the meaning of rate, pitch, and volume.
2. Ask participants to form groups of four, and choose partners within the group.
3. Distribute discussion topics to each pair.
4. Allow three to five minutes for each discussion. Have both groups use the same tape for the two three-to-five-minute discussions.
5. Ask participants to play the tapes all the way through.
6. Have each group of four listen to the two conversations, stopping the tape when necessary to provide feedback to the two individuals involved. Each participant begins to complete his or her self-assessment sheet.

7. Participants should then be instructed to finish completing their self-assessment sheets.
8. Lead a final discussion in which participants share their findings and make summary comments about voice and its role in delivering effective service.

***

VOICE SELF-ASSESSMENT

- The overall attitude I projected during my conversation was _____.
- I displayed the following emotions during the conversation: _____, _____, and _____.

Check only those statements that apply to you:

- In terms of volume:

  _____ I am easy to hear: I project my voice well and I am quite loud.

  _____ I am generally easy to hear, although at times my voice fades away.

  _____ I can be heard, but my voice is often soft and my partner has to listen closely to hear what I say.

- In terms of pitch:

  _____ My pitch is generally very high for my gender and age.

  _____ My pitch is generally very low for my gender and age.

_____ I don't tend to vary my pitch very much in conversations.

_____ I vary my pitch quite a bit in conversations.

• In terms of rate:

_____ I have a tendency to speak fairly quickly.

_____ I have a tendency to speak rather slowly and thoughtfully.

_____ I have a tendency to speak quickly when I become excited or emotional.

_____ My pace is regular and consistent.

_____ My pace varies according to what I am talking about.

• Overall:

_____ I am quite satisfied with my voice.

_____ I use adequate vocal variety when I speak.

_____ I am a bit too monotone when I speak.

_____ I convey appropriate attitudes and emotions when I speak.

_____ There are a few aspects of my voice that I need to work on before I will be satisfied with the way I sound.

• My action plan:

***

CONVERSATION STARTERS SHEET

Assign one of these situations to each pair, or allow them to generate their own topic. Although it is best if the two pairs in each group have different topics, several groups can use the same conversation starters.

• Your spouse has called to tell you about a leak in the roof. Although you're very concerned, the call has come at an inopportune moment and you really want to call him or her back. He or she insists on telling you every detail of the problem.

• A customer feels he or she has been overcharged. The customer realizes that you may not be able to resolve the problem, but he or she needs to talk about the situation to someone in your organization.

***

Endnotes

Acuff, J. (2004). *The Relationship Edge in Business: Connecting with Customers and Colleagues when it Counts*. Hoboken, NJ: John Wiley & Sons.

Albrecht, K. (1988). *At America's Service*. Homewood, IL: Dow Jones-Irwin.

Albrecht, K. & Zemke, R. (1985). *Service America*. Homewood, IL: Dow Jones-Irwin.

Anonymous. (1993). Employees' customer-service pride helps raise guest-satisfaction ratings. *Personnel Journal, 72*(8), 17.

Anonymous. (2006). The CIA: Preparing the next generation of foodservice leaders. *Nation's Restaurant News, 40*(18), S16–S18.

Bamford, D. & Xystouri, T. (2005). A case study of service failure and recovery within an international airline. *Managing Service Quality, 15*(3), 306–324.

Berta, D. (2005). Empowered staff thrives at fine-dining Panzano. *Nation's Restaurant News, 39*(37), 59–60.

Bill, T. (2006). Customer care scheme for 2012 Olympics. *Caterer & Hotelkeeper, 196*(4431), 9–12.

Blanchard, K., Heil, G., & Tate, R. (1989). *Legendary service*. San Diego, CA: Blanchard Training and Development.

Blanding, W. (1989). *Customer service operations*. Washington, DC: International Thomson Transport Press.

Blumberg, D. F. (1991). *Managing service as a strategic profit center*. New York: McGraw-Hill.

Bowen, D. E. (1990). *Service management effectiveness*. San Francisco: Jossey-Bass Publishers.

Bowen, J. T. (1997). A market-driven approach to business development and service improvement in the hospitality industry. *International Journal of Contemporary Hospitality Management, 9*(7), 334–340.

Bowen, D. & Johnston, R. (1999). Internal service recovery: Developing a new construct. *International Journal of Service Industry Management, 10*(2), 118–132.

Bowen, J. & Ford, R. (2004). What experts say about managing hospitality service delivery systems. *International Journal of Contemporary Hospitality Management, 16*(7), 394–403.

Brady, D. (2006). *!#@ the e-mail. Can we talk? *Business Week, 4012*, 109.

Cannon, D. (2002). Expanding paradigms in providing internal service. *Managing Service Quality, 12*(2), 87–101.

Chezzi, D. (2000). Get etiquette. *Maclean's, 113*(40), 12.

Coggins, A. O. Jr. (2004). *What makes a passenger ship a legend: The future of the concept of legend in the passenger shipping industry.* Dissertation: Virginia Polytechnic Institute and State University. p. 488.

Congram, C. A. (1991). *The handbook of marketing for the service industries.* New York: AMACOM.

Czepiel, J. A., Solomon, M. R., Suprenant, C. F., & Gutman, E. G. (1985). Service encounters: An overview. In Czepiel, J. A., Solomon, M. R., & Suprenant, C. F. (Eds.). *The Service Encounter,* Lexington, MA: Lexington Books..

Davis, S. III. (2005). The customer service opportunity. *Lodging Hospitality, 61*(14), 36.

DeNise, Antoinette. Starwood introduces new-age gizmo for hotel guests. *Meeting News,* August 15, 2005. http://www.allbusiness.com/transportation-communications-electric-gas/4238009-1.html

Disend, J. E. (1991). *How to provide excellent service in any organization.* Radnor: Chilton Book Company.

Edmondson, V. (2006). Organizational surveys: A system for employee voice. *Journal of Applied Communication Research, 34*(4), 307–309.

Ford, R. & Heaton, C. (2001). Managing your guest as a quasi-employee. *Cornell Hotel and Restaurant Administration Quarterly, 42*(2), 46–55.

Fox, S. & Madden, M. *Pew Internet and American Life Project Survey* January 2005, May–June 2005, and September 2005. http://www.pewinternet.org/index.asp

Gatling, A. (2005). In casual-dining segment, opportunities abound for frontline leadership training. *Nation's Restaurant News, 39*(31), 22–25.

Goodman, G. (2000). *Monitoring, measuring, and managing customer service.* San Francisco, CA: Jossey Bass, Publishers.

Grönroos, C. (1984). A service quality model and its marketing implications. *European Journal of Marketing, 18*(4), 36–44.

Heath, C. & Heath, D. (2006). The curse of knowledge. *Harvard Business Review, 84*(12), 20–37.

Hochschild, A. R. (1983). *The managed heart.* Berkeley: University of California Press.

John, B. (1997). A market-driven approach to business development and service improvement in the hospitality industry. *International Journal of Contemporary Hospitality Management, 9*(7), 334–351.

John, J. (2003). *Fundamentals of customer-focused management.* Westport, CT: Praeger Publishers.

Koteff, E. (2006). Health care industry could use a prescription for true hospitality from foodservice peers. *Nation's Restaurant News, 40*(32), 23.

Krazmien, M. (1999). *Teaching the bear new tricks: A comparison of behavior modeling and lecture-based service training in a Russian hotel.* Thesis written in fulfillment of the Master of Management in Hospitality, Ithaca, NY: Cornell University.

Lashley, C. (1999). Employee empowerment in services: A framework for analysis. *Personnel Review, 28*(3), 169.

Lauer, C. S. (2006). Back to the basics. *Modern Healthcare, 36*(43), 22–23.

LeBlanc, C. & Mills, K. (1995). Competitive advantage begins with positive culture. *Nation's Restaurant News, 29*(39), 22–23.

Lewis, B. & McCann, P. (2004). Service failure and recovery: Evidence from the hotel industry. *International Journal of Contemporary Hospitality Management, 16*(1), 6–23.

Liu, C. & Chen, K. (2006). Personality traits as antecedents of employee customer orientation: A case study in the hospitality industry. *International Journal of Management, 23*(3), 478–486.

Lovelock, C. (2001). A retrospective commentary on the article "New tools for achieving service quality." *Cornell Hotel and Restaurant Administration Quarterly, 42*(4), 39.

McDougall, G. H. & Levesque, T. (1999). Waiting for service: The effectiveness of recovery strategies. *International Journal of Contemporary Hospitality Management, 11*(1), 6–17.

McIntyre, K. S. (2005). *Understanding a climate for customer service.* Dissertation: Colorado State University. p. 114.

Murdick, R. G., Render, B., & Russell, R. (1990). *Service operations management.* Boston: Allyn & Bacon.

Paraskevas, A. (2001). Exploring hotel internal service chains: A theoretical approach. *Journal of Contemporary Hospitality Management, 13*(5), 251–260.

Paraskevas, A. (2001). Internal service encounters in hotels: An empirical study. *International Journal of Contemporary Hospitality Management, 13*(6), 285–293.

Parker, G. M. (1990). *Team players and team work.* San Francisco: Jossey-Bass Publishers.

Phillips, P. & Louvieris, P. (2005). Performance measurement systems in tourism, hospitality, and leisure small medium-sized enterprises: A balanced scorecard perspective. *Journal of Travel Research, 44*(2), 201.

Rosander, A. C. (1989). *The quest for quality in services.* Milwaukee: Quality Press.

Rosheim, E. (2005). Closing the communication gap. *Training, 42*(9), 46.

Rowe, M. (1994). Hyatt does a reality check. *Lodging Hospitality, 50*(9), 30–33.

Scudamore, B. (2006). Rah! Energy. *Profit, 25*(4), 23–31.

Sherman, D. H. (1988). *Service organization productivity management.* Hamilton: The Society of Management Accountants of Canada.

Spector, A. (1999). Taco Bell launches sweeping CHAMPS retraining effort. *Nation's Restaurant News, 33*(12), 4–7.

Teare, R. (1990). *Managing and marketing service in the 1990s.* London: Cassell Educational Limited.

Tschohl, J. & Franzmeier, S. (1991). *Achieving excellence through customer service.* Englewood Cliff: Prentice Hall.

van der Does, L. & Caldeira, S. (2005). *Nation's Restaurant News, 39*(29), 16–18.

van der Does, L. & Caldeira S. (2006). "Ambassadors" keep the focus on customers. *Nation's Restaurant News, 40*(1), 12–14.

Varoglu, D. & Eser, Z. (2006). How service employees can be treated as internal customers in hospitality industry. *The Business Review, 5*(2), 30–36, Cambridge.

Watkins, E. (2002). Service in the age of the Internet. *Lodging Hospitality, 58*(2), 4–5.

Watkins, E. (2005). At your service. *Lodging Hospitality, 61*(6), 26–28.

Watkins, E. (2005). Invest in your most important assets. *Lodging Hospitality, 61*(12), 4–6.

Wilson, M. (2006). What recruiters look for in on-campus interviews. *Black Collegian, 37*(1), 33–36.

Woods, R. (1987). Understanding and improving service in the hospitality industry. Seminar presentation to Koala Inns of America, May 27.

Young, C., Corsun, D., & Shinnar, R. (2004). Moving from fire-fighting to fire prevention: What service organizations need to know. *International Journal of Contemporary Hospitality Management, 16*(1), 27.

Zemke, R. & Schaaf, D. (1989). *The service edge: 101 companies that profit from customer care.* New York, NY: Penguin Books.

2

COMMUNICATING IN ORGANIZATIONS

The greatest problem in communication is the illusion that it has been accomplished.
—George Bernard Shaw

Most conversations are simply monologues delivered in the presence of a witness.
—Margaret Miller

The most important thing in communication is to hear what isn't being said.
—Peter F. Drucker

CHAPTER OUTLINE

Introduction

Communication Model
   Message Channels
   Roles of Receiver and Sender
   Feedback

Improving Oral and Written Communication
   Avoid Confusion When Choosing Words
   Be Brief and Precise
   Know When to Use Redundancy
   Choose the Right Time and Place

Speaking Effectively
   Creating Vocal Variety
   Pronunciation and Fluency
   Silence

Nonverbal Communication Dimensions
   Appearance
   Posture and Positioning
   Proxemics
   Touching
   Gestures
   Facial Expression and Eye Contact
   Chronemics

Effective Listening
   Importance of Listening
   Factors that Influence Listening
      Age
      Gender
      Personal traits
      Physical and psychological states
      Noise and external distractions
   Brownell's HURIER Listening Model
      Hearing
      Understanding
      Remembering
      Interpreting
      Evaluating
      Responding
   Building Listening Skills

LEARNING OBJECTIVES

After reading this chapter, you will be able to do the following:

1. Discuss the five dimensions of the communication process: phenomenology, message channels, roles, feedback, and listening.
2. Understand and implement the steps needed to improve oral and written communication.
3. Describe the difference between language and paralanguage.
4. Explain the four functions of nonverbal communication.
5. Name the seven ways one can communicate nonverbally.
6. List and discuss two reasons managers should improve their listening skills.
7. Discuss the factors that affect a person's ability to listen to others.
8. Understand the six components of the listening process, as described by the HURIER Listening Model.
9. Describe several steps managers can take to improve their memory.

Opening Scenario

Brady is the marketing director for Rikko Hotel and Spa at a popular beach in South Carolina. He has recently been focusing on training the staff to understand that marketing is everybody's job. It seemed that his biggest marketing challenge was the staff itself. There were instances where customers had complained of inadequate or inattentive service. He requested and received the support of his manager in this endeavor. He distributed a survey to understand the staff's current views on this idea. He was looking for feedback in all forms, speaking with managers in all areas, and letting it be known that all comments were welcome. The surveys gave him very positive comments regarding the staff's willingness to participate in this program. However, one of the housekeeping staff heard an assistant manger tell the chef that he thought Brady was pretty clever to get everyone else working on his job. Soon the entire staff had changed its view of the "Everyone Is Responsible for Marketing" campaign, and when Brady tried to proceed with his program he was met with opposition and resentment.

BOX 2.1

Michael Chiu, President of Prima Donna Development Corporation and Prima Hotels, gave us his perspective of communication within the hospitality industry.

"Communication is all about an effective manner by which a message is conveyed. Cultural and language barriers present a constant set of obstacles in the diverse hospitality workforce, which is very labor intensive. Inherent in the process is the methodology employed; however, achieving the desired end-result ought to be the overriding criterion for a successful engagement. For an engagement between the initiator and receiver to be successful, it is vitally important to really listen to what you hear, but don't hear only what you are listening for. Say what you mean and mean what you say. What has been said must be followed up by action, and act consistently on what you have been saying all along. Reinforcing the message by action or deed is the most critical tool in communication that will yield positive results and engender loyalty. The ingredients that contribute to a successful oral or written communicative process are the eight qualifiers that must be answered in the communication itself. They are: How, When, Where, Why, Who, How Much, For Whom, and For What."

INTRODUCTION

Despite the fact that people begin to express themselves and indicate their needs from the time they are born, most individuals remain surprisingly poor communicators. Research shows that misunderstandings caused by poor communication are occurring more frequently than people think, and such misunderstandings cause more headaches for managers than any other single factor. One reason why people communicate poorly is that they are rarely taught good communication skills. Most people unconsciously absorb their ability to communicate without paying attention to whether their techniques really work.

In the most fundamental sense, a manager's job is to coordinate the work of employees. This can't be done unless the manager can communicate effectively. Of course, a manager's uses for communication go beyond simply giving directions. A manager must be able to receive feedback from subordinates and listen to the next level of the organizational hierarchy. A hospitality manager must also be able to communicate with and receive feedback from her guests. In this chapter we will cover both interpersonal and organizational communication to give you the necessary tools to navigate these often rough waters.

In what ways did you first learn to communicate? Have you had instruction in communication? What did it involve?

COMMUNICATION MODEL

Transcript of an *actual* radio conversation of a U.S. naval ship with Canadian authorities off the coast of Newfoundland (released by Chief of Naval Operations, October 10, 1995):

AMERICANS: Please divert your course 15 degrees to the North to avoid a collision.

CANADIANS: Recommend **you** divert **your** course 15 degrees to the South to avoid a collision.

AMERICANS: This is the Captain of a US Navy Ship. I say again, divert **YOUR** course 15 degrees to the North.

CANADIANS: No . . . I say again, you divert **YOUR** course.

AMERICANS: THIS IS THE AIRCRAFT CARRIER *USS LINCOLN*, THE SECOND LARGEST SHIP IN THE U.S. ATLANTIC FLEET. WE ARE ACCOMPANIED BY THREE DESTROYERS, THREE CRUISERS, AND NUMEROUS SUPPORT VESSELS. I **DEMAND** YOU CHANGE YOUR COURSE 15 DEGREES NORTH —**THAT'S ONE FIVE DEGREES NORTH**—OR COUNTERMEASURES WILL BE TAKEN TO ENSURE THE SAFETY OF THIS SHIP.

CANADIANS: **THIS IS A LIGHTHOUSE . . . YOUR CALL.**

The above example illustrates clearly how quickly and completely communication can break down. Further it shows that breakdowns in communication can lead to dire consequences. Whether you are a ship at sea or a hotel chain, poor communication can run you aground. To become more aware of the intricacies of communication that most of us take for granted, it helps to examine the components of the communication process.

In the most basic version of the communication process, an individual sends a message, the message is received by a second individual, and a response is returned to the sender of the message. To make the model more complete, we add several other dimensions, including message channels and individual roles. In the following section we discuss each of these topics, and by the end of it we will have a more comprehensive understanding of this complex process.

Message Channels

The **channel** used to transmit a message has a direct impact on how that message is perceived. Business communication can be sent through the following **channels:**

Verbal:

Spoken words—conversations, meetings, lectures

Written words—memos, handbooks, newsletters, emails, signs

Mediated communication—with the use of technology

Non-verbal:

Body language—hand gestures, facial expressions, touch, posture

Actions—work habits, timing, use of personal space

Visual symbols—charts, graphs, graphics

Environments—boss's office, corner café, hospital room

It is crucial to choose the appropriate channel for a message. For example, don't read someone a list of 100 numbers when they could be concisely summarized in a chart. Also, don't send a graph for a thank-you note. When addressing an issue that may cause conflict, written communication may be less confrontational than oral communication.

Do you have a favorite communication channel? One you prefer to use and find effective?

Roles of Receiver and Sender

The roles and status of two individuals affect the way that a message is communicated between them. People of low status are expected to show deference and are often intimidated by those of higher status, like our sea captain. When status differences are large, the communication process will tend to have more formality than when roles are equal. If the receiver and sender are friends, they will communicate with greater warmth and openness than if they are coworkers or acquaintances.

Feedback

Feedback is any message that the sender receives back from his or her partner and interprets. Without feedback, we would never know if our messages had been understood in the manner we intended. Feedback can come through all of the channels mentioned above. It can take the form of simply maintaining eye contact or the form of a lengthy verbal statement. Some feedbacks, such as a pertinent response or a nod of the head, indicate that the receiver understands the sender. Other feedbacks indicate that there was a misunderstanding. For instance, if one person says, "Do you have any objections to the new proposal?" and another person responds with, "I think I have a few of them in my freezer," chances are the message didn't get through. A look of confusion or responses such as "I don't understand" or "Me speak only pig Latin" are obvious indicators of unsuccessful communication. Feedback to a successful communication can indicate agreement or happiness, or disagreement, discontent, or lack of interest.

Expanded Communication Model

To fully grasp the complexities involved in the communication process, we can incorporate message channels, roles and status, and listening into our model, as shown in Figure 2.1. This

FIGURE 2.1   Expanded communication model

model takes into account the way in which the intended meaning of the message gets distorted by the sender's "message manufacturer," the choice of channels, the way the message gets distorted by the receiver's "listening filters," and the way the receiver formulates feedback.

> Give an example of a situation in which your message was distorted by the receiver. What happened? Was there anything you could have done as the speaker to have prevented this from happening?

Message Filter	Listening Filter
Personality	Personality
Attitude	Attitude
Relative Role	Relative Role
Status	Status
Non-Verbal Behavior	Interpretation of Receiver

IMPROVING ORAL AND WRITTEN COMMUNICATION

We are surrounded by words. They pour out of our mouths, our radios, our televisions, and our Ipods. They cover the pages of our newspapers and books. They bombard us from billboards and road signs. We have learned to transmit them around the world and through outer space at the speed of light. Without words we could not think or communicate in the way we are accustomed. Words serve one of two purposes, depending upon where they are. If they are inside our minds they are being used for thinking or what is called intrapersonal communication. Most of our communicating, however, is done with other individuals—whether face-to-face or through distance channels or even in books. When you think about it, it becomes obvious that there are a lot of words out there communicating! One very rough estimate puts the tally at 100,000,000,000,000,000 (that's one hundred quadrillion). In such a word-oriented world, the necessity of being an effective communicator is evident. In this section we present five general guidelines for effective communication and then separately examine written, spoken, and nonverbal communication skills.

> Do you believe that our vocabulary constrains our thinking? That is, do you agree that if you don't have a word to express an idea, then you don't formulate the idea?

Avoid Confusion When Choosing Words

The basis of most misunderstandings that arise in the communication process can be summed up as follows: *Meanings are in people, not in words.* In our section-opening vignette, clearly the ship captain felt that his meaning should be the accepted one by virtue of his position and rank. Unfortunately, he did not realize that his current position was pointing at a lighthouse.

In many cases such as this, the speaker is perceived more clearly than the words spoken. In other words, if a word falls in a forest and nobody reads it, it doesn't have any meaning.

CATHY   **by Cathy Guisewite**

Words take on meanings only when they are received into brains. By themselves, words are simply ink marks on a piece of paper or sound waves in the air. This seems quite trivial until we come to the crux of the issue: words don't mean the same thing to all people. The meaning that a word triggers when it is received in your brain is often different from the meaning that it triggered in the sender's brain. We often fail to consider the connotations that words carry; it is important to recognize that the message that one person sends is not the same message that the other person receives.

In addition, every discipline has its own dictionary of jargon and technical terms. These are words that may be known only by those who work in the subject and rarely have precise dictionary definitions. Such words should generally be avoided when communicating. Because they are ill-defined and are known only by a select few, they are subject to misinterpretation. The only exceptions to this rule would be if you were absolutely certain that all people with whom you are communicating agree to the word's meaning, or if the term is defined immediately after it is introduced. Before you use jargon or technical terms, ask this question to yourself: Do I want to show off or do I want to communicate? Some examples of jargon concocted by those who chose to show off:

Wood Interdental Stimulator—Government term for toothpick.

Experienced Cars—Automotive euphemism for used cars.

Normally Occurring Abnormal Occurrence—The nuclear industry's description of something that goes wrong all the time.

Therapeutic Misadventure—Medical jargon for an operation that kills the patient.

Be Brief and Precise

If we draw out the communication process longer than necessary, we risk losing our audience. When we are bored, we tune out. While it is important to be brief, it is even more important to be precise. If you say to your administrative assistant, "Please have that report done in the near future," do you mean that it should be done by next Tuesday or some time within the post-modern era? All too often, communication is blocked because the sender hasn't precisely planned what he or she wants to say, or doesn't say precisely what one planned.

If you want to be precise, you have to know exactly what you want to communicate. You should ask yourself such questions as, "What do I want to say?" "Why am I saying it?" and "To whom should I say it?" Before you even begin communicating, make sure that these questions have all been answered.

Know When to Use Redundancy

When someone says, "What do you mean by that?" in the course of a conversation, and you re-state what you just said but in different words, the person usually understands you the second time. Redundancy in business communication helps to clear the kind of misunderstandings that make people say, "What do you mean by that?"

When a message is sufficiently complex, it may help to repeat it in different words or from a different perspective. But be careful; too much or unnecessary repetition is boring. Use your judgment. When the same message gets sent several times, people get tired of hearing it; they may even feel you are insulting their intelligence. Redundancy can make people lose interest because you keep saying the same thing again and again.

> Think of a speaker you know who is very clear and precise, and then someone you know who can't seem to express himself or herself regardless of how many words are used. What are the differences in communication effectiveness?

Choose the Right Time and Place

When and where you choose to communicate can have an important impact on the success of the communication. In business communication, it is best to deliver your message at a time when:

1. The organization perceives a need for what you have to say.
2. There will be minimum delay between when people receive the message and when they must take action.

Suppose that you have devised a new incentive program to motivate the kitchen staff. You should not suggest your plan to your supervisor right after the kitchen staff picnic, when morale is high anyway. Rather, wait until the organization perceives that the kitchen staff needs to be motivated.

Choosing where to deliver your message is equally important. If you want to communicate as an equal to someone who is of either higher or lower status than you, you might be better off speaking to them outside of the workplace where your status is not as evident. You should also decide if your message will be more effective if you seek out the person with whom you wish to communicate, or if you invite that person to your office.

> Describe a situation where someone tried to talk with you at a bad time or in an awkward place. Did it influence communication effectiveness?

SPEAKING EFFECTIVELY

Generally we focus on the content of our communication and tend to neglect the quality of the speech itself. Certainly, the content of our messages is important but spoken language goes beyond merely uttering sounds. Oral communication comprises two equally critical components: language and paralanguage. **Language** refers to the words that we speak. **Paralanguage** refers to the way that we say these words. Paralanguage includes attributes that contribute to vocal variety, pronunciation, and silence.

Creating Vocal Variety

A speaker who uses inflections, rate, and volume effectively has what is called vocal variety. This variety makes it easier for listeners to pay attention and to distinguish main points from supporting details in a message.

> **Inflection:** Inflection is the pattern of vocal pitches used when speaking. Unchanging pitch (the absence of inflection) is called a monotone. Most people think that the use of inflection makes the voice more animated and more interesting to hear. Inflection can also be used to indicate which words are most important as you are speaking.
>
> **Rate:** Most people have a natural rate at which they usually speak. However, when people are feeling a particular emotion their vocal speed tends to change. Usually, speech slows down when people are depressed or bored and speeds up when they are happy or anxious. Speaking too slowly or quickly can be a deterrent to communication.
>
> **Volume:** The volume at which we speak helps to emphasize parts of a message. For example, we can speak softly and then emphasize a point by shouting, or we can speak loudly and then emphasize a point by whispering. Both methods draw attention to the part of the message that is spoken at a different volume.

Pronunciation and Fluency

Mispronounced words such as "dese," "dat," "nothin'," and "Febuary" are often interpreted as clues to educational background. **Pronunciation** can also give clues about which part of the country or which part of the world you come from originally. One can intentionally modify a dialect or drawl in order to communicate more effectively with a wider range of people.

Fluency refers to one's ability to speak articulately without excessive use of fillers such as "um," "ah," "ya know," and long pauses. Fluent speakers are impressive. They show confidence and the ability to concentrate on their train of thought and express it eloquently. Lack of fluency, although it does make one less polished, should not be seen as a sign of poor intelligence. Creative thinkers often have so many things running through their minds that it is difficult for them to follow one train of thought. We think at rates of 1,000–2,000 words per minute but can only speak at rates of 100–200 words per minute. Therefore, we must sort out 90 percent of what is in our heads. "Um"s and "ah"s give us the time to do that. However, do not feel obliged to fill pauses in your train of thought. Often it is best to stay silent.

Silence

Silence can be an effective communication tool. Like variations in speech volume and punctuation in written communication, silence can be used to enhance messages. A pause draws the listener's attention to what you will say next. Silence as a response is also an effective form of feedback. Silence can mean many things; it can communicate unutterable astonishment or unutterable disgust. Because it can mean such vastly different things, you must make sure that your use of silence has the desired effect.

How do you use silence in your daily communication?

NONVERBAL COMMUNICATION DIMENSIONS

Sumiko had been waiting for weeks to make this important call home to her family in Japan. It was nearly six months since she had spoken to them, and she was anxious to tell them all about her recent interviews. After finishing her second year in a hospitality program in Singapore, she had flown directly to the States to look for a summer job as a front desk clerk.

While her dream was to work at the Lucky Lady on the New Jersey shore, she wasn't certain what she should say to her parents about her interview that morning. All she knew was that the entire experience made her confused and uncomfortable.

First, the woman whom she met there was not dressed properly at all! She had on a very colorful blouse that all the men stared at when she walked by their desks. She did not seem at all interested in Sumiko and did everything so quickly that Sumiko was unsure what was happening. Mr. Peters, the director of human resources, spoke much too loudly and used big gestures that were almost frightening. It seemed that, even when sitting in his office chair, Mr. Peters took up a huge amount of space as he stretched his arms in the air to make his points. When he finally got up to escort Sumiko to her next meeting, he put his hand on her shoulder and stood so close Sumiko thought she might faint. But, how would she explain all of these feelings to her mother? Perhaps would it be best to just say the interview went well?

Humans have an elaborate **nonverbal language** that does most of the talking for us. Indeed, Mehrabian (1972) did a study in which he determined that total meaning is communicated 93 percent by paralinguistic, facial, and body cues, and only 7 percent by the words themselves. Experts say that our society is increasingly relying on visual information to gain understanding. Newspapers, while still primarily verbal, have become far more visually stimulating. People rely on television and other visual formats to get information about the world. In schools, children are experiencing a far more visually oriented curriculum than did their parents. We are learning to interpret visual meaning to a greater extent than our predecessors did and we need to be acutely aware of the nonverbal messages we send.

It is advantageous for the hotel manager to know how to send and interpret nonverbal cues. Knowing how to interpret nonverbal cues enables managers to determine employees' emotional state, their feelings, and how they perceive their role. Also, nonverbal messages are generally believed; it is difficult to lie nonverbally. Nonverbal communication serves the following four functions:

1. *Expresses emotion.* Facial expressions and hand gestures are especially useful for expressing emotion. Rarely do we hear someone say, "I am feeling angry with a touch of jealousy." Rather, we can "read it all over his face."
2. *Communicates the nature of the relationship.* How close we stand to someone when conversing indicates our feelings toward that person as well as our relative organizational status. Gestures and expressions can also communicate how comfortable we feel with someone.

3. *Affects verbal meaning.* If our verbal and nonverbal messages are in agreement, the two messages will reinforce each other and our communication attempts are likely to succeed. If, however, the verbal message contradicts the nonverbal message, research shows that the nonverbal message will be believed. For example, if someone says, "I'm so glad to see you!" and complements the verbal message with a warm smile and a handshake, you are likely to get the impression that she is indeed glad to see you. If, on the other hand, she contradicts the message by looking the other way and sneering, you are likely to feel unwelcome, despite the verbal message.

4. *Substitutes or replaces verbal communication.* When a particular situation makes verbal communication impossible or inappropriate, we use nonverbal communication. For example, the catcher can't yell to the pitcher's mound, "Throw a curve ball now!" without letting the batter hear; instead he uses hand signals. Waving at someone who is too far away to hear you say "Hello" serves a similar purpose. Rolling your eyes incredulously at a friend to discreetly communicate your thoughts about a third person or nodding your head to communicate agreement to a speaker without interrupting him are substitutes for verbal communication.

Almost every movement of the body and every action that we make can be interpreted as a form of nonverbal communication. In the following sections, we will explore seven categories of nonverbal communication.

> Think of a situation where you have tried to manipulate or manage your nonverbal communication. How successful were you?

APPEARANCE

We tend to infer a great deal about people from their physical appearance. These inferences often reflect stereotypes and biases which can ultimately influence our business judgment. For example, research shows that taller people get paid more than shorter people with the same qualifications.

Although there is little we can do about our natural body shape or facial features, we should be aware of the aspects of our appearance that we can readily change. For example, the way we dress reflects our personality and our status. People who dress meticulously are likely to be perceived as careful and organized on the job. However, people who are excessively fashion-conscious might be perceived as ostentatious or overly concerned about other people's opinions of them.

People of higher status in organizations tend to wear more expensive clothes than those of lower status. The general manager's "uniform" communicates higher status than the uniform the sanitation workers wear. Clothing can also be a barrier to communication in some situations. For example, suppose a manager decides to tour the hotel with the hope of getting to know the staff on an informal basis. If he does so in an expensive three-piece suit, he is likely to be perceived as less approachable than if he were to dress more casually.

> Under what circumstances do you intentionally try to create a particular image through your appearance? Do different generations perceive appearance in different ways?

Posture and Positioning

The way that you hold your body says a lot about your personality and your state of mind at a particular time. An erect attentive posture shows alertness, poise, and interest. A careless, distracted posture shows lack of interest and perhaps even laziness. Some postures, such as slouching, can be complex to interpret. Slouching can be interpreted as humiliation, submissiveness, or just plain boredom. Although psychologists have developed rules about the meaning of various postures, you will probably find that just from experience and from the context of a given situation, you can infer the meanings of different postures.

You have undoubtedly noticed many variations in the way that people position themselves relative to others. These positions are often indicative of certain attitudes. For example:

- A group which forms a closed circle and faces inward probably doesn't want others to join them.
- Leaning toward a person and facing him or her usually indicates that one is glad to be communicating with that person.
- Lifting one's head and straightening one's shoulders indicates a feeling of superiority.
- When people who are communicating hold postures that are similar to one another, it indicates that they are in agreement and feel positively toward each other.

Proxemics

Most animals display a characteristic called territoriality. Territoriality is the selection of a region that an animal will defend from invasions of outsiders. **Proxemics** is the study of how people space themselves relative to one another—how far we will allow someone into our "personal territory." There are "appropriate" distances between people for different kinds of interaction.

As you can see in Figure 2.2, the more intimate we are with someone, the closer we allow that person into our space. When people encroach on our space, we feel uncomfortable

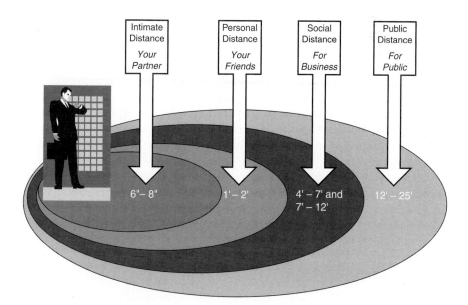

FIGURE 2.2 Territorial proximity

and pressured and perhaps even intimidated or aggressive. However, the distances in Figure 2.2 may differ depending on which culture an individual is from. These differences are further discussed in Chapter 3.

Touching

Western culture tends to discourage touching in public. Touching is reserved for private places and for those with whom we are intimate. However, there has been a trend toward more acceptance of touching because it is a good way to communicate closeness and openness.

One rather elaborate ritual that we have devised to allow people to touch each other is the handshake. We infer things about people from the way they shake hands. A firm handshake is considered assertive and confident; a weak handshake is listless, submissive, and generally "wimpy." In organizations, people of higher status touch those of lower status more often than the other way around. For example, the general manager is more likely to pat the front desk clerk on the back and say, "You're doing a fine job."

Gestures

Gestures are communicative movements. They are usually made with the hands, arms, and head. We gesture when we are talking or listening or when verbal communication is inappropriate. Although different cultures use gestures to varying degrees, many gestures have similar meanings in most cultures. A clenched fist almost always means aggression. Tapping one's fingers usually indicates anxiety or boredom. Opening one's hands is widely recognized as a gesture of sincerity. Nonetheless, some gestures are far from universal. For example, the American hand signal for "okay" would be interpreted by a Brazilian as something quite obscene.

Facial Expression and Eye Contact

When conversing with someone, we usually look at their face more than any other part of their body. The many versatile muscles in the face make it an ideal structure for communication, for we can shape our faces into countless different expressions. It should be noted that of all the modes of nonverbal communication, the face is the one we lie with the most easily. This is because we are generally more conscious of our faces than the rest of the body.

It has been said that the eyes are "the windows to the soul." If we know how to read the messages that people send with their eyes, we have a useful "window" to people's attitudes and emotions. **Eye contact** between two people can communicate (1) that they wish to communicate; (2) that one is looking for feedback from the other; or (3) that one wants to put the other under stress.

Eye contact is generally avoided when people are being deceptive, dishonest, competitive, or when they simply dislike each other. Another time people avoid eye contact is when their personal space has been invaded to the extent where they feel uncomfortable. For example, in a crowded elevator, people usually look at the floor. It has been found that people in high status positions tend to look at people while talking to them but not while listening to them.

Under what circumstances do you find it difficult to maintain eye contact? How does it affect you as a speaker when no one is looking at you?

Chronemics

Like money, time can be spent, saved, and must not be wasted. We keep a clock in sight, and have schedules, working hours, and deadlines. **Chronemics** concerns the things that people communicate through their use of timing. In the corporate world, being on time is considered essential. Those who are habitually late are considered unreliable, disrespectful, and careless. In other situations, promptness is undesirable. One is not supposed to arrive at a cocktail party precisely at the time on the invitation but rather "fashionably late." An additional convention about the use of time is that people who are of high status are allowed to be late for meetings with people of lower status, but people of lower status must not "keep the boss waiting." Chronemics is used to communicate status or degree of respect.

EFFECTIVE LISTENING

Shaul had been unconvinced of the value of listening training until two of his servers, who completed a ten-hour seminar, were transformed by the experience. As F&B Director at an up-scale seafood restaurant, Shaul had little faith in training of any sort. He learned all the skills he had through years of work experience, and he had been confident that he could show his staff anything they needed to know—especially something as simple and natural as listening! After all, what was there to learn? The changes he saw in Shannon and Petra, however, had him seriously rethinking his position.

"What did they teach you in that listening seminar?" Shaul asked when he met with the women for a debriefing. "You two have been amazing since taking that course—our customers can't say enough about your professional and caring service. How do you do it?"

"Well," Petra replied, "First, I now focus my full attention on the guest! I suddenly realized that I was only half listening when I took an order. I'd be watching some little kid play with her food or thinking about whether my car was going to start . . . now, I give my customers my complete attention, and they can tell the difference. It's so rare these days!"

"For me," Shannon explained, "It was all about getting the order right. I used to make so many mistakes because I just wasn't sure what someone meant—and then, you know, guests are always changing their minds. After the seminar, I learned it was okay to ask questions or to repeat the order so I could be sure everything was just the way the customer wanted it. Now, I never have to go back to the kitchen a second time. Everyone is happier!"

"We also learned some pretty cool memory techniques," Petra added. "And we pay close attention to the person's nonverbal cues so we know if they need us to suggest an option or further describe the dish."

"It sounds like there's a lot to learn, and practice," Shaul concluded. "Maybe the two of you could talk to your coworkers at our next staff meeting to see if anyone else might be interested in this listening seminar."

"Sure," the two women immediately agreed. "Then we'd be by far the best restaurant in town!"

Your listening skill is a key factor in determining both personal and professional success. As a supervisor, you must be prepared to analyze and synthesize information, make decisions, create relationships, and deal wisely with your staff. To accomplish this, a high level of communication competence is required.

You've probably always realized that training was necessary to speak effectively—to express your ideas clearly, to convince, and to motivate. But, have you ever really learned to listen? Hospitality researchers have studied supervisory listening skills and the results are revealing. While listening is one of the key behaviors in maintaining quality service, in creating an effective team, in developing your employees, and in problem-solving, it is also one of the most poorly developed. For example, human resource managers ranked listening as the "most troublesome yet important" communication skill. Fortune 500 training managers agreed, calling poor listening one of the "most important problems" facing their organization.

In spite of the recognition of its importance, listening is still the most neglected among all communication skills. Although it's likely that you spend almost twice as much time on the job listening as you do on speaking, reading or writing, the time devoted to teaching listening is much less than that devoted to other communication skills.

Importance of Listening

Listening serves two interdependent purposes:

1. *Effective listening helps you accomplish tasks with fewer misunderstandings.* If you listen carefully, you are more likely to order the right number of drinks, clean the appropriate room, and make accurate staffing plans. Effective listening saves you time and money as it increases the likelihood that you will have accurate information on which to base your decisions.
2. *Effective listening builds relationships.The quality of your relationships is affected by the quality of your listening skills.* If you demonstrate a sincere interest in your employees' ideas and problems, they will feel better about the quality of their work experience. The best way for you to indicate that you value your employees and their opinions is by listening to what they have to say.

Listening is a key tool of empowerment. Excellent supervisors learn to listen well and, in doing so, they create a supportive and positive environment in which to work. When supervisors listen, employees participate in problem-solving and feel that they have a greater stake in the department or organization's success. The positive relationships that result also contribute to increased morale and team effectiveness.

Your listening behavior can positively influence your work group, your department, and your organization. The consequences of good listening are far reaching. All it takes is knowledge of some basic principles, and then practice in applying the principles to your specific workplace setting.

Do you feel you are a better listener when you are interested in accomplishing a task or in building a relationship? Why?

Factors that Influence Listening

Your listening—and your employees' listening—is affected by a number of factors. Some of the factors you can control, others you can't. Some problems are caused by stress and things going on in your mind, others result from the environment itself. For a number of years researchers have explored the factors that appear to influence listening effectiveness. Among the most useful for you to know about are:

AGE   Listening ability is affected by the individual's age. Young children and the elderly are two groups that have distinct listening profiles, particularly with regard to memory functions. While children have trouble concentrating, older employees may not store information efficiently and so find it difficult to retrieve at a later time. The rate of information processing also slows down as an individual gets older.

GENDER   Differences in listening ability exist between men and women! For example, if women are taught that appearance is important, they are likely to pay more attention to messages that have to do with neatness or cleanliness. To the extent that interests are gender based, this also affects listening. It is likely that the average man would pay more attention and listen more effectively to stories concerning football or tractors or electrical repairs than would most women. However, as you can imagine, we can't always explain why men and women hear different things when someone speaks.

PERSONAL TRAITS   Personality dimensions, such as extroversion and introversion, influence listening ability. If someone is impatient and nervous, her listening behavior and challenges will be quite different from someone who is described as low-key or mellow.

PHYSICAL AND PSYCHOLOGICAL STATES   Physical states such as fatigue, stress, and strong emotions can also affect your listening ability. If you're upset about something or not feeling well, you can't devote your full energy to listening. It is important to understand how your physical or psychological state might be influencing your listening behavior. In some cases, the wisest decision might be to postpone the listening task until you are better able to handle this type of activity.

NOISE AND EXTERNAL DISTRACTIONS   It's difficult to concentrate, and to listen, when there are a lot of things going on around you. Telephones, people talking, or even music can create distractions that prevent you from focusing on the intended message.

> What factors do you find regularly influence your listening effectiveness? Explain in as much detail as possible.

Brownell's HURIER Listening Model

Listening is a complex activity that is largely covert. You can't really "see" someone listen. You can see *indicators* of listening, but not the actual listening process itself. How many times have you made eye contact with someone, nodded, and smiled, but didn't hear a word the person said?

In addition, listening isn't just one simple process but a system of several interrelated components. Therefore, it's sometimes difficult to know how to think about listening or how to go about improving your behavior. It's not unusual to find supervisors who think they can improve employees' listening simply by shouting, "Listen!!"

The **HURIER model** is presented below (Brownell, 2006). It suggests that there are six different elements of the listening process. Each component is developed by acquiring appropriate attitudes, learning relevant principles, and developing specific behaviors. Each letter of the word "HURIER" represents a different component: hearing, understanding, remembering, interpreting, evaluating, and then, responding.

HEARING   Hearing involves the accurate reception of verbal messages. In order to hear, you must focus your attention on the speaker and concentrate on what she has to say. It is particularly difficult to concentrate on a lengthy or complicated message when your employee is foreign or has difficulty speaking. Unless you accurately hear what was said, however, the listening process quickly breaks down.

UNDERSTANDING   Listening comprehension is different from reading comprehension. As with any other skill area, listening comprehension can be improved with practice. When listening to your employees, one of the most useful ways to improve understanding is to perception check. Ask your employee if your understanding of her point of view or idea is correct. Specialized vocabularies also interfere with comprehension. Don't avoid asking others for an explanation if a word they are using is unfamiliar to you.

REMEMBERING   Although you might think that memory is a separate ability from listening, memory is essential in order for you to apply what you have heard. Learning long- and short-term memory techniques can have a high payoff; recalling a new employee's name can be rewarding for both of you. The time you spend improving your memory will be well worthwhile; remembering information about someone is a form of compliment, illustrating that you care about them as an individual.

INTERPRETING   **Empathic listening** is one of the most valuable supervisory skills you can develop. When you listen empathically, you do two things. First, you take into account the total communication context so that you are better able to understand the meaning of what is said from the other person's point of view. This involves attention not only to the substance of a message, but also to the nonverbal cues that convey emotional meaning. Second, empathic listeners let their partner know that he or she has been understood by demonstrating supportive nonverbal behaviors in their response.

EVALUATING   It is impossible not to evaluate, to some extent, almost everything you hear. You listen from a unique point of view and are influenced by your past experiences and predispositions. It is therefore essential that you work to remain as open-minded as possible. Particularly, as the workforce becomes increasingly diverse, it is essential for supervisors to identify bias, stereotyping, propaganda, and other factors that may influence the conclusions they draw. Effective listeners, as you might suspect, try to minimize the influence of their own viewpoint until they have first understood the speaker's ideas.

RESPONDING   The quality of your listening is often judged by the nature of your response. The HURIER model incorporates your response as an integral part of the listening process because that's how your employees determine whether or not you have listened to them. Effective communicators recognize the range of alternative responses available to them and assess the situation to determine the most appropriate thing to say in each specific case.

> Which listening component of the HURIER model is most important for the type of listening that is important to you?

Building Listening Skills

There have been volumes of research about how to listen well compiled by authors such as Brownell (1988). Much of this research has been distilled into practical principles. Five of the most useful are described below.

Principle 1: Pay attention to the speaker. Really paying attention to someone means that you listen to everything that person communicates, both verbally and nonverbally. Good listening requires concentration. It's easy to become distracted when someone else is speaking, especially if you have a lot on your mind. One reason why you have this problem is because you think too fast! You can process information at least three or more times faster than someone can speak. That means you have a lot of spare thinking time, and it's very tempting to use those extra moments to reflect on other tasks, review your day's activities, decide what to have for dinner, or any number of things! Here are some tips for improving your concentration:

- mentally repeating what was said
- take a sincere interest in people and ideas
- think about how you can use the information you hear
- be as actively involved in the conversation as possible; ask questions, take notes

External distractions can also make it difficult to listen well. Always make sure you are ready to listen. If you let someone begin to speak while you are still gathering forms, finishing a project, or talking to a coworker, you are likely to miss important information. Take as much control of the listening situation as you can. Get organized to listen, and let your employee know when you are ready so you can give her your undivided attention.

Principle 2: Let the speaker know that you are paying attention. It is very hard to open up to someone who listens silently and expressionlessly. To let someone know that you are listening, you must give the appropriate verbal and nonverbal feedback. Your facial expressions and posture should reflect your interest in what the speaker has to say. Lean toward the speaker and maintain eye contact. Nod your head to express your understanding. If you don't understand, say so. Asking for clarification helps you to understand the speaker's intended meaning and gives the speaker the impression that you really want to understand the message.

Principle 3: Listen to the entire message. You've probably encountered an employee who seemed to take forever to answer questions, or who gave you twice as much information as you needed. You want to move the person along so that you don't waste valuable time, but the employee insists on going at his or her own pace.

Interruptions are also likely to occur when you disagree with someone and become emotionally involved—you become anxious to present your arguments or side of the story. Or perhaps you simply get excited about a topic of conversation and break in with your own experiences and ideas.

Think twice before you interrupt. Not only does it upset the speaker, but you've moved the focus from your employee onto yourself. You're demonstrating a concern for meeting your own needs. Always be sure that you realize the consequences interruptions may have on your relationship as well as on your accurate understanding of the message.

Principle 4: Take notes. It can be helpful to jot down notes in personal conversations as well as when listening to more formal lectures. There are times when it may not be appropriate, particularly if an employee is discussing some personal issue that he or she wants held confidential. If you are making a commitment to do something for a person, however, writing it down not only will help you to remember but also will give your employee the feeling that you want to understand.

Principle 5: Practice memory techniques. There are a variety of memory techniques that you can learn and apply to on-the-job situations. The payoff for improving your memory is tremendous. Two common memory techniques are **imagery devices** and **mnemonic devices.**

Imagery

Use both your visual and your auditory senses. There are many types of visual imagery techniques. One of the simplest is to see what you are trying to remember. If you leave your glasses next to your computer, you might visualize a robot with a computer head wearing your glasses. If you make that image vivid in your mind, then when you think to yourself, "What did I do with my glasses?" an image should come to mind immediately!

Imagery is also helpful in remembering names. You need to look directly at the person you are greeting rather than thinking about what you plan to say next. Repeat his or her name, and then try to form some visual or verbal association. The more you practice, the easier this process will become.

Mnemonic Techniques

Mnemonics are memory aids, such as formulas, rhymes, and other devices. How do you remember the number of days in each month? The letters associated with the lines and spaces in music? These are mnemonic devices that, once learned, stay with us forever.

> What have you learned from these five principles that you can apply to improve your personal listening effectiveness?

COMMUNICATING IN THE FORMAL ORGANIZATION

An organization can be perceived as a complex message-processing system in which messages are constantly flowing in all directions. Communication can be transmitted directly from sender to intended receiver as in our opening scenario when Brady distributed his surveys; or transmitted indirectly as when the housekeeper overheard negative comments about the program. Sometimes it flows through formal channels. Brady did this in his written request to the general manager to begin the program. Other times it is transmitted informally as when the kitchen staff discussed the new program.

Messages can travel up the corporate hierarchy from an hourly employee to the vice president, or down the corporate hierarchy as when the vice president sends a message to all hourly workers to attend a meeting regarding marketing. Messages are taken in from outside the organization. Brady had received reports of numerous customer service problems which were beginning to affect the hotel's reputation. Finally, messages are sent out to the environment, as when Brady advertised a new slogan in conjunction with his program "Rikko Hotel: A Hospitality Haven."

The efficiency and effectiveness of the organizational "message processing system" is crucial to the success of the overall organization. In any organization there is a formal communication network and an informal communication network. The formal communication network is generally depicted by an organizational chart like the one shown in Figure 2.3.

The chart indicates who is responsible to whom, who makes the most important decisions, and the relative status of employees. The formal communication network follows the links depicted in the chart. It is designed intentionally by the company. Message transfer within this network follows prescribed company policy. By contrast, the grapevine is not intentionally designed. Instead, it is a natural consequence of the social interactions among an organization's employees.

The formal communication network is a firmly structured hierarchy, with messages traveling in three directions: upward, downward, and horizontally. Upward communication occurs when a subordinate sends a message to a superior. Downward communication occurs when a superior sends a message to a subordinate. Horizontal communication occurs when one member of the organization communicates with a colleague of equal rank.

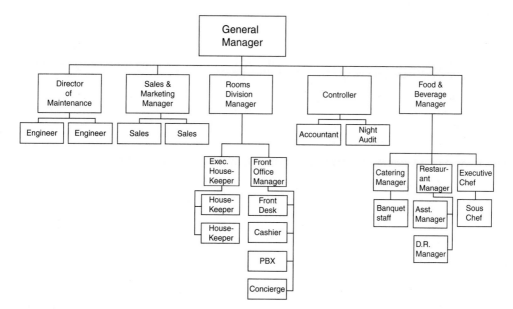

FIGURE 2.3 Organizational Chart

Diagram your position within the formal structure of an organization where you have recently worked.

Upward Communication

Upward communication is the means through which superiors stay in touch with the ideas, attitudes, grievances, and opinions of their subordinates. An effective upward communication system, in addition to providing important information and feedback to management, also enhances a subordinate's feeling of participation in the organization.

Despite the well-documented values of upward communication, some managers may be afraid that what they will hear from employees will be unfavorable, or perhaps they believe that their subordinates don't have anything of value to say. However, managers who do not use upward communication are losing valuable information that subordinates could provide.

The following three suggestions will improve upward communication in an organization:

1. Encourage your staff to communicate with you.
2. Respond.
3. Avoid communication barriers.

1. *Encourage Your Staff to Communicate with You.* Make it clear to your staff that you value their opinions and that you really want to hear what they have to say. Suggestion boxes and questionnaires are a step in that direction. An open-door policy that is truly open is another good way to encourage upward communication. The best way, however, is to schedule frequent meetings with each subordinate. All of the methods mentioned above should be utilized. The more channels you create for upward communication, the better. For example, a person may express himself more candidly in a questionnaire than in a meeting with the boss.

2. *Respond.* When employees believe that their suggestions are never taken out of the box, their questionnaires are never looked at, and no one ever *does* anything in response to their complaints, they become frustrated and may not bother with upward communication in the future. Therefore, it is imperative that you respond to your employees.

The most gratifying response for employees is when you use their suggestions, or remediate the problem that necessitated a grievance. However, when this is not possible, you must still explain why you can't use a suggestion or solve a particular problem. This lets your employees know that you considered what they had to say, and respected their opinion.

3. *Avoid Communication Barriers.* A large, impressive desk in an office can be intimidating to an employee of low organizational status. If status differences between superior and subordinate are particularly blatant, upward communication will be blocked. For example, even in companies with professed "open door" policies, it is unlikely that a custodian in uniform will feel comfortable walking in on the vice president in a three-piece business suit—regardless of how open the vice president's door might be. Indeed, the custodian would probably by screened out by a receptionist.

Another barrier to upward communication is physical distance. In large hotels and hotel chains especially, the corporate offices are often quite remote from individual properties. The best way to avoid these barriers is to leave your plush office and personally seek out your employees.

> Identify what you consider to be one of the biggest challenges to employees who strive to communicate upward in their organization.

Downward Communication

Any message that is sent through the formal communication links from a person of higher status to a person of lower status is an example of **downward communication.** It occurs, for example, when a manager asks her administrative assistant to type a memo, when the front desk manager gives directions to the other front desk employees, or when the general manager makes a speech to the whole staff. Downward communication is primarily concerned with "getting the job done." It may consist of instructions that specifically tell an employee what to do, or it may consist of information that helps an employee make a decision. Downward communication also serves an important role in establishing the corporate culture.

One barrier to successful downward communication is that the message gets increasingly distorted at each level in the formal network. The process is similar to the game "rumor" or "telephone," where a message is whispered from one person to another down a long line of people until the last person says the version of the message that they heard. The last person's version is usually quite different from the original. By the time the message reaches the employee, 80 percent of the message is lost.

Poor downward communication is a serious problem for an organization. Subordinates who get distorted messages or no messages at all from their managers will be confused about what they are supposed to do. Such confusion is frustrating to subordinates. It is equally frustrating to management if subordinates are not doing what they want them to do. However, often employees are not doing what management wants because, as a result of poor downward communication, they were never told what to do.

We offer four techniques that will improve downward communication in an organization:

1. Establish trust.
2. Use redundancy and multiple channels.
3. Make the message important to the employee.
4. Don't overload.

1. ***Establish Trust.*** Subordinates who mistrust their superiors are likely to treat messages from that superior in ways that reflect their lack of trust. If an employee is supposed to pass a message on, information may be filtered or the meaning distorted. If the message is intended for a specific employee, it may not be delivered. An employee who does not trust the formal communication network may rely instead upon the grapevine for information.

   To establish trust you can:

   a. ***Allow your employees to get to know you.*** Mistrust can be caused by a lack of contact and misunderstanding between people.
   b. ***Be honest.*** Don't make the picture look any brighter or grimmer than it is. If you always exaggerate the seriousness of something in order to motivate your employees, or try to cover up negative information, your employees will stop believing you.
   c. ***Explain why.*** Don't be mysterious. When giving directions explain why you are giving them.

2. ***Use Redundancy and Multiple Channels.*** As we discussed in the first part of this chapter, repeating a message aids the receiver's understanding and ability to remember. We suggested that you should state your message in two different ways or from two different perspectives. You can also use two different channels to achieve redundancy. Suppose you want to communicate newly formed organizational goals to all of

your employees. You could begin by writing a memo to be distributed to everyone, follow up on the memo with personal contact, and then make posters that list the goals.

3. *Make the Message Important.* The perspective of a subordinate differs from the perspective of a manager. What is important to one may not be important to the other. If you want your subordinates to pay attention to what you are saying, you must try to make the message interesting to them. For example, suppose that you are instituting a new benefit plan. The reasons why you consider the plan important are that it will increase motivation, cost less than the old plan, and give you more prerogatives. Your employees would consider it important because it offers more benefits to good workers and a larger pension. When explaining the new plan to your employees, don't get so caught up in what is important to *you* about the plan that you fail to concentrate on what is important to *them.* Explain the pros and cons from their perspective first. Then, after you have explained what is important to them, it is also good to explain why the plan is important to you.

4. *Don't Overload.* People have limited capacities for internalizing and responding to messages. If an employee is besieged by piles of memos, incessant phone calls, and constant meetings, then information overload occurs. Miller and Hawes explore people's responses to information overload. Some of these responses are:

   1. *Error*—"It doesn't matter if it's done right; I just want to get it done."
   2. *Queuing*—"I can't deal with all this paperwork; I'm just going to let it pile up" (and up, and up).
   3. *Filtering*—"I'll do the important stuff now and let the rest of it rot."
   4. *Delegation*—"Let someone else do it." (I understand Mikey actually likes it!)
   5. *Escape*—"Forget this, I'm going to Bermuda."

When are you most likely to experience message overload? What happens when there are too many options—what is your response?

Horizontal Communication

Horizontal communication is the type of information processing that occurs between people of equal status in an organization. Usually horizontal communication serves the purpose of coordinating the functions of different departments within the organization. Horizontal communication links are not typically depicted on an organization chart; such charts typically show only the upward and downward links. In the organizational chart depicted in Figure 2.3 imagine there are horizontal communication links between several departments. Without these links it would take one upward, two horizontal, and one downward link for the Executive Housekeeper to communicate with the Director of Maintenance.

The following two guidelines will aid horizontal communication within an organization:

1. Reward good horizontal communication.
2. Make sure interdepartmental competition is constructive.

1. *Reward good horizontal communication.* Organizations often have rewards for those who contribute to effective upward or downward communication. Rarely do they reward good horizontal communication.

2. ***Make sure interdepartmental competition is constructive.*** Often organizations establish competitions between different departments in order to increase motivation. Such competitions have their advantages and their drawbacks. One serious drawback is that they can engender hostility between competing departments. Competing departments may not want to share resources or information with each other. Also, when departments are competing, employees tend to see things from the narrow perspective of their own department instead of from the perspective of the entire organization. These drawbacks hinder horizontal communication. When instituting interdepartmental competition, make sure that the competition is not hindering horizontal communication or cooperation in general. Always stress that the competition is for the good of the whole organization, not just one department.

> Which type of formal communication do you think is most challenging—upward, downward, or horizontal? Give your reasons.

THE GRAPEVINE

The term "grapevine" is derived from the days of the Civil War. In those days the army communicated using telegraph wires strung from tree to tree in such a way that they resembled a grapevine. Messages that traveled through these wires often got mixed up. Hence, the term **grapevine** came to be associated with garbled messages.

Like the grapevine used during the Civil War, the modern organization is strung together in a haphazard fashion because it is composed of informal links that cross status and departmental boundaries, making up an organization's **informal communication network.** However, unlike the grapevine in the Civil War, the grapevine in modern organizations can be surprisingly accurate. This is not to say that it is entirely dependable as a source of information, but it is more dependable than most people assume. When the topics discussed are non-controversial, the grapevine is correct 75 percent of the time. The grapevine is also the fastest disseminator of information in the organization. While it may take months for an official message to get from one person to another, it probably takes only a couple of hours before the whole organization knows that the boss is divorcing his wife.

Some managers who are concerned about rumors flowing through the grapevine would like to eliminate it altogether. This is both impossible and undesirable. It is impossible because the grapevine is an unavoidable consequence of people interacting socially. It is undesirable because it is an essential channel for organizational communication. The grapevine can distribute valuable information quickly by bypassing the formal links. Another reason why it is undesirable to eliminate the grapevine is that the grapevine is necessary for a healthy social climate in the organization.

The manager, instead of trying to eliminate the grapevine, should try to eliminate rumor. The grapevine is generally a positive aspect of an organization; it is the rumors that are negative. The best way to reduce rumor is to increase downward communication. For example, suppose the management has decided to lay off one kitchen worker. If the manager does not make this known to all employees through formal downward links, he runs the risk that a rumor might develop that says, for instance, that the entire kitchen staff is being fired. By using downward communication management can prevent outlandish rumors from developing.

Summary

In this chapter, we discuss two different types of communication: interpersonal and organizational. A hospitality manager has two primary jobs: (1) to coordinate the work of employees and (2) to handle difficult situations with the organization's customers. Thus, effective communication is a necessity for hospitality managers. We make a number of suggestions for improving oral and written communication.

We also discuss the importance of nonverbal communication. Research has shown that only about 7 percent of communication is verbal, the remaining 93 percent is through some form of nonverbal cues. We discuss several different forms of nonverbal communication.

Not only is it important for a manager to effectively communicate, it is also necessary to possess effective listening skills. We provide a number of principles managers can use to improve listening effectiveness.

We also examine the formal and informal communication networks that exist within an organization. There are three types of communication in an organization's formal communication network: upward, downward, and horizontal. Communication will be more effective within an organization if a manager encourages all three of these types. The grapevine is an informal communication network that exists in many organizations. While many managers try to eliminate the grapevine, we suggest that they merely try to eliminate rumors and improve the accuracy of the information flowing through the grapevine.

Key Words

channel *33*
language *37*
paralanguage *37*
inflection *38*
pronunciation *38*
fluency *38*
nonverbal language *39*

proxemics *41*
eye contact *42*
chronemics *43*
HURIER model *46*
empathic listening *46*
external distractions *47*
imagery devices *48*

mnemonic devices *48*
upward communication *50*
downward communication *51*
horizontal communication *52*
grapevine *53*
informal communication
    network *53*

Exercises

Exercise 1   Dealing Out Bad News

Category: Communication

Objective: To help participants practice skills for communicating undesirable news

Group Size: Three participants

Time Frame: 45 minutes

Materials: Index cards, paper, pens

Procedure:

1. Explain the objective of the exercise:

   In the hospitality industry, as elsewhere, we often need to tell our customer or coworker something that they do not wish to hear. For example, a waitperson may need to explain that a desired entrée is no longer available, or a cleaning person may need to tell both the executive housekeeper and customer that a personal item was broken in the process of cleaning the room. How does one overcome reluctance and nervousness and communicate the facts honestly but in a diplomatic manner?

   Role playing provides an opportunity to practice tactful methods of conveying bad news. Constructive feedback from those observing the role play will help to further refine these skills.

2. Divide the participants into groups of three.
3. Give each participant four index cards.
4. Write examples of open-ended sentences on the board, such as:
   - There is something I need to tell you about . . .
   - I am not sure how to say this, but . . .
   - I hate to tell you that . . .
   - This is awkward, but . . .
   - I don't know how to say this . . .
5. Each participant writes down one sentence on each of the four cards beginning with any of the open-ended prompts. Encourage them to draw examples from their own workplace experience. Collect the cards.
6. Each participant draws a card.
7. In each group, one person plays a role using the sentence on the card, and another person acts as the coworker or customer. The third person observes and critiques the exercise. After each play, the participants rotate their roles. The process continues until each person in the group has played each role. Observers should take notes on what went well and what could have gone better in the role play.
8. A class discussion should follow the exercise highlighting the strengths and weakness of various responses to the situations in the role play.

Exercise 2   Are You Listening?

Category: Communication

Objective: To illustrate how nonverbal communication and listening skills affect a speaker

Number of Participants: Groups of Four

Time Frame: 20 minutes

Materials: none

Procedure:

Divide participants into groups of four. Assign each participant a role without letting the other group members know which participant has which role.

The roles are as follows:

Storyteller. This participant is told to tell their favorite jokes or a short humorous story. The jokes or story should last for approximately three minutes.

Avid Listener. This participant is told to listen very attentively, giving nonverbal cues that they are listening, such as leaning forward, nodding, eye contact, and smiling.

Apathetic Listener. This participant is told not to listen to the speaker. For example, the listener might look out the window, hum a tune, stand up and sit a lot, doodle, etc.

Aggressive Non-Listener. This participant is told to be overly inattentive to the speaker. For example, this participant might make or receive a cell phone call, exhibit hostility to the speaker, attempt to strike up conversations with other listeners or move physically too far from the speaker.

After the storytellers complete their stories, group discussion about the effects of the various roles ensues. The following discussion questions may help stimulate conversation among the participants:

- How do the storytellers describe each of the listeners?
- Which listening types have people most often dealt with in the past?

- What are some useful strategies speakers might employ to refocus less than attentive listeners?
- As a listener, which techniques could you employ to get someone speaking to you to feel most comfortable and open to speaking?

Exercise 3   Honestly Lying

Category: Communication

Objective: To practice detecting verbal and nonverbal cues in communication styles

Number of Participants: Any number divided into groups of four

Time Frame: 30 minutes

Materials: "Honestly Lying Cards" (copy onto cardstock from following page)

Procedure:

Divide participants into groups of four. Each participant takes an "Honestly Lying Card" and will take a turn speaking for one minute about the topic on their card. Prior to speaking, the participant chooses whether they will tell the truth or lie. After each person speaks, the other participants are allowed one minute to ask questions to help them determine whether the person was telling the truth. The group then votes on whether or not they believe the speaker was telling the truth. The speaker then tells if the vote was correct and the play continues with the next participant speaking. Cues as to

whether a speaker is telling the truth may include body language, voice confidence and inflection, eye contact, and pacing. However, a speaker may intentionally alter these cues in order to mislead their audience.

Following this exercise, the class discusses the experience. Discussion topics might include the following:

- Which body language cues might help you determine when a person is lying to you?
- Which voice cues might help you determine when a person is lying to you?
- If one of the speakers was successful in deceiving the group either of their truthfulness or lying, what aspects of their presentation were most convincing?
- If your job necessitates that you convince someone of your truthfulness, which techniques might help you to convey that honesty?
- As a hospitality manager, how might understanding nonverbal communication help you in your job?

***

Honestly Lying Card	Honestly Lying Card
My favorite actor . . .	The worst thing I ever did in a sports game . . .
Honestly Lying Card	Honestly Lying Card
My favorite food . . .	The best book I ever read . . .
Honestly Lying Card	Honestly Lying Card
The best movie I ever saw . . .	My most memorable experience at a restaurant . . .
Honestly Lying Card	Honestly Lying Card
The most valuable lesson I learned from my mother (or father) was . . .	My earliest childhood memory is . . . .

***

Exercise 4 Identity Crisis

Category: Communication

Objective: To learn about questioning strategies used to gain information

Number of Participants: Any number in groups of five or six

Time Frame: 15 minutes

Materials: Adhesive labels with the names of famous individuals printed on them

Procedure:

Divide the participants into groups. Place a label on the back of each group member without telling the person the name on their own back. The participants look at each other's backs, then sit in a circle and take turns asking yes/no questions to determine their identity.

After the exercise, the groups discuss the following points:

1. How did you begin your line of questioning?
2. Which kinds of questions were most useful?
3. What did this exercise tell you about communication?

Famous People		
Hillary Rodham Clinton	Britney Spears	Saddam Hussein
Usher	Mike Meyers	Abraham Lincoln
Tom Cruise	Albert Einstein	Bill Gates
Elvis Presley	George Washington	Fidel Castro
John F. Kennedy	Bono	Martin Luther King, Jr.
Marilyn Monroe	William Shakespeare	Martha Stewart
Benjamin Franklin	John Stewart	Mother Theresa
Paul Revere	Beethoven	Queen Elizabeth II
Warren Buffet	King Henry VIII	Steve Irwin

Endnotes

Blumentritt, R. & Hardie, N. (2000). The role of middle management in the knowledge-focused service organization. *Journal of Business Strategies*, *17*(1), 37–48.

Borchgrevink, C. & Susskind, A. (1996). Beverage communication: A pilot study of the experiences and preferences of restaurant customers. *The Hospitality and Tourism Educator*, *8*(1), 19–23.

Brownell, J. (1988). *Building Active Listening Skills*. Englewood Cliffs, NJ: Prentice Hall, Inc.

Brownell, J. (1992) Hospitality managers' communication practices. *The International Journal of Hospitality Management*, *11*(2), 111–128.

Brownell, J. (1998). Effective communication in multicultural organizations: A receiver-defined activity. In C. R. Lovitt (Ed.). *Redefining professional communication as an international discipline: Implications for teaching and research*, Amityville, NY: Baywood Publishing Co. pp. 171–187.

Brownell, J. (2006). *Building active listening skills*. Boston: Allyn & Bacon, Publishers.

Brownell, J. & Reynolds, D. (2002). Strengthening the purchaser–supplier partnership: Behaviors that make a difference. Report sponsored by the Center for Hospitality Research, Cornell University, and Richmond Events.

Gallivan, M. (2001). Meaning to change: How diverse stakeholders interpret organizational communication about change initiatives. *IEEE Transactions on Professional Communication*, *44*(4), 243–266.

Keleman, M. (2000). Too much or too little ambiguity: The language of total quality management. *Journal of Management Studies, 37*(4), 483–498.

Knapp, M. (1988). *Communication in human interaction.* New York: Holt, Rinehart, & Winston.

Mehrabian, A. (1972). *Silent messages.* Belmont, CA: Wadsworth Publishers.

Miller, J. & Cardy, R. (2000). Technology and managing people: Keeping the "human" in human resources. *Journal of Labor Research, 21*(3), 447–461.

Moody, J. Stewart, B., & Bolt-Lee, C. (2002). Showing the skilled business graduate: Expanding the tool kit. *The Journal of Business Communication, 65*(1), 21–36.

Olaniran, B. A. (1994, February). Group performance in computer-mediated and face-to-face communication media. *Management Communication Quarterly, 7*(3), 256–282.

Phyllis H. P. (2001, July). I have a dream: Communicating a vision helps managers become leaders. Pharmaceutical Executive: Pharmaceutical Executive Careers, 28–30. Retrieved January 23, 2008, from ABI/INFORM Global database. (Document ID: 75871673).

Rosenfeld, L. B. & Civikly, J. M. (1976). *With words unspoken: The nonverbal experience.* New York: Holt, Rinehart, & Winston.

Smith, J. (1999). Do your employees know the plan? *Management Review, 88*(9), 11–14.

Stamp, G. (1999). A qualitatively constructed interpersonal communication model: A grounded theory analysis. *Human Communication Research, 25*(4), 531–547.

Stuart, J. & Thomas, M. (1986). Dialogic listening: Sculpting mutual meanings. In J. Stewart (Ed.). *Bridges not walls: A book about interpersonal communication.* New York: McGraw-Hill Publishers. pp. 192–210.

Sypher, B. D., Bostrom, R. N., & Seibert, J. H. (1989). Listening, communication abilities, and success at work. *The Journal of Business Communication, 26*(4), 293–303.

Tubbs, S. L. & Moss, S. (1994). *Human communication.* Eastern Michigan University: McGraw Hill.

Wetlaufer, S. (2001). Can we talk? *Harvard Business Review, 80*(3), 12.

Williams, D. (2001). Communicate our leadership agenda. *Executive Excellence, 18*(12), 10–15.

3

UNDERSTANDING THE DIVERSE ENVIRONMENT

If man is to survive, he will have learned to take a delight in the essential differences between men and between cultures. He will learn that differences in ideas and attitudes are a delight, part of life's exciting variety, not something to fear.
—Gene Roddenberry, Quoted in an Aardvarque greeting card, Santa Barbara, Calif., 1971

CHAPTER OUTLINE

Introduction

Understanding Individual Differences
    Differences in Perception
        Experiences influence perception
        Expectations influence perception
        Other perceptual filters
    Unobservable Cultural Differences
        Values
        Time
        Space
        Context
        Relationships
        Work attitudes

Specific Behavioral Differences
    Overcoming Resistance to Taking Initiative
    Reluctance to Speak Out
    Working Toward Cross-Cultural Understanding
    Ineffectiveness of Conventional Incentives

Business Culture

Techniques for Managing a Diverse Workforce
    Communicating with Sensitivity
    Developing Empathy
        Self-awareness
        Cultural sensitivity
        Relational abilities
    Becoming More Adaptable
    Asking More Questions

Improving Cross-Cultural Skills
    Orient Employees to the Work Environment
    Educate Workers and Supervisors Regarding Cultural Differences
    Provide Language Classes
    Encourage Employee Input
    Develop Support Groups
    Create It

Stereotypes and Cultural Biases

Summary

LEARNING OBJECTIVES

After reading this chapter, you will be able to do the following:

1. Understand the benefits of a diverse workforce, which includes enhanced productivity, utilizing diverse frames of reference, fostering creativity and problem solving, and developing empowerment paradigms for all employees.
2. Discuss barriers to valuing diversity and methods for overcoming them.
3. Explain how cultural identity is formed.
4. Explain the importance of values and how they may affect your employees at work.
5. Discuss three values that may differ among the employees of a diverse workforce.
6. Describe three behavioral differences managers may observe when working with employees from another culture, or of a different age or gender.
7. List the steps you would take to manage the three behavioral differences you described in objective 6.
8. Understand the three components of empathy and describe one action you could take to become more empathic.
9. Identify four strategies a manager can adopt when trying to establish a more effective and efficient diverse work environment.
10. Discuss three common attitudes/cultural biases managers of a diverse workforce should avoid.

Scenario: Josh's Juncture

Josh, a new vice president for a chain of hotels, organized a meeting of international food vendors thinking that getting products directly from their home countries will give his company an edge. He was pleased to meet with each of them in his hotel in New York. The first to arrive was Ahmed. Josh greeted him warmly, but as they conversed he became uncomfortable as Ahmed was clearly stepping in too close to him and had him backed into a corner. Next, Mario arrived. His coffee products from Brazil had a wonderful reputation. Josh stepped around Ahmed and reached out to shake Mario's hand. He was surprised when Mario embraced him. He thought he would further bond by offering his greeting in Spanish. Mario looked at him quizzically and replied in Portuguese. Kwan from Korea arrived almost at the same time as Mario. Josh stepped out of Mario's embrace and moved to embrace Kwan in the same manner, but Kwan stepped back with a stiff and alarmed expression. Josh decided he would shake the hands of his remaining guests. Hans from Germany, Harish from India, and Henry from Canada also arrived. It was ten minutes past the scheduled start of the meeting, but Josh was reluctant to begin as Aracelli from Mexico had not yet arrived. He waited five more minutes, and then, sensing impatience on the part of his other guests, particularly Hans who was standing like a sentinel next to his seat, he began the meeting. Josh spoke quickly to move things along after his late start. He was nearly through his introduction when Aracelli arrived, slightly miffed that they had begun without her.

Josh's unfamiliarity with cultural norms and values made for a very uncomfortable meeting for his guests as well as for himself. He could have vastly improved his situation by learning that Arabs are comfortable in smaller personal spaces, not all South Americans speak Spanish, Koreans are not comfortable with physical contact especially in first introductions, Germans wait to be asked to sit by their hosts, and in Mexico timetables are very loose.

INTRODUCTION

The hospitality industry has and will continue to have a global perspective. Business and service interactions will require increasing levels of cultural sensitivity. Current projections predict an increasing diversity of the U.S. labor force. According to recent reports, the American workforce comprised of Hispanics, Asians, and other minorities is approaching 30 percent and is projected to continue to increase (Bureau of Labor and Statistics, 2006). Outside of the United States, multinational corporations are expanding their operations and an increasing number of managers are facing the challenges of managing culturally diverse work teams.

For hospitality managers, the implications of a culturally diverse workforce are twofold. First, the hospitality industry attracts a diverse workforce. Second, the diverse workforce serves customers with different needs and backgrounds. This phenomenon creates a challenging managerial environment. Nonetheless, if managed effectively, diversity can create a significant competitive advantage by developing a resourceful, creative, and flexible workforce that can be the foundation for a hospitality organization's long-term success. In order to successfully train and keep diverse employees, managers must gain as much insight as possible into this source of labor and cultivate a wide range of interpersonal skills.

However, the interest level of hospitality managers in diversity issues shows signs of decline. *Hotel and Motel Management* reports the drop in attendance at diversity conferences organized by the Hospitality Industry Diversity Institute (HIDI), which is sponsored by the American Hotel & Motel Association and *Hotel & Motel Management*, among others. In particular, the attendance at the HIDI conference dropped nearly 50 percent in just two years. In an attempt to regain interest, the HIDI decided to merge its conference with the Multicultural Foodservice and Hospitality Alliance. Conferences early in the twenty-first century have attracted more participants, but have been light on the hotel industry participation. These signs of lack of interest in diversity efforts suggest that there is a need for hospitality managers to understand the powerful implications of workforce diversity. "How can you leverage diversity to the bottom line?" is the question that was addressed during the 2000 conference (Hospitality Leaders, 2000). The answer to this question starts with hospitality managers building on the strengths of workforce diversity while recognizing potential problems.

In this chapter we summarize important facts and principles related to diversity as it impacts the hospitality industry, and explore how these findings can be applied to a diverse workforce. First, how culture affects individuals in a work group is explained. Second, challenges and potential benefits related to a hospitality workforce that is diverse in age, culture, and gender are examined. Third, research on workforce diversity is analyzed to explain how diversity can affect the workforce. Finally, implications for hospitality managers are presented together with specific recommendations for building a diverse and effective workforce. These recommendations focus on three distinct levels: personal, departmental, and organizational.

> Why might conflicts be divided into personal, departmental, and organizational? How is it useful to managers?

UNDERSTANDING INDIVIDUAL DIFFERENCES

Maria was pleased to have been invited to the first planning meeting of the events committee at the large resort hotel where she worked as a marketing associate. The events committee was responsible for coordinating all company social activities, including holiday parties. This was a real change for her, having begun her career in a small rural village in Mexico, and she was grateful for the opportunity to be involved.

The particular topic at hand was how the company was going to recognize its vice president of marketing, Juan Santos, who was retiring at the end of the month. Maria had intended to just listen to her coworkers' ideas at this first meeting without sharing her personal views. However, as the discussion progressed, she found it difficult to remain silent. Peter suggested putting on a talent show, where employees could volunteer to sing or dance or read jokes. Caitlin wanted to have a casino theme, where participants could gamble and win prizes. Sean argued for roasting the guest of honor; he thought it would be fun if several employees gave short speeches about particularly memorable experiences.

Maria felt that she knew Mr. Santos better than anyone else in the room, and she was horrified at the suggestions she heard. Mr. Santos was a kind, generous, and distinguished gentleman. She doubted that he would be comfortable with any of the ideas that had been presented. Rather, Maria believed an appropriate celebration would involve a formal ceremony and serious recognition of Mr. Santos' accomplishments. How could these people think that Mr. Santos would enjoy being embarrassed? It sounded to her like this celebration was designed for the participants, not for the guest of honor. Maria could not be silent any longer. She raised her hand high in the air.

Differences in Perception

You may have heard the phrase, "From the other person's point of view, he or she is probably right!" The perceptual process, the way we select and then interpret stimuli in our environment, greatly affects how we see the world and how we respond to events. While the exact nature of perceptual differences is often difficult to determine, we do know that no two people experience the world in exactly the same manner.

EXPERIENCES INFLUENCE PERCEPTION   Perhaps the most important influence on our perceptions is our past experiences. There's a story told that when people who grew up in the jungle saw an elephant at a distance, they remarked at how very small the animal was. What they didn't realize, because they had no prior experience with that perspective, was that things look smaller as they get farther away. They assumed, at first, that they were simply looking at a little elephant.

This chapter discusses the issues and challenges of managing a diverse workforce, of understanding and motivating people whose backgrounds are quite different from one another. As the above example illustrates, growing up in cultures with different traditions, languages, and social environments is likely to create significant perceptual differences as well. Several of these dimensions will be discussed in detail later in this chapter.

EXPECTATIONS INFLUENCE PERCEPTION   To some extent, too, individuals see what they expect to see. This is called selective perception. Often, people have preconceived notions about how smart someone is or how capable they are of doing a good job. In other instances, an employer might be biased toward someone who came from a particular university or who has had prior experience in a particular field. In such cases, the person in question can either do no wrong or can't seem to do anything right—at least in the eyes of the biased beholder. In the most damaging cases, such expectations lead to what we call stereotyping and cultural bias. Managers who either demonstrate stereotyping themselves, or allow their employees to stereotype, are creating obstacles to individual, team, and organizational well-being.

Give an example of how your past experiences have influenced your perception of some event or person. Describe both the specific experiences and how they influenced your understanding of the event.

OTHER PERCEPTUAL FILTERS   Every person is constantly influenced by a range of internal and external factors. These might include their attitudes, values, interests, gender, age, and—importantly—culture. You are influenced by the specific situation and how comfortable you feel in your environment. The nature of these filters and the impact they have determine your judgments and conclusions.

For instance, put yourself in the place of a convention planner. You get instructions from the client about table settings, decor, food, and decorations. You believe that you are following her directions and, when you finish, you feel good about how everything turned out. You even checked with two of your coworkers who also complimented you on putting together a professional looking arrangement. Unfortunately, when the client sees your work, she is horrified! She describes it as "cluttered," "fragmented," and "disturbing." Where did you go wrong? Keep in mind that it's never a matter of "right" or "wrong." It's simply how various individuals perceive a situation. The more you know about the people you work with, the better able you will be to anticipate their responses to various options.

In this chapter we explore the complexities of the diverse workplace. Understanding perceptual differences, as you will discover, is a prerequisite to effectively managing a diverse workforce.

Unobservable Cultural Differences

Every society develops its own set of norms and passes them on from one generation to the next. From our earliest days we begin to gain an understanding of the difference between good and bad. From our elders, we learn the basic guidelines for social interaction and the values of work and honesty. These culturally distinct instructions help to form an intangible set of beliefs and assumptions about the world and provide a framework for conducting even the most mundane transactions. In short, culture is the learned, shared, and compelling norms of a society, based on a culture's specific set of attitudes, values, and beliefs.

Identifying explicit cultural differences such as dress, eating habits, and language is relatively simple. Successfully managing a diverse workforce, however, requires recognizing and working with both overt and subtle cultural characteristics that influence an individual's work performance. These could include norms of politeness, norms for group interaction, openness about feelings, use of voice and gesture, and feelings about power. Several important cultural differences that are not readily observable are discussed.

Have you traveled to or lived in another country? What were some of the important differences you noticed that affected your interactions and comfort?

VALUES   **Values** are enduring beliefs. Every culture has a unique system of values. Values form the core of a culture. It is from values that almost every other facet of society arises: lifestyle, customs and practices, and, in some cases, language. Values are signposts that reflect

*"In the interest of cultural diversity, we've hired Jason,
here, who owns a number of hip-hop CDs."*

what a society or culture really cares about, what they live, fight, and die for, and how they behave. Values can be divided into two distinct types. **Instrumental values** represent acceptable behaviors to be used in achieving ends—for example, honesty, self-discipline, or courage. **Terminal values,** on the other hand, represent goals to be achieved or end states such as peace, wisdom, or respect.

Some values are universal and transcend almost every culture and society. For example, desires for physical comfort and human companionship are valued from culture to culture. Other values are more unique to one particular culture, or are given different priorities on a hierarchy of values in individual cultures. Values of self-reliance and independence from family are highly treasured in American society, while these have low priorities in other countries, particularly in Asia.

Differences in values among various cultures create differences in individual value systems. These differences in values can have profound effects on how diverse workers can be managed, and how productivity within organizations can be assessed and maximized. The study of diverse cultural values and how these values affect working relationships among cross-cultural employees is important for four primary reasons (Thiederman, 1990).

1. *Values dictate needs.* Felt needs of a person are determined to a great extent by cultural values. Without knowledge of the needs of their diverse employees, managers' efforts in motivating them will be greatly compromised.
2. *Values dictate what is perceived as a problem.* The perception of a problem is often influenced by values. For example, to the Asian worker, the tendency to remain silent or failure to ask questions despite lack of understanding does not present a problem. To a German manager, this type of behavior would be problematic as it is contrary to the values of openness and directness.
3. *Values dictate the solutions to problems.* Values also influence how problems are solved. For example, some cultures are nonconfrontational. An individual from one of

these countries might try to solve an interpersonal conflict by requesting a transfer to a new department. He or she places a high value on maintaining harmony in the workplace and perceives a loss of this harmony if a direct confrontation takes place. An individual from a more direct or confrontational culture would likely perceive this as cowardly and evasive, preferring to deal directly with problems.

4. *Values dictate expectations of behavior.* Different cultures expect different types of behavior as a result of their cultural values. For example, some workers will expect their managers to take time to chat with them and take an interest in their personal lives. An American manager may not be aware of this and may inadvertently appear apathetic and cold.

> Identify three values you hold. Would these be shared by members of other cultures? Why or why not?

TIME   Cultures differ in perceptions and behavior with respect to time. In Japan, decisions are made slowly through group consensus, while in Ethiopia the longer it takes to reach a decision, the greater its importance. Many cultures value a two-hour siesta during the middle of the workday and are casual about getting to work at a designated time.

As you will see in Chapter 6, Americans view time as a precious commodity that should be used efficiently, wisely, and never be wasted. Americans are taught that being "lazy" and "idle" are not desirable traits. This view about time is transferred into the workplace and affects the way routine business activities are conducted. In America, meetings must begin promptly and a conclusion must be reached within prescribed time limits. Information transferal cannot wait and is communicated by email, telephone, or facsimile. Even performance evaluations reflect the importance of time. Employees are judged on promptness and on the ability to perform tasks within specific time constraints and deadlines. Recognizing that the concept of time is not uniform among cultures provides a basis for understanding and working with cultural differences.

SPACE   An inappropriate use of space in social or work situations can cause individuals to feel awkward or uncomfortable. Individuals from Arab countries generally stand 12–18 inches apart when engaged in conversation, whereas Americans stand approximately 24 inches apart. While a person from Saudi Arabia might regard the American's distance as a sign of rejection, an American might be uncomfortable interacting at such a close distance.

In many countries, space is a sign of prestige. It is something that is protected, increased, and, in the hospitality industry, sold. The large corner office with a good view is at the top of the prestige hierarchy. By contrast, individuals from other cultures wonder how managers can supervise from behind closed doors and place managers in a central location, such as at the head of a table or in the center of a room (Copeland and Griggs, 1985).

Differences in perceptions of touching can also present problems to the uninformed manager. To many native Asians, touching is taboo. For example, patting an individual from Thailand on the back is considered highly inappropriate and touching his or her head may constitute a great offense. The regard for interpersonal distance is conditioned by one's native culture and is often difficult to perceive in the process of supervising others. Status, gender, age, and other factors also contribute to differences in the level of comfort individuals feel with touching and being touched.

Do you mind being touched on the arm or shoulder in professional situations? How, in general, do you feel about touching someone in business contexts?

CONTEXT   The particular business environment also shapes individual behavior. In some countries, results are paramount. In American companies, the employee who maintains high standards but is unsuccessful at task completion is generally overlooked when promotion time rolls around. An American manager who is able to generate strong company loyalty among subordinates but who achieves only low profitability will probably enjoy only a short tenure at his or her organization. On the other hand, the individual who produces tangible results will be lauded and is likely to rise rapidly through the corporate ranks.

While some cultures are results oriented, other cultures emphasize process. In many societies, individual accomplishments are gauged by the integrity with which they are performed. In East Asia, for example, sincerity, group harmony, and the ability to cultivate a strong work team are regarded as being more important than profits or efficiency (Copeland, 1985). One difficulty noted in supervising a culturally diverse workforce is that individual priorities may differ. While the manager in a results-oriented culture may consider only results, the diverse employee may regard the process of achieving these results to be equal or greater in importance than the actual outcome.

RELATIONSHIPS   Some cultures place a high value on individual freedom and mobility. Moving from one job to another, across oceans and continents, is regarded as natural and necessary for professional development. In contrast, those in many societies rely on family, friends, and even (to a certain degree) on employee–employer relationships for security. Concerns regarding relationships in the workplace, therefore, are important for all managers to consider. While in some cultures a transfer is seen as a long-awaited career advancement, in other cultures—especially those where children support their parents and where everyone is expected to contribute to the local community—relocating to a distant property away from family and friends may be culturally unacceptable.

WORK ATTITUDES   Some cultures uphold the belief that each individual is the master of his or her own destiny. As a result, individuals strongly identify with their professions and regard their jobs as a means of attaining personal goals. However, in many parts of the world, self-determination is of little consequence. In Muslim countries, for instance, the will of Allah governs an individual's life. Muslims would question why anyone would struggle to get ahead when their destiny has already been determined by greater forces. In Southeast Asia, Buddhist tradition regards the desire for material possessions and selfish gain as the root of suffering. Why would anyone seek advancement and higher status when such attainments only propagate personal suffering?

Some cultures may be quite willing to take work home from the office, to commit weekends to corporate business, and to fill graveyard and weekend shifts in order to climb the corporate ladder. However, it is unreasonable for managers to assume that all workers will possess this strong orientation toward career attainment.

You've heard of work–family balance. Do you think Americans have a particularly difficult time balancing their job and their family? What can be done to help encourage balance?

SPECIFIC BEHAVIORAL DIFFERENCES

Overcoming Resistance to Taking Initiative

Some cultures view employee initiative, or empowerment, as essential to organizational effectiveness. If employees from all cultures are to begin to take personal initiative, they must be coached and educated. Some individuals in our own culture, many women and minorities, may not have been raised to take initiative, either. Below is a list of suggestions for how managers can encourage employee participation and independence:

1. Managers can emphasize that acting independently signifies dedication and loyalty rather than defiance and disrespect. While it will take some employees more time to adjust, sound and consistent cultural education and exposure will help them to become more proactive.
2. Managers can encourage and support employees who take initiative even when they make mistakes. This support is crucial, because an employee who suffers humiliation from making a mistake will hesitate to take another initiative. The manager must be able to correct the mistake and at the same time let the employee "save face." Sincere encouragement will help reduce the fear of embarrassment and give the employee the courage to take other initiatives.
3. Managers can praise employees when they do take initiative so that the behavior is reinforced and continued.
4. Managers can clarify to employees exactly what is expected of them and what the appropriate opportunities are for taking initiative. This will help prevent misguided efforts on the part of the employee to be proactive and save them from embarrassment.

Reluctance to Speak Out

In some cultures, individuals are reluctant to criticize or make negative statements, even when asked to do so for a legitimate business purpose. If a particular task is not completed on time, the individual may accept the blame and not explain the mitigating circumstances, such as the lack of necessary supplies or the poor performance of the subordinate staff.

Managers may interpret an employee's silence as guilt or even deceit. They must realize that the reason for the reluctance to speak up is to avoid hurting feelings or causing the humiliation that comes when one is faced with such a dilemma.

Managers must also be aware that employees may be confused and may not ask for clarification. To avoid this dilemma, the manager can observe nonverbal communication and body language to better empathize with employees who do not share their cultural norms. Common signs that an individual has not understood might include:

- repetitive nodding and smiling
- repetition of "yes, I understand"
- distracted facial expressions
- failure to ask any questions

If employees demonstrate these behaviors, the manager can review the instructions to ensure that opportunities for questions have been provided in a safe environment. Concern for helping individuals feel comfortable is important because it shows respect for the employee's personal beliefs. Respectful communication will lead to future cooperation and greater productivity.

There are several steps managers can take when dealing with diverse employees who are reluctant to express their confusion or problems.

1. Managers can communicate respect for the employee. By demonstrating respect for the individual's beliefs, the manager gives the employee a sense of psychological safety as the threat of being disapproved of is removed.
2. Managers can communicate to employees that they need to know the facts of a situation at all times, especially in serious problems.
3. Managers can respond positively to negative comments made by employees. This may be difficult to do, but management will appreciate honesty, and this will help to encourage it.

Describe an example of when you have felt confused—in a class or a work situation—but were reluctant to ask a question or let others know you needed more clarification. What could the instructor or manager have done to make you more comfortable and confident?

Working Toward Cross-Cultural Understanding

Coworkers, managers, and guests may lose confidence or become frustrated when trying to communicate with an employee who is difficult to understand. This problem is exacerbated when the conversation is conducted over the phone. Some employees may also tend to ignore words that they cannot catch, causing communication breakdowns.

Education provides the best solution to this problem. It is necessary to involve the entire staff for the education to be fully effective. The staff should be taught

- to share responsibility when there is a breakdown in communication;
- to speak slowly and distinctly to other associates and customers;
- to minimize the use of slang;
- to watch for signs of lack of understanding.

All managers should be taught

- the specialized vocabulary of the industry;
- that the entire staff accepts responsibility for the success of communication;
- to admit any lack of understanding;
- to pay attention to common errors of pronunciation.

Ineffectiveness of Conventional Incentives

The theory of motivation holds that workers are motivated when their perceived needs are met in their work environments. Managers who motivate effectively are those who are able to sense the central needs of their employees and find ways to meet these needs in the organizational context.

Problems in motivating employees arise from not knowing what the central needs of individual employees are. This issue is heightened when managers deal with diverse employees. It is not uncommon for managers to be confounded by the lack of responsiveness to conventional incentives demonstrated by some employees. Many Vietnamese workers, for example, would prefer not being promoted if it meant that they would have to discontinue working with the people in their group. On the other hand, a promotion or recognition in the company newsletter will motivate most American employees. A Japanese worker would pass the credit for individual achievement to the group he worked with on a specific project.

In assessing the needs of a diverse workforce, it is all too easy for managers to project their own culture-specific needs onto others. This is especially true when there is no conscious effort on the part of the manager to educate himself or herself on the cultural background of each employee. It is crucial to avoid such projections of one's own cultural beliefs and needs. The more educated and sensitive a manager is to diverse employees, the more effective and productive these employees will be.

Have you worked with employees from another culture? In what ways were they similar to you? In what ways were they different?

BUSINESS CULTURE

Thus far we have been discussing **societal culture,** the enduring primary socialization that takes place early in life. It includes the values, ideas, and behaviors encouraged in the family, at school, and in the community. Another form of culture is **business culture.** This is a form of socialization that includes the rules of business, code of conduct, and more specialized beliefs about business. For example, the New York business culture is significantly different from the Boise, Idaho, business culture even though both are American.

As a hospitality manager, you are in a key position to influence the culture of the organization which you serve, whether it is a four-star hotel or a rural restaurant. The history, size, **diversity** of employees, recruitment, selection, and promotion activities all serve to form the behavior patterns in an organization. Stories, slogans, rituals, and ceremonies are just a few of the ways in which an organization expresses its culture. Management determines the standards, priorities, and reward systems which promote and maintain a healthy business culture.

TECHNIQUES FOR MANAGING A DIVERSE WORKFORCE

Great achievements are not born from a single vision but from the combination of many distinctive viewpoints. Diversity challenges assumptions, opens minds and unblocks our potential to solve any problem we may face.

—Anonymous

Managers who maintain the belief that people are people, and that business is business, are ignoring the influence that culture has on individual perceptions and behavior and, as a result, create barriers to effective management of a diverse workforce. In an exhaustive study, Hofstede (1980) compared the dimensions of power distance, uncertainty avoidance, individualism, and masculinity among 40 nations. Hofstede concluded that individuals and organizations are "culture-bound" as each of these four factors varies by country. He further suggested that these differences cause individuals to become more responsive to leadership, job design, and motivational and planning techniques compatible with their basic cultural assumptions.

BOX 3.1

Examples of Hofstede's dimensions

	High countries	Low countries
Power distance (psychological distance)	Philippines, Mexico, Venezuela, India, Latin America	New Zealand, Israel, Austria, Denmark
Uncertainty avoidance	Malaysia, Italy, Indonesia, Japan	United States, Norway, Australia
Individualism (decision-making freedom in work)	United States, Canada, Great Britain, the Netherlands	Japan, Israel, Malaysia, Columbia
Masculinity–feminity (traditional roles)	Masculine: Latin America, Austria	Feminine: United States, Norway, Sweden, Denmark

In countries where **power distance** is moderate, such as the United States, people at different levels in the corporate hierarchy are regarded as equals. This belief in equality is demonstrated in the workplace by the use of participatory decision making. While participation seems natural in these countries, it is not shared internationally. In countries where power distance is high, such as in Latin America, supervisory and subordinate roles are clearly distinguished. In these countries, individuals do not regard themselves as being equal to their seniors and expect their supervisors to have directive management styles.

As the following examples illustrate, while a manager may have good intentions, implementation of certain managerial techniques may produce unintended results when used with individuals from other cultures.

1. Feeling that a pat on the back would make employees feel more motivated, a manager continually "patted" his employees. Asian workers in his department were uncomfortable being touched and actively avoided him.
2. A manager, pleased with a technique developed by a Native American employee, praised her in front of her peers. The employee was humiliated and did not return to work for three weeks.
3. A manager attempted to delegate to his Filipino employees by asking them to inform him of any equipment problems. Rather than tell their manager of the problems, they manipulate the equipment.
4. A new immigrant, pleased with her new job, presented her manager with a gift. Concerned about ethics, the manager declined the gift. The employee was so insulted that she quit.
5. A manager attempted to implement participatory management with a group of Hispanic workers. Rather than cooperation, this resulted in ego battles and insubordination.

Do you believe that too much of a big deal is made about cultural differences in the workplace? Do you think that it's just a matter of everyone following organizational policy and forgetting about their cultural background? Explain your view.

Communicating with Sensitivity

Vivek had been the assistant front desk manager for nearly six months. Marty, his supervisor, was pleased with Vivek's progress and had given him a new responsibility—scheduling all front desk employees. Vivek was excited about this opportunity and enjoyed the challenge. Within a few weeks, however, Marty could see there was a problem. Vivek was clearly giving priority to his male employees. Whenever a woman would make a request, Vivek would tell her that the company came first and that she should adjust her personal plans accordingly. However, if a man asked for a favor, Vivek would try hard to give him the hours he needed. Marty realized it was time to talk with Vivek about this issue. As Vivek was packing his things to leave for the day, Marty called him into his office.

Marty introduced the conversation by saying, "I don't want to keep you long, but there is an important matter we need to discuss."

"Sure," Vivek said, as he closed the door and sat down in front of Marty's desk.

"You are doing a great job with the scheduling. We have plenty of employees during busy periods, and no one is sitting around during off-peak times. However, there is one thing I have noticed. It seems to me that our male employees are able to take time off when they need it. The women, however, frequently have their requests for schedule changes denied. Does it seem that way to you?"

Vivek thought for a moment. "The men have a big responsibility. They must work to support their families, and it is difficult for them to fit in the other things they have to do—car repairs, appointments, trips. The women do not need to work. My position is, they can either adjust to my schedule or find another job. It's that simple."

"I thought maybe that was your view," said Marty. "It's good that we're having this talk because here in the United States, men and women need to be treated in exactly the same manner. There are even laws to make sure this happens. Working women need their jobs just as much as the men do. We have single mothers supporting two or three young children. They need time off for doctor's appointments and school-related meetings. Their job is very important to them."

"I have noticed that the women take their jobs very seriously," said Vivek. "I did not intend to be unfair."

"I am sure you didn't," said Marty.

"Now that I know about this situation, I will be sure to treat all of my staff in the same manner."

Whether leading meetings, training new employees, or engaging in daily operations, communication is the primary medium for conducting business. The ability to communicate effectively, as we emphasized in Chapter 2, is an important skill that is difficult to achieve even with a homogeneous workforce. Managing a culturally and ethnically diverse workforce significantly increases the complexity of this process.

Obviously, spoken language is important. The inability to communicate verbally not only hinders performance but can also cause anger and frustration. As we have seen, cultural filters may cause different individuals to attribute different meanings to the same spoken words.

In addition to implicit meanings attributed to spoken communication, nonverbal communication is also culturally determined. Managers must realize that gestures, facial expressions, and body movements can have different interpretations to individuals with different national origins. Laughter, smiling, and tone of voice are also culturally conditioned. Even eye contact has different meanings to individuals from different parts of the world. For example, in Middle Eastern cultures, extensive eye contact is the accepted norm, while Native American individuals avoid eye contact with their elders as a sign of respect. Americans generally perceive a lack of eye contact to mean that a person is shifty or is trying to hide something, while an excess of eye contact tends to create discomfort.

Developing Empathy

Dilemmas related to diversity are not confined to the managerial realm. Immigrating to a foreign country creates physical and often psychological distance from one's native culture. To a native, the country's external environment is relatively predictable. To a new immigrant, this certainty is minimal. Going to the market can be a harrowing event; navigating an unfamiliar city can be frustrating and intimidating. Even immigrants who have resided in a country for many years may be challenged by the demands of functioning in the workplace.

Cultivating management skills for a diverse workforce requires that managers develop empathy. Empathy refers to understanding and relating to the experiences and feelings that individuals encounter as they become acclimated to a new work environment. Empathy is not giving advice or reassuring words; rather, empathy implies that managers closely listen to their employees and anticipate the difficulties they will encounter. Developing empathy in the context of cross-cultural management includes gaining self-awareness and cultural sensitivity in addition to refining one's relational skills.

SELF-AWARENESS It is important that a manager understands oneself in order to relate better to both guests and employees whose cultural background is different from one's own. Gaining insight into oneself helps to uncover personal beliefs, values, and behavior patterns. With this understanding, managers can begin to distinguish cultural differences and can develop a foundation for viewing other cultures more objectively.

CULTURAL SENSITIVITY Cultural sensitivity evolves from understanding the values, traditions, and beliefs of another culture. Building on this understanding, managers can begin to see situations from another person's perspective. Recognizing these differences in perspective helps to create possibilities for more effective multicultural management. For example, a manager who supervises a large Asian population may wonder why a newly implemented individual incentive plan is failing to motivate employees. An understanding of cultural differences would indicate that many Asians are not attracted to incentives focusing on personal achievement. Building on this knowledge, a manager might attempt to institute teams and alter the performance evaluation system so that it rewards group attainments.

In addition, sensitivity will help provide insight into the meanings that workers attribute to a manager's actions and comments. Through sensitivity, managers can begin to see situations from multiple perspectives and alter their management styles accordingly. Rather than trying to restructure the culture so that it conforms with the system, sensitivity will help managers adapt their techniques so that they are compatible with a given culture.

RELATIONAL ABILITIES   Awareness of another culture's values and customs provides a framework for understanding behavioral differences. Relational abilities, however, extend beyond having a "feeling" for a given culture. Managers must be able to accept individual differences without passing judgment. To be effective, managers must possess a willingness, as well as a capacity, to work with people whose beliefs, values, and norms of conduct differ distinctly from their own.

> Do you believe that you have a high or low ability to empathize? Explain your response by giving a concrete example. Do you think people are born with this ability?

Becoming More Adaptable

Effective managers develop the ability to view situations from a broad perspective and to view problems as challenging opportunities rather than as problems. When discussing how to work with a diverse workforce, managers emphasized that what is needed is flexibility. One of the most important attributes is to accept suggestions from subordinates as well as from supervisors when they are practical.

Managers must be able to integrate a wide range of perspectives, to unify culturally diverse employees into a cohesive work unit, and to solve problems within different frameworks. Understanding cultural differences provides a strong foundation for supervising a diverse workforce. However, it is also important to recognize and respond to individual needs and desires. Managers must not only understand cultural differences, but they must also be able to evaluate, anticipate, and prepare for changes that will affect each individual.

Asking More Questions

Cultivating management skills is an ongoing learning process. Even if you have learned a new language, engaged in cultural studies, become more aware of issues related to gender and age bias, and acquired some sensitivity to cultural differences, this does not mean that you have become an expert. The more inquisitive you are with new and existing diverse employees, the more you will learn about individual aspects of your employees, and therefore you will gain their respect and loyalty. By asking questions and keeping an open mind, you can continually expand your understanding of individuals and their backgrounds.

> Do you typically ask a lot of questions? What can others do to either encourage or inhibit you from feeling comfortable in this manner?

IMPROVING CROSS-CULTURAL SKILLS

Whether at the property or corporate level, the ability to work with individuals from all cultures is a vital aspect of the hospitality industry. Empathic management is not confined to a single occasion or a specific department. Effectively working with individuals from a wide variety of nations is an ongoing process that requires commitment at all levels of the organization. When managers were asked about effective strategies for reducing barriers to understanding and establishing a more effective and efficient multicultural work environment, the following themes emerged:

Orient Employees to the Work Environment

Orientation programs for a culturally diverse workforce need to extend beyond an introduction to corporate policies and procedures. While it is important to communicate basic job expectations and the layout of the physical plant, all employees need to gain an awareness of the corporate culture. At the supervisory level, managers need to be alerted to the types of challenges they will encounter. Line employees, who work with many diverse employees, also need to understand how cultural diversity influences the workplace.

Educate Workers and Supervisors Regarding Cultural Differences

Employees and managers must be sensitized to different cultures if they are to be productive. Through films, seminars, and discussions, members of the workforce can gain insight into different value systems and styles of conduct. While these are important educational tools, it is also important to acknowledge that individuals will not always fit into textbook classifications. In order to avoid **stereotyping,** employees and supervisors should also be alerted to the fact that each employee is an individual with distinct needs and desires.

> If you were asked to design a training program for all employees on cultural sensitivity, what specific topics would you include?

Provide Language Classes

Managers must continually provide direction and elicit responses from coworkers and subordinates. From a practical standpoint, language skills provide the basic means for relating and accomplishing tasks in the multilingual hospitality workplace. By offering language instruction, your organization will encourage managers to enhance their communication skills.

Language training does not need to be restricted to management. Providing opportunities for employees to learn a second language is beneficial to both employees and the organization. As employees become more comfortable with their linguistic capabilities, their confidence will increase. Not only will they be able to understand and carry out instructions with greater ease, they will also be able to respond and interact more effectively with guests.

Encourage Employee Input

Employees may be hesitant to approach their supervisor and mention problems that stem from cultural differences. Furthermore, without an exchange of information, managers can only speculate about what their employees need. One of the most straightforward methods for learning about individual needs and about factors that influence individual behavior is to ask.

A variety of methods, such as surveys, suggestions boxes, group meetings, and one-on-one meetings, can be used for gaining employee input. The most appropriate method of soliciting information will depend on the cultural composition of the workforce and the information that is being sought.

Develop Support Groups

Individuals have a need to interact with other people with whom they have shared values and perspectives on the world. Organizations can help their employees adapt to the workplace and to their new country by developing cultural support groups. These groups provide individuals with the opportunity to raise questions and discuss problems with others who have had similar experiences.

In addition to having numerous functions that are relevant to their members, support groups can have a positive impact on the organization. For example, each hospitality organization can encourage group members to develop and implement their own language training programs. Groups can also design educational programs about their country of origin which are, in turn, presented to other support groups and management. By providing meeting space, offering funding, and demonstrating an ongoing interest in group development and maintenance, these groups can be implemented in hospitality organizations.

Create It

You may wish to use this "Create It" model for situations in which cultural sensitivity is required. Use the letters that spell out the words "Create It" to develop harmony within diversity.

BOX 3.2

Curiosity	to learn about other cultures
Recognition	of your own biases and stereotypes
Empathy	put yourself in your employees shoes and understand how they feel
Acceptance	of individual differences
Team building	creating synergy among employees who are different from one another
Explain	make certain everyone understands the company's goals
Invest	in people
Training	constantly

STEREOTYPES AND CULTURAL BIASES

Stereotyping is the belief that people in a specific group share similar traits and behaviors, negative and positive. Its function is to rationalize our behavior in relation to that group. Listening to a person's language, observing their facial features, noting their age or gender, or learning an individual's national origin can lead to false assumptions. Managers should understand that people who speak a particular language can come from many different countries. Even if a manager correctly identifies a person's country of origin and has some understanding of their culture, this does not mean that the person will conform to cultural generalizations. In the same way, one cannot assume skill level or energy level based on an individual's age or gender.

Stereotyping can create barriers to effective management of diverse employees since it reduces organizational efficiency and hinders individual development. If assumptions about a person are based on cultural heritage, rather than on skills and abilities, improper job placement can result. Poor placement, in turn, limits an individual's contribution to the organization. Moreover, each individual has needs and desires that, although affected by culture, age, or gender, are specific to that person. Just as managers would not assume that one type of reward will satisfy every male American or that one career path characterizes every female American, the same is also true for individuals from different ages and backgrounds. Incorrect generalizations about an employee's needs and desires can limit personal growth and job satisfaction.

In general, people tend to make certain assumptions about those from other cultures. Or worse, they may hold certain biases and prejudices against these cultures. An **ethnocentric** person believes that his or her own way is the best way, viewing the known culture as superior. The manager needs to be aware of his or her own attitudes toward employees of different cultures and to resolve any conflicts therein if he or she hopes to manage these employees effectively.

The following are points on some common stereotyping assumptions:

Point 1: Before you can be effective in management, you must be sensitive to the reality of diversity. It is all too easy for managers to overlook this issue and treat each employee in the same way. If an organization or company aims to thrive, it is essential that its managers learn how to manage and motivate their increasingly diverse employees effectively. The acknowledgment of diversity would then be the first step toward achieving such an objective.

Point 2: In discussing and practicing management of a diverse workforce, keep in mind that any statement or observation about a certain culture, gender, or age group is a generalization. The statements and observations should only serve as guides in helping manage and motivate your employees. It is important that you personalize your approach by treating each employee individually. Making sweeping assumptions or using stereotypes could lead to embarrassment or feelings of alienation if the manager fails to take into account the individual's specific background and needs.

Point 3: It is common for an employee with a heavy accent to be perceived as uneducated, unassimilated, or having difficulty understanding English. Such assumptions are often untrue, and should not be made. In dealing with employees with heavy accents, it is important to be aware that understanding the vocabulary and grammar of a language is often easier than pronouncing that language.

Point 4: Above all else, it is critical for you to be empathic toward your diverse employees. Too often, managers unwittingly project their own biases onto such employees, inviting personal bewilderment and frustration as they realize that their management styles are ineffective. Empathy is the first step toward understanding why employees behave and respond the way they do, and lays the foundation for a willingness to educate oneself about the uniqueness of each employee.

Point 5: As a manager, you must always communicate trust and respect for the culturally rooted values of your employees. By understanding and respecting the values and beliefs among diverse employees, the manager builds an environment in which these employees feel safe from disapproval and ridicule. This in turn leads to greater willingness and responsiveness on the part of the employee to change or modify behavior to increase effectiveness.

Summary

In this chapter we discuss the need for managers to reevaluate their interpersonal abilities and adapt their managerial styles as the hospitality industry continues toward globalization. In order to successfully manage a diverse workforce, managers, who themselves may have a wide range of cultural backgrounds, must become sensitive to the role that culture, age, and gender plays in individual beliefs and perceptions. Obviously, managers cannot learn about every aspect of every culture. They can, however, gain sensitivity and learn to better manage fundamental differences.

Through awareness of subtle cultural characteristics and insight into one's own beliefs, biases, and management style, knowledge of communication issues related to culture, age, or gender can be used to enhance one's managerial effectiveness. We make several suggestions for managers as they try to establish a more effective diverse workforce.

We warn about the dangers of stereotyping when working with a diverse workforce. Many individuals do not conform to cultural, gender-, or age-related generalizations. If managers attempt to categorize their employees, they risk hindering organizational efficiency and employee development. We recommend that managers personalize their managerial styles and treat each employee with sensitivity and respect.

Key Words

values *64*
instrumental value *65*
terminal value *65*

societal culture *70*
business culture *70*
diversity *70*

power distance *71*
stereotype *75*
ethnocentrism *77*

Exercises

Exercise 1   Label Exercise

Objectives:

- To develop awareness of the role stereotypes play in our behavior
- To engender a norm of openness and sharing

Group Size: 8–22 participants

Time Frame: 30 minutes

Procedure:

1. In advance of the training session, trainer writes personality descriptor labels on Post-it notes. Labels include "aggressive," "witty," "shy," "depressive,"
"boisterous," "flirty," "disdainful," "know-it-all," "confused," "passive," "talkative," "impatient," and "stern."

2. Participants sit in circle and trainer pastes one label on each participant's forehead.

3. Participants have a group discussion on a topic of their choice.

4. Debrief: After about 15 minutes, trainer stops the discussion and participants are asked to discuss how they were being perceived. How easy was it to figure out how you were "labeled?" When someone is "labeled" in a particular way they often live out that label. Did that happen in your group?

Endnotes

Baskerville, R. (2003). Hofstede never studied culture. *Organizations and Society, 28*(1), 1–12.

Bureau of Labor and Statistics. (2006). September 28, 2007 <http://www.bls.gov/cps/labor2006/home.htm>

Chang, L. C. (2003). An examination of cross-cultural negotiation using Hofstede framework. *Journal of Academy of Business, 2*(2), 567–571.

Copeland, L. & Griggs, L. (1985). *Going international.* New York: Random House. pp. 11–16.

Dickson, M. W., Hartog, D., & Mitchelson, J. (2003). Research on cross-cultural context: Making progress, and raising new questions. *Leadership Quarterly, 14*(6), 729–741.

Fullerton, H. N. Jr. (1999). Labor force projections to 2008: Steady growth and changing composition. *Monthly Labor Review,* 19–32.

Girlando, A., Anderson, C., & Zerillo, J. (2004). An examination of Hofstede's paradigm of national culture and its malleability: Italy and US thirty years later. *Journal of Transnational Management Development, 10*(1), 23–47.

Goldstein, J., & Leopold, M. (1990, November). Corporate culture vs. ethnic culture. *Personnel Journal, 89*(11), 84.

Gong, W., Li, Z. G., & Stump, R. L. (2007). Global internet use and access: Cultural considerations. *Asia Pacific Journal of Marketing and Logistics, 19*(1), 57–73.

Hofstede, G. (1980). *Culture's consequences: International differences in work-related values.* Beverly Hills: Sage Publications. pp. 71, 118, 149, 190, 372–390.

Hofstede, G. & McCrae, R. R. (2004). Personality and culture revisited: Linking traits and dimensions of culture. *Cross-Cultural Research, 38*(1), 52–70.

Higley, J. (2000). Hospitality leaders promote diversity during conference. *Hotel and Motel Management, 215*(16), 2–5.

Leo, C., Bennett, R., & Hartel, C. (2005). Cross cultural differences in decision making styles. *Cross Cultural Management, 12*(3), 32–64.

Malai, V. & Speece, M. (2005). Cultural impact on the relationship among perceived service quality, brand name value, and customer loyalty. *Journal of International Consumer Marketing, 17*(4), 7–22.

Masterson, B. Murphy, B. (1986). Internal cross-cultural management. *Training and Development Journal, 40*(4), 58.

Merritt, A. (2000). Culture in the cockpit: Do Hofstede's dimensions replicate? *Journal of Cross-Cultural Psychology, 31*(3), 283–302.

Singh, S. (2006). Cultural differences in, and influences on, consumers' propensity to adopt innovations. *International Marketing Review, 23*(2), 173–197.

Soares, A. M., Farhangmehr, M., & Shoham, A. (2007). Hofstede's dimensions of culture in international marketing studies. *Journal of Business Research, 60*(3), 277–291.

Thiederman, S. (1988). Breaking through to foreign-born employees. *Management World, 17*(3), 22–29.

Thiederman, S. (1988). Managing the foreign-born workforce: Keys to effective cross-cultural motivation. *Manage, 40*(3), 26.

Thiederman, S. (1990). *Bridging cultural barriers for corporate success.* Massachusetts/Toronto: D.C. Heath and Company. p. 82.

Triandis, H. C. (2004). The many dimensions of culture. *The Academy of Management Executive, 18*(1), 88–102.

4

THE POWER OF TEAMS IN HOSPITALITY

CHAPTER OUTLINE

Introduction

Teams in Hospitality Management
    The Benefits of Teams in Hospitality
    The Importance of Teambuilding

Types of Teams in Hospitality Management
    Interdepartmental Teams
    Cross-Functional Teams
    Task Force
    Self-Directed Teams
    Upper Echelon Teams
    Quality Teams

Characteristics of Teams
    Group Norms
    Group Cohesiveness
    Groupthink
    Risky Shift
    Social Loafing
    The Linking Function of Teams

Dimensions of Team Behavior
    Task Dimension
    Relationship Dimension
    Individual Needs Dimension

First Steps to Building an Effective Team
    Increasing Member Trust
    Creating an Appropriate Team Environment
    Establishing and Clarifying Team Goals

Teambuilding and the Problem-Solving Process
    Identify the Problem
    Gather Information
    Interpret the Data
    Plan for Change
    Implement the Plan
    Solicit and Provide Feedback

Leading Your Team
    Select Team Members
    Anticipate Challenges
    Assess Your Team's Performance
    Leader Task Behavior
    Leader Relationship Behavior
    Observing and Facilitating Team Communication

LEARNING OBJECTIVES

After reading this chapter, you will be able to do the following:

1. Define a team and describe the key ways in which teams differ from groups.
2. Explain why teamwork is necessary for success in the hospitality industry specifically.
3. Identify the characteristics of both effective and ineffective teams.
4. Describe task functions and maintenance functions and why each is important to team performance.
5. Identify specific task-related roles and specific relationship-related roles.
6. Name and describe the types of teams common to hospitality organizations.
7. Explain the importance of communication and trust to teambuilding.
8. Discuss the steps in building teams through the problem-solving process.
9. Describe the advantages and potential concerns in using technology to facilitate team functioning.

Scenario for Application: Lucinda's Frustration

Lucinda made her way to the housekeeping department at the Royal Palm Hotel at 5:30 a.m., as usual. After a few hours of assorted tasks, she began cleaning rooms on her designated floors—10 and 11. Upon entering room 1053, she discovered that the occupants, a young couple, were still sleeping. Somewhat irritated, she shook her head and quietly closed the door, muttering under her breath about the "front desk messing up again." She was tired of constantly being embarrassed. When she finished her shift, Lucinda stormed up to the front desk manager and gave him a piece of her mind. The manager, a young Hotel School grad, replied defensively, "If you had bothered to check the register, you would have known that the party in room 1053 decided to extend their stay."

    Is Lucinda part of a team? Perhaps it might not appear to be the case at first. How could Lucinda improve her value to the team?

INTRODUCTION

In hospitality organizations, teams are an essential component of almost every activity. The hospitality industry is a high-contact service setting that places physical, mental, and emotional demands on its employees. In such a fast-paced and uncertain environment, effective teamwork at all levels is essential. As you can see from Lucinda's situation at the Royal Palm Hotel, if the ball gets dropped as the service process moves from one department or individual to the next—in this case from the front desk to housekeeping—employee relationships are harmed and the guest experience ultimately suffers as well.

Identify an experience you've had in a hospitality organization—for instance in a restaurant, hotel, or airline—where service suffered because employees weren't working together effectively?

We define a team as a group of individuals who have established mutual trust and open channels of communication. Communication and trust are the foundation of team life and enable individuals to work together effectively to accomplish a task or to solve a problem. If there is trust among employees, then they can work in concert to perform their respective duties and provide excellent service to guests. While you may at first think of teams as simply small groups, we have extended the concept to encompass all levels of interaction that require trust and communication among members. Teams, while most commonly a cluster of four to eight individuals, can also be viewed as all employees who work together within a larger organizational or departmental context.

Teams are not always created by physical proximity. What a general manager may mistakenly regard as a team is often simply a group of individuals who are working *next* to each other, rather than *with* each other. To be a true team, employees must share a common goal and participate in the give-and-take of ideas. Members must also develop trust in one another and share information freely. The Royal Palm Hotel scenario portrays a lack of teamwork that happens again and again throughout service organizations. When goals are ambiguous and communication infrequent or unclear, trust is lost, misunderstandings arise, and relationships are damaged.

Employees in a service environment are much more than a group of individuals serving the needs of a demanding clientele. Effective service providers must become a tightly choreographed, multi-functional and cross-disciplinary team, constantly in contact and communication with one another. Think of teams as differing from other collections of individuals in the following ways:

- Teams share leadership roles
- Teams uphold individual accountability
- Teams have a unified and compelling purpose
- Teams create collective work products
- Teams encourage active discussion
- Teams measure performance by assessing collective work outcomes
- Teams discuss and perform real work together.

In this chapter you will learn about the benefits of building strong and well-functioning teams and the characteristics that distinguish them from simple groups of employees. In addition, you will better understand the importance of balancing task and maintenance functions and of building effective teams through a multi–step problem-solving process. Finally, you will consider the effect of technology on team performance. Armed with this information, you will be prepared to effectively develop and lead the various teams you encounter—a process we refer to as teambuilding.

Does the prospect of being a team leader appeal to you? Have you led teams in the past?

TEAMS IN HOSPITALITY MANAGEMENT

To keep pace with constant change and to meet the evolving needs of an increasingly demanding market, hospitality managers recognize the importance of teams in getting work done and in gaining and maintaining a competitive advantage through excellent service.

The Benefits of Teams in Hospitality

Just as teamwork often determines which team will win a sporting event, teamwork can be a crucial factor in the success of a hospitality organization. In sports, teams of greatly talented individuals have been beaten by players of more modest ability who work as a cohesive unit. In hotels, restaurants, and clubs many teams of employees will give the consistently superior service that pleases guests, while individual "star" performers will lead to uneven levels of service across the organization. The essence of teamwork is that the whole can be greater than the sum of its parts.

Can you think of a high-performing team to which you have belonged? How did it make you feel to be a member?

Some of the benefits of teams over individuals working independently are listed in Box 4.1.

The Importance of Teambuilding

As previously explained, **teambuilding** is the process of establishing trust and opening communication channels among a number of individuals who share a common purpose or goal. Teambuilding is not a new idea; the importance of teamwork in the business world has been emphasized repeatedly. For example, Peters and Waterman believe that teams are "the basic organizational building blocks of excellent companies." In the same manner, the well-known management consultant Peter F. Drucker stated, "Teams are . . . highly receptive to experimentation, to new ideas, and to new ways of doing things. They are the best means available for overcoming functional insulation and parochialism."

Teambuilding can ease tensions between departments and make it easier to improve service at all levels, melding staff members into an effective unit. Whether a manager is new to the job or is a seasoned professional, the ability to create a cohesive team out of an increasingly diverse workforce is an essential management competency. Such teambuilding improves employees' satisfaction and productivity, enabling them to handle complex challenges. Employees will also respond more quickly to new situations and are likely to make better decisions in circumstances where multiple perspectives are required.

BOX 4.1

Benefits of Teams Over Individuals

1. Higher quality decisions resulting from pooling of resources
2. When judgment is required, multiple views are surfaced and considered
3. Difficult or complicated tasks can be partitioned and individuals can focus on specific areas of expertise
4. Teams encourage the creative handling of complex tasks
5. Higher motivation through group interaction

What do you consider to be the most significant benefit of teambuilding?

TYPES OF TEAMS IN HOSPITALITY MANAGEMENT

Teams serve a wide variety of functions and can be created at all organizational levels. In addition to viewing the entire organization as a team, there are also interdepartmental teams, and task forces. Some teams are formed at the "upper echelon"; others, such as quality teams, monitor specific organizational processes. Perhaps one of the most important types is a problem-solving team. These individuals move through a structured process either to address a specific organizational dilemma or to improve the organization's own team functioning. Several of the most common types of teams are described below.

Interdepartmental Teams

Often a department, such as Reservations, will experience a particular problem or take on a specific task. Imagine that suddenly computers at the front desk were replaced and all attendants now had to learn to operate an entirely new software system. What is the best way to go about training everyone in a short period of time? Such a question might well be put to an **interdepartmental team** composed of several front desk staff, the assistant manager, and any others in the department who have a stake in the outcome and who could contribute to the creation of an acceptable and workable proposal.

Cross-Functional Teams

Organizational structures run both vertically and horizontally. You may be most familiar with the vertical structure, which often focuses on an increasing scope of authority from line employees, to supervisors, to department managers, and finally to the organization's senior executives. The organization's horizontal structure, on the other hand, concerns its various functional areas such as finance, marketing, food and beverage, and so forth. Communication among functional areas, due to potentially conflicting goals and distinct areas of expertise, is often most problematic. **Cross-functional teams** are critical to solving many organizational problems, but conflicts inevitably arise if goals are not shared or if members feel threatened.

What would you guess would be one of the major challenges confronted by a cross-functional team?

Task Force

Task forces are formal teams created by management for the purpose of exploring a specific topic or problem. Most often, a task force exists only until the team has made its recommendation or until the problem has been resolved. Goal clarity is particularly important for a task force, as the team is often accountable to a larger body and is working under compressed time constraints to develop its recommendation or report. The most high-performing task forces are composed of members with diverse backgrounds and areas of expertise so that multiple perspectives can be brought to bear on the task. Examples of a task force might include one set up to recommend a policy for handling vacation requests or selecting a new employee uniform.

Self-Directed Teams

Self-directed, or self-managed, **teams** have decision-making responsibility and, as their name suggests, manage themselves as they tackle organizational challenges. As companies flatten and employees take increasing responsibility for organizational quality and effectiveness, self-directed teams have become a major tool of cutting-edge hospitality companies.

In addition to direct benefits from the work self-managed teams do, organizations that depend on self-directed teams to make important decisions and to solve organizational problems also enjoy the higher morale and increased productivity this form of empowerment provides. Such teams work over an extended period of time to develop expertise and identify goals. This framework requires a progressive and open organizational environment and has proven effective in numerous instances.

Would you enjoy being part of a self-directed team, or do you prefer having a designated leader for your group? Why?

Upper Echelon Teams

Upper echelon teams are a type of self-directed team, most often composed of senior executives who focus on strategic-level issues. Researchers believe that the values and competencies of upper echelon team members have a significant influence on the direction of the organization. In this regard, it is particularly important that these teams represent multiple viewpoints and consider all perspectives represented by the employee population. The more diverse the team, the better able it will be to make wise decisions regarding the future of the organization.

Quality Teams

Often line employees, who are responsible for implementing the organization's policies and practices, are in the best position to identify problems as they arise. **Quality teams** are composed of employees at various organizational levels who come together to discuss and address issues related to such processes as customer satisfaction, facilities, or employee benefits. While quality teams often do not have decision-making authority, they serve a valuable function in bringing critical problems—and often recommendations—to the attention of management.

It should be clear that knowledge of teams and how they function is key to organizational productivity and employee satisfaction. As you can imagine, your personal effectiveness and the ability of your work group, department, division, or organization to meet its goals depends in large measure on your ability to develop and lead teams. An understanding of teams and of the role you play in facilitating productive team dynamics will give you a clear competitive advantage in the complex, fast-paced hospitality environment. You will discover that your ability to develop and lead teams is valuable. As a manager or supervisor, it is your responsibility to ensure that your employees work collaboratively. In this chapter we explain how you can build your staff into a team that will run your organization effectively, complete challenging projects, and deliver excellent service.

Give an example of how one of the above types of teams might help a resort hotel increase its business.

CHARACTERISTICS OF TEAMS

Sonya glanced quickly at her watch. "Almost time to go," she said as she leaned back against the front desk.

"I don't want to keep you," Tony apologized as he, too, became aware of the time.

"Oh, not a problem," Sonya reassured him. "We never start on time. Phillippe doesn't care if we sneak in late, just so long as we share our doughnuts! Reservations Department meetings are definitely all about the food!"

"Must be nice," Tony replied. "Not the same in Marketing, that's for sure. Carri runs—how should I put it—a 'tight ship'! She doesn't even like it when we bring in coffee! She has everything planned out—we each report on our progress since the last meeting, bring up any problems we're having with our customers or other departments, and help her set the agenda for the next meeting. We talk about her behind her back, but actually we get a lot accomplished. We even have a 'Devil's Advocate' requirement— every time there's a suggestion made, at least two members of the team have to pose objections. We work together pretty well, and she definitely keeps us on our toes!"

"That's amazing!" Sonya replied, shaking her head. "No one ever disagrees in our team because it would just prolong the session. In addition, Petra and Nish just sit there staring into space. I don't think they have a clue what's going on. Well, guess I better go get the coffee and doughnuts or the meeting will be over before I even get there! Hope I remember where it is!"

Effective teams always function as part of the larger organizational system no matter how small or isolated individual members may sometimes feel. Since the team is a component of the department, division, or some other larger unit, it affects and is affected by all other components. While a team reflects and is profoundly affected by the company's culture, it also develops a unique culture of its own under the influence of its member composition, tasks, reward system, and leadership.

To better understand the team process, it is first necessary to consider several dimensions of group dynamics. You should now be thinking of a team as a collection of individuals, held together by effective communication and trust, who share a common purpose, and who hold themselves mutually accountable for accomplishing specific goals.

Group Norms

Over time, individuals working together develop a set of rules, or norms, to keep members' behavior in line with the shared attitudes, values, and goals that are developed through the team experience. Group norms are defined as a set of assumptions, or expectations, that members have concerning what behavior is good or bad, appropriate or inappropriate, allowed or discouraged within the context of the specific team. Norms may be explicit or implicit. They affect such dimensions as the length of meetings, the range of acceptable decision-making strategies, or even the type of language used at meetings.

If you want to ensure that your team develops healthy and productive norms, you can focus one of your early meetings on clarifying, or making explicit, how the group will go about its task—whether to increase profitability for the entire organization or increase guest satisfaction in the formal dining room. During this discussion, you would agree on the answers to questions such as those listed in Box 4.2.

Your willingness to tailor your behavior to conform to the group's expectations, or norms, is determined by the strength of your desire to be a member.

BOX 4.2

Questions that Help Identify Team Norms

- What is the consequence to members who are late?
- How will strong differences of opinion or personal conflicts be handled?
- How will the group progress when members don't show up?
- What happens when members don't do what they said they would do?
- What is the consequence if members don't make the group tasks a high priority?
- How will the group handle members who dominate the discussion or who don't participate?
- How will time be managed?
- How will meeting times be established?

Group Cohesiveness

The perception of group attractiveness that brings individuals together is called "cohesion." When **cohesiveness** is strong, there is a willingness on the part of all members to trust one another and to sacrifice personal gain to further the team's goals. Team norms and cohesiveness, then, combine to shape the performance expectations that influence member productivity.

If a team consists simply of a collection of individuals, each pursuing his or her individual interests, the group will lack cohesion and will not function effectively. Some of the key factors that influence group cohesiveness are presented in Box 4.3.

When norms are strong and when they favor high productivity, cohesiveness then provides the social pressure needed to encourage members to excel. A group requires a personal commitment from all members if it is to develop a strong culture and attain its most difficult goals.

BOX 4.3

Factors that Influence Team Cohesiveness

- The degree to which attitudes and values are shared; those who share the same beliefs are more likely to be attracted to one another
- The extent of agreement on group goals; shared goals encourage members to work together productively
- The frequency of interaction; frequent interaction encourages mutual understanding
- The group size; small groups are more likely to be cohesive than larger ones
- Recognition; a favorable evaluation for effective performance reinforces feelings of pride in membership
- External threats; threats from outside of the group can serve to strengthen the group's cohesiveness

Groupthink

Groupthink, a term first presented by Irving Janis, is defined as the tendency of members not to disagree with one another or to examine ideas critically. This circumstance can seriously harm team functioning. Symptoms of groupthink include the tendency to discount negative information and, in some cases, the willingness to ignore ethical consequences of the group's decisions. Perhaps most striking is the pressure members feel to share the views of other group members. When groupthink is strong, no one speaks out, disagrees, or critically evaluates suggestions. The symptoms of groupthink are listed in Box 4.4.

Ironically, cohesive teams are most susceptible to groupthink. When individuals like and respect each other, they are also prone to feel that it is more important to agree with their teammates than to make a good decision. When team morale is high and groups believe they can do no wrong, decisions are often made quickly and without sufficient deliberation. High stress, time constraints, and the absence of clear norms for how decisions are evaluated also encourage unhealthy conformity. Generally, multicultural teams experience groupthink less frequently because individual members have inherently different perspectives.

The consequences of groupthink can be serious. They include failure to evaluate risks, biased information processing, and a failure to establish contingency plans, since the group often has not realistically assessed its risks and options. Therefore, it is wise to take reasonable measures to eliminate or reduce this tendency. Below are some suggestions that may help groups make better decisions:

- ensure an open climate for discussion
- implement a specific decision-making process
- seek dissenting voices, through a devil's advocate or other technique
- do not mistake silence for consent—draw out all members and hear their views
- get feedback from informed individuals outside of the group
- provide enough time for group members to understand the problem and its implications fully.

BOX 4.4

Symptoms of Groupthink

Symptom	Description
Invulnerability	Members feel they are safe and protected from ineffective action
Rationale	Members ignore warnings by rationalizing their own or others' behaviors
Morality	Members believe their actions are inherently moral and ethical
Stereotypes	Members view opponents as stupid or evil and thus unworthy of or incompetent at negotiations around differences in positions or beliefs
Pressure	Members pressure all individuals in the group to conform to the group's decisions; they allow no questioning or arguing of alternatives
Self-censorship	Members do not express any questions about the group's decision
Unanimity	Members perceive that everyone in the group has the same view

Identify a specific situation when you were a victim of groupthink. How did it affect your participation in the team? How did it affect the team's decision-making process?

Risky Shift

Another phenomenon that affects group process is called **risky shift.** Risk taking is a critical personal variable in team functioning. When risky shift is operating, the group's tendency is to take a position that is more risky than any individual member would have taken independently. For example, imagine a chain of restaurants that serve traditional "home-cooking." This type of fare is rather high in fat and cholesterol, but has been popular with customers in the past. At a meeting of managers, a question arises as to whether to offer healthier fare and eliminate some of the more unhealthy items from the menu. Individually, no manager wants to be saddled with a decision of this magnitude. When questioned individually, everyone said, "Why change if we are currently successful?" Changing the offerings could lose the chain's devoted clientele. On the other hand, people are making healthier choices in general and the chain could become obsolete. After a group discussion, and knowing that no individual will be credited with the decision, the group decides to change the menu.

Researchers propose that risky shift occurs for any of the following reasons:

1. The responsibility for the decision is diffused among all group members.
2. High risk takers are generally more persuasive and influential, convincing other members of the group to adopt their position.
3. There may be social desirability of risk as a cultural value.

It has been established that risk taking is important to maintaining organizational effectiveness, and risky shift occurs when the group collectively agrees on a course of action that is more extreme than they would have made if asked individually. In this way, risky shift can be beneficial, provided that the person overseeing the group is aware of the risky shift phenomenon and carefully assesses the merits and potential dangers of risky ideas.

Social Loafing

Have you ever been in a group where morale was low due largely to one or two individuals who just weren't doing their share of the work? **Social loafing** occurs when a team member fails to participate fully in the group's activities. The social loafer frequently contributes less time, thought, or other resources to the team's effort. Social loafing not only results in the group losing potentially valuable contributions from the loafer but it also affects members' perceptions of equity, since the loafer often receives equal recognition and benefits for substantially less work.

Social loafing is thought to occur for two primary reasons. First, because of the dilution effect or the tendency of team members to feel submerged within the group, they believe that their contributions do not make a difference. The other explanation, the immediacy gap, is a dynamic that causes an individual member to feel isolated from other team members and from the team's outcomes. This is most likely to occur when a member is unclear about the team goals or believes that he has little in common with other team members.

Because social loafing is one of the most prevalent and disruptive group member behaviors, it is important to create a strategy to deal with this issue. While there are no guarantees, the more accountable you can make each team member, the more difficult it will be for the social loafer to avoid doing his or her share of the work. Assigning specific tasks to each individual and asking for a report back to the group, or implementing a formal verbal or written self-assessment may solve, or at least reduce, social loafing.

> Under what circumstances do you find yourself "social loafing?" Is there anything that might have been done to change this behavior?

The Linking Function of Teams

Linking is the central work function that coordinates and integrates all the other work functions. In mature teams, every team member spends some time working on linking activities. High-performance teams are generally characterized by excellent "linking" skills.

There are three main forms of linking: external linking, internal linking, and informal linking. **External linking** has been associated with managers who take on an "organizational politician" role and who represent the team to more senior decision makers. These managers are excellent negotiators who make sure that adequate resources are available for the team to achieve excellence. **Internal linking** is performed by managers who are good at integrating and producing work arrangements among team members, ensuring that all participants are updated on key issues and that communication is smooth and sufficient. This creates a high degree of team cohesiveness and cooperation.

Finally, informal linkers excel at allocating work. **Informal linking** is facilitated by employees who have frequent interaction across departments and thereby ensure that plans are implemented effectively and work is handled collaboratively.

> Draw a diagram that illustrates how a department manager might demonstrate a specific linking function.

DIMENSIONS OF TEAM BEHAVIOR

There are two fundamental types of behaviors performed in teams as members go about making decisions and solving problems. These are referred to as **task functions** and **relationship, or maintenance, functions.** While task functions help members accomplish the goal at hand, relationship functions keep the interaction among members progressing smoothly.

Task Dimension

Members assume task roles to facilitate and coordinate team efforts. Most commonly, the group task is to define and solve a specific problem. Each group member may, of course, take on more than one role throughout the course of the team's life; in fact, one member may assume all or most of the different roles that have been identified. While the roles listed below (Box 4.5) are self-evident from their titles, they also provide examples of the types of tasks group members routinely perform.

As members work to accomplish tasks, they have an impact not only on each other's behaviors but also on team members' interpersonal relations. The relationships that develop among group participants affect the overall group culture and can either facilitate or block the group's progress in achieving its goal.

BOX 4.5

Common Task Behaviors

Information seeker asks for clarification of suggestions made by group members in terms of factual accuracy; may also request facts pertinent to the problem being discussed

Information giver offers facts or generalizations

Opinion giver states his or her beliefs with regard to a suggestion that has been made

Elaborator spells out suggestions in terms of examples and tries to determine how an idea would work out if adopted by the group

Coordinator shows or clarifies the relationships among various ideas and tries to coordinate activities of group members

Orienter defines the position of the group with respect to its goals by summarizing what has occurred; identifies departures from agreed-upon directions or goals

Evaluator-critic subjects the accomplishment of the group to some standard of group functioning

Energizer motivates the group to action and attempts to stimulate the group to higher quality activity

Procedural technician expedites group movement by doing things for the group such as distributing materials or rearranging the seating

Recorder writes down suggestions and discussion outcomes; serves as the group's memory

Relationship Dimension

In addition to clarity regarding the task itself, focusing on group process encourages an emphasis on the relationship aspects of a team—how members feel about one another. Just because you have brought individuals together does not mean that they will function together effectively. Personal relations include how people feel about each other, expectations with regard to member behaviors and loyalties, assumptions employees make about other team members, and the personal problems that arise as individuals seek to work cooperatively.

Unless participants establish relationships that encourage each employee to draw on his or her individual experience and expertise to benefit the team, the group may in fact be less effective than would individual members working on the problem separately. Fear of rejection and poor relationships can create unproductive conflict, hostility, or other problems.

Specific behaviors that encourage or harm members' interpersonal relationships, and thereby either increase or hinder group productivity, are listed in Box 4.6.

Think of a specific team you have been on. Did you demonstrate more task or relationship behaviors? Why do you think this is the case? Is this true of all teams to which you belong?

Individual Needs Dimension

Think of any group to which you have belonged, and you are likely to recall individuals who were overly defensive, unproductive, or who either competed with their peers or withdrew

BOX 4.6

Maintenance or Relationship Behaviors

Encourager	praises, agrees with, and accepts the contributions of others
Harmonizer	mediates differences between other members and attempts to reconcile disagreements; relieves tension in conflict situations
Compromiser	may demonstrate such behaviors as offering to yield his or her status or admitting that an error has been made
Gate keeper	attempts to keep communication channels open by facilitating participation by other group members or by proposing the regulation of the communication flow
Standard setter	expresses standards for the group or applies standards in evaluating the quality of the group's process
Observer	keeps records of various aspects of group process and proposes interpretations of the group's activities
Follower	goes along with the group passively, accepting others' ideas

entirely. Why do you suppose some members become enthusiastic and involved while others remain silent or daydream? Failure to satisfy **individual needs** can bring about one of the most common blocks to group effectiveness—the hidden agenda. Hidden agendas refer to the motives of team members who work on two levels at once, the surface level and the hidden agenda level.

In addition to hidden agendas, there are a variety of other dysfunctional roles team members play that are important to recognize and address. These include "blocking," "attacking," "withdrawing," and "joking." Blockers, constantly raise objections to whatever is proposed, attacking and questioning the competence or motives of their fellow group members. An individual who covers up his or her feelings, or does not respond to ideas that are presented in the group, harms both cohesiveness and productivity. You may have personally witnessed how joking or other inappropriate humor distracts the group from its task. The most common individual roles are listed below. These behaviors are readily identified, as they occur to some extent in nearly all group situations. As a team leader, it will be your responsibility to ensure that they do not undermine the effectiveness of your team dynamics.

BOX 4.7

Individual Needs and Dysfunctional Behaviors

Aggressor	deflates the status of others and expresses disapproval of the values, actions, or feelings of other group members
Blocker	is negativistic and resistant, disagrees and opposes without reasons or attempts to bring back an idea after the group has rejected it
Recognition-seeker	works in various ways to call attention to himself or herself, whether through boasting, dominating with personal achievements, or acting in unusual ways
Self-confessor	uses opportunities that arise in the group to express personal, nongroup oriented feelings or insights
Ego-centered	makes a display of his or her lack of involvement in the group's processes. This may be cynicism, disinterest, fooling around, or other nonproductive behaviors
Dominator	tries to manipulate the group through flattery, giving directions in an authoritative manner, or interrupting others' contributions
Help-seeker	attempts to gain sympathy from other group members through expressions of insecurity, confusion, or other unreasonable behaviors
Special interest pleader	speaks for a disenfranchised group, often cloaking his or her own prejudices in the stereotype which best suits his or her individual needs
Joker	distracts the group from its task

Recognizing personal motives is the first step in dealing with unhealthy member behaviors. This requires confronting members through positive, open exchanges and helping them to deal with issues that might threaten their self-interests. If a supportive group climate has developed, group members will learn to trust one another and the chances for successful confrontation and conflict management will increase.

> Give an example of an occasion where you have had strong "individual needs." What were the circumstances? How did it affect your participation?

FIRST STEPS TO BUILDING AN EFFECTIVE TEAM

You need not be experiencing major problems to derive benefits from a formal teambuilding effort. Even when employees are functioning *well* as a team, you should consider teambuilding to help a well-functioning team improve. Teambuilding can make an already successful team even more productive, especially when there is a high degree of task interdependence as is characteristic of hospitality organizations. For example, the maintenance department repairs the rooms that housekeepers clean and the front desk staff sells. If the customer is to receive the best possible service, these departments must all cooperate with each other.

Yet, even in organizations with a well-coordinated staff, the front desk workers may sometimes unnecessarily pressure the housekeepers to speed up room cleaning, and the housekeeping department may complain that the maintenance staff leaves behind a mess when it does repairs. In cases like these, teambuilding among department heads and among the employees of different departments can help employees to understand each other's tasks. With the greater trust and understanding that results from teambuilding, each individual will be better able to anticipate how his or her actions on the job will affect the jobs of others. This can enable an effective organization to become an exceptional one.

Increasing Member Trust

Teambuilding is not an easy process, since it involves taking both personal and professional risks. Employees often fear that their jobs will be in jeopardy if they say what they really think is wrong with the way a team or an organization is functioning. It must be made clear to members that the aim of the teambuilding process is to develop **trust.** Employees must be encouraged to discuss any factors that are blocking this essential ingredient, even though the discussion may be painful. It is important for a manager or supervisor to reassure the team members that they have nothing to fear and to secure their cooperation and commitment prior to the first team meeting. One way to do this is to ask each person individually and publicly for his or her support.

Trust is often the core team issue that managers must address. It is almost always at least part of the problem in every dysfunctional team. There is no magic cure for lack of trust. Trust is established over time. It accumulates from observations and judgments of everyday, routine interactions. Yet, trust can disappear in a few seconds. When managers think about dealing with lack of trust they are dealing with "**undiscussables.**" This can be defined as a problem or issue that someone hesitates to talk about with those who are essential to its resolution. As people take the opportunity to talk about undiscussables, the number of undiscussables goes down and trust goes up.

There are many symptoms of a trustless team. Among the most common are:

- poor communication habits as exhibited by a lack of openness and an unwillingness to really listen;
- cliques, or subgroups of team members who exclude others;
- poor follow-through and failure to keep commitments or take agreed-upon actions;
- guarded information flow by excessively controlling information;
- hidden agendas, where objectives and actions of a certain group are not shared with the entire team; and
- end-runs, wherein certain actors avoid those people who should legitimately be involved in a decision, request, or communication.

As soon as you notice that any of the above have occurred in your team, it is essential to bring this symptom to members' attention so that it can be addressed and resolved.

> Which of the symptoms of poor trust have you experienced most frequently? What member behaviors most affect your willingness to develop trust in a team?

Creating an Appropriate Team Environment

It is important that the team meet in a place that is considered **neutral territory.** Physical surroundings carry many powerful psychological associations. People usually feel more secure in their own offices, for example, and most employees will consider the person behind the large desk or at the head of the table to be in a position of authority. Therefore, to promote communication among team members, your sessions are most productively held in a more informal setting where everyone feels comfortable.

It is also crucial that teambuilding sessions be free from distractions and interruptions. It takes time for an atmosphere of trust to develop; phone calls or other interruptions can significantly impede the team's progress. For this reason, some organizations hold periodic teambuilding sessions at a remote location that is free of distractions where members can focus their complete attention on the group dynamics and revitalize their team activities.

As you will discover, the rewards of teambuilding are many. Increased motivation and the ability to react rapidly to the changing business environment are just two benefits of promoting team spirit. Everyone wants to be a member of a winning team, but final victory in the championships can come only from a full season of training, development, and teamwork.

> Recall a time when you were uncomfortable due to some feature of your environment. Describe the setting in detail. How did it make you feel?

Establishing and Clarifying Team Goals

There will be numerous occasions when you will find yourself responsible for creating and leading teams. One of the keys to effective teambuilding is the establishment of clear, shared, and measurable goals. **Goal clarity** implies that there is a specific performance objective that enables members to determine when the goal has been attained. Goals improve team performance by producing higher levels of effort and planning than could be expected when goals are unclear or too vague. The sense of accomplishment that comes from making progress toward a specific goal then increases members' intrinsic satisfaction and motivates them to work even harder.

In addition, members must believe that the goal embodies a worthwhile and important result; the goal must be what researchers have called "elevating." When goals are perceived as important, members—and the team as a whole—find them challenging. Elevated goals make a difference and present a sense of urgency. Members feel excited and energized by the process, and the focus of all participants is on the team's common objective and ultimate success.

Goals either can be assigned or can emerge from the team dynamics. Most scholars agree that participatory goal setting increases confidence, which, in turn, increases member motivation. When a team believes it can accomplish a task, members push themselves to high performance. Participatory goal setting also channels anxiety into motivation, and generally increases members' confidence. Both of these factors lead to greater commitment to achieve the goals that have been set.

In addition, you can increase commitment by reinforcing the importance of the goal, making the goal public to other organizational members, and instilling confidence in the team that the goal is attainable.

> What are some other consequences of a team process when members are unclear about their goals or purpose?

TEAMBUILDING AND THE PROBLEM-SOLVING PROCESS

Mark, General Manager of the Skylook Lodge in the Endless Mountains, covered his face with his hands in frustration. What could have gone wrong? He had put together the best possible problem-solving team. He had made all the necessary resources available to them and even provided lunches on several occasions when meetings ran into the noon hour. These were all bright, creative managers. He looked around the room at the seven team members, shaking his head. "Okay. We messed up on this one," Mark suddenly announced, breaking the silence. "But I need to know—why? What happened? Everyone understood the problem—our information systems, especially reservations, were hopelessly outdated. We gathered information, made site visits, listened to sales presentations, hired consultants . . . we analyzed the information in light of Skylook's needs and priorities. We considered everything; we created a comprehensive, detailed plan. We did a great job."

Mark's dilemma is becoming too typical of strategic problem-solving efforts. While the process of reaching a solution is given tremendous attention, the team stops short of the final but critical steps—the design and execution of an implementation plan and feedback processes. Good ideas don't become good processes automatically. Solutions require attention and effort to implement; neglecting this essential step spells doom. In the case of the Skylook Lodge, doom came in the form of angry guests and frustrated employees, resulting in low satisfaction and a steadily falling bottom line.

While teambuilding is an ongoing managerial function, it is important to recognize teams in crisis situations that require immediate and appropriate attention. There are a number of signals that indicate that employees are not functioning as a team. These include low productivity, poor service quality, a decrease in customer or member satisfaction, hostility and conflicts among departments, and an increase in the number of requests for transfers. Confusion about work assignments or general apathy also might indicate that individuals are not working as a team. You know your staff is experiencing problems when employees frequently claim, "Nobody tells me anything." Teambuilding, therefore, is a multistage process undertaken with the goal of creating and maintaining a high degree of trust and open communication among members.

Identify the Problem

The first step is to identify the problem you wish to solve. The team's goals must be defined and the employees' commitment to them and to the teambuilding process must be secured. Without your employees' willingness to examine the problems they face and to recognize the need for change, a teambuilding effort is probably doomed.

Gather Information

After you have identified the team goal or problem and you have fostered an environment conducive to teambuilding, the second step is to begin gathering information about the problem at hand. There are three main ways to gather data:

1. Hold a meeting to air grievances;
2. Conduct a survey;
3. Bring in an outside consultant.

An open "clear the air" session can be difficult to orchestrate effectively. You may find that no one is willing to risk giving opinions regarding the organization's problems. The second method of data gathering, conducting a survey, is less threatening and more likely to yield pertinent information.

Taking a survey gives you or the team leader the advantage of knowing what conflicts and difficulties the team might face in advance of the team meeting. The survey might indicate that you, the team leader, or some other supervisor is considered one of the team's primary problems. With the survey information, you can get the first discussion "rolling" by mentioning a common problem and asking for the team's ideas. The leader can set a nondefensive tone during the meeting by bringing up some of the main survey findings about himself or herself. By doing so, the leader shows the team that it is okay to discuss problems that relate directly to management.

If the manager or supervisor is considered to be one of the team's main problems, it is a good idea to bring in an outside consultant. It may also be necessary to bring in a consultant if the problems facing the team are likely to cause heated discussion.

Interpret the Data

In step 3 of the teambuilding process, the manager assembles the data and communicates it to team members. It is helpful if the new information can be presented on a flip chart so that the team can discuss each item in turn. The discussion can be largely free-form, but as team leader your job is to encourage participation from all team members—calling on them by name if necessary. Be sure to allocate substantial time for this step, because each member of the team requires an opportunity to elaborate on his or her views on each topic.

What other problems are likely to arise at this stage of the process?

Plan for Change

Once your team has thoroughly analyzed the information, it can begin step 4—planning for change. Like the other parts of the teambuilding process, this can be a challenging activity. Because most team members will have their own ideas about how to make changes, each person must be willing to compromise. By now, the team members have already spent time together discussing problems, so they should be able to work together as they establish plans for eliminating factors that are blocking their effectiveness.

Although team members may be eager to resolve the matter at hand and jump directly into problem solving, the team must first attend to procedural matters and establish norms for team functioning. One of the early agenda items is to determine how decisions will be made. For example, the team should decide whether all team members will have an equal vote on each issue or whether the votes of those who are most directly affected should carry more weight.

At this point, the team also establishes objectives and makes plans for achieving them. Say, for example, that more frequent communication is one objective. The team may decide to improve communication by holding weekly meetings and by circulating detailed agendas in advance.

If there are areas of conflict, the team can develop specific strategies to overcome them. Recall our opening hotel example. A frequent area of conflict lies between the housekeeping department and the front desk staff. Through the teambuilding process, these two departments might resolve their differences by working out a schedule and a mutually satisfactory process.

Implement the Plan

When the group has formulated its plan for solving problems or improving service, it is ready for step 5—implementing the plans. During this period, the team should continue functioning according to the guidelines it has set for itself. Employees who have not been part of the teambuilding sessions should be fully informed and involved in the plan. For example, the executive housekeeper should get a list of the rooms that are vacant from the front desk staff at the beginning of the shift and clean those first. In this case, the process of obtaining a list of vacant rooms from the front desk staff prior to cleaning them can be repeated until all of the rooms have been cleaned.

Solicit and Provide Feedback

This critical step—feedback to team members—is sometimes ignored. If your team is comprised of managers, for example, you might rate its success by how subsequent management decisions affect the organization's bottom line. When your team is composed of food servers or front desk staff, it is more difficult to assess the team's success because it is more difficult to link team outcomes and recommendations to subsequent action plans. You will remember our discussion of feedback from Chapter 2.

LEADING YOUR TEAM

Now that you have been introduced to a number of principles that will help you better understand team dynamics, it is time to think more specifically about your team leadership role. The following section provides some guidelines and considerations for selecting team members, anticipating challenges, and providing the types of support your team needs to accomplish its task, while benefiting from the expertise and insights of all team members.

Select Team Members

Selecting members of your team is one of your most important considerations. Your general manager may want to build a team of his or her department heads, while they in turn may build a team of their staff. If you are a department head, you may choose individuals you directly supervise, or you might consider gathering members from several departments for your teambuilding activities.

The selection of a team's membership depends on the way jobs are interrelated. As mentioned earlier, interdepartmental teambuilding can reduce conflicts between departments. You may want to select specific team members to work on a particular project based on the different skills and expertise each person brings to the project. The important thing to remember is that you can't overestimate the importance of who is on a team, as the composition influences the level of expertise, the likelihood of conflict, and the degree to which various viewpoints are represented.

Would you rather be on a team where everyone was friends or where everyone had a different perspective on the problem? Explain.

Anticipate Challenges

Imagine you are now ready to leave your office and meet with your team for the first time. It is likely that you will be anxious about how this first session will progress. Don't worry— some anxiety is to be expected. Even the most experienced team leaders feel a bit nervous as they prepare to lead important team efforts. After all, team dynamics are never completely predictable and the outcomes are never certain.

For example, William J. Crockett, a former manager in the U.S. Department of State, wrote of his anxiety before his first teambuilding session. He acknowledged that he was concerned about the risks that such a meeting might hold. Recognizing that he depended upon all members of his team, he knew that conflicts were inevitable and he would like to have avoided or reduced hard feelings that might have resulted in some members withdrawing or resigning.

Other managers have also expressed concern regarding the well-known principle that a manager should not discuss an employee's performance, especially his or her weaknesses, in front of the employee's peers. Yet, a teambuilding session will probably involve exactly that. If you feel these concerns, recognize that they are legitimate and normal. Through experience, however, you will discover that the rewards of encouraging a team to work together more effectively through open and honest communication far outweigh the risks involved.

What do you find most challenging about leading an important team process? What would be your main concerns or anxieties?

Assess Your Team's Performance

Team leaders are always actively engaged and are constantly assessing their teams along three related dimensions.

- The team's productivity; that is, whether the team meets or exceeds the expectations of the organization.

BOX 4.8

Guidelines for Effective Team Leaders

1. Communicate clearly and often
2. Solicit input from other team members toward making decisions
3. Remain accessible to employees
4. Treat team members with respect
5. Give constructive feedback and truly listen
6. Accept ownership for team decisions
7. Regularly evaluate the effectiveness of the team

- Team member satisfaction, which can be determined by whether or not team members have feelings of competence and believe there are possibilities for long-term growth.
- Team synergy, which can be assessed by the team's effectiveness at achieving its goal (task behaviors) and compatibility (maintenance behavior).

Managers who take group process for granted often fail to lead their teams productively. This can be the result of any number of factors, but most often occurs because these leaders:

- are too eager to please team members;
- are confused about their role;
- have a tendency to avoid serious problems; or
- exhibit a lack of commitment to the team.

On other occasions, team leaders may demonstrate dysfunctional behaviors that inhibit healthy and productive interactions. Some of the most common problems include showing favoritism, displaying a lack of sensitivity to individual members' circumstances, or becoming inflexible in decision making. As a team leader, you will be most effective when you adhere to the several simple guidelines listed in Box 4.8.

Leader Task Behavior

In addition to the general guidelines given above, effective teambuilding requires that leaders apply a specific set of task and maintenance behaviors among those that were discussed earlier. With regard to task behaviors, the first is initiation. The team leader must both propose goals and tasks and define a group problem when it arises. The second task behavior is that of seeking information or opinions, which requires the leader to ask for facts, feelings, and information relevant to concerns of team members. The third task behavior is clarifying and elaborating. In other words, managers are responsible for clarifying or crystallizing ideas and comments if they are not easily understood by some of the team members. The fourth behavior is summarizing; this is a major management behavior that facilitates the teambuilding process. Every 15 minutes or so, the team leader summarizes the group's discussion to prevent the team from backtracking or meandering.

Leader Relationship Behavior

An important maintenance behavior in the teambuilding process is harmonizing. A leader who seeks to build a cohesive team must reconcile disagreements, reduce tension, and encourage team members to explore differences. The second key maintenance behavior is gate-keeping or helping to keep communication channels open. Effective team leaders facilitate input from less assertive team members, thus "opening the gate" for quiet people to express their views. The third behavior is encouraging. An example of encouraging would be that, after a quiet person has spoken, the leader expresses support such as, "That's a good point." This helps ensure that the next time a quiet person feels the impulse to speak, he or she will remember the words of encouragement and share ideas with greater confidence. The fourth and final behavior is compromising. This maintenance behavior requires offering solutions to problems that accommodate different perspectives from the group. Every group needs its leader to demonstrate both task and maintenance behaviors.

As a team leader, would you be most comfortable demonstrating task or relationships behaviors? Explain your response.

Observing and Facilitating Team Communication

It is also useful for a leader to observe communication patterns among team members so that he or she knows how best to respond to the team at any given point. An experienced manager is able to answer the following questions:

1. Who talks? For how long? How often?
2. Whom do people look at when they talk? The person whom people look at has the power in the group.
3. Who talks after whom, or who interrupts whom? The person whom people talk over has little status in the group.
4. What style of communication is used (assertions, questions, tones of voice, gestures)?
5. What is the body language of the team members? Who is sitting with their arms across their chest? Who is looking out the window? Who is tapping their feet and pencils?

These observations provide clues to other important things that may be going on in your team, such as who is leading whom or who influences whom.

Managers can use a variety of team situations, such as department meetings, to increase information sharing and communication. A well-structured meeting can be highly beneficial as meetings generate a spirit of unity and cooperation that contributes to the formation of a collective identity. Meetings also increase individuals' commitment to decisions and help to define and promote the collective goals of the organization. Meetings provide a forum for the generation of new ideas, enhance creative ideas during team problem solving, and enhance communication by creating a pool of shared knowledge.

The manager influences the effectiveness of meetings by investing time and energy into preparing for and conducting them. The first step is to notify participants well in advance. Have a well-defined purpose: "For this meeting to be successful, we need to accomplish . . . ." Prepare a written agenda with a realistic time schedule for each item. If there are items that employees need to think about in advance of the meeting, distribute that list early. In order to maintain the focus of the meeting, select only participants who have direct interest in the items to be discussed.

When conducting a meeting, be clear and precise in your aims and agenda. Begin promptly by stating the purpose of the meeting. Once the goals are clear, present the agenda and time schedule. As the meeting progresses, make sure no one monopolizes the discussion. Summarize frequently and relate the progress in the discussion to the initial objectives. Near the end of the meeting, check for understanding of any conclusions drawn. Decide what actions are to be taken. Record the plan of action and assign the persons responsible for carrying out these plans.

TECHNOLOGY AND TEAMS

Advances in technology have affected numerous aspects of organizational life. For instance, technology has affected communication systems and decision-making processes. It has had an impact on employees' time management and on the ability to deliver high quality customer service. Here, we explore the ways in which technology influences group dynamics.

As a hospitality manager, you will certainly find yourself leading or at least participating in teams that make use of one or more forms of technology. The term **team virtuality** is increasingly used to refer to the extent to which team members use virtual tools to coordinate team processes and implement team decisions. While it may seem a natural progression, the use of technology can be problematic and leaders must acquire new skill sets to effectively manage the dynamics of teams with a high degree of skill. The skills of coaching and boundary spanning have been found to be particularly important to successful technology implementation within a team context.

Factors that Influence Virtual Team Effectiveness

In addition to leader behaviors, equally important to team effectiveness is an organizational culture that supports communication and trust among team members. The most productive teams have been trained to use the required technology so that a high level of member competence is developed. Simulated virtual teams, in particular, enable potential team members to become familiar with the technology. Issues of trust and access to communication tools both affected team member productivity and satisfaction.

Lurey and Raisinghani (2001) studied best practices in virtual teams and discovered that team member relationships had one of the strongest correlations with effectiveness. Other researchers agree, emphasizing that team leaders must continue to focus on the human relations aspect of teamwork and not allow decisions to be driven by technology alone.

In addition, it appears that team performance is highly dependent upon the fit between the communication channel(s) being used and the nature of the task. Also of importance is the team's process and the leader's style. When considering best practices of teams whose members are widely dispersed, culture differences must also be taken into consideration. The behaviors that work in one culture context may not be as effective in another, and team members must be prepared to address and respond to intercultural team dynamics, whether interacting face-to-face or through technology.

Have you had experience as a member of a virtual team? If so, how effective was the team's effort? If not, would you look forward to this opportunity?

Dimensions that Facilitate and Hinder Virtual Team Performance

In Chapter 8 we will discuss creativity, an essential characteristic of high performing leaders and their teams. Clearly, the potential for creativity is increased in virtual teams where individuals from a variety of different contexts come together to problem-solve. In fact, some researchers and practitioners believe that the creative aspect of virtual teams far outweighs any constraints such teams may experience.

As we have seen, perhaps the greatest block to teamwork is lack of communication. When employees feel isolated, they avoid talking with each other, and you can end up with a staff of individuals who are all cooperating according to their own concept of individual job requirements. Obviously, this attitude makes functioning as a team extremely difficult, and it results in low productivity, employee dissatisfaction, and erratic service. This is a danger to watch out for, especially in virtual teams, where the team members may be geographically isolated from one another and meet only in a virtual sense in teleconferences and Internet communication.

Summary

In this chapter we discuss what makes an effective team, and the process of building and maintaining an effective team. We define a team as a group of individuals who have established mutual trust and open channels of communication, allowing them to work together effectively to accomplish a task or to solve a problem. We emphasize that in the consumer-driven world of the hospitality industry, developing teamwork is the source of a valuable competitive advantage.

Teambuilding is important for many reasons. It can ease tensions between departments and make it easier to improve service at all levels of the organization, and it can create the opportunity for employees to respond more quickly to new situations. Recall that "team" refers to a collection of individuals who are brought together for a specific purpose and who hold themselves mutually accountable for accomplishing specific goals. Goals improve team performance by producing higher levels of effort and planning than could be expected when goals are unclear or too general.

We discuss in detail six dimensions of teams that can help to identify strengths and weaknesses. These include:

- Group norms
- Group cohesiveness
- Groupthink
- Risky shift
- Social loafing
- The linking function of teams.

Using these dimensions, appropriate teambuilding activities can be implemented.

We also discuss task functions versus relationship functions. The task dimension concerns the group members' contributions toward accomplishing their stated objectives; the personal relations dimension refers to the building of group-centered attitudes and morale as the group discusses its task.

Finally, we look at the issue of trust, which is a problem factor in almost every dysfunctional team. Trustless teams exhibit a lack of openness and an unwillingness to really listen and often have subgroups of team members who exclude others.

Key Words

teambuilding *85*
interdepartmental team *86*
cross-functional team *86*
task force *86*
self-directed team *87*
upper echelon teams *87*
quality teams *87*
cohesiveness *89*

groupthink *90*
risky shift *91*
social loafing *92*
external linking *92*
internal linking *92*
informal linking *92*
task function *93*
relationship function *93*

individual needs *95*
trust *96*
undiscussables *96*
neutral territory *97*
goal clarity *97*
team virtuality *104*

Exercises

Exercise 1   iflycytravel.com Case

Category: Building Teams

Objective: To identify the key components of building group dynamics

Number of Participants: 20

Time Frame: 50 minutes

Materials: One copy of the iflycytravel.com case and one feedback form per participant

Procedure:

1. Distribute the iflycytravel.com and ask each participant to read it (15 minutes).
2. Ask for four volunteers to act as two executives from iflycyber.com and travelux.com who have been charged with the task of developing a strategy to facilitate the transition and integration of the merger.
3. The four volunteers have 15 minutes to provide a game plan to ameliorate the current situation.
4. The remaining participants are observers to the problem-solving team and complete the "Observer's Feedback Form."
5. Debrief and discuss the relevant issues raised in this case (20 minutes).

DISCUSSION QUESTIONS

- Why wasn't the iflycytravel.com corporate staff a team?
- What does it take to be a team?
- What teambuilding suggestions would you recommend?
- How will trust be developed among the staff members?

***

OBSERVER'S FEEDBACK FORM

A. Watch the role play carefully and make notes in the space provided below prior to the general review and discussion.

The Problem-Solving Executive's Behavior & Comments

Iflycyber.com   Travelux.com

B. Please indicate the appropriate rating scale, such that '1' represents excellent and '5' poor.

1. Did the executives identify the key problems?
   1 _____   2 _____   3 _____   4 _____   5 _____
2. Did they assess the team's strengths and weaknesses?
   1 _____   2 _____   3 _____   4 _____   5 _____
3. Did they set specific performance goals to be accomplished by the unified team?
   1 _____   2 _____   3 _____   4 _____   5 _____
4. Did they hold themselves accountable for the team's results?
   1 _____   2 _____   3 _____   4 _____   5 _____
5. Did they create solutions to address the redundancy issues among the departments and staff members?
   1 _____   2 _____   3 _____   4 _____   5 _____
6. Did they set a common vision or goal for the newly formed company?
   1 _____   2 _____   3 _____   4 _____   5 _____

***

IFLYCYTRAVEL.COM: CASE

Octopus Inc. is a technology conglomerate that owns *iflycyber.com,* the premier online travel solutions website. *Iflycyber.com* manages a portfolio of online travel services that targets all markets and areas of the travel business. Recently, Octopus acquired *travelux.com,* a competitor whose expertise lies within the luxury travel segment. The newly created company, *iflycytravel.com,* would place them in a unique position as the only all-services dot-com travel company in the marketplace. While this position will greatly leverage iflycytravel.com, the newly merged companies are under tremendous pressure to streamline operations, improve productivity, and expand their market base. Further improvements have been mandated to integrate functions and eliminate redundancies across the company.

The strategic plan for the newly merged iflycytravel.com is to withdraw from all the ancillary businesses, such as tour operations and concierge services, in order to concentrate on the online flight and hotel reservations, car rentals, and time-share opportunities. These focused efforts involve streamlining the technologies and operations across the two companies to increase profitability. These ambitious goals and organizational changes put tremendous pressure on iflycytravel.com's president and CEO, who has been overwhelmed in restructuring the pieces of the newly merged company, and developing a team from the chaos which could persevere and accomplish its assigned mission.

The iflycytravel.com merger has created a multitude of significant structural and interpersonal changes that Octopus and the financial engineers of the merger had not even contemplated. These include (1) considerable increase and redundancy in management personnel and structure (2) a new CEO with ambiguous power and goals (3) changing operating procedures and responsibilities and (4) uncertain reward systems and career paths. These externally initiated changes led to a multitude of internal changes in organizational culture, interpersonal relationships, structural uncertainty, and career opportunities.

The executive staffs are extremely competent in their areas of expertise, but they are dependent on each other to make the organization function effectively. The different styles of staff members, coupled with the anxiety and resentment, which has rapidly developed regarding the ambiguity of careers and power bases, have led to minimal communication and distrust of others' intentions, disorganization, and low productivity. The merger has transformed two effectively functioning teams into one group of disorganized and competing individuals.

This is especially true of the executive staff, which is made up of the president, vice president, financial and legal division directors, and their immediate staffs. The need to streamline and increase profitability means that all of the current group, which represents officers of both the previous *iflycyber.com* and *travelux.com* companies, would not remain at the end of the year because of the considerable redundancies. The politics, lack of trust, fear and hostility, and considerable differences from previous corporate cultures and behavioral styles have created a group of territorial infighters. Clearly, the iflycytravel.com corporate staff is not a team.

Exercise 2   Dyadic Encounter

Category: Teambuilding

Objective: To get members of a team to know each other

Number of Participants: 10–30

Time Frame: 10 minutes for interviewing, and two minutes per person to introduce their partner

Procedure:
The group divides into pairs. Pair with someone you know the least. Interview the person with whom you are paired with the following questions:

1. What have you done at work that makes you most proud?
2. What is the most humorous situation that occurred at work?
3. What is one fact about yourself that no one would know?
4. What is one item about yourself that is untrue?

You have five minutes for each person to interview the other (10 minutes altogether). Then after the interviews are completed, introduce your partner to the rest of the team, giving answers to each of the four questions.

Exercise 3   Can We Share?

Category: Problem solving

Objective: To help participants seek ways to solve a problem creatively using negotiations and team effort

Group Size: 4–6 participants in each group

Time Frame: one hour

Materials*:

A copy of instruction sheet for each group

Ruler

A pair of scissors

Glue

Compass

A roll of string

2 rolls of ribbons

2 pens

2 sheets of blue construction paper

4 sheets of white construction paper

2 sheets of yellow construction paper

2 sheets of red construction paper

12 balloons

Procedure:

- Prepare a set of materials for each group. For example:

  Group 1

  Ruler

  Pen

  1 piece of blue construction paper

  2 pieces of white construction paper

  Group 2

  A pair of scissors

  1 piece of blue construction paper

  2 pieces of yellow construction paper

  3 balloons

  Group 3

  Glue

  Pen

  1 piece of red construction paper

  2 pieces of white construction paper

  Ribbons

Group 4

Compass

1 piece of red construction paper

String

9 balloons

- Divide participants into groups of 4–6, and give each group a set of materials.
- Explain to the groups that they are to prepare for a small party hosted by an important customer of the hotel whose daughter is having a birthday party this evening at the hotel. Their task is to prepare a creative tabletop setting for the party by completing the task described on the instruction sheet written by the "6-year-old birthday-girl." The groups can work with other groups to share the resources. Since time is not on our side, the first to complete the task will receive the best appraisal.
- Hand out the instruction sheet.
- After the exercise, debrief with the class on how they overcame the shortage on resources in order to accomplish the task. Key questions may be:
  - Cooperation—How did the group cooperate to complete the task?
  - Competition—What are the natures of competition that you observed?
  - Negotiation—Describe the negotiation procedure with other groups. What went well, and what went wrong?
  - Shared feelings—How did you feel about the process?

Instructions from the Client

Dear Staff,

This is my 6th birthday, and the party is VERY IMPORTANT. Please make the following to the specifications.

- Centerpiece for the table with at least 3 balloons and lots of ribbons.
- 1 Welcome card, 15 inches by 10 inches, using at least 3 colors.
- 2 cone-shaped hats which are 20 inches in diameter.

Thank you!

Source: Adapted from "It's Not Fair!" by Kirby, A. (1992). *The Encyclopedia of Games for Trainers*, Amherst, MA: Human Resource Development Press.

---

*materials are subject to number of groups and the task assigned to the group members.

Exercise 4   Team Tactics

Category: Teambuilding

Objectives:

- For participants to learn to work in a team toward the achievement of a common goal, especially when team members have differing viewpoints
- For participants to realize the value of a cohesive team, and that a team of people can sometimes arrive at a better solution to a problem than individuals

Number of Participants: Any number, with a minimum of four

Time Frame: 45 minutes (depending on the number of participants)

Materials:

One copy of the scenario (attached)

Paper

Flipchart

Markers

Procedure:

1. Divide all the participants into teams of four or five, and have them sit together.
2. Read the scenario (attached) aloud.
3. Have participants take five minutes to prepare written responses.
4. Have participants convene in their teams and prepare a cohesive response to the situation. Allow 10–15 minutes for this task, and have teams write their responses on flipcharts.
5. Teams present their responses to the entire group, and comment on the process that their particular team went through in order to reach a consensus. Presentations should last no longer than three minutes.

Variations:

The scenario can be adapted for any department or area of the hospitality industry. Moreover, the validity of this exercise can be enhanced with a real-life example from whatever department or specialty the participants come from.

Scenario: (Read Aloud)

You are the Guest Service Manager at a luxury chain hotel, and you have just received an email from your General Manager advising you that the corporate office has just given you $100,000 to create a training initiative for all hotel employees that will improve overall guest satisfaction. Since guest satisfaction has been steadily declining for all five of the chain's hotels in your region, the Vice President of Hotel Operations would like to see your proposal before he or she authorizes the release of the money. The Vice President would like to see a detailed list of exactly how the money will be spent, with approximate costs beside each expense. The General Manager has suggested that you first come up with a proposal yourself, then meet with the Guest Service Managers of all five of the neighboring hotels to come up with one consistent proposal that will meet the needs of all the hotels in the region.

Some examples of what the Vice President is looking for are:

- Spend $X to have a guest service specialist lead a training session at the hotel.
- Spend $X to research the guest service programs of our closest competitors.

Debrief: Discuss the programs that each team designed and discuss which team was the most creative. Then have that team discuss its process.

Source: Adapted from "Team Building:" Scannell, E. & Newstrom, J. (1994). *The Complete Games Trainers Play.* New York: McGraw Hill Inc.

Endnotes

Anonymous (2002). Creating a customer-focused management team. *Paper, Film and Foil Converter*, Chicago. pp. 4–19.

Berger, F. & Vanger, R. (1986). Building your hospitality team. *Cornell Hotel and Restaurant Administration Quarterly, 26*(2), 82–90.

Bertolotti, F., Macri, M., & Tagliaventi, M. (2005). Spontaneous self-managing practices in teams: Evidence from the field. *Journal of Management Inquiry, 14*(4), 366–385.

Bragg, T. (1999). Turn around an ineffective team. *IIE Solutions, 31*(5), 49–55.

Chidambaram, L. & Tung, L. (2005). A study of social loafing in technology-supported groups. *Information Systems Research, 16*(2), 149–171.

Chip, R. (1999). Team ghostbusters. *Strategy and Leadership, 27*(1), 44–51.

Cox, S. (2003). Building dream teams. *Nursing Management, 34*(1), 58–59.

Crockett, W. J. (1980). Team-building—One approach to organizational development. *Journal of Applied Behavioral Science, 6*(3), 292.

Doolen, T., Hacker, M., & Van Aken, E. (2003). The impact of organizational context on work team effectiveness. *Transactions on Engineering Management, 50*(3), 285–292.

Drucker, P. F. (1974). *Management: Tasks, Responsibilities, Practices.* New York: Harper & Row. p. 567.

Edmondson, A. (2003). How team leaders promote learning in interdisciplinary action teams. *The Journal of Management Studies, 40*(6), 1419–1431.

Henttonen, K. & Blomqvist, K. (2005). Managing distance in a global virtual team: The evolution of trust through technology-mediated relational communication. *Strategic Change, 14*(2), 107–119.

Hutchins, R. (1996). Globalwork: Bridging distance, culture, and time. *Human Resource Development Quarterly, 7*(3), 297–303.

Janis, I. L. (1982). *Groupthink: Psychological Studies of Policy Decisions and Fiascoes.* Second Edition. New York: Houghton Mifflin.

Kirkman, B. & Mathieu, J. (2005). The dimensions and antecedents of team virtuality. *Journal of Management, 31*(5), 700–706.

Larson, C. E. & LaFasto, F. M. (1990). *Teamwork: What Must Go Right, What Can Go Wrong.* Newbury Park, CA: Sage Publications.

Larsen, K. & McInemey, C. (2002). Preparing to work in the virtual organization. *Information and Management, 39*(6), 445–462.

Livermore, C. (2006). Creativity in virtual teams—key components for success. *Journal of Global Information Technology, 9*(1), 69–73.

Lu, M., Watson-Manheim, M., Chudoba, K., & Wynn, E. (2006). Virtuality and team performance. *Journal of Global Information Technology Management, 9*(1), 4–24.

Lurey, J. & Raisinghani, M. (2001). An empirical study of best practices in virtual teams. *Information and Management, 38*(8), 523–537.

Palleschi, B. & Heim, P. (1980). The hidden barriers to team-building, *Training and Development Journal,* 14–18.

Peters, T. J. & Waterman, R. Jr., (1982). *In Search of Excellence,* New York: Harper & Row. p. 126.

Pfeiffer, J. E. N. (2004). *Creativity in Virtual Teams—Key Components for Success.* New York: Wiley Publishers.

Provo, J. (1996). Team effectiveness and decision making in organizations. *Human Resource Development Quarterly, 7*(3), 291–296.

Pyona, P. (2005). Information technology, human relations and knowledge work teams. *Team Performance Management, 11*(3/4), 104–113.

Raudenbush, L. M. (2000). A cross national comparison of effective leadership and teamwork: Toward a global workforce. *Human Resource Development Quarterly, 11*(2), 207–211.

Rico, R. & Cohen, S. (2005). Effects of task interdependence and type of communication on performance in virtual teams. *Journal of Managerial Psychology, 20*(3/4), 261–275.

Thamhain, H. (2004). Team leadership effectiveness in technology-based project environments. *Project Management Journal, 35*(4), 35–47.

Tran, V. & Latapie, H. (2006). Four strategies for team and work structuring in global organizations. *The Business Review, 5*(1), 106–111.

5

GROUP PROBLEM SOLVING AND DECISION MAKING

CHAPTER OUTLINE

Introduction

Understanding Group Problem Solving
  Facilitating Problem-Solving Groups
  Strategies for Effective Group Problem Solving
  Investigating Contextual Influences
  Establishing the Ground Rules for Group Problem-Solving Behavior
  Managing Breakpoints
  Item Contingent Model
  Benefits of Group Problem Solving

Theories of Group Decision Making
  Vigilant Interaction Theory
  Centralization of Authority Hypothesis

Factors That Affect Group Decisions
  Emotions
  Participation
  Information Exchange

Methods for Group Decision Making
  Unstructured Techniques
  Structured Techniques
    Dialectical inquiry
    The stepladder technique
    The vote model
    Consensus mapping
    Garbage can model
  Technology and Group Decision Making

Understanding the Impact of Group Dynamics
  Conformity
  Groupthink
  Deviance
  Deindividuation
  Power

Group Versus Individual Decision Making
  When to Make a Group Decision
  When to Make an Individual Decision

Summary

LEARNING OBJECTIVES

After reading this chapter, you will be able to do the following:

1. Define problem solving and how it differs from decision making.
2. Discuss the three strategies managers should use for effective group problem solving.
3. Understand the item contingent model and its two primary assumptions.
4. List the benefits of group problem solving versus individual problem solving.

5. Discuss when to make a decision individually and when to make a decision in a group.
6. Describe two of the factors that affect a group's ability to make decisions.
7. Name and discuss three methods a manager can use when making a group decision.
8. Explain how group dynamics can affect group decision making.
9. Discuss three of the problems associated with group problem solving and decision making.

Scenario: Difficult Dilemma

A downturn in the market has made it necessary for the Galaxy Hotel to lay off two staff members. The executive team of the Galaxy Hotel is sitting in the conference room trying to determine which two staff members to lay off. The group has identified four employees to consider for termination: Fred Clark; Claude Harris; Martha Rogers; and Roscoe Turner.

Fred Clark is a mechanic who attends night school. He is very creative and has earned three innovation awards for his superior performance in mechanical tasks. However, Fred received his first warning when he missed two days of work to attend an African-American political march after he was denied time off.

Claude Harris works in the Food and Beverage Department as a cook. Over the past year his supervisors have complained that his work performance has declined, although still above minimum standards. His supervisors suspect that part of the problem is that his wife is terminally ill and the doctors estimate that she will not live more than a year. However, Claude has expressed that he would like to continue working and he will improve his performance.

Martha Rogers is a single mother who has been working at Galaxy Hotel for one and a half years as the executive housekeeper. She is a favorite with her peers at work and keeps the morale of the housekeepers high. However, her attendance has only been fair because of work missed when her children were sick.

Roscoe Turner works as a receiving clerk. He has been picking up extra shifts and working part-time because his wife is pregnant and he needs the extra money. He has had perfect attendance, but has received marginal work performance evaluations. Roscoe's supervisors say that he does not seem as intelligent as other employees and needs extra supervision on assignments that require independent thinking.

The executive team is trying to decide what process to use in determining who will be laid off and who will stay. What process would you use?

INTRODUCTION

> The man who is denied the opportunity of making decisions of importance begins
> to regard as important the decisions he is allowed to make.
>
> —C. N. Parkinson

This quote suggests that it is important to include employees in the process of problem solving and decision making on issues that impact them. Effective managers understand the factors at work in the interactions of group members and in the process of group problem solving and decision making. It is important for managers to know when they should make decisions in a group and when they should make decisions individually. As you can see from the opening scenario, there are many variables that go into problem solving and decision making. These variables include the employees, the competency of the managers, and the situation.

In this chapter we will offer the resources to determine which method of problem solving and decision making to use. We will examine decision making as one of the components of problem solving. Then, we will explore strategies that managers can use in the process of problem solving and decision making. We will identify the benefits of group problem solving and decision making versus individual problem solving and decision making. The factors that influence a group's ability to solve problems and make decisions will be discussed; moreover, the role of group dynamics will be explored. There are multiple methods that managers can use to make decisions; we will discuss these in detail to provide insight into the framework that managers can use in group problem solving and decision making.

What are some of the groups to which you belong? Do you enjoy group activities?

UNDERSTANDING GROUP PROBLEM SOLVING

Problem solving is a multi-phase process involving a series of steps which usually begins with information gathering and which leads to the implementation of a final decision. The decision making process is the step within the larger problem-solving process where a particular option is chosen. Problem solving is concerned not only with this step but with other steps of analysis, implementation, and evaluation.

Facilitating Problem-Solving Groups

Facilitative influence is a stimulus that helps a group to coalesce around a solution. A hospitality manager can use organizational strategies such as a discussion agenda or a procedural format as a facilitative influence. Facilitative problem solving is most effective when the problem to be solved is complex, requiring higher level thinking skills such as synthesis, analysis, and evaluation. This level of complexity in problem solving may be referred to as functional potential.

Facilitative influence depends on:

1. the type of task: when a task is simple, the discussion agenda or procedural format is of less consequence.
2. functional potential: strategies that permit groups to deal with more complex types of problems lead to higher quality solutions. These more complex types of problems may be referred to as **critical function tasks,** which include:
   a. analyzing a problem carefully;
   b. establishing criteria for an effective solution; and
   c. evaluating the positive and negative qualities of alternatives in light of the criteria (Hirokawa, 1989).

Strategies for Effective Group Problem Solving

Strategies for effective group problem solving, referred to above as facilitative influence, can take a number of forms. Hospitality managers must understand that the problem solving process will be unique to the problem at hand and must be ready to modify the process according to the needs, direction, and progress of the group.

A typical sequence follows:

1. Prior to the group's first meeting, the manager should prioritize the aspects of the problem to be solved. Influences on the participants and on the problem must be taken into consideration.
2. A framework for solving the problem should be established either by the manager or as the first task assigned to the group.
3. The manager must frequently monitor the progress of the group, requiring feedback on the process, and establishing continuing goals or directions for the group.

> Do you find yourself doing a lot of problem solving individually? How about in groups? What are some specific problems that your group has addressed? Were you happy with the outcome?

Investigating Contextual Influences

One of the most difficult aspects of managing problem-solving groups is understanding the influences or biases that individuals bring to the group. The best way for a manager to ascertain these kinds of influences is through familiarity with their staff and the everyday interactions within their workplace. This kind of understanding can expedite solutions to difficult situations by enabling the manager to take into account and plan for the covert factors which will play into the decision making process. Managers should be aware of the following:

- *Group members' preliminary thinking about the issue.* Do they have preconceptions or biases toward the announced agenda? Do the members view the meeting as a formality/ritual or do they expect to get real problem solving done?
- *Interpersonal diversity may prove to be a challenge.* Employees will always bring with them their individual values and opinions. Refer back to our discussion of this issue in Chapter 3.
- *Relational and personal agendas brought to the group by members.* Only part of what occurs in a meeting is immediately related to the deliberations at hand. Understand that under the guise of discussing organizational business, people are also acting out the role they wish to play in the organization and expressing their feelings toward other people at the meeting. People will pursue hidden social agendas regardless of (or even despite) problem-solving procedures advocated by the manager.
- *The group will be affected by the interest other groups in the organization have in it and how participants relate to those other groups (to assess what boundary activities are likely to occur).* People in problem-solving groups seek not only to meet personal needs, but also to serve the needs of other groups with which they are simultaneously affiliated.
- *Existing patterns of behavior for problem-solving groups within the particular organizational culture and within society in general (to assess what facilitation strategies will be accepted—and which will be resisted as inappropriate, despite their logical fit).* A group's corporate culture implicitly limits what can occur in that group. What social rules will constrain members? Does the company follow participative or directive management?

Establishing the Ground Rules for Group Problem-Solving Behavior

The job of the manager is to establish the rules for interaction among the group participants without asserting his or her opinion to the exclusion of all others. In order to function effectively, the participants in the group must feel that they are in a protected social environment where their ideas will be accepted and fairly considered without threat of negative social repercussions. To the extent that a manager can create and maintain this environment, the solutions will be diverse, creative, and viable. An effective manager is capable of striking this balance between managing the structure of the discussion and allowing for the free exchange of ideas and solutions.

1. Prior to the group's first meeting, the manager's primary task is to set the parameters for the problem-solving process. This would include a structure for discussion. The problem must be clearly defined either by the manager or as the first task assigned to the group.
2. Before the group begins work on the problem, the manager must set clear expectations for group discussion. Basic rules of discussion as well as how to handle the conflicts that will inevitably arise would be covered in the process. In this way, conflict is recognized as an expected and necessary part of the process and is, therefore, less apt to cause a breakdown in finding the solution to the problem. At the same time, managers should define their own role in the process, be it participant, observer, or facilitator.
3. A further prerequisite to group work is a discussion of the various perspectives on the problem that participants may hold. Understanding other perspectives may help to establish a framework for discussion. This is where a manager's familiarity with the issues surrounding a problem becomes key. The manager is able to provide a broad overview that individuals within an organization may not see.

Managing Breakpoints

No group can work nonstop. A breakpoint is a convenient time at which to make a change or interruption. A hospitality manger must use breakpoints to the advantage of the process rather than as an interruption. For example, rather than schedule a coffee break for exactly 10:15, an effective facilitator would watch for a time around 10:15 to initiate a break. When managing breakpoints, one should watch for the following:

- *Normal breakpoints in the group's interaction.* An appropriate moment might be when a portion of the problem is solved, discussion has died down, or a point has come where individual reflection may be more advantageous than group discussion. When activities resume, little intervention is required on the part of the manager to keep the process moving forward.
- *Sometimes a breakpoint will occur when something has been left unresolved.* The unresolved issue may be a point of discussion or it could be a conflict between participants at a more personal level. In this case, an intervention which involves a review of the pertinent facts of the discussion or some conflict resolution between the participants may be required. It is sometimes necessary to go backward a little before the group can proceed.
- A disruptive breakpoint is an unplanned disruption in the group's progress based on a conflict or a process failure. The manager must firmly reestablish the objectives of the process while mediating concerns and conflicts within the group. These points must not be viewed as a disaster because they are sometimes a prelude to a breakthrough.

Item Contingent Model

In the **item contingent model,** performance is determined by group resources and strategies for their use. Performance is equal to resources minus process losses. Member task knowledge is an essential component of group problem solving. Group experts are the resources (Bottger, 1988). According to the model, groups perform well when they use their members' task knowledge. The item contingent model partially integrates the decision scheme approach and the process model. The process model measures how groups search for and identify knowledge. The decision scheme approach measures the extent to which knowledge is used. The item contingent model is based on two assumptions:

1. A view must be shared by a minimum of two members to ensure it is properly evaluated.
2. Where a majority view exists, it tends to dominate group decision making.

This model implies that, in some circumstances, the use of a decision-making pair might be better than individual or group decision making. Specifically, the model suggests using two experts to make decisions of a professional nature.

Benefits of Group Problem Solving

The use of the problem-solving process leads to:

- a quicker problem identification;
- a better problem definition;
- a more complete problem analysis;
- an increased number of alternatives for problem resolution; and
- a broader acceptance and support for the decision made (Longnecker et al., 1995).

Managers might be tempted to simplify the problem-solving process by handling the problem themselves or assigning it to one individual. By doing so, the manager loses out on the many advantages groups bring to the problem-solving process. Group problem solving is superior to individual problem solving in that groups have a greater sum of knowledge and information and a greater number of approaches to a problem. Employees who participate in problem solving are more likely to accept and comprehend the decision or solution. Furthermore, some researchers believe that groups are more confident than individuals (Sniezek, 1992).

> Think of an example of a problem-solving group to which you have belonged. How confident were you of the decision that was made? Why is that the case?

THEORIES OF GROUP DECISION MAKING

Now that we have examined the process and benefits of group problem solving, we will turn our focus to decision making, one of the last steps a group will take when solving a problem. In the following section, we will discuss the theories that group members can use to make effective decisions.

Vigilant Interaction Theory

In the past, experts believed that group interaction was a channel through which the true determinants of group decision performance were able to exert their influence. Now, theorists realize that interaction plays an active role in determining group decision outcomes. According to vigilant interaction theory, "the manner in which group members *talk* about the problems, options, and face the group affects the way they *think* about those problems, options, and consequences, which, in turn, ultimately determines the quality of final choices they make as a group" (Hirokawa, 1992). The group's critical thinking process influences the quality of the decision.

Group interaction processes can contribute to faulty decision making, leading to the group's failure to consider and recognize the positive quality of available choices. For example, it can cause the group to overlook important negative qualities of available choices, resulting in the group's overestimation of the negative benefits of available choices (Hirokawa, 1992).

Centralization of Authority Hypothesis

Lee was the assistant manager of Envel Tourism Company. When he was first promoted, he considered it a mark of status for an assistant manager to make most of the decisions. However, his manager believed that input from the entire staff would make the company run more effectively. Accordingly, Lee began to use groups to submit ideas for certain decisions. His staff began to feel more and more comfortable coming to him with ideas and suggestions. Lee started to think group decision making was perhaps a good idea after all.

Then one day a guest was injured on one of the buses used by Envel to transport guests. The driver claimed the guest had been intoxicated and careless. The guest claimed Envel was to blame for arranging an all-day drinking cruise followed by a precarious bus ride up a steep mountain slope. She threatened an expensive law suit. The central office publicly supported Lee's office, but was privately concerned.

With the current situation in the hands of company lawyers, Lee rallied his staff to come up with ideas to prevent similar occurrences in the future. Unfortunately, he seemed to be the only one suggesting ideas. The others would either agree with him or be noncommittal. After a long and fruitless meeting he still had only his own ideas and solutions to work with. Frustrated, he thought about how hard it is to know when to use group input and when to make the decision himself.

According to the centralization of authority hypothesis, when a group is making a decision under stress, subordinates will transfer the responsibility of the decision to the manager, while the manager becomes less likely to accept input from subordinates. The authority is centralized to the manager (Driskell and Salas, 1991). Driskell and Salas's study proposed the alternative hypothesis—that under stress, *all* group members become more receptive to task information provided by others (Driskell and Salas, 1991). The study's results supported the alternative hypothesis, discovering that status was a significant determinant of group interaction.

As expected, low status group members were much more likely to defer to the decision inputs of high status group members, and higher status group members were less likely to defer to subordinate group members. Low status members became even more willing to defer to others when under stress. High status group members under stress become more receptive to the task inputs of their partner, whereas high status group members become *more* likely to attend to the task contributions of other group members in decision making. This result is contrary to the centralization of authority hypothesis. The fast pace of hospitality organizations makes it particularly important for teams to work well under stressful conditions.

Groups can make better decisions under stress by:

1. increasing the level of participation and influence of subordinate members;
2. reducing the performance expectation gap between subordinates and managers;
3. recognizing that the subordinate group member's deferential behavior is a manifestation of a cooperative group status process rather than as an individual affliction;
4. altering the behavior of both the high and low status group members;
5. building team cooperation that involves high and low status members;
6. using realistic training that simulates the potential overload under stressful conditions—this will be especially helpful for team leaders (Driskell and Salas, 1991).

> How does stress affect you as a decision maker? What happens when most group members become stressed?

FACTORS THAT AFFECT GROUP DECISIONS

Emotions

The ability of a group to think clearly is affected by high levels of emotion. Because emotions affect the ability of a group to think clearly, the range of ideas is reduced when group members' emotions are at a high level. The advantages of groups that do not have a high level of emotionality are as follows:

- They are more energetic.
- They consider a wider range of ideas.
- They are less stressed.
- They are seen by members as more effective.

Participation

An advantage of making decisions in a group is that it allows more involvement by more people and therefore more people will have a stake in the decision. It is known that groups make better decisions than individuals except for a very knowledgeable individual; in that case, the individual should make the decision. The assembly effect occurs when the group is able to accomplish a task that could not have been accomplished by an individual. However, when comparing the number of hours it takes for a group versus an individual to complete a task, the individual is usually more productive. The time requirements for group decisions and tasks, the associated cost to the organization in terms of salary, and the opportunity cost of each individual focusing on the decision rather than other necessary job tasks must be weighed against the benefits of participation in the group.

As discussed in chapter 4, **Social loafing,** a negative effect of group decision making, may occur in a group, as individuals allow the group to "carry them;" however, when decisions are made individually, the person making the decision is the responsible entity. Social loafing is especially prevalent if the individuals of a group believe their decisions cannot be identified.

Studies have found some reasons for the relative slowness of groups. Therefore, it may be beneficial to use a group when there is a simple task requiring a quick response (Shaw, 1981). In addition, if learning constitutes a critical goal of the activity, group participation may yield faster learning results than individual efforts. There is also evidence of group superiority in making simple decisions.

Information Exchange

Group members have dual or competing motives because they act both as individuals and as group members. Silver's (1995) two-stage model illustrates this dualistic information exchange well.

Stage 1: Individual members can lose status if they give information that they know will receive negative evaluation, especially if this negative evaluation comes from high status group members. An individual will often only give information that allows him or her to maintain his or her status. This type of information exchange helps the individual, but it may hurt the group.

Stage 2: The group member will take a chance and go beyond this minimum level of information exchange in order to contribute to group decision quality. "The increment the member accepts is proportional to his or her status, and is the basis for the initiation of ideas and negative evaluations" (Silver, 1995).

Information exchange happens under the following requisite conditions:

1. Members occupying positions in a group have some basis to judge their own relative status position.
2. Members are motivated to avoid status loss—the motive to avoid status loss is greater than the motive to gain status.
3. Members are motivated to contribute to the group objective.
4. Members expect that the amount and type of information they send will influence the amount and type of information that they will receive. Thus, they at least implicitly recognize the causal relationship between information initiation and evaluation by others (Silver, 1995).

Ideas and negative evaluations contribute the most to the quality of group decisions; however, sending both of these information types has higher expected status costs than sending data, questions, or positive evaluations. Most information exchanges will be messages of low risk (i.e., data), whether or not the information contributes to the task. In an effort to maintain their status, members will not initiate negative evaluations. High status members will receive more positive evaluations because of their position.

In groups with large status differences between members and low commitment to group objectives by medium and low status members, there are a:

1. very low proportion of ideas or negative evaluations;
2. high proportion of positive evaluations sent to high status members; and
3. high proportion of blanks (low participation).

Groups will produce the highest quality decisions when the ideas and negative evaluations occur in an ideal proportion. The exact proportion will depend on the status distribution in the group, the type of decision, and the group's interaction history. Negative evaluations are less harmful if they are distributed to members in proportion to the number of ideas these members have initiated.

> Do you believe that your participation is affected by higher-status members of your team? If so, what behaviors of group members influence your interaction?

METHODS FOR GROUP DECISION MAKING

The first objective of group problem solving is to make maximum use of resources brought by each individual member, including any added group potential. The second objective is the generation of a high level of motivation for carrying out the group's decision in each and every member (Hoffman et al., 1995). Group size will determine the amount of resources and group diversity will determine the range of resources. Diverse memberships bring a variety of perspectives on a problem, leading to higher quality solutions. Groups with different personalities, leadership abilities, and points of view, have been shown to be more creative and innovative than groups with more similar member characteristics. Diversity will also increase the tension in the groups. Groups often become more homogeneous as they age.

Unstructured Techniques

Consensus technique is an informal approach which "encourages the expression of cognitive conflict among group members without providing an explicit structure for group interaction" (Priem et al., 1995). The group is instructed to "be suspicious of early agreement, to encourage each member to fully express his or her opinions, and to treat disagreement as a positive part of the decision-making process" (Priem et al., 1995). The goal is to strive for consensus among all members, not opting for a "majority rule, coin flips" or other techniques to reach recommendations (Priem et al., 1995).

Structured Techniques

When a group uses **methodical decision-making methods,** it adheres to a highly structured and systematic decision-making process (Neck and Moorshead, 1995). Groups that use structured techniques are less likely to fall into the groupthink trap, since structured techniques promote constructive criticism, nonconformity, and open-mindedness within the decision-making group (Neck and Moorshead, 1995). Without adequate decision-making procedures, highly cohesive groups will make poor decisions (Neck and Moorshead, 1995). Examples of structured techniques include parliamentary procedure, alternative examination procedure, and information search procedure.

Expert-based technique is an alternative to structured technique. Experts make the decisions. When a group works on well-structured tasks, structured techniques lead to more effective decisions than expert-based techniques (Priem et al., 1995).

The appropriate techniques for group decision making depend upon decision quality factors, situational factors related to the problem, the decision context, and the group itself (Priem et al., 1995). In certain circumstances, strong consensus among decision makers and/or strong commitment to a course of action may not be appropriate. The influence and expertise of some decision makers may outweigh the dissent of other group members, overriding relatively less informed reasons for disagreement (Bonner et al., 2002). In the next several paragraphs, we will discuss examples of structured decision-making techniques.

DIALECTICAL INQUIRY   The first step in the **dialectical inquiry** process involves the division of the major group into two subgroups. The first subgroup independently develops recommendations for the problem, lists the assumptions on which these recommendations are based, and then presents these recommendations and assumptions to the second subgroup. Next, the second subgroup develops new assumptions that are counter to those presented by the first subgroup, then develops new recommendations from these new assumptions, finally presenting these counter-assumptions and new recommendations to the first subgroup. The last step comprises both groups debating until they can agree upon a set of assumptions; the entire group works on these assumptions to come up with the group's final recommendation.

Dialectical inquiry helps improve decision making structurally; the division into two different groups increases the level of cognitive conflict expressed *during* group discussion. Furthermore, this cognitive conflict is focused on substantive, task-related matters rather than socioemotional issues, so its expression is helpful (Priem et al., 1995).

THE STEPLADDER TECHNIQUE   The **stepladder technique** improves group communication and decision making by ensuring that every member contributes to the decision-making process. The process is delineated as follows:

Stage 1: Two group members (the initial core group) work together on a problem.

Stage 2: A third group member joins the core group and presents his or her preliminary solutions for the same problem.

Stage 3: The fourth group member joins the core group and presents his or her preliminary solutions.

Stage 4: The four members discuss until they come to a final group decision.

The number of stages increases or decreases, depending on the number of members. The structure can change to accommodate larger groups. For example, two members, instead of one, can enter a stage.

Several prerequisites need to be implemented to ensure the success of the stepladder technique. First, before each group member enters the group, they must be given the group's task and sufficient time to think about the problem. Second, the entering member must present his or her preliminary solutions before hearing the core group's preliminary solution. This constant verbalization and reiteration of group members' ideas will increase comprehension, understanding, and retention of information. Third, after each additional member joins the core group, the group needs sufficient time to discuss the problem. Fourth, the group should not come to a final decision until the entire group has formed.

The stepladder technique prevents group deficiencies in five ways:

- The technique facilitates communication by all members.
- Because members can no longer hide behind others' contributions, the technique cuts down on social loafing. A study found that stepladder group members work significantly harder on their task than their counterparts in conventional groups (Rogelberg et al., 1992).

- The constant addition of a new person generates new ideas and possibly some helpful controversy. Disagreement that arises in a structured setting fosters critical thinking. Groups that freely evaluate ideas and confront controversy come to better decisions.
- The structure's communication mandate gives members the opportunity to reveal their knowledge. "If expertise is made known, the group may allocate more time for the best member to express ideas and concerns. Recent research suggests that when best members are allocated more time for communication, group decision quality is likely to be enhanced" (Rogelberg et al., 1992).
- By continuously remaking decisions, the group will come to a higher quality decision.

The stepladder technique is most useful when the decision to be made is easily definable and it has not been subdivided. In addition, the technique is most practical when information is required from each member, and no one member contains exclusive information that results in the group waiting for that member's entry. Finally, when simultaneous participation is not a prerequisite and the process is not being conducted under urgent time pressure, the stepladder technique allows for group development through multiple steps.

There are, however, some limitations to the stepladder technique. First, members need equal status, or all members must be assigned randomly to entry positions. Second, the technique needs to be modified to the number of group members.

The stepladder technique has proven successful when implemented into the group decision-making process. For example, groups that have used this approach "were highly satisfied with the structure, felt that everyone agreed with the group solution, felt their solution was high in quality, and felt comfortable with the climate produced by the technique" (Rogelberg et al., 1992). Rogelberg's study found that "stepladder groups produced significantly higher quality decisions than did conventional groups (in which all members entered and worked on a problem at the same time). Stepladder groups' decisions surpassed the quality of their best individual members' decisions 56 percent of the time. In contrast, conventional groups' decisions surpassed the quality of their best members' decisions only 13 percent of the time" (Rogelberg et al., 1992).

> Would you enjoy participating in a group that is using the stepladder technique? Explain.

THE VOTE MODEL The **vote model** is a goal-based decision-making framework based on an interpersonal model. The agent's goals include both personal goals and adopted goals for interpersonal relationships; however, the agent must resolve conflict by making trade-offs. The relative priorities of the goals drive the decision process. The vote model is a descriptive qualitative and quantitative approach.

The vote model process of decision making initially begins with members basing voting decisions on their set goals. The goals in this domain are issues that may be specific proposals, such as funding for childcare, or abstract values such as fairness. The stances on issues have a *side,* and a level of *importance.* The consequences of a stance on a given issue are represented as stances on other issues. Finally, the consequences of voting for or against a given bill are also represented as stances. Member stances are derived from three sources: explicit personal credo, implicit voting record, and adopted constituency agendas.

There are nine principles to the vote model of decision making:

1. *Decision trade-offs*. Because a member has many goals and limited resources, he or she cannot realistically achieve all goals. In the effort to achieve some goals, members will have to make trade-offs, compromises, and sacrifices.
2. *Goal decomposition*. Members can choose which goals to pursue first by breaking goals down into their original elements.
3. *Principle of importance*. The importance of a goal is proportional to the resources that the agent is willing to expend in pursuit of that goal.
4. *Resource decomposition*. Resources are also decomposed into primitive elements to use to compare and reason.
5. *Cognitive resources*. Members can allocate cognitive resources, such as attention and memory, in the pursuit of goals.
6. *Cooperating agents*. Members interact with other members through interpersonal relationships.
7. *Principle of interpersonal goals*. Adopted goals are processed uniformly as individual goals, with a priority determined by the importance of the relationship.
8. *Organizational relationships*. The principle of interpersonal goals may be extended to include goals adopted from institutions and organizations.
9. *Goal-based decision making*. An alternative to quantitative decision analysis is a model of decision making based on an agent's goals.

CONSENSUS MAPPING

Madeleine, head of human resources, was concerned about the motivation level of the middle managers and their supporting staff. Their motivation was average, but she wanted it to be exemplary. She called a meeting of the middle managers. Madeleine decided to use the nominal group technique (NGT) method for the meeting. She asked each middle manager to survey themselves and their employees, asking what factor had been the most motivating for them in the last year, and to ensure that the replies would be anonymous. After the managers compiled these replies, they were to email them to Madeleine. She had her secretary print each idea out separately on Post-it notes. While many were repeated more than once, the ideas were as follows:

- *Salary increase*
- *When Molly covered for me to pick my sick child up from school*
- *Ted in the kitchen keeps everybody's spirits up*
- *Bonuses for positive guest feedback*
- *When a guest praised me in front of everybody at the front desk*
- *The four-day work week*
- *Customer service seminar*
- *Time spent going over my job with the boss*
- *Switching to Tony's department*
- *Getting away for a while*
- *My supervisor always has good things to say about my work*
- *World Service Business Conference*
- *Switching to day shift*

- *My friend got laid off with no notice and I know that would not happen here, so, I guess, job security*
- *Flex time*
- *When I was allowed to oversee the stockbroker's convention*
- *Now that I've been working for three years, I get three weeks' vacation*
- *The on-site day care*
- *Generous maternity leave policy*
- *When my supervisor showed me how Manny's work looked better than mine*
- *The employee picnic—it helps to have fun time outside of work*
- *Being put on the strategic development team*
- *My promotion*
- *Overtime pay for extended days*
- *Being allowed to use the gym in the hotel during nonpeak hours*
- *Working the same shift as my husband*

After reading them aloud, Madeline divided the managers into three groups of five. Each individual was given a set of the motivating factors and they arranged them into clusters according to their own classification system. Then the individuals rejoined their group and discussed the similarities and differences in their clusters. As a group they must agree upon a system of classification for the ideas. Most people found it easy to cluster issues related to time, money, or professional gain. The other category, related to collegial relationships or praise, was more difficult to define. There were disagreements when one factor could fit in several different categories. Madeleine gave them pieces of yarn that they could use to connect related ideas in separate categories. While there were still disagreements, eventually two of the managers relented and joined the others in order to avoid a stalemate. Next each smaller group presented its results to the entire group. Two representatives were chosen from each group to blend the results of the three groups into a final consensus map (Figure 5.1). This group was also asked to prioritize and sequence the motivational strategies that would be actionable within the next year. All members would meet again in a week to review the results of the representatives' work and to discuss implementation of their ideas.

Consensus mapping is an exciting approach to decision making that helps groups structure and organize their ideas. It builds on techniques like NGT which generate ideas, but do not go the next step to organizing them. When in the idea-structuring phase of consensus mapping, processes like the round-robin listing of individual ideas (characteristic of NGT) is discontinued since it tends to result in team members' internalizing specific group norms. Those who facilitate consensus mapping should assume a low profile, stepping in only to keep members engaged and on task. This relationship allows participants to interact freely. Consensus mapping depends upon an extensive list of ideas relevant to the topic of concern. It unfolds as small task groups of 5–9 participants oversee and guide the process. Consensus mapping works particularly well on complex problems, as it directs the team's attention to interrelationships and the sequencing of ideas. Consensus mapping also encourages individuals with different perspectives to arrive at a shared understanding of the problem and achieve a mutually agreeable solution (Boroush et al., 1985). Consensus mapping assumes that a task group has already generated a list of ideas, clarified the meaning of those ideas, and conducted a preliminary evaluation (i.e., ratings or prioritization). There are two key steps to consensus mapping.

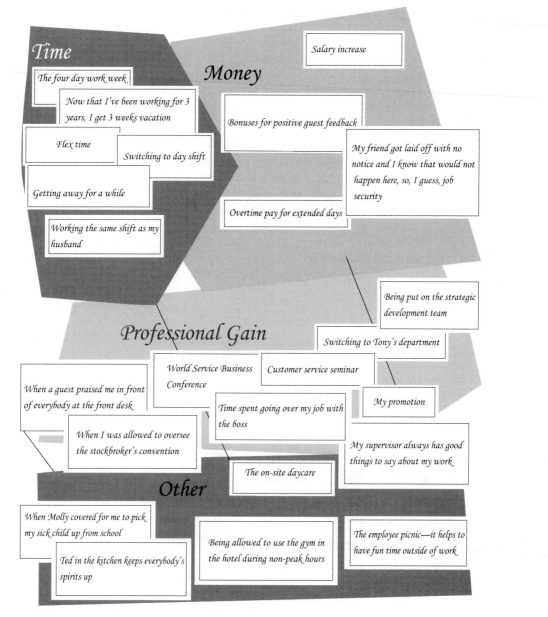

FIGURE 5.1   Final consensus map

Step 1 involves the group making a unified classification scheme that identifies many of the key parts of the problem. "The goal of this search should be an agreed upon structuring of the problem or solution that includes a *classification scheme* for the generated list of ideas. . . . Once this scheme has been agreed on, the individual items can be re-prioritized by the group using a numerical rating scheme as in NGT" (Boroush et al., 1985). Step 2 comprises creating a "strawman map" to display the structural interrelationships and time dependencies among *all* of the categories and ideas generated by the group. The group should not exercise evaluative judgment by pruning ideas or designing the overall structure to a specific end (the strawman map is a springboard, not a solution). Materials or "props" used to develop the consensus map should be given special consideration. For instance, use an approach that facilitates manipulation and modification (i.e., use a Smartboard, if available, or large sheets of newsprint to represent the categories and Post-it notes to represent specific ideas). The benefit of consensus mapping is that the key results of the discussion are automatically documented, which does not happen in ordinary free-flowing conversation.

GARBAGE CAN MODEL   "In the **garbage can process,** it is assumed that there are exogenous, time-dependent arrivals of choice opportunities, problems, solutions, and decision makers. Problems and solutions are attached to choices, and thus to each other, not because of any means-ends linkage, but because of their temporal proximity. At the limit, for example, almost any solution can be associated with almost any problem—provided they are evoked at the same time" (March and Olsen, 1986). The garbage cans are such choice opportunities as contract meetings, budget committees, and compensation decisions. Choice opportunities collect decision makers, problems, and solutions. Within this process, decision makers are involved in one choice opportunity at any one time, but they move from one choice opportunity to another.

Decision makers are characterized by their arrival times (when they first enter the system), the amount of energy required to solve them (ability to solve problems), and their access to choice opportunities (decision structure). "Problems, solutions, decision makers, and choice opportunities are linked initially by virtue of the times of their arrivals on the scene, and the possibilities available at those times. The linkages change over time as problems, solutions, and decision-makers move from one choice opportunity to another, and as choices are made. Thus, the results produced by the system depend on the timing of the various flows and on the structural constraints of the organization" (March and Olsen, 1986).

Choices in the garbage can model are made in three different ways:

1. *Oversight.* "Sometimes a choice opportunity arrives and no problems attach themselves to the choice. All the problems in the system are attached to other choices. In this situation, a choice is made with a minimum of time and energy. It resolves no problems" (March and Olsen, 1986).
2. *Problem resolution.* In this circumstance, "there are problems associated with a choice opportunity, and the decision makers attached to the choice bring enough energy to

meet the demands of those problems. The choice is made and the problems are resolved" (March and Olsen, 1986).

3. *Flight.* "Sometimes a number of problems are associated with a choice opportunity for some time. Since they collectively exceed the energy of the decision makers attached to the choice, the choice is not made. When another choice opportunity becomes available, the problems leave the initial choice to attach themselves to another (i.e., people take their salary grievances to another forum). After the problems are gone, the original choice is made. It resolves no problems" (March and Olsen, 1986).

What did you find most interesting about the garbage can model? Was there any aspect of the model that caused you to think, "Yes, that's so true!"? What was it?

Technology and Group Decision Making

Managers have been using technology to assist in their decision making for many years. Expert systems, a form of artificial intelligence, are computers programmed with decision rules which then become a primary source of knowledge in the decision-making process. Similarly, decision support systems are computer and communication systems that process data and consequently reduce the time managers require to respond to problems that arise.

More recently, group decision support systems (GDSS) have become an important business tool. Effective group problem solving is critical in today's globally diverse and widely distributed organizations. The decision support systems (GDSS) use computers in either face-to-face or dispersed meetings. The technology depersonalizes responses and allows members to share information more freely. Many software packages are now available, including *Groupware*, which has direct business applications. Groupware has been particularly useful in balancing member participation. One company discovered that 20 percent of their team members did 80 percent of the talking. By using a GDSS, those team members who had been less verbal participated actively and equally from their computer terminals.

Technology has enabled individuals to work remotely in virtual teams. This term refers to groups of individuals who are geographically dispersed but who are able to work together on a common task. In addition to GDSS, Internet and intranet systems are also used to support virtual team activities. For example, the Internet video phone company SightSpeed is known for its web-based video calling or conferencing service, an option that delivers two-way video communications. SightSpeed also offers a video email service, an option that has increasing uses—including political campaigns.

While the technology is now available for teams to work together remotely, some theorists are concerned that bureaucratic, highly structured organizations may not be taking advantage of the flexibility and intellectual capital that virtual teams make possible. The vision of virtual environments is to provide organizational members with a space where they can meet as if they were in the same room and help their companies make better decisions through technology. When that vision is realized, organizations will undoubtedly improve their overall performance.

Of all the techniques described, which do you believe is the most effective most of the time—in other words, if you had to use just one technique all the time, which would it be?

UNDERSTANDING THE IMPACT OF GROUP DYNAMICS

Social influence plays a critical role in a group's progress and sustainability. **Conformity** within a group results from the members' desire or feelings of compulsion to live and behave within the norms of the group. Often, we look upon a cohesive, nonargumentative group as a "good group." While this may be the case, strong group unity can lead group members to go along with the group's decisions simply to avoid damaging the harmonious nature of the group. Whether or not a group has formal, established hierarchies of power, certain members tend to emerge as more charismatic and influential players in the decision-making process. Powerful group members are seen as more likable, receive a greater amount of intragroup communications, and are likely to have others follow their wishes (Shaw, 1981). Understanding the various types of relationships that may develop in group settings empowers employees and leaders to consider these dynamics thoughtfully while forming groups for particular tasks. It also provides keys to repair the damage when intragroup conflict arises.

Conformity

Conformity can result from normative or informational influence. Conformity as a result of normative influence stems from an individual's need for social acceptance and approval. Such conformity, however, does not penetrate deeply. The individual acts as he or she feels is expected by others and complies with such expectations but does not internalize. Normative conformity occurs when the group has the power to punish or reward the individual for his or her behavior (Hogg and Abrams, 1988). For example, an individual speeding down the highway slows down when he or she sees a police car. This behavior results from a fear of punishment, not from a sudden realization that it is dangerous to speed. Similarly, an employee may follow standard procedures when his or her supervisor is present, yet disregard them at other times.

Informational influence, on the other hand, leads to conformity resulting from an individual's need to be correct. Unlike normative influence, informational influence leads to an "internalization of beliefs, attitudes, and behaviors" (Hogg and Abrams, 1988). When employees know the reasons behind standard procedures (i.e., safety or security), and want to do things right for the reasons given, they will follow the rules more closely at all times, regardless of supervision. It is therefore very important to understand the difference between normative and informational influence. Creating rules and regulations without giving the reasons and philosophies behind them can create conformity and surface compliance but not commitment. Management has a much greater likelihood of gaining true behavioral changes by communicating honestly with employees rather than simply mandating new procedures.

Reitan and Shaw found that several factors affect the level of conformity to group norms: personality characteristics of group members, nature of the stimuli evoking the response reflecting conformity, situational factors, and intragroup relationships (Shaw, 1981).

Personal factors also influence the level of conformity:

- Less intelligent people conform more than intelligent people.
- People who tend to blame themselves for what happens to them conform more than those who tend not to.
- Authoritarian people conform more than those who are nonauthoritarian (Shaw, 1981).

Other research has found the following variables to be correlated with the propensity to conform:

- low self-esteem;
- high need for social support or social approval;
- need for self-control;
- high anxiety; and
- feelings of inferiority or relative low status in the group (Hogg and Abrams, 1988).

These findings should not be taken as evidence that people react in the same way in various situations. Conformity is most likely to occur when:

- the task at hand is ambiguous;
- the task is strongly related to the group's "existence and function;"
- the task is focused on the "right answer" rather than on individual thoughts or beliefs; and
- the group places great importance on "group cohesiveness" (Hogg and Abrams, 1988).

When an individual has faith in the abilities of the group, he or she is more likely to conform to group pressures and influence (Shaw, 1981). Therefore, a group that has performed successfully in the past is more likely to have members who display behavior that conforms.

> Think of someone you know who readily conforms in group situations. Do they fit the characteristics listed above? Explain.

Groupthink

Pressure for conformity is a strong component of Janis's explanation of **groupthink**—"the mode of thinking people engage in when concurrence seeking becomes so dominant in a cohesive in-group that it tends to override realistic appraisal of alternative courses of action" (Janis, 1982). This desire to conform leads to less than optimal decision making. Those afflicted with groupthink will make efforts to support appropriate, conforming behavior, and punish deviant views or opinions (Janis, 1982). Other symptoms of groupthink include:

1. limiting of discussion to only a few options without considering a range of alternatives;
2. failure to reevaluate decisions made even after being informed of risks regarding the decision;
3. little discussion of reducing costs of undesirable alternatives;
4. minimal attempts to gain information from experts within the organization regarding possible gains and losses;
5. very strong interest in facts which support the chosen alternative and disregard of those which oppose it; and
6. little discussion of how the chosen alternative could fail to work as planned. As a result, minimal time is spent creating contingency plans (Janis, 1982).

Janis proposes, among other things, that a devil's advocate be assigned in groups to reduce the likelihood of groupthink. This devil's advocate will be expected to dispute other members and thus will have different norms to abide by than the others. Sometimes these devil's advocates arise naturally in groups, to the consternation of other group members.

If you were to make a promise to yourself that you would personally try to help your group avoid groupthink, what exactly would you do to fulfill it?

Deviance

As group members fight to maintain group stability and equilibrium, group pressure for conformity is often strong. Nevertheless, **deviance** from expected norms does occur. Behavior is considered deviant when it violates the behavior expected of a person as a member of a group. Social deviance does not necessarily connote a negative or "bad" action, but simply an action that contrasts with group norms. Deviance can actually be a positive force. Minority views, while not necessarily correct, can "foster the kinds of attention and thought processes that, on balance, permit the detection of new truths and raise the quality of group decision making and performance" (Worchel et al., 1992). Just as the designated "devil's advocate" assists in reducing the risk of groupthink, normal deviation from norms within groups can bring about new ideas and fight stagnation. In some cases, however, norms in organizational subgroups may be at odds with those of the organization. For example, while the management desires the highest possible rate of production, one study showed that working quickly and producing at a higher rate than norm production rates for a group led the overly industrious worker to be ridiculed by other group members (Shaw, 1981).

Deindividuation

Deindividuation occurs when people are "prevented by situational factors present in a group from becoming self-aware . . . and are blocked from awareness of themselves as separate individuals and from monitoring their own behavior" (Paulus, 1980). The theory of deindividuation as it relates to deviance relies on the assumption that self-awareness is required to identify and analyze differences between one's behavior and norms or standards for behavior. When a person is all-consumed within a group and loses self-awareness, he or she is more likely to act in a deviant manner. Other research has shown that deindividuation reduces a person's ability to see another within the group as an individual as this reflects perception of the group as a whole.

Power

Individual influence within a group can have negative or positive outcomes. A strong personality—a "natural leader"—may be just what a group needs to propel itself toward its goals. Influential persons can persuade, motivate, and coordinate the efforts of other individuals. However, power and influence within a group can run amok. Consider the occasions on which an individual seems to take power within a group by force, fostering resentment from other members. In other instances, individuals are so reluctant to take a strong leadership position that the group flounders aimlessly, never reaching its goals. Influence and power play important roles in an individual's satisfaction with the group and in the group's overall productivity.

Influence within a group comes from power, authority, or persuasion. A powerful individual within a group has the ability to get their way, even when they encounter resistance. Such situations do not usually occur in normal organizational groups. Authority is established when others accept it by voluntarily complying with the authority's wishes. An example of this type of relationship is the boss–subordinate relationship. Persuasion also depends on voluntary compliance, but occurs when an individual "arouses the perception and exercise of choice among the various alternatives" (Barker, 1979).

When an individual is formally designated as a leader, that person attains structural power—power that derives from the design of a higher authority. In contrast, personal power comes from personal characteristics that make an individual influential (Fisher, 1990). Within so-called leaderless groups, certain individuals gain more power than others simply because of their charismatic personal characteristics. On the other hand, a person who is designated as a leader, yet lacks the necessary personal or technical characteristics, may not gain a great deal of power within the group. Individuals who possess powerful personal characteristics, then, can overcome structural power and challenge formal hierarchies within groups.

Leaders do not always lead the group to effective decisions. In fact, formally appointed leaders can sometimes limit discussion within groups although they usually can ensure the hearing of a minority, but correct viewpoint. Individuals whose knowledge or abilities are perceived as "critical contingencies" of the organization often attain power disproportionate to their position within the organization. Departments within an organization whose activities are directly linked to profit gain more prestige than departments that carry out behind-the-scenes functions. Similarly, group members who play a direct, important role in propelling the group toward its goals will be more influential than other group members. Organizational studies have shown that certain functions within an organization attain more power than their hierarchical status would grant due to irreplaceability, centrality, or ability to control and generate resources. For example, maintenance workers in a hotel have a great deal of power because they are able to fix the hotel equipment. Applying these organizational findings to small groups, we can analyze power within the group as it relates to each individual's strengths. For example, a group whose task is to develop financial projections will grant more power to an individual with skills specific to that area. Similarly, the only group member who has critical statistical analysis skills will be seen as important and irreplaceable.

This type of power can shift within a group as the group's goals and needs change. A quality improvement team will likely defer to the member with food and beverage knowledge when dealing with an issue related to a food and beverage outlet but will be more influenced by the housekeeping employee when trying to solve a rooms-related problem. Powerful group members are perceived as being able to hurt or help less powerful group members.

The contours of power, deviance, and conformity within groups can decisively shape the effectiveness of group work in any type of organization, from faculty committees in university departments to planning groups in voluntary organizations to executive committees in top corporations.

> Do you enjoy having "power" in a group, or do you prefer not to have responsibility for group outcomes? Explain.

GROUP VERSUS INDIVIDUAL DECISION MAKING

There are several factors that must be considered when deciding whether to make a decision alone or to involve others in the process. Below we have provided some basic guidelines managers should follow when trying to decide whether they should make a decision in a group or individually. These guidelines are based on the required quality of the decision, the level of acceptance by others in order to implement the decision, and time constraints.

When to Make a Group Decision

Group participation may be more appropriate than individual decision making in the following scenarios:

1. *When the quality of the decision is critical.* A group of people working on a decision reduces the possibility of error or omission of information in the judgment or reasoning processes. In addition, a group of individuals will have a greater pool of information to draw from when making the decision.
2. *When acceptance of the decision by other individuals or groups is necessary to implement the decision.* When individuals are involved in the decision itself, a sense of ownership arises. These individuals will work hard to ensure that the decision is implemented and carried out properly.
3. *When group members are trusted to carefully consider the decision.* Individuals whose responsibilities will be greatly affected by the decision will likely take the decision seriously and put the appropriate time into making an optimal decision. Also, individuals who have successful track records in group decision making will be more trusted with a current decision (Locke et al., 1994).

When to Make an Individual Decision

Individuals may be better suited to make decisions than groups under the following circumstances:

1. *When the individual has the information necessary to make a good decision.* When an individual has the necessary information, it may be more effective to make the decision alone. The presence of confidential or sensitive information in the decision process may decrease the desirability of involving other individuals.
2. *When there is an applicable solution that has worked well in the past.* If a situation seems similar to an instance in the past where a decision has worked well, a similar solution may be utilized without the participation of others.
3. *When there are time constraints.* Strict time limits may make the inclusion of other individuals in the decision process less desirable. In such instances, an individual may be forced to make the decision alone. Caution must be taken, however, as the time factor can become a convenient excuse for the exclusion of others in decision making.

It seems at times that groups and teams are assembled just for the sake of creating a group; because it seems like "the right thing to do." It is critical to ensure that group participation is critical to the task at hand. Research conducted by Rosabeth Moss Kanter indicates that participation in decision making should be utilized to "allow knowledgeable individuals to contribute to a decision, to address conflicting approaches or views, or to gain new sources of expertise and experience." On the other hand, when one individual has much greater knowledge on a subject than others, when there are serious time limits, or when individuals are able and wish to work alone, a nonparticipative approach will be more appropriate.

Think of a good decision that you made alone—one that you are confident could not have been made as effectively if discussed by a group. What was it? Why was it best determined individually?

Summary

In the process of group problem solving and decision making, the prime factor to bear in mind is that all groups and all situations are not alike. To choose the appropriate strategy for your particular problem, you must evaluate the dynamics of group interaction, the information that must be evaluated in order to come to a decision, and the amount of time in which decisions must be made. We have provided you with some of the keys to making these evaluations and to structuring the process of problem solving and decision making. Above all, remember to be flexible in the application of these techniques and allow the group to be dynamic in innovating for your own situations, using these tools as a basis for action.

Key Words

problem solving *115*
facilitative influence *115*
critical function tasks *115*
item contingent model *118*
social loafing *121*
consensus technique *122*

methodical decision-making
    methods *122*
dialectical inquiry *123*
stepladder technique *123*
vote model *124*
consensus mapping *126*

garbage can process *128*
conformity *130*
groupthink *131*
deviance *132*
deindividuation *132*

Exercises

Exercise 1   Process Observation: Analyzing How a Group Operates

Category: Group Process

Objectives:

- To acquaint the group members with the various dimensions of a group's process
- To provide the group members with feedback concerning their group's process
- To offer the group members an opportunity to observe process variables in meetings

Time Frame: 35 minutes in addition to the time that the regular meeting consumes

Materials:

1. A copy of the "Process Observation Report Form" for each group member
2. A pencil for the designated process observer

Physical Setting: Any room in which the group regularly meets

Procedure:

1. At the beginning of a meeting, the leader explains that it is useful to analyze the process by which a group operates and accomplishes things. The leader states that, accordingly, for the next several meetings one member will observe (but not participate), analyze the group's functioning, and report his or her observations at the conclusion of the meeting. The leader also clarifies that the members will take turns observing and that each observer will record his or her observations on a specific form for that purpose. (Five minutes.)

2. The leader distributes copies of the "Process Observation Report Form" and reviews the form with the group, eliciting and answering questions about it. (Fifteen minutes.)

3. The leader chooses a volunteer to serve as the first observer and gives this person a pencil. All other members are asked to put their observation forms away and to concentrate on the business of the meeting.

4. After the business of the meeting has been concluded, the leader asks the observer to report on his or her observations about the group's process. Then the leader elicits reactions from the remaining members.

***

Process Observation Report Form

Group _____ Date _____

Interpersonal-Communication Skills

1. Expressing (both in words and without words)

2. Listening

3. Responding

Communication Pattern

4. Direction (one person to another, one person to the whole group, all through a leader)

(continued)

5. Content (expression of thoughts and ideas; expression of feelings)

Leadership

6. Major roles (record names of group members)

_____ Information processor (requested facts, helped the group analyze and summarize what was happening)

_____ Coordinator

_____ Evaluator (helped the group evaluate its work during the meetings)

_____ Harmonizer (sought to maintain harmony)

_____ Gatekeeper (kept communication flowing, encouraged participation and sharing)

_____ Follower (passively went along with the group)

_____ Blocker (blocked the group's progress)

_____ Recognition seeker

_____ Dominator (dominated the discussion)

_____ Avoider (avoided confrontation and difficult issues)

7. Leadership style

_____ Democratic (leader encouraged everyone to participate and to contribute to decisions)

_____ Autocratic (leader guided the entire process and made all decisions without asking for the team's input)

_____ Laissez-faire (leader took a "hands-off" approach and let the members do what they wanted)

8. Response to leadership style

_____ Eager participation _____ Low commitment _____Resistance

_____ Lack of enthusiasm _____ Holding back

Climate

9. Tone of the meeting (How did the meeting "feel?" Were the group members at ease and comfortable with one another? Did they cooperate to accomplish the purpose of the meeting?)

10. Cohesiveness (Did the group members function as a unit?)

Goals

11. Explicitness

12. Commitment to agreed-on goals

(continued)

(continued)

Situational Variables

13. Group size (Were all the people here who should have been here? Was anyone absent who should have been included?)

14. Time limit (Was a time limit set for the meeting? Were time limits set for specific discussions? Did the group adhere to the set limits?)

15. Physical facilities (Was the size of the room adequate? Was it equipped with everything the group members needed during the meeting?)

Observer's Reactions

16. Feelings experienced during the observation

17. Feelings at this moment

18. Hunches, speculations, and ideas about the process observed

***

Exercise 2   Communication in Problem Solving and Decision Making

Category: Group Decision Making

Objectives:

- To offer the team members an opportunity to observe their communication patterns while they work as a team to solve a problem
- To allow the team members to explore interpersonal influence in problem solving

Time Frame: Approximately one hour

Materials: Blank paper and a pencil for each team member

Physical Setting: A room in which the team members can work without interruption. Writing surfaces and comfortable chairs should be provided.

Procedure:

1. The leader explains to the team members that during this activity they will work together to solve a mathematical problem and that they must arrive at consensus.[1] The team members are urged to pay attention to how the team arrives at the conclusion so that they can later discuss the process that emerges. (Five minutes.)

2. The leader states the mathematical problem as follows: "Three men rented a hotel room for $9 each, including all taxes and fees. When it was time to check out, they had $30 dollars among them, but it was all in five dollar bills. So they gave the bellman one of the fives to get it changed into singles. When the bellman brought the singles, they gave him two of them as a tip. So, in all, they paid $9 × 3 = $27 to the hotel and $2 to the bellman for a total of $29. What happened to the other dollar?"

[1]A consensus decision is one that all team members can accept, regardless of how satisfied they are with it. Each member's opinion must be heard; no "majority-rule" voting, bargaining, or averaging is allowed.

After stating the problem, the leader distributes paper and pencils, tells the team members to begin solving the problem, and asks them to let him or her know when they have the solution.

3. When the team members indicate that they have a solution, the leader ensures that they are all in agreement, asks for the answer (the three men have it), and then asks one member to explain the process of arriving at the conclusion. (If the team members become preoccupied with the answer itself or the mathematics involved, the leader should focus their attention on the team process instead.) (Five minutes.)

4. The leader leads a discussion of the communication issues by focusing on such behaviors as the following:

   • reacting negatively to the phrase "mathematical problem" and establishing artificial constraints;
   • leaving the problem solving to "experts" (self-proclaimed or otherwise);
   • adopting pressuring tactics in reaching consensus;
   • using "teaching aids" in convincing others (scraps of paper, paper and pencil, real money);
   • feeling distress if a wrong conclusion is reached;
   • using listening checks and other communication skills techniques; and
   • refusing to set aside personal opinion in order to reach consensus. (Twenty minutes.)

5. The leader leads another discussion, this time focusing on the patterns of communication that were reflected in the experience, such as influence behaviors, tendencies toward one- or two-way communication modes, personal or team issues that interfered with task accomplishment, and behaviors that facilitated or hindered communication. Subsequently, the implications of these patterns for the team's future functioning are considered.

Exercise 3 Group Decisions: Examining and Changing the Process

Category: Group Decision Making

Objectives:

• To examine how the group typically makes decisions
• To plan changes in the group's decision-making process

Time Frame: One to one and a half hours

Materials:

1. A copy of the "Group Decisions Information Sheet" for each member
2. A copy of the Group Decisions Check List for each member
3. A copy of the Group Decisions Interpretation Chart for each member
4. A pencil for each member
5. A newsprint flip chart and a felt-tipped marker

Physical Setting: A room with a chair and a writing surface for each group member. Each member should be seated so that he or she can see the other members as well as the leader and the newsprint flip chart.

Procedure:

1. The leader introduces the activity by explaining its goals.

2. Each member is given a copy of the "Group Decisions Information Sheet" and is asked to read this sheet. (Five minutes.)

3. After all members have read the information sheet, the leader leads a discussion on its content and elicits and answers questions about it. (Five minutes.)

4. Each member is given a copy of the "Group Decisions Check List" and a pencil. The leader discusses the checklist instructions with the members, eliciting and answering questions as necessary. (Five minutes.)

5. The leader asks each member to complete the checklist independently. (A minimum of five minutes.)

6. After all members have completed the task, the leader distributes the "Group Decisions Interpretation Chart," eliciting and answering questions about the instructions on the chart. The leader then asks each member to complete the interpretation chart. (Five minutes.)

7. While the members are working independently, the leader copies the "Group Decisions Interpretation Chart" onto newsprint. After all members have completed their task, the leader asks them to take turns reading the numbers they have circled. The leader records the numbers on the newsprint chart.

8. The leader identifies the decision-making style or styles that the members indicated as most typical in their group and leads a discussion on how

these styles have affected the team's decisions. (Ten minutes.)

9. The leader asks each member to choose the decision-making process that he or she would prefer for group meetings and to share the reasons for that choice with the other members. (Three minutes per group member.)

10. While the members are presenting their preferences, the leader records them on newsprint, noting their frequency and rank-ordering them.

11. The leader instructs the members to decide which decision-making process(es) they will use in their group meetings. If the members need help, the leader may refer them to the "Group Decisions Information Sheet" for clarification of the various processes. (Twenty minutes.)

12. When the decision has been made, the leader asks the group members to identify the process they used in arriving at the decision. The leader then asks them to identify some actions that could be taken in the next group meeting to ensure that the selected process(es) will succeed. As the members discuss these actions, the leader records salient items on newsprint, along with names of any members responsible for the actions. The leader then gives the sheet to a group member for reference at the next group meeting. (Even if there is unanimity from the beginning on what process should be used, the leader asks the members to identify actions that could be taken in the next meeting to ensure that their preferred process will work.)

Source: Adapted from Francis, D. & Young, D. (1979). *Improving Work Groups: A Practical Manual for Team Building.* San Diego, California: University Associates.

(Reproduced from *The Encyclopedia of Team-Development Activities (page 131).* Edited by J. William Pfeiffer. Copyright © 1991 by Jossey-Bass/Pfeiffer, San Francisco, CA.)

***

Group Decisions Information Sheet

One of the most important questions regarding decision making is "Who actually decides?" From answers to this question, the following five decision-making processes can be clearly identified:

1. **Individual decision.** One person, normally the manager, actually makes a decision. Others who are involved in the situation are expected to abide by the decision.

2. **Minority decision.** A few of those involved in a situation meet to consider the matter and make a decision, and this decision is binding for all concerned.

3. **Majority decision.** More than half of those involved in a situation make a decision, and it is binding for all concerned. Many political and democratic organizations use this principle.

4. **Unanimous decision.** Each person fully agrees on the action to be taken, and everyone concerned fully subscribes to the decision that is made.

When people are involved in making a decision, they are much more likely to be committed to that decision than if some other person—or small group—makes a decision on their behalf. Therefore, going up the decision-making scale (from individual decisions to unanimous decisions, as outlined above) increases commitment, although it also increases the difficulty in arriving at an agreement.

***

Group Decisions Check List

Instructions: Think about the ways in which your team typically makes decisions, and then read each of the statements below. Choose at least three and no more than five statements that are most typical of your team. Circle the number that precedes each of your choices.

1. When decision making is necessary, a few of us usually get together and take care of it.

2. The senior team member usually decides, and the question is settled.

(continued)

3. All group members are encouraged to express their views, and we attempt to include something for everyone in the decision.
4. A decision typically is not made until everyone somewhat agrees with it.
5. We frequently let the majority rule.
6. The person in charge of the task makes the decisions.
7. Often all of the group members agree on a decision and support it wholeheartedly.
8. A small clique runs everything in our group.
9. A decision is made only when most of the members agree on a particular course of action.
10. We do not make a decision until every member of the group is completely in agreement with it.
11. Our members are allowed to air their views, but our manager makes the decision.
12. A few of our group members usually dominate the group.
13. A decision is not made unless every member of the group can accept it to some extent.
14. A numerical majority is required before decisions are made.
15. A decision is not made unless every member of the group actively supports it.

***

Group Decisions Interpretation Chart

Instructions: After you have marked three to five statements on the "Group Decisions Check List," circle the same numbers below in the "Statement Numbers" column. Write the total number of circles in each row in the "Total Circles" column. (Be sure to count your circles; do not count the numbers inside the circles.) The style corresponding to the highest score in the "Total Circles" column represents a typical decision-making style among the members of your group.

Statement numbers	Total circles	Representative style
2, 6, 11		Individual
1, 8, 12		Minority
5, 9, 14		Majority
3, 4, 13		Consensus
7, 10, 15		Unanimous

***

Exercise 4   Individual or Team Decision

Category: Group Decision Making

Objectives:

- To assist managers to determine when a team approach is appropriate
- To provide a framework for assessing stages of team development

This activity helps to increase problem-solving skills, managerial insight, and team-building skills.

Method: Managers constantly need to evaluate when they should be directive and when they should use a team approach in which responsibility for decisions is shared by members of the work group. An individual approach connotes speed, decisiveness, and discipline, whereas the team approach suggests commitment, resourcefulness, and balance. One of the principal factors in the choice of decision-making style is the stage of development of the work team. This activity provides a format for examining those stages of development and making an informed choice of the most appropriate approach to decision making.

Ask several members of your team to complete the "Team Development Questionnaire." The results will be helpful in assisting you to evaluate your decision-making style and its appropriateness to the development level of the team.

***

TEAM DEVELOPMENT QUESTIONNAIRE
Write a clear definition of the team to be evaluated below and then complete the questionnaire with respect to that team.

Team under review:

Place a mark on each line to indicate your view of the present development of the team in relation to the factors described below.

1. Technical Skill
The degree to which team members possess the technical competence necessary to do the job

Low Skill						HighSkill
0	1	2	3	4	5	6

2. Effectiveness
The degree to which the team is capable of a high level of achievement in output and quality

Low						High
0	1	2	3	4	5	6

3. Creativity
The degree to which the team is able to solve complex problems or create new processes

Low						High
0	1	2	3	4	5	6

4. Resourcefulness
The degree to which the team identifies useful resources and uses them appropriately

Low						High
0	1	2	3	4	5	6

5. Responsiveness
The degree to which the team responds quickly to changes in priorities

Low						High
0	1	2	3	4	5	6

6. Initiative
The degree to which the team will undertake assignments and resolve problems without outside motivation

Low						High
0	1	2	3	4	5	6

(continued)

7. Enthusiasm
The degree to which members develop a team approach and are positive about the team and its work

Low   High
0   1   2   3   4   5   6

8. Closeness
The degree to which members are open and friendly with each other

Low   High
0   1   2   3   4   5   6

9. Leadership Style
The degree to which the leader's personality and skills promote a team approach

Low   High
0   1   2   3   4   5   6

10. Constraints
The degree to which there are external factors that undermine the development of a team approach

Low   High
0   1   2   3   4   5   6

Scoring
Add up your scores and mark the total on the line below

A	B	C	D
0	15	30	45	60

The following analysis is one indication of the decision-making style most likely to be effective in relation to the team at this time.

Style A: The team is at a low stage of development. The leader will need to take a firm and directive approach while taking active steps to develop a team approach.

Style B: The team is still below average in terms of team development, but has made some progress. Views can be solicited, but important decisions generally are best made by the team leader.

Style C: The team is developing and can participate in a wide range of decision-making processes although it still needs some guidance and support.

Style D: The team is well developed and can be expected to cope competently with a wide range of decisions.

(Reproduced from *The Unblocked Boss: Activities for Self-Development* Mike Woodcock and Dave Francis San Diego, California: University Associates, Inc., 1981.)

***

Endnotes

Anderson, A. H. (2006). Achieving understanding in face-to-face and video-mediated multiparty interactions. *Discourse Processes, 41*(3), 251–252.

Baskerville, R. (2003). Hofstede never studied culture. *Organizations and Society, 28*(1), 1–12.

Bonner, B. L., Bauman, M. R., & Dalal, R. S. (2002). The effect of member expertise on group decision-making and performance. *Organizational Behavior and Human Decision Processes,* 88, 719–736.

Boroush, M., Hart, S., Enk, G., & Hornick, W. (July 1985). Managing complexity through consensus mapping: Technology for the Structuring of Group Decisions. *The Academy of Management Review, 10*(3), 587–600.

Bottger, P. & Yetton, P. (1988) An Integration of process and decision scheme explanations of group problem solving performance. *Organizational Behavior and Human Decision Processes, 42*(2), 234–249.

Cane, A. (February 28, 2007). Decision making software in the fast lane: Programs developed to select the right option in motor racing are being adopted by business. *Financial Times.* 4–5.

Chang, L. C. (2003). An examination of cross-cultural negotiation using Hofstede framework. *Journal of Academy of Business, 2*(2), 567–571.

Copeland, L. & Griggs, L. (1985). *Going International.* New York: Random House. pp. 11–16.

Creelman, J. (2007). Becoming world class: How IBM delivers shareholder returns. *Business Performance Management Magazine, 5*(1), 5–8.

Dickson, M. W., Hartog, D., & Mitchelson, J. (2003). Research on Cross-Cultural Context: Making Progress, and Raising New Questions. *Leadership Quarterly, 14*(6), 729–741.

Driskell, J. E. & Salas, E. (1991). Group decision-making under stress. *Journal of Applied Psychology,* 76, 473–478.

Fisher, A. B. (1990). *Small Group Decision Making: Communication and the Group Process,* New York: McGraw-Hill Publishing. p. 223.

Friedman, P. G. (1989). Upstream facilitation: A proactive approach to managing problem-solving groups. *Management Communication Quarterly,* 3, 33–50.

Fullerton, H. N. Jr. (1999). Labor Force Projections to 2008: Steady Growth and Changing Composition. *Monthly Labor Review,* 19–32.

Girlando, A., Anderson, C., & Zerillo, J. (2004). An examination of Hofstede's paradigm of national culture and its malleability: Italy and US thirty years later. *Journal of Transnational Management Development, 10*(1), 23–47.

Goldstein, J. & Leopold, M. (November 1990). Corporate culture vs. ethnic culture. *Personnel Journal, 89*(11), 84.

Gong, W., Li, Z. G. & Stump, R. L. (2007). Global internet use and access: Cultural considerations. *Asia Pacific Journal of Marketing and Logistics, 19*(1), 57–73.

Goebbels, G. (2002). *Team work in distributed collaborative virtual environments*, University of Pretoria, Dissertation, AAT 0804319, 193.

Hare, A. P. (1992). Group, Teams and Social Interaction. *Theories and Applications,* New York: Praeger Publishers.

Hirokawa, R. Y. (1989) Facilitation of Group Communication, *Management Communication Quarterly,* 3, 71–92.

Hirokawa, R. Y. & Rost, K. M. (1992). Effective group decision making in organizations: Field test of the vigilant interaction theory. *Management Communication Quarterly,* 5, 267–288.

Hoffman, R. R., Shadbolt, N. R., Burton, A. M., & Klein, G. (1995). Eliciting knowledge from experts. A methodological analysis. *Organizational Behavior and Human Decision Processes.*

Hofstede, G. (1980). *Culture's Consequences: International Differences in Work-Related Values.* Beverly Hills: Sage Publications. pp. 71, 118, 149, 190, 372–390.

Hofstede, G. & McCrae, R. R. (2004). Personality and culture revisited: Linking traits and dimensions of culture. *Cross-Cultural Research, 38*(1), 52–70.

Higley, J. (2000). Hospitality leaders promote diversity during conference. *Hotel and Motel Management,* 4.

Hogg, M. A. & Abrams, D. (1988). *A Social Psychology of Intergroup Relations and Group Process.* Routledge. p. 166

Janis, I. L. (1982) Groupthink. *Group Dynamics,* 239.

Leo, C., Bennett, R., & Hartel, C. (2005). Cross cultural differences in decision making styles. *Cross Cultural Management, 12*(3), 32–64.

Locke, E. A., Latham, G. P., & Winters, D. C. (1994). Cognitive and motivational effects of participation: A mediator study. *Journal of Organizational Behavior,* 15(1), 49–63.

Longnecker, H., Daigle., R. & Feinstein, D. (1995). *Successful Application of Principle-Centered Leadership in the Information Systems Project Course.* In Proceedings of the Twelfth Information Systems Education Conference, Charlotte, NC. pp. 194–200.

Malai, V. & Speece, M. (2005). Cultural impact on the relationship among perceived service quality, brand name value, and customer loyalty. *Journal of International Consumer Marketing, 17*(4), 7–22.

March, J. G. & Olsen, J. P. (1986). Garbage can models of decision making in organization. In James G. March and Roger Weissinger-Baylon (Eds.). *Ambiguity and Command: Organizational Perspectives on Military Decision Making.* Mansfield, MA: Pitman Publishing. pp. 11–35.

Masterson, B. & Murphy, B. (1986). Internal cross-cultural management. *Training and Development Journal, 40,* 58.

Merritt, A. (2000). Culture in the cockpit: Do Hofstede's dimensions replicate? *Journal of Cross-Cultural Psychology, 31*(3), 283–302.

Molinari, D. L. (2004). The role of social comments in problem solving groups in an on-line class. *The American Journal of Distance Education,* 18(2), 89–93.

Neck, C. P. & Moorshead, G. (1995). Group think remodeled: The importance of leadership, time pressure, and methodological decision procedures. *Human Relations,* 48, 537–557.

Paulus, P. B., ed. (1980). *Psychology of Group Influence.* Hillsdale, N.J.: Lawrence Erlbaum Associates, Inc. p. 210.

Priem, R. L., Harrison, D. A., & Muir, N. K. (1995). Structure conflict and consensus outcomes in group decision making. *Journal of Management,* 21, 691–710.

Ranieri, K. L. (2004). Toward group problem solving guidelines for 21st century teams. *Performance Improvement Quarterly,* 17(3), 86–106.

Rogelberg, S. G., Barnes-Farrell, J. L., & Lowe, C. A. (1992). The Stepladder Technique: A structure facilitating effective group decision making. *Journal of Applied Psychology,* 77(5), 730–737.

Shaw, M. E. (1981). *Group Dynamics: The Psychology of Small Group Behavior.* Third Edition. New York: McGraw-Hill.

Silver, S. D. (1995, September). A dual-motive heuristic for member information initiation in group decision making: Managing risk and commitment. *Decision Support Systems, 15*(1), 83–97.

Singh, S. (2006). Cultural differences in, and influences on, consumers' propensity to adopt innovations. *International Marketing Review,* 23(2), 173–197.

Soares, A. M., Farhangmehr, M., & Shoham, A. (2007). Hofstede's dimensions of culture in international marketing studies. *Journal of Business Research, 60*(3), 277–291.

Sniezek, J. A. (1992). Groups under uncertainty: An examination of confidence in group decision making. *Organizational Behavior and Human Decision Processes,* 52, 124–155.

Thiederman, S. (1988). Breaking through to foreign-born employees. *Management World Journal,* 17(3), 22–29.

Thiederman, S. (1988). Managing the foreign-born workforce: Keys to effective cross-cultural motivation. *Management Journal, 40*(3), 23–28.

Thiederman, S. (1990). *Bridging Cultural Barriers for Corporate Success.* Massachusetts/Toronto: D.C. Heath and Company. p. 82.

Triandis, H. C. (2004). The many dimensions of culture. *The Academy of Management Executive, 18*(1), 88–102.

Worchel S., Wood, W., & Simpson, J. A. (1992). *Group Process and Productivity.* Sage Publications. p. 100.

6

MANAGING TIME

Voltaire, the great French writer and philosopher, posed an interesting question in his book *Zadig: A Mystery of Fate*.

The Grand Magi asked Zadig,

> *"What, of all things in the world,*
> *Is the longest and the shortest,*
> *The swiftest and the slowest,*
> *The most divisible and the most extended,*
> *The most neglected and the most regretted,*
> *Without which nothing can be done,*
> *Which devours all that is little and enlivens all that is great?"*

Without hesitation, Zadig answered, *"Time."*

CHAPTER OUTLINE

Introduction

How Managers Manage Their Time

Principles of Time Management
    Completing a Time Management Skills Assessment
    Conducting a Time Analysis
    Analyzing Personal Time Management Behaviors

Improving Time Management Skills
    Spending Time on Important Tasks
    Identifying Time Traps

Three-Pronged Time Management Attack
    Fight Procrastination
    Learn the Keys to Effective Delegation
    Eliminate Interruptions
        Calls
        Visitors
        Paperwork
        Mail

Technology and Time
    Prevalence of Individual's Technology Use
    Technology and Potential Time Management Concerns
    Increased Organizational Responsiveness to Time Management Needs

Balancing Work and Family
    Characteristics of the Hospitality Workplace
    Advancement Opportunities and Time Requirements
    The Importance of Family Time
    The Organizational Impact of Work/Family Time Issues

Summary

LEARNING OBJECTIVES

After you read this chapter, you will be able to do the following:

1. Define what we mean by time management.
2. Identify common causes of poor time management in the hospitality industry.
3. Describe Pareto's Rule.
4. Discuss the implication of Pareto's rule on time management.
5. Identify the three unique aspects of time as a resource.
6. Differentiate between effective and ineffective time analysis.
7. Understand the importance of prioritization and delegation as key management tasks.
8. Elaborate on the factors that determine when to delegate tasks.
9. Discuss five of the "How to Delegate" principles.
10. Determine which kinds of interruptions are appropriate and which are not.

11. Outline strategies for reducing or eliminating inappropriate interruptions.

12. Describe four principles for effective and time-efficient meetings.

13. List methods of reducing paperwork.

Green House Co., Ltd.

Green House Group (GHG) was started in 1947 and marked its 60th anniversary in 2007. GHG operates 14 hotels and 504 restaurants and takeout shops throughout Japan, and 28 restaurants in Korea and Taiwan. The Green House Co., Ltd., also owns Cini-Little Japan (a foodservice facility and design consulting company) and Horwath Asia-Pacific Japan (a hotel consulting company) under their license agreements. A major part of Green House's activity is contract food service for businesses and organizations, schools, hospitals and nursing homes, and company recreation facilities, which totals 1,493 stores, besides restaurants. The group also sells food products, daily necessities, and food facility equipment. The total sales volume of the group reaches US$1 billion. Green House has a total of 3,667 employees, including all contract food service sections, hotels, and consulting companies. Green House Foods Co., Ltd., operator of the restaurant and takeout shops division, has 570 employees. Green House placed 4th in the contract food service industry in a 2005 ranking. Green House holds top-class market share and has the largest number of stores in public offices of listed companies in the industry. Green House has contracts with Japan's leading companies and public offices, such as Toyota headquarters in Tokyo, Mitsubishi Motors, Tokyo Stock Exchange, and Tokyo Metropolitan Police Department. The executive team consists of Chiaki Tanuma, President and CEO, nine managing directors, and five directors. Broadly, the organization is comprised of subsidiaries of four divisions, which are businesses and industries, hospitals and nursing homes, restaurants and takeout shops, and hotels.

We interviewed Chiaki Tanuma, President and CEO of Green House:

Interview with President and CEO Chiaki Tanuma

Question: *How do you, as the President and CEO of Green House, manage your time?*

Answer: I define what we want the company to be 10 years from now. Medium- and long-term business plans (for the next 3 to 5 years) are important. However, what executives need now is to define clearly what the company wants to be 1 year from now. First, I define the company's goal 1 year from now, and then focus on time management for the next half year, 3 months, 1 week, and 1 day to achieve my goals.

I also impose on myself previews, reviews, and a Plan, Do, Check, Action review (PDCA) of every day, every week, and every month. Many companies have 1 or 2 meetings every month to check if they have done as they planned and consider improved action for next month. However, I do not believe 12 to 24 cycles of PDCA meetings annually is enough. We need to do PDCA more often to improve the accuracy of the management. If we do PDCA once a week, we will have 52 cycles annually and if we do it every day, we will have 200 cycles. My daily routine consists of: preview my schedule in the car on my way to the office every morning, PDCA time management every day, and review my schedule in the car on the way home.

Question: *How do you encourage your managers and employees to manage their time?*

Answer: People tend to forget the goals that they or their company set for a year from now because they are tied up all day by their work. It goes without saying that process management is

(continued)

(continued)

important to achieve a goal. In my company, executives and head office staff place an emphasis on keeping the set time limit for reaching a goal. I consider time in business to be a part of a budget, just like sales profit. Executives need to have the ability to manage time as a budget. For example, if a group of 5 people do a job in 10 hours, it means that it takes 50 hours in total. The total cost to finish the job will be clear by calculating the labor cost of the 5 people per hour. If we can reduce the time to 40 or 30 hours, it is an achievement for management. There is an old saying, "time is money." I tell the employees that time is a cost and using time management to control cost will move them one step further in business.

Question: *Is there a difference between American and Japanese concepts of time?*

Answer: Although everyone has 24 hours a day equally, how it is consumed depends on each person. For both Americans and the Japanese, the important point is how they use their limited time.

Question: *How do you achieve balance among work, family, and exercise?*

Answer: That is not easy for me because everyday I want to finish up what I was supposed to do. Even after I get home, I often sit up until midnight, or sometimes all night, to look over documents. I use the summer and winter holidays to relax and spend time with my family.

Scenario: Tim's Time Troubles

Tim Corella manages a mid-priced family restaurant in the Harriot Hotel. His restaurant has a steady clientele from the city as well as business from the travelers staying in the hotel. He has three assistant managers and a competent staff. However, his days seem to fly past, and he can never catch up with all that must be done. He frequently works late and often takes additional work home with him. His wife, Sarah, complains that he has no time for her or their two young daughters. Tim says, "This is the job I've dreamed of, but now that I have it, it seems to consume my whole life! How is it that I know other managers that have similar jobs, but also seem to have time for family and friends?"

Yesterday was a typical example. Tim started out in a positive frame of mind. He promised Sarah that the whole family would go out for pizza and bowling that evening at the Stop, Drop, and Roll Bowling Alley. Tim arrived at work at 8:00. His main goals, in addition to his usual daily duties, were to interview and hire two new prep persons, price the new menu, prepare next week's forecast, and prepare the employee schedule. This seemed reasonable enough for a nine and a half hour shift.

When he arrived at work, Lisa, one of his assistants, said she was concerned that certain types of wine were running low. Tim had begun the wine inventory two days ago but had not had time to complete it. Bill, the head waiter, told him that a representative from the Lion's Club had called regarding their dinner at the restaurant later in the week. During the course of the day, a couple of unscheduled vendors requested his time. Sarah phoned a couple of times about their evening plans. Tim did not want to be rude, but he felt like telling Sarah that the more often she interrupted his work, the less likely their plans for the evening became. His friend Tony also

(continued)

(continued)

called to say that they had not enjoyed a round of golf in months. Then, near the end of lunch, a $95 discrepancy appeared at the register. It turned out to be an input error, but Tim spent half an hour counting receipts and verifying entries until the mistake was found. By evening, Tim was tired and still had not completed enough of his scheduled work to feel he could go home at 5:30. He called Sarah to let her know. Then Bill went home sick, and Tim had to take over the remainder of Bill's shift, working the floor and unable to complete his own tasks. By 10:00 pm, Tim was headed home with the unfinished work in his briefcase.

INTRODUCTION

What is **time management?** Simply stated, it is putting time to the best possible use. But when one considers time management more thoroughly, it becomes apparent that it is not time, but one's self that must be managed. Though simple in concept, time management can be very difficult to implement. The subject has been explored extensively in articles and books, but the problem of poor time management still haunts today's manager.

In this chapter we will discuss the common causes of poor time management. Managers often do not accurately judge the effectiveness of their time management skills. Thus, we suggest that managers analyze how they spend their time and we provide a framework for conducting a time analysis. After we describe the time analysis process, we discuss how managers in the hospitality industry can improve their time management skills. Delegating the less important tasks can leave managers with more time for completing important tasks. We describe **interrupters** as a large consumer of a manager's time and suggest methods for reducing inappropriate interruptions. Finally, we provide tips for conducting effective and time-efficient meetings. After reading this chapter, you should have a better grasp on how to manage your time effectively.

> How would you rate yourself as a time manager? Explain.

HOW MANAGERS MANAGE THEIR TIME

How do hospitality managers manage their time? The answer, for the most part, is "poorly." The results of a study by Ferguson and Berger (1984) found that, more often than not, restaurateurs felt they lacked the knowledge of adequate time management. This is a major problem affecting the restaurateur in his or her role as manager. As most would agree, until you learn to manage your time, nothing else will matter because time is the essence of managerial effectiveness.

Ninety-four restaurateurs responded to the question, "How well do you manage your time?" Four basic categories (poor, fair, good, and excellent) segmented the responses. The parameters of the categories reflected the relative degree of "time management" the restaurateur felt was practiced. The "poor" category consisted of managers' responses indicating no planning or forethought whatsoever. The "fair" category included managers who did plan or attempt to plan, but only in a casual way. The "good" category included those managers who consistently planned, using a day timer and looking forward into upcoming weeks. The "excellent" category included those managers who not only used a day timer but also prioritized and updated their schedule. Using this framework, over 50 percent of the restaurateurs fell into the "poor" category, about 20 percent into the "fair," 15 percent into the "good," and 12 percent into the "excellent" category.

In another study, Berger and Merritt (1998) found that, of a sample of 74 restaurant managers, virtually all claimed to use time management principles daily (only 5 percent said that they did not). Of the 69 respondents who apply time management principles, well over two-thirds (46) ascribed at least a 15 percent increase in positive bottom-line results to time management, and 24 attributed 20 percent of bottom-line strength to time management. However, the same study indicated that managers give low ratings when asked to rate the effectiveness of their time-management skills. Forty rated themselves poor in time management effectiveness, while 13 gave themselves a rating of fair. Nine said their effectiveness was good, and 12 rated the effectiveness of their time-management skills as excellent.

PRINCIPLES OF TIME MANAGEMENT

Improving your effectiveness and efficiency requires a thorough understanding of time. Porter focuses his discussion of time management on the principles of time, which are as follows:

1. Time is a unique resource. It exists only in the present instant, and time past is gone forever.
2. Time is irreplaceable and, in the long run, inelastic. We may try to expand the hours in the "busy day" season, but in the long run such a burst is not sustainable.
3. Because time past is gone forever, there seems to be only one dimension in which time can be managed effectively—that is, the future. In other words, plans must be made today for the effective use of time that will pay off in the future.

Some theorists would advise that you begin with time, not tasks. And they do not start out with planning; they begin by finding out where their time actually goes. They attempt to manage their time and to cut back unproductive demands on that time. Finally, they consolidate their 'discretionary' time into the largest possible continuing units.

Completing a Time Management Skills Assessment

Many managers do not realize that they have poor time management skills. Completing a time management assessment, as discussed later in this chapter, would allow managers to more accurately understand their habits. A good assessment you can use is the *Time Mastery Profile* developed by Dr. Merrill Douglas and Dr. Larry Baker. The time management dimensions they recommend are listed in Box 6.1.

Why do restaurant managers do so poorly when it comes to time management? Mainly because they don't have the time to think out properly what their days will actually be like. They constantly manage in an "interrupt" mode.

If we review Tim's profile, his weaknesses become obvious. Although he begins his day with a good attitude, he does not evaluate the cause of the underlying frustration with his job: his poor time management skills. He has a vague idea of his daily goals, but he is not specific about how they will be completed and keeps no record of his accomplishments. Tim seems to be reactive rather than proactive. He does not prioritize, and drifts from task to task as they arise, often driven more by interruptions than by planned or scheduled tasks. Rather than delegating tasks to his subordinates and co-workers, Tim is given tasks to do, for example the wine inventory and the busboy issue. His team is running in a backward direction. It is no wonder that Tim is overwhelmed!

BOX 6.1

Dimensions of Time Management

- **Attitudes**—The extent to which you believe you can control or influence the things that happen in your life;
- **Goals**—How often you set goals for yourself and how frequently you meet those goals;
- **Priorities**—The degree to which you finish difficult, more important tasks before completing more enjoyable tasks;
- **Analyzing**—How frequently you observe where you spend your time;
- **Planning**—The amount of time you spend planning your day;
- **Scheduling**—How specific you are when setting times for the events you have planned;
- **Interruptions**—The degree to which you are flexible in changing your plan to accommodate interruptions;
- **Meetings**—How effective and organized your office meetings are;
- **Written communication**—The extent to which you sort your paperwork and keep your office organized;
- **Delegation**—How often you assign tasks to your subordinates;
- **Procrastination**—The extent to which you push off projects that are difficult and time consuming;
- **Team time**—How frequently your team and you analyze the use of time during meetings.

Although our example is hypothetical, Tim exemplifies the very real time management troubles of many restaurateurs. But are the restaurant managers alone? Not really. A sample of 900 managers in nine countries attending company and public training workshops encountered the same problems that put the restaurant manager into the **interrupt mode,** including telephone interruptions, meetings, unexpected visitors, poor delegation, and crises. So the question becomes, "How can the restaurant manager become more effective in managing his or her time?"

Time management consultants often apply the 80/20 theory first proposed by Vilfredo Pareto. This theory simply says that 80 percent of a manager's efforts produce only 20 percent of the results and vice versa; that is, 20 percent of the efforts produce 80 percent of the results. If "interrupters" are reduced, any manager can strive for a higher level return on his or her time. With knowledge of time management and its unique character, and with a reduction in the number of interrupters through elimination, delegation, or reduction, the manager will become more efficient.

Of the dimensions mentioned in Box 6.1, which do you anticipate will be most relevant to your time management efforts?

Conducting a Time Analysis

The average restaurant manager spends 35 percent of his or her time in unscheduled meetings, 17 percent in desk sessions, 13 percent on telephone calls, and 6 percent on touring the operation (Ferguson and Berger, 1984). But this only points out how the time is being allocated; it does not specify the importance of the activities with respect to the manager's goals. This is where the restaurant manager must do an additional piece of research. The day must be closely reviewed and its events recorded to determine exactly where the time has gone. This process is known as **time analysis** and is a critical first step to managing time effectively.

Some of the managers surveyed already used time analysis. They stated that they were currently using a day planner or a "to do" list. In our scenario, Tim simply had a mental list of four tasks he hoped to accomplish. But this is only the beginning. In an effective time analysis, the manager records the day's events in 15-minute intervals, prioritizes each event, and separates events into groups such as unscheduled meetings, scheduled meetings, and telephone calls. For practical purposes, the manager can list the categories at the top of the time log and simply record the number of the category in the 15-minute time slot. It is important to record the function as it happens, rather than at the end of the day or at lunch. This is because the average manager will tend to forget the ordinary day-to-day events in the work day. As an example, Figure 6.1. presents a time log of Tim's day.

Date
Goals: **Priority Codes:**

1. Hire two new prep persons   A = Important/Urgent
2. Price new menu   B = Important/Not Urgent
3. Finish liquor inventory   C = Urgent/Not Important
4. Arrange Lion's Club dinner   D = Routine
5. Prepare next week's forecast
6. Prepare employee schedule   **Action Codes:**

                                                   1 = Scheduled Meeting
                                                   2 = Unscheduled Meeting
                                                   3 = Desk Session
                                                   4 = Telephone
                                                   5 = Tour

Time	Action	Priority	Disposition/Results
8:00	3	D	Opened and read mail
8:15	3	D	sorted mail
8:30	3	D	coffee break with John
8:45	1	B	Sage vendor/discussed prices
9:00	1	B	Texas meats/prices, quality
9:15	1	A	read over applications w/John
9:30	2	B	salesman about new advertising
10:00	3	A	final applications
10:15	1	A	set up 4 interviews/3:00–4:00
10:30	3	D	coffee w/Lisa/forecast for week

FIGURE 6.1   Sample time log

10:45	4	D	wife called
11:00	2	D	wait staff w/schedule questions
11:15	5	B	check out kitchen/lunch
11:30	1	D	Lunch
11:45	5	D	walk the floor/help servers
12:00	4	D	wife called
12:15	2	A	customer insists on speaking about dissatisfaction with rude busboy
12:30	2	C	tried to fix dishwasher until repairman arrives
12:45	2	B	waiter questioned me about wine shortage
1:00	2	C	notice unemptied garbage in bathroom/seek out maintenance worker
1:15	4	C	phone dishwasher repair company again
1:30	2	A	$95 balance discrepancy/count receipts
1:45	2	A	still counting receipts
2:00	1	D	Oversee the lunch closing
2:15	3	A	priced beef entrees
2:30	3	A	Finished half of menu pricing
2:45	4	C	Tony called about Sunday golf
3:00	2	D	discussed hockey game w/Bill
3:15	2	B	day/evening events w/Bill
3:30	1	B	talked w/2 applicants
3:45	4	A	Texas meats will deliver tonight
4:00	1	B	Finished interviews/hired 2
4:15	2	B	Lions President/Thursday meeting
4:30	2	B	Lions President/Thursday meeting
4:45	2	A	Repairman for dish machine
5:00	2	B	discussed contingency w/Bill
5:15	2	D	talked w/Lisa before leaving
5:30	4	D	called wife/no dinner
5:45	2	B	discussed week's forecast w/Bill
6:00	3	B	Worked on week's forecast
Evening	3	B	Finished forecast
	2	B	Bill home sick/I worked floor

FIGURE 6.1   (continued)

> If you don't have time to do it right,
> When will you find time to do it over?

At the end of the day, Tim can refer to the time log and summarize what was actually accomplished toward achieving his stated goals, and how much time was spent doing so. Although initially time-consuming, this process is necessary to construct a more detailed picture of his day and of how effectively time was used to achieve his goals. Figure 6.2 illustrates this function.

Goal	Total Time Spent	Completed	Percent of Day
1. Hire 2 prep persons	60 min	Y	10.5
2. Price new menu	15 min	N	2.6
3. Finish liquor inventory	0 min	N	0
4. Arrange Lions Club dinner	30 min	Y	5.3
5. Next week's forecast	60 min	N	10.5
6. Employee schedule	15 min	N	2.6
7. Other			68.5
Total time spent toward goals:	225 min		31.5

FIGURE 6.2 Tim Corella's daily effectiveness

Note: 1 day equals 9.5 hours or 570 minutes.

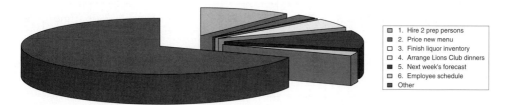

GRAPH 6.1 Daily effectiveness

As Graph 6.1 illustrates, Tim spent almost 70 percent of his time on pursuits other than his stated goals. While some of this time was spent on routine tasks associated with his job performance, much of it could have been delegated to others or skipped entirely.

Analyzing Personal Time Management Behaviors

Table 6.1 further categorizes Tim's activities to help him see what kinds of work he is performing for what percentage of his scheduled day.

Tim spent nearly a quarter of his day in unscheduled meetings. However, one day will not show a pattern. Using this system, a manager can begin keeping a log of daily

TABLE 6.1 How Tim Spends His Time		
Category	*Minutes spent*	*% of day*
1. Unscheduled meetings	120	21.1
2. Scheduled meetings	225	39.5
3. Desk session	105	18.4
4. Telephone	90	15.8
5. Tour	30	5.3
Total	570	100.0

activities for one week. At the end of the week, the manager can tabulate the amount of time spent on each category and estimate the effectiveness of each day. This will give the manager some idea of what consumes time in the typical workday. Figure 6.3 illustrates how this is done.

Let us assume that a manager has been working on a time log for one week and is ready to summarize the results in the weekly performance and allocation report (see Figure 6.3). A breakdown of the various categories on the log will show where the manager's time was spent. The manager must then probe further and analyze how effectively he or she had used the time toward achieving desired goals.

Weekly Time Category Log										
	Mon		**Tues**		**Wed**		**Thurs**		**Fri**	
Category	**Time**	**%**	**Time**	**%**	**Time**	**%**	**Time**	**%**	**Time**	**%**
1. Unscheduled meetings										
2. Scheduled meetings										
3. Desk session										
4. Telephone										
5. Tour										

FIGURE 6.3   Weekly time category log

Let's begin by investigating the manager's goal performance. We will look at the manager's areas of effectiveness and analyze daily duties, determining which were absolutely necessary and which could have been delegated. The manager should ask, "Did I spend enough time, or too much time, on a particular activity?"

If you were to create large categories into which many of your activities could be clustered, what would they be?

IMPROVING TIME MANAGEMENT SKILLS

Spending Time on Important Tasks

The daily effectiveness chart in Figure 6.2 shows the amount of time spent on each goal. By comparing this to the relative importance or priority of each goal, the manager can decide in each case whether the proper amount of time was spent. Naturally we tend to spend more time on things we enjoy doing and to put off the things we don't enjoy. Because of ingrained habits, most executives have difficulty differentiating time spent on

the enjoyable goals from that spent on not enjoyable goals, since both result in the same feeling of accomplishment. One way this problem might be eliminated is to mark the often neglected essentials as more urgent by setting a task of the week (TOTW). The trick is to take something from the bottom of your pile and promise yourself that you will make the time to finish it during the week. Mentally pledging yourself to a TOTW will help you resist the false appeal of trivial things that appear to be urgent. When you analyze your time logs you may find that you spend almost no time on your high priority goals. Only a written record will enable you to understand how your time is actually being spent. Your memory can be self-deceiving!

Drucker (1961) recalls asking an executive before doing a time analysis how he perceived his time was being spent. The executive firmly stated that his time was divided into three categories, with an equal amount spent on each. After his administrative assistant brought in the time analysis that she had been keeping for him for six weeks, the executive could not believe that it was his. He discovered that he had spent almost no time on any of the three groups that he would have selected. With the effectiveness chart, the executive will be able to determine which goals are more important, how much daily time was spent on each, and how much time was needed to complete them. Figure 6.2 shows that the executive chose hiring two prep people as a more important task than doing the liquor inventory. By periodically reviewing his own activities, the executive could monitor time spent in relation to **goal priority** and make more informed decisions about those priorities. He would be relying less on habits and more on facts.

Identifying Time Traps

When reviewing the time log, the manager should analyze it for wastes of time, gaps in any process, and tasks that could have been eliminated, delegated, or reduced. Should the manager be opening the restaurant mail? Is planning out next week's forecast by discussing it at 8:00 a.m. and 5:00 p.m. as effective as preparing it between 5:30 and 6:15 p.m.? Does the value of the manager's time justify watching the repairman fix the dishwashing machine?

Ultimately, only the restaurant manager himself can answer these questions. We can only show the manager what to look for and suggest possible changes he or she could make. By targeting specific areas in which the time spent should be reduced, the manager initiates more efficient time management.

An end-of-week analysis can help the manager monitor his progress. By segmenting the week into daily percentages and then calculating a weekly average, the manager can track the week's performance and adjust accordingly. Time logs should continue to be maintained, even if on a random basis. It is human nature to fall back into bad habits and forget about such things as conscientious time management.

Have you ever kept a time log? What challenges would you anticipate?

THREE-PRONGED TIME MANAGEMENT ATTACK

While the methods described are an important first step to more productive work activity, there is still more to be done. We recommend a three-pronged attack to initiate the most effective personal time management system. These steps involve (1) fighting procrastination, (2) delegating, and (3) eliminating as many interruptions as possible.

Fight Procrastination

Few of us recognize our bad habits because we are not consciously aware of them. When a new and better practice is conceived, it should be implemented as soon as possible. This reduces the chance of the new practice being lost again to the subconscious mind. The new practice should contrast with the old so as to obviate the need to perform the old. Furthermore, when initiating a new practice, the manager must commit to following through with it. A public announcement of the change will usually suffice. Once begun, there can be no excuses for avoiding the new practice.

The human failing most closely associated with poor time management is that of procrastination. Most people procrastinate to some extent; there is always something you would rather do than the distasteful task at hand. **Procrastination,** most experts agree, is something to be recognized and faced. The following six guidelines (Box 6.2) have proven helpful to thousands of managers.

Once procrastinators have begun working, a related habit is not completing a task or a decision the first time through. Each time a manager picks up an old unfinished task, he must re-familiarize himself with it all over again. This not only wastes time but in many instances reduces the quality of the task accomplished or the decision made.

BOX 6.2

Fight Procrastination One Step at a Time

1. View procrastination as a major problem, not a harmless hang-up.
2. Select one task where procrastination derails you and master it.
3. Set priorities and focus on one task at a time.
4. Create deadlines for yourself.
5. Don't avoid the most difficult problems.
6. Don't let the tendency to be a perfectionist paralyze you.

All the manager's original fresh ideas about the task might not be recalled to assist the final execution. An effective manager follows through with an initiated task until it is accomplished.

> Under what circumstances are you likely to procrastinate?

Learn the Keys to Effective Delegation

By looking at Figure 6.2 and Table 6.1, it appears our manager Tim Corella is ineffective at allocating time toward the things that matter, that is, toward daily goals. Some of these goals were not even addressed, while much of his time was spent on less relevant matters. Tim must take a hard look at these goals and ask some pointed questions. "Were these goals really necessary in the first place? Were they important enough to warrant a major portion of the day?" Tim might respond that *all* the goals were important and had to be accomplished for effective control and management. But then he should ask *whose* time was needed to complete these crucial goals. For instance, did Tim have to finish the liquor inventory, or could somebody else have done it? Was it so important and sensitive that it required the attention of a management person? Does Tim feel that in order to control the operation he has to complete the employee schedule? The busboy incident could have been handled by Bill, the head waiter. Someone from maintenance should have seen about the garbage and dishwashing machine. Clearly these kinds of duties could have been delegated to either an assistant manager or another person in authority such as the chef or head waiter; the manager has wasted valuable time doing the work of others. As many experts note, a manager who does not delegate is not managing.

We will now describe how the manager can delegate effectively. Where does this process begin? Analysis of the time log should be the first step. Before delegating tasks, the manager must identify where his or her time is being spent and which tasks could be performed by somebody else. Managers who delegate effectively follow the guidelines below.

BOX 6.3

Guidelines for Effective Delegation

- Establish targets and strategies that will lead to successful accomplishment of clearly defined visions and goals.
- Establish successful delegation experiences for their employees by shifting responsibilities gradually and praising successful accomplishment of these tasks.
- Create a cooperative working environment where coaching, tutoring, and mentoring relationships are a natural part of the delegation process.
- Provide employees with all of the necessary information and resources to accomplish the tasks delegated.
- Ensure that employees have a feeling of ownership and authority with the tasks they are given through clear directives, access to other aspects of the project, and clear feedback on the success of the task accomplished.
- Do not supervise too closely; employee initiative leads to creativity in the organization.
- Do not delegate only when you are overworked, but rather continuously.

Effective **delegation** is a prerequisite for building a smoothly operating team. This is because:

1. Delegation allows the manager more time for thinking and planning.
2. The person closest to the activity is best able to make decisions.
3. Delegation encourages subordinates' initiative and makes use of their skills.
4. Initiative, in turn, improves morale.
5. Delegation reduces decision-making time, as it eliminates the need to consult the superior.
6. Delegation develops subordinates skills by permitting them to apply knowledge gained from training programs and meetings.

The manager must remember that delegation involves the transfer of authority and decision-making, not of actual responsibility. There are different levels of delegation, and the manager must determine to what degree he or she wants to delegate authority. The degrees of delegation in Box 6.4 were developed by W. H. Nesbitt of Westinghouse Corporation:

BOX 6.4

Degrees of Delegation

1. Investigate and report back. The employee gathers facts; the manager then takes appropriate action.
2. Investigate and recommend action. The employee recommends action based on fact finding or specialized knowledge. The manager evaluates the recommendation and takes appropriate action.
3. Investigate and advise of action planned. The employee makes decisions based on investigation. The manager evaluates the decision and approves or disapproves.
4. Investigate and take action; advise of action taken. The manager gives employee control over decision; the manager requires reports to keep informed.
5. Investigate and take action. The manager allows the employee full control over decision making and has complete faith in the decision.

When delegating, the manager should be aware of certain limitations or rules. First, the delegating manager must follow through and find out the results of his or her delegation. This is important not only for the task itself but also for the manager's understanding of his or her subordinates' capabilities. The manager who delegates tasks beyond the scope of his or her employees defeats the ends of those tasks and negates the act of delegation in the eyes of the employees.

The delegating manager also needs to set standards of performance so that the subordinate can track his or her own progress toward completing the task. The manager must also develop ways by which to monitor the subordinate's progress. Such monitoring may take the form of written reports or verbal communication in meetings.

The delegating manager relinquishes many operational tasks. Although this frees up one's time for "managing," he or she is still responsible for the smooth running of the entire operation. By setting levels of operating performance, the manager can monitor the operation and be alerted to any abnormal changes.

You now know the degrees of delegation as well as its advantages and limitations. Time log analysis should give the manager a clear idea of how his or her time is being spent. Using the above guidelines, the manager can then investigate which tasks to do and which can be delegated. Think of tasks as falling into three categories. In the first category is work that can be done only by the manager. In the second is work that can be delegated immediately. In the third is work that can be delegated as soon as there is someone capable of accomplishing it. The manager should know the capabilities of his or her subordinates so that work in the second category can be delegated and accomplished immediately. The nature and amount of work in the third category will tell the manager what the staff's training needs are; as this training progresses, the manager will have more time for "managing." Once these two categories of work have been addressed, the manager can concentrate on eliminating the interruptions.

Is delegation something that can be learned, or does it just come more naturally to some people?

Eliminate Interruptions

In the hospitality industry, customer interruptions are a necessary and welcome aspect of the services we provide. These are not the interruptions we address in this section. Rather, managers must seek to eliminate unnecessary or inappropriate interruptions during the workday, while providing timely and attentive service to customers.

CALLS   A well-trained administrative assistant is the manager's first and most effective line of defense. Since occasional emergencies and other situations always arise, the administrative assistant needs to be able to distinguish important calls and be aware of key individuals the manager should speak to immediately. The manager needs to set aside a period at the end of the day for returning calls, since most people are in a hurry to leave the office and are far more inclined to adhere to the business at hand than to chat.

VISITORS   Another interrupter in the manager's workday is the unscheduled meeting or "walk-in" visitor. Restaurant managers often spend three and one-half times more on unscheduled meetings than other managers (35 percent versus 10 percent). In fact, such meetings take up more of the restaurant manager's day than any other single activity. Consequently, they must be reduced to the point where the manager is once again in control of his or her workday. If the visitor insists on seeing the manager, the manager should come out of one's office and meet the visitor on neutral ground, thus preventing the visitor from sitting down and tying up a long period of time. Should the visitor persist in idle conversation, the manager can begin his or her on-the-floor rounds, thus letting the visitor know politely but unmistakably that his or her time is up.

While an open-door policy is valuable for promoting open communications, the manager must have some uninterrupted work time. Many managers now find that it is beneficial to have a second office, or a hidden retreat where they can work uninterrupted for extended periods of time. Although a second office is not common in restaurants, where space is usually at a premium, a desk or a table in the attic or the basement would work. If this is not possible, the manager should spend certain mornings at home.

Scheduled meetings are a time waster for the restaurant manager that can be reduced through planning and prioritizing issues. Each time a meeting is held, a record of the time spent per person and the hourly salary of the persons attending should be kept. This can be tabulated to determine the total cost of the meeting and compared to the actual results or outcome of the meeting. If someone other than the manager calls the meeting, that person should be given a copy of the cost and should analyze the impact of it on the daily operating performance. The astute manager will be able to determine if the benefits derived from the meeting outweigh the costs. The probable outcome would be fewer meetings of a more productive nature.

All too often, meetings are held on an open basis so as to receive as much input as possible. Sometimes this can cause them to become unstructured rambling instead of the information forum that they were designed to be. To reduce the chance of a meeting getting out of control, the manager and staff must be well prepared before it commences. This task is in the control of the manager, who can set up detailed agendas to follow, and assign persons to comment on certain topics. Once the agenda is complete, the meeting should cease. If a topic outside the agenda arises, the manager should severely limit discussion of it and instead schedule those topics on the next agenda. If it is of extreme importance, it should be discussed with the appropriate people after the meeting has been concluded. This way, people who will not be involved can return to their own tasks and not have their time wasted. Before the meeting is adjourned, the manager should give a briefing as to the issues and responsibilities for the next meeting so each person will be prepared.

The manager should also be aware of other peoples' time. How often have you been asked to attend a meeting that wasted your time? Often a copy of the minutes is as informative as the meeting itself. Keep this in mind whenever you schedule a meeting. Require attendance only of those who will be contributing to the agenda and ask others if they would like to attend. This will allow others to evaluate how the meeting will affect their time and will prevent anyone from feeling left out.

If the meeting is informal, of short duration, and consists of only a few persons, the manager may elect to hold a "stand up" meeting. When required to stand throughout the meeting, people tend to say only what really needs to be said. This will help ensure that the meeting doesn't last longer than necessary.

PAPERWORK   Incoming paperwork is another problem faced by restaurant managers. One day's absence from the desk can result in a stack of correspondence and memos that takes two days to sort and answer. People seem actually to take advantage of the manager's day off to overload him or her with unusual amounts of material. This perception is true in a sense because throughout a working day, the manager is constantly sending verbal replies to the queries of others.

The manager can eliminate a large portion of wasted time by reviewing all incoming paperwork. While reviewing the paperwork, effective managers organize it into three categories: one that requires action, one that requires reading, and one that should be thrown out. When going through the first group (action category), the manager should respond to each one individually. Action should be taken before the next one is read. The second group (reading category) should be separated into two piles: those that require passing on and those that need filing. The third group should be discarded. The emphasis is on handling each piece of paper one time only.

Sometimes the work done by others that is submitted is inadequate and needs to be redone. The following proven strategies should alleviate the manager's burden of revising poor work:

1. Have your staff redo the work on the job.
2. Educate the staff to minimize problems in the future.
3. Make sure the staff person knows the job requirements and timetables.
4. Make sure people are not over–committed. Over-commitment leads to unfinished work and cutting corners.

MAIL   Once the manager is on a mailing list, amounts of junk mail seem to increase steadily. The administrative assistant can eliminate this problem also by opening all mail and forwarding only the important pieces. This can then be roughly sorted by the manager in order of importance and be dealt with appropriately. Another trick would be to use different forms of the restaurant's or manager's name when subscribing to publications, ordering them through vendors, and other correspondence. This will identify the source of the incoming mail and will help the sorting process in terms of importance.

In the past, what has been the most effective way of handling interruptions? Is there someone you know who interrupts you frequently? Are you dealing effectively with this situation?

TECHNOLOGY AND TIME

As today's college graduates enter the workforce, we can expect the use of all recent technologies, especially those readily accessible such as email and instant messaging to increase substantially for both internal and external communication (Strom, 2006; Blackwell, 2006). What does this increase mean for an employee's time management?

Prevalence of Individual's Technology Use

Statistics show that at least 10 percent of workers spend more than four hours a day on email. An important time management feature of this medium is what is called "broadcasting capability" or the vast number of recipients that can be reached with one message almost instantly.

Unlike email, instant messaging is akin to real-time chat and appears to be the technology of choice for today's busy hospitality professionals. With presence-awareness technology, IM programs indicate when someone is online, which increases the likelihood over email of getting an immediate response. Users also can set "away messages," which is like a do-not-disturb sign. The average IM lasts 20 seconds, making this communication technology an efficient way to get quick answers to quick questions.

Given its characteristics, it is not surprising that IM is becoming increasingly prevalent in the workplace, joining email as among the most frequently used business communication channels. The increasing workplace applications of these two technologies have profound implications for an individual employee's time management. While on the one hand they have the potential to save time, they also distract and often blur the distinction between personal and professional communications.

The BlackBerry also expands an individual's reach and connects to a company's server (Lake, 2005). Starwood, for example, offers guests in some hotels a device similar to a BlackBerry called StayInTouch. StayInTouch enables guests to contact the concierge as well as their buddy list from home through instant messaging. Employees can rely on a manager to be available through this type of wireless device nearly all of the time. This connection allows managers to answer quick questions, even while in a meeting or out of the office. Portable technologies expand the reach of those looking to stay in touch—everywhere.

Which technologies do you use regularly? Do you feel it helps or harms your time management?

Technology and Potential Time Management Concerns

There is no question that the new technology is pervasive and exploding, bringing with it individual-, unit-, and corporate-level time management challenges never before encountered in the hospitality workplace. Few recent developments have so clearly distinguished the Net Generation from their more senior counterparts. Recognition of the potential problems associated with runaway technology is growing. Fifty–eight percent of employees, for instance, admit sending IMs for personal use during the workday. As Primeaux and Flint (2004) suggest, the question becomes, "Should employers push IM out of the workplace, or encourage its use?"

Email and IM may not always be the most effective means for accomplishing workplace goals. Too often, communicators rely on channels with which they are familiar or which are the most efficient rather than those that best accomplish their purposes. A hospitality employee accustomed to contacting friends and family online may find it difficult to determine when a telephone call or a face-to-face meeting may be the most effective means of accomplishing the task.

There are many occasions where IM and email save time and create efficiencies. There are also many occasions, however, where the technology develops a life of its own and consumes its user. If every time an employee sits down to work, he or she checks email, this and similar habits can be a distraction and waste valuable time. Those who fail to organize their files may also find that much time is spent looking for past communications.

Increased Organizational Responsiveness to Time Management Needs

Increasingly technology plays a role in organizational flexibility and in the company's ability to respond to employee time requirements. While in some instances such advances may depersonalize the organizational environment, computerized workstations and other developments make new options available to those who require alternative work routines and more flexible work schedules. The need for all employees to work long hours or at a particular workstation is reduced; a variety of tasks may be performed at home when computers are linked and employees are online. Work can more easily be shared when databases are established and readily accessed. Although guest contact will remain a critical aspect of service delivery, an increasing number of functions in the hospitality industry will likely be streamlined and automated.

BALANCING WORK AND FAMILY

Management positions produce significant time management challenges as employees attempt to balance family and career. The demands of a supervisory role and the requirements for job advancement have created significant obstacles for hospitality professionals who aspire to senior-level positions. This is due, in part, to the nature of the hospitality workplace itself.

Characteristics of the Hospitality Workplace

The unique characteristics of hospitality organizations make them among the most challenging for employees who seek to advance their careers while maintaining active involvement in family activities. Literature that addresses challenges in the hospitality workplace has established this industry as among the most demanding (Brownell, 1994). What factors make the hospitality industry so difficult?

In many instances, the hospitality culture contributes to interactions that family-oriented employees find stressful. Long and irregular hours cut into family time. Since promotions and job advancement frequently require relocation, many hospitality employees experience pressing financial concerns. In addition, issues affecting women in the workplace appear particularly significant to hospitality employees as they strive to balance work and home responsibilities.

Hospitality employees find themselves confronted with continuous crises and a great deal of daily uncertainty. Uncertainty creates high levels of job stress. Service delivery in the hospitality industry is a matter of meeting guests' expectations and responding appropriately to unanticipated events. Problems arise in the kitchen that require immediate attention; twenty more guests attend the banquet than were expected; the computer creates serious over-booking problems; a guest slips and falls on the diving board. Due to this uncertainty and the reactive nature of service delivery, hospitality management is not a 9:00 a.m. to 5:00 p.m. job. Success in the industry demands long hours and requires a great deal of crisis management and problem solving.

Financial concerns are also key for employees with family responsibilities. Wages in hospitality organizations are generally below those found in other types of industries. This makes expenses associated with child care and other family necessities particularly stressful.

Advancement Opportunities and Time Requirements

Employees realize that there are opportunities for them to advance in this rapidly growing industry, but they often feel that the requirements—long hours, stress, loss of quality time with their family—are not worth the potential benefits of a hospitality career. The hospitality litera-ture is now rich with first-hand accounts of men and women, at all levels, who have pursued careers while attending to family concerns (Witham, 1992; Umbreit and Diaz, 1994). Trends of the twenty-first century are likely to increase, not reduce, the work and family tensions that have been building for several decades.

The Importance of Family Time

It would be misleading to assume that family and work balance is only a woman's concern. One study concluded that eight out of ten employees would choose a position that provides time for their family over fast-tracked career advancement or better salaries. Over half of all men typically report that they experience family and job conflict. The problems of making time for family responsibilities are especially profound for the increasing numbers of single parents in the hospitality workforce.

While managers have always looked ahead at managing relationships that affect their spouse and their children, new demographics now require them to look back as they become primary caregivers to their parents as well. The number of those in mid-career who must be concerned with the welfare of an aging family member is increasing steadily. The cost of managing family relationships across generations makes home life particularly stressful for those in the middle.

As employees work longer, and as retired workers reenter the workforce, attention to life stages is a particularly critical concern. Although single parents, teenagers, and the elderly may work side-by-side, their personal needs for time may vary dramatically. The "workaholic" generation is being replaced by young people who seek quality of life and insist that their work does not consume their entire life. While their supervisors and older co–workers describe them as "indifferent" toward the workplace or "selfish" about their personal needs, the shift in demographics may well be accompanied by even more family-friendly policies and the flexibility that allows employees to feel comfortable managing their personal and professional lives.

The Organizational Impact of Work/Family Time Issues

Stress from balancing personal and work responsibilities is likely to result in substantially reduced performance as employees suffer the consequences of anxiety and depression. Family balance is becoming one of the most critical issues of the twenty-first century. Family problems that become time management problems in the workplace threaten a company's competitiveness and profitability. While organizations may talk of sensitivity to employee needs, no company is likely to ignore its bottom line. Researchers repeatedly conclude that the difficulties faced in managing personal and work responsibilities frequently result in reduced performance.

Progressive organizations are beginning to understand the strong link between work/family balance and productivity. Organizations of the future are likely to discover that their competitive edge is not in salary or facilities, but in their responsiveness to the growing emphasis on family concerns.

> What do you anticipate as your most difficult work–family balance issue? Can you take measures to reduce this conflict?

Summary

In this chapter we have shown the manager how to break old habits, how to delegate tasks, and how to eliminate interrupters. With proper implementation, we are confident that even good time managers will benefit from these techniques. It all begins with the time log and a proper analysis of how time is spent. Though itself time-consuming, the time log will produce lasting benefits in better habits, more effective delegation, and fewer interruptions.

Where does the manager go from here? The answer is simple. The manager must use the freed time to manage, that is, in planning, organizing, coordinating, and controlling. The manager must be prepared to take these "new" blocks of time and use them to plan for the future.

Eleven Hints for Effective Time Management

1. Write down a daily list of things to do; make a new one each day.
2. Implement a quiet hour for thinking, planning, and doing important tasks.
3. Group similar tasks.
4. Set short- and long-term goals with deadlines for each.
5. Set priorities on a daily basis. Rank tasks in order of priority of importance.
6. Do the important tasks; delegate the urgent and not-so-urgent. Avoid over-committing yourself.

(continued)

(continued)

7. Organize the paperwork: things requiring action, things to be read and passed on, things that can be thrown out.
8. Avoid procrastination.
9. Do unpleasant, distasteful, or dreaded tasks first.
10. Recognize when you are wasting time and take appropriate action.
11. Control the interruptions (phone calls, meetings, drop-in visitors).

Source: Adapted from Mishra and Misra, 1982

Key Words

time management *150*
interrupters *150*
interrupt mode *152*

time analysis *153*
goal priority *157*

procrastination *158*
delegation *160*

Exercises

Exercise 1   Beating Procrastination

Objectives

- To recognize signs of procrastination
- To identify ways to overcome procrastination

Number of Participants: 10–30 participants in a group

Time Frame: 30 minutes

Materials:

- "Self-assessment: Am I a Procrastinator?" worksheet for each participant
- "Analyze Your Procrastination" worksheet for each participant
- Flip chart and markers

Procedure:

1. Review the material on procrastination. Give participants five minutes to fill out "Self-Assessment: Am I a Procrastinator?"
2. Ask for a show of hands for those who scored 6 or more points under the first column, then 4 or more points under the first column. Write the numbers on a flip chart. Identify this group as people who may find work on beating procrastination particularly helpful. Emphasize that we may have time management deficiencies we don't recognize and that those who did not score high may still find it useful to practice behaviors that will help them avoid procrastination.
3. Ask participants to form small groups of four to six members. Direct them to review their responses and discuss specific examples of times they demonstrated the various behaviors listed on the assessment.
4. Ask participants to focus on **one** of the examples generated by the group, and to develop a plan that would have helped to overcome procrastination in that particular case. Groups that finish early may move on to another example.
5. Tell participants to spend a few minutes looking over the worksheet, "Analyze Your Procrastination." Ask them to jot down notes to themselves in the blanks, and then to share some of their thoughts and advice with other members of their group.

***

SELF-ASSESSMENT: AM I A PROCRASTINATOR?

	Agree	Neutral	Disagree
1. I invent reasons and look for excuses for not acting on a really tough problem.	_____	_____	_____
2. It takes pressure to get me to move on with a complex assignment.	_____	_____	_____
3. I take half measures which will avoid or delay unpleasant action.	_____	_____	_____
4. There are too many interruptions and crises that interfere with my accomplishing big jobs.	_____	_____	_____
5. I avoid forthright answers when pressed for an unpleasant decision.	_____	_____	_____
6. I have been guilty of neglecting follow-up aspects of important action plans.	_____	_____	_____
7. I try to get other people to do unpleasant assignments for me.	_____	_____	_____
8. I often feel too tired (upset, nervous, etc.) to do the large and difficult tasks that face me.	_____	_____	_____
Total Responses	_____	_____	_____

(continued)

If you checked "agree" three or more times it's likely that you're procrastinating more than your colleagues. The news is that simply increasing your awareness of procrastination is the first step in overcoming this tendency.

***

ANALYZE YOUR PROCRASTINATION

1. Think of the kinds of tasks that you are most likely to put off.
2. Is there a common pattern? Do you put off tasks that involve figures? That involve conveying bad news? That will result in interpersonal conflict?
3. Identify your most common "delay tactics."

   1.

   2.

   3.

   4.

4. How can you use the techniques you have learned so far to "fight" procrastination?

Experiment to find solutions that work for you!

***

Exercise 2   Personal Tendencies and Time Management

Objective: To identify personal tendencies that affect time management behaviors

Number of Participants: 10–30 participants

Time Frame: 30 minutes

Materials: Flip chart, markers, "Personal Tendencies and Time Management" worksheet

Procedure:

1. Ask group members to think about their typical responses to situations and to select the word that best describes their behavior: *procrastinator*, *perfectionist*, or *impulsive*. Remind them that this is a *forced choice*. Even if they feel all words equally characterize their behavior, they must select just one for the purposes of this exercise.
2. Distribute the "Personal Tendencies and Time Management" worksheet. Ask group members to reflect on their choice and to think of some examples of how they have demonstrated their behavior at work. These examples should be noted on their worksheets.
3. Put participants into small groups according to the adjective they selected. You may have two or

three groups representing one of the adjectives and only one group for another of the adjectives. Groups should have from three to five members. (If only one person has selected one of the adjectives, have them make another choice so they have discussion opportunities.)

4. Ask groups to spend approximately five minutes talking about how the adjective they selected describes their behavior.
5. Then, ask each group to generate a list of the time management problems individuals who exhibit their particular characteristic are *likely* to have. This does not mean that each group member feels he or she experiences this problem, just that such a problem may arise because of the personal characteristic. Groups have another ten minutes to complete this aspect of the activity.
6. Ask one member from each group to report on the potential time management problems his or her group generated. Record the problems on a flip chart and discuss. Remind participants to be aware of the potential time management problems associated with their particular tendency.

***

PERSONAL TENDENCIES AND TIME MANAGEMENT

1. Which adjective best describes your behavior?

   Procrastinator

   Perfectionist

   Impulsive

2. Record some specific examples of when you demonstrated this characteristic at work.
3. What time management problems *might* this personal tendency cause?
4. Which of the above potential time management problems have *you* experienced?

***

Exercise 3   My Style, My Time

Objectives

- To encourage participants to consider their personal style and how it influences their time management
- To encourage participants to view their behaviors creatively
- To provide an opportunity for participants to compare and contrast their style with others', and to discuss some of the characteristics that may influence their time management

Number of Participants: Up to 40 participants in each group

Time Frame: 30 minutes

Materials:

- "Open-Ended Choices" sheet for each participant
- Flip Chart and markers

Physical Setting: Flexible seating for small groups

Procedure:

1. Distribute the "Open-Ended Choices" sheet and ask participants to select the item that best describes them. Some participants will have trouble doing this exercise because they think literally about their behavior. It may be necessary to give some examples regarding why an individual might choose, for instance, "here" over "there." Emphasize that this is a forced choice. Participants must select one of the items in each pair.
2. Ask participants to give some thought to their choices and jot down some of the reasons why they selected each alternative. A "Public Fishing" person, for instance, may talk about the fact that he or she always likes other people around and doesn't mind it when others use his or her desk, supplies, etc. A "No Trespassing" person, on the other hand, may become stressed when others stand too close or he or she may have a high need for privacy.
3. Ask all participants to stand in a straight line in the center of the room. Take each pair of items in turn, and ask participants who chose the first item to take a step to their right, and those who chose the second item to take a step to their left. After you have gone through the list, note those pairs where you had a fairly even split among participants.
4. Select one pair of items and ask participants to form small groups with others who agreed with their choice. For instance, all "yes" people would be together and all "no" people would be together.
5. Allow approximately ten minutes for participants to briefly share why they chose the item they did, and then to talk about its implications for their time management. One participant from each group is asked to summarize the group's findings.
6. Record the potential time management concerns generated by each group on a flip chart.
7. Repeat this process with one or two more pairs: Ask participants to gather in small groups according to their choices (four or five people per group), discuss the item, and then report to the larger group. Record the group's summary on a flip chart.
8. Close the activity by asking participants to summarize what they learned about themselves and how their personal style may affect their time management.
9. Ask participants to set a personal goal regarding either some action they can take or some behavior they would like to modify to manage their time more effectively.

***

OPEN-ENDED CHOICES

Thinking Creatively About Yourself and Your Time

Are You More . . .	
A Leader	A Follower
Public Fishing	No Trespassing
Yes	No
Here	There
Rose	Daisy
Now	Later
Just coming	Just going

***

Exercise 4   Values Auction

Objectives

- To become more aware of your values and the extent to which your values and your behavior are consistent
- To compare your values with those of other session participants

Number of Participants: Up to 40 participants in each group

Time Frame: 30 minutes

Materials:

- A "Values Auction for Time Management" sheet for each participant.

Procedure:

1. Lead a general discussion and review of the importance of identifying personal and organizational values.
2. Explain that everyone will attend a values auction where various values will be auctioned to the highest bidder.
3. Distribute copies of the "Values Auction for Time Management" sheets, and review the directions. Ask if anyone has questions.
4. Allow approximately five minutes for participants to review the list of values and to estimate the amount they will bid on each item.
5. Display a copy of the "Values Auction for Time Management" sheet, where you will record the amount spent on each item.
6. Begin the bidding. Take bids until no one raises the amount. Then, record the amount of the top bid and the name of the person who got the item. Continue for each item.
7. When the bidding is over, lead a discussion of the following questions:
   - Who did not end up with any items? How does that person feel?
   - Which item went for the most money? Why do you think that is?
   - How close was your estimate to the amount you actually ended up bidding on various items? What explains the discrepancies?
   - How did bidding on values make you feel? Was it upsetting to only be able to bid on some of items and not others?
   - How did you make decisions about which items to bid on?
8. Ask for general comments and questions from the group.

***

A VALUES AUCTION FOR TIME MANAGEMENT

You have in front of you twenty 10 dollar bills—$200. You can spend this money in whatever way you wish to try to "buy" items on the list below. You must spend the money in $10 units, and must use the entire sum in making your "estimate" list. When involved in the actual auction, however, you are free to adjust your estimates and spend the money in another way.

	Actual	Estimate
1. Assertive ability		
2. Unlimited office space		
3. Unlimited patience on the job		
4. Ability to delegate		
5. Greater ability to relax		
6. Magic to overcome procrastination		
7. A perfectly organized workplace		
8. A terrific sense of humor		
9. A more carefree attitude		
10. Two hours a day for yourself		

***

Endnotes

Berger, F. & Merritt, E. (1998). No time left for you: Time-management strategies for restauranteurs. *Cornell Hotel and Restaurant Administration Quarterly, 39*(5), 33.

Blackwell, L. (2006). Instant messengers grow up and go to work. *PC World, 24*(2), 66.

Brownell, J. (1994). Women in hospitality management: General managers' perceptions of factors related to career development. *International Journal of Hospitality Management, 13*(2), 101–117.

Buchanan, R. (1977). How to effectively delegate. *Food Service Marketing, 39*(12), 54–56.

Cooper, E. (2004). Make your time pay: How can you squeeze more productivity out of the work day? Here's how one broker uses technology to maximize his time. *On Wall Street, 14*(7), 1–2.

Dobbs, R. & Gibbs, J. (2003). How has technology changed the way you allocate your time? *Texas Banking, 92*(6), 33–35.

Donkin, R. (March 29, 2001). Communications leave senses working overtime: E-mail and mobile phone technology are contributing to diminished attention in the workplace, but there are ways to cope: [Surveys edition]. *Financial Times,* 10. Retrieved January 27, 2008, from ABI/INFORM Global database.

Douglas, M. & Baker, L. (1984). *Time Mastery Profile.* New York: Performax Systems International, Inc.

Drucker, P. (1961). How to be an effective executive. *Nation's Business, 49*(4), 34–37.

Fulford, M. D. & Herrick, A. (1994). Women at work in hospitality: Fair notice for the nineties. *Hospitality and Tourism Educator, 6*(4), 25–30.

Glasgow, F. (1995). Mobility matters. *Resident Abroad,* 20–23.

Godin, S. (1995). *Wisdom, Inc.: 26 Business Virtues That Turn Ordinary People into Extraordinary Leaders.* New York, NY: HarperCollins Publishers, Inc.

Gold, S. & Poftak, A. (2004). 7 time-saving tools. *Technology and Learning, 24*(11), 18–29.

Kelly, K. & Kelly, J. (1994). Multiple dimensions of meaning in the domains of work, family, and leisure. *Journal of Leisure Research, 26*(3), 250–274.

Kridel, M. (2002). Time management and technology: Two steps forward and one step back? *Infotech Update, 11*(3), 1–4.

Lake, M. (2005). *How BlackBerry Conquered the World*. CNN. March 23, 2005. Retrieved on March 26, 2006 from http://www.cnn.com/2005/BUSINESS/03/23/blackberry.rim/.

Leahy, T. (2004). The technology transformation. *Business Finance, 10*(4), 19–23.

Mackenzie, R. A. (1972). *The Time Trap*. New York: McGraw-Hill.

McGirt, E. (2006). Getting out from under. *Fortune, 153*(5), 89–94.

Mcginn, D. (2007). Taming to-dos: A new book offers tech tips for working smarter. *Newsweek, 149*(4), E.06.

Nichols, J. (2001). The Ti-Mandi Window: A time-management tool for managers. *Industrial and Commercial Training, 33*(3), 104–109.

Olsen, F. (2006). Time management in a BlackBerry world. *Federal Computer Week, 20*(1), 46–49.

Primeaux, R. O. & Flint, D. (2004). Instant messaging: Does it belong in the workplace? *Intellectual Property and Technology Law Journal, 16*(11), 5–7.

Rowh, M. (2006). Beat the clock. *Career World, 35*(3), 24–27.

Saunders, C., Van Slyke, C., & Vogel, D. (2004). My time or yours? Managing time visions in global virtual teams. *The Academy of Management Executive, 18*(1), 19–33.

Towers, I., Duxury, L, Higgins, C., & Thomas, J. (2006). Time thieves and space invaders: Technology, work and the organization. *Journal of Organizational Change Management, 19*(5), 593–607.

Umbreit, W. & Diaz, P. (1994). Women in hospitality management: An exploratory study of major and occupational choice variables. *Hospitality Tourism Education, 6*(4), 7–9.

Witham, G. (1992). A crack in the ceiling: Sills named president of colony resorts. *Cornell Hotel and Restaurant Administration Quarterly, 33*(1), 9.

Spira, J. (2005). The high cost of interruptions. *KM World, 14*(8), 1–3.

Strom D. (April 5, 2006). I.M. Generation is Changing the Way Business Talks. *New York Times*, G4.

Welterten, M. (2003). Technology time management. *Grounds Maintenance, 38*(9), 4–6.

Whetten, D. & Cameron, K. C. (2002). *Developing Management Skills*. Fifth Edition. New York: Harper Collins.

7

MANAGING STRESS

If you ask what is the single most important key to longevity, I would have to say it is avoiding worry, stress and tension. And if you didn't ask me, I'd still have to say it.

—George Burns (1896–1996)

CHAPTER OUTLINE

Introduction

The Nature and Role of Stress
    The Nature of Stress
    The Role of Stress
    The Forbes Continuum of Underload/Overload

The Consequences of Excessive Stress
    Physiological Consequences
        Heart disease
        Hypertension
        Headache
        Formation of ulcers
    Psychological Consequences
        Anxiety
        Depression
        Sleep disturbances
    Behavioral Consequences
        Increased smoking
        Alcohol and drug abuse
        Accident proneness
        Violent tendencies
        Eating disorders

Stress in Individuals
    How We Cause Our Own Stress
    The Effects of Change and Uncertainty
    Individual Differences and Stress
    Type A Personality and Stress
    Take Responsibility for Reducing Your Stress

The Importance of Managing Stress
    Internal Control Techniques
        Relaxation response
        Meditation
        Stress inoculation
        Humor as a stress reliever
    External Control Techniques
        Time management
        Exercise
        Diet and nutrition

Hospitality Industry Innovations
    Wellness Programs
    Training Management to Deal with Employee Stress
    Hotel Spas
    Restaurant Offerings
    Hospital Stress Management and Stress Reduction for Patients and Staff

Summary

LEARNING OBJECTIVES

After you read this chapter, you will be able to do the following:

1. Explain the nature and role of stress.
2. Identify the consequences of excessive stress.
3. Describe at least two manifestations each of physiological stress, psychological stress, and behavioral stress.
4. Discuss the importance of managing stress.
5. Contrast internal control techniques with external control techniques.
6. Demonstrate the relaxation response, progressive muscle relaxation, and other internal control techniques.
7. Explain the stress inoculation technique.
8. Delineate the multiple benefits of external control techniques in addition to stress management.
9. Present industry trends in the management of stress in at least three sectors of the hospitality industry such as hospitals, hotels, and restaurants.

Scenario for Application: Simmering Stress

Judith is the general manager of a hotel in a metropolitan area. This hotel caters to tourists and business travelers, and has convention facilities. The past summer had been particularly busy with a record number of conventions booked and the hotel running at near capacity. One of the most recent convention groups had been particularly difficult to satisfy, complaining about everything from the size of the tables in the conference rooms to not enough juice variety on the breakfast buffet.

Judith sensed an escalating level of tension and deteriorating morale among her staff. Several staff members had complained to her about the increased workload. There had been a heated argument among three members of the kitchen staff that required management intervention. The incidence of employee sick leave had increased, and even on the job, several employees regularly suffered from headaches and chronic flu symptoms.

Suspecting that stress was a developing problem among her staff, Judith decided to hold a series of meetings with employees in the different work areas of the hotel to explore this concern further. At these meetings, employees were asked to air their concerns about the circumstances that were creating stress in their jobs. As might be expected, there were a vocal few expressing the most obvious concerns, or else small personal concerns. Breaking these meetings into small group brainstorming sessions yielded better results, and Judith felt she was getting a clear picture of the stress problems among her staff.

Using the information collected in these meetings and in meetings with middle managers, Judith concluded that job-related stress was a serious problem in several areas of the hotel staff and that she needed to help resolve this situation before it led to a decline in what was otherwise a very successful year for her hotel. After identifying the problem, she sought the help of a consultant well versed in handling job stress issues. This consultant was a faculty member at a local university who taught courses on job stress and organizational behavior.

(continued)

(continued)

The first step was to initiate an anonymous survey to complete the picture that Judith had begun. This survey indicated that, in addition to the stresses already identified, employees felt they were often put to blame for an error made by a manager or by a client. There seemed to be a sense of powerlessness among the staff in general, and the middle managers did seem to lack confidence in their employees. After reviewing all of the information and touring the facility, the consultant suggested offering several workshops to educate the staff and the management about job stress—its causes, effects, and prevention. Analysis of the survey data suggested that three types of job conditions were linked to stress complaints among workers (Farren, 1999):

1. unequal and sometimes unrealistic workloads;
2. low levels of support from supervisors; and
3. lack of worker involvement in decision making.

Having pinpointed these problems, Judith and the consultant developed and prioritized a list of actions to correct the sources of stress. Examples of these actions included:

- greater participation of employees in work scheduling to reduce unrealistic workloads;
- preshift meetings between workers and managers to establish clear communication and give workers the opportunity for input on situations as they arise; and
- ongoing workshops on stress management techniques.

What are some of the most stressful situations you encounter? Identify and describe two of them.

INTRODUCTION

The hospitality industry is an inherently stressful environment because employees have to work when their peers don't: weekends, nights, holidays. In addition to long, late hours, employees have to be "on" all of the time. Tuning into the customer's needs: does the customer want a leisurely meal or does she just want to be in and out as quickly as possible? Hospitality employees have to check their emotional baggage at the door. The repercussions of a server raising his or her voice in frustration to a guest are far greater than if a mechanic kicks an automobile bumper when he or she makes a mistake. In a hotel the front desk staff must avoid the "top of the head" syndrome as they relate to the computer for check-in purposes rather than making eye contact with the guest checking in. Face-to-face contact with clientele adds an element of stress to any industry, but is particularly critical in the hospitality industry as so much of the business is generated by goodwill. Employees are the primary means of generating goodwill.

THE NATURE AND ROLE OF STRESS

Stress in the workplace has become a major problem with significant ramifications for corporate profits and employee well-being. As a result of employee stress, companies are experiencing costly problems such as employee turnover, higher rates of absenteeism, and decrease in morale. The National Safety Council and the American Institute of Stress estimate that as many as one million employee absences every day are stress–related, and that stress plays a major factor in 80 percent of work-related injuries and in 40 percent of workplace turnover. According to the American Institute of Stress and the American Psychological Association, stress costs organizations many billions of dollars a year.

The growing incidence of stress in industry is mainly attributable to two factors:

1. increasing competitiveness in businesses and
2. inability of most managers to manage stress in their workplaces.

There is little managers can do about the increasing competitiveness in the business world. Rather, managers need to learn to control the level of stress in their own working lives and the working lives of their employees by being aware of the nature of stress, its role and importance, the consequences of excessive stress, and techniques for controlling stress. The more managers are aware of the need to control stress in their workplace, the better equipped they are for dealing with both the stress in their own working lives and the stress in their employees' lives.

In the following sections, we will first explore the nature of stress and how the body reacts to it. Then we will discuss the importance and role of stress, followed by a discussion on the consequences of excessive stress. Last, we will present methods and techniques that hospitality managers can utilize to manage stress in the workplace effectively.

The Nature of Stress

For our purposes a stressful situation can be defined as any threatening external stimulus that elicits an immediate response from the body. Such a response, commonly known as the **stress response,** consists of a pattern of physiological and biochemical responses that originally had survival value in primitive times. For example, primitive humans facing stress in the form of an approaching saber-toothed tiger reacted by fighting it or by running away. Accordingly, the stress response is also known as the **fight or flight response.**

The body of a person faced with a stressful situation reacts in the following ways in order to prepare the person either to "fight" or to take "flight:"

1. The body's respiration increases so that more oxygen is provided to the blood.
2. The heart pumps faster to redirect more blood to the muscles and brain. Consequently, blood pressure increases.
3. The muscles tense and there is an increased sense of alertness.
4. There is a release of increased amounts of glucose and fatty acids from their storage sites into the bloodstream to provide extra energy that may be needed.
5. Adrenaline is secreted and circulated around the body to put all body parts on ready alert.

From the above reactions, we can see that the body generates a good amount of energy during the "fight or flight" response. Therefore, if the energy generated is continuously utilized ineffectively, the body will eventually suffer. It is therefore imperative for managers to manage the level of stress in their workplace in order to modulate the stress responses. Managers need to understand how the stress in their lives can be managed to enable their employees and themselves to achieve a high level of productivity.

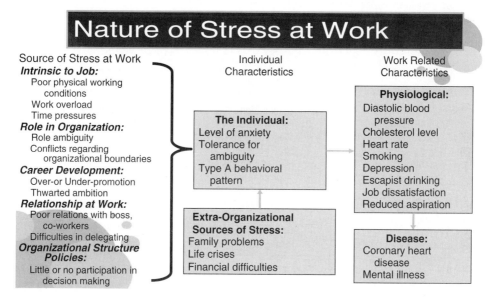

FIGURE 7.1 Nature of stress at work

Figure 7.1 indicates how the interaction of workplace stressors and individual characteristics can result in physical manifestations of stress.

The Role of Stress

Adopting the right attitude can convert a negative stress into a positive one.

—Dr. Hans Selye

Although **stress** is a naturally occurring event in everyone's lives, it is a common notion that stress is a bad thing. Actually, stress and its consequent responses are not, in and of themselves, a problem. In fact, a certain amount of stress can have a positive influence on productivity. When properly managed, the stress response can lead to improved performance.

It is important to note here that different people require different levels of stress to motivate and stimulate them to optimum performance. What constitutes excessive stress to one person may be a normal amount to another person. However, for all individuals, there is a breaking point in the correlation between stress and performance at which the amount of stress becomes counterproductive. If the body is stressed too frequently and too intensely, it reaches a state of exhaustion. The body's exhausted state can cause a person to tire mentally as well, thus clouding one's thinking, impairing proper decision making, and generally lowering one's performance. Individuals vary with respect to the level of stress their bodies can handle before they suffer negative effects.

How much stress do you find optimal? Do you become disoriented easily, or do you need a good amount of stress to stay motivated?

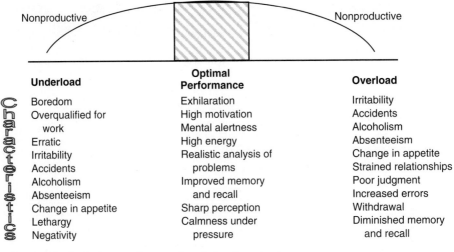

	Underload	Optimal Performance	Overload

C
h
a
r
a
c
t
e
r
i
s
t
i
c
s
	Boredom
	Overqualified for
	   work
	Erratic
	Irritability
	Accidents
	Alcoholism
	Absenteeism
	Change in appetite
	Lethargy
	Negativity
		Exhilaration
		High motivation
		Mental alertness
		High energy
		Realistic analysis of
		   problems
		Improved memory
		   and recall
		Sharp perception
		Calmness under
		   pressure
			Irritability
			Accidents
			Alcoholism
			Absenteeism
			Change in appetite
			Strained relationships
			Poor judgment
			Increased errors
			Withdrawal
			Diminished memory
			   and recall

FIGURE 7.2 The Forbes continuum of underload/overload

The Forbes Continuum of Underload/Overload

An effective manager watches for signs that the employees are operating under an acceptable level of stress. Figure 7.2 is useful in identifying behaviors and characteristics that are indicative of stress levels among employees. Note that some behaviors, such as absenteeism, are identified under both underloaded and overloaded individuals. Judgments must be made on a collection of evidence rather than the identification of a single characteristic.

It is important for managers to note that stress can be harnessed for beneficial effects. It can be managed through an understanding of how excessive stress manifests itself. In order to do this, managers need to be cognizant of the behavioral, psychological, and physiological consequences of mismanaged stress. In the following section, we discuss these three major categories in detail.

THE CONSEQUENCES OF EXCESSIVE STRESS

Prolonged periods of stress can result in a state of **distress,** in which individuals can face damaging consequences to both their mental and physical well-being. The many adverse consequences of excessive stress can be classified as **physiological, psychological,** and **behavioral.**

Physiological Consequences

In recent years there has been an increased amount of research into the relationship between stress and diseases such as heart disease, stroke, cancer, asthma, hypertension, diabetes, headache, and back pain. Here, we explore four of the body's responses to stress: heart disease, hypertension, headache, and formation of ulcers.

HEART DISEASE Work stress was directly linked to heart disease and diabetes in a major British study (Aboa-Éboulé et al., 2007). In fact, men in stressful positions for 14 years or more were almost twice as likely to develop heart disease and diabetes as those not in stressful work environments. The researchers emphasized that it's not just concerning people who report being stressed at work, it's also about an individual's sense of control, the pace of work, and the extent to which the individual has support in the workplace. Managers have to oversee these three dynamics with respect to their employees. When a manager perceives an employee to be suffering from stress, he or she must make an effort to adjust the amount of control an employee has over tasks, provide additional support for the employee, or adjust the pace of the employee's tasks.

HYPERTENSION   Hypertension is one of the most obvious consequences of prolonged stress. For example, one 20-year study concluded that men at the highest levels on the stress scale were twice as likely to have high blood pressure as those with normal stress. The effects of stress on women's blood pressure are less well documented. Such factors as high job stress and lack of career success have been linked to high blood pressure in both men and women. High blood pressure forces the heart to work harder as it pumps blood through constricted arteries. This pressure on the arteries may cause kidney failure, liver disease, cardiovascular disorders, as well as ruptured blood vessels, and the resulting aneurysms can be fatal (Aboa-Éboulé et al., 2007).

HEADACHE   Stress is an identified trigger for headaches, including migraine headaches. Hard work followed by a period of relaxation can cause a phenomenon referred to by the Mayo Clinic as the **weekend migraine.** Managers should be aware of this type of stress-related headache. Overstressed employees may be having little or no recovery from their job if an exhausting workweek is alternating with weekends filled with suffering (Quick et al., 1997).

FORMATION OF ULCERS   In spite of recent research which cites the presence of *Helicobacter pylori* as the sole cause of ulcers, or lesions in the inner wall lining of the stomach, ulcers can result from the higher production of stomach acids that stress may cause. Current thinking focuses on the relationship between stress and the presence of *H. pylori.* Ulcer attacks are associated with stress and frustration; attacks are often triggered by major stressor events like death of spouses, divorces, and getting fired from jobs. Patients suffering from ulcers report increased pain in stressful times, and ulcers are more resistant to treatment in times of stress (Levenstein, 1998).

It is important to note here that the above physiological consequences could have purely physical causes like improper diet and lack of exercise. It is advisable for the individual to see a doctor to determine if the causes are physical or stress related, or a combination of both.

What physical signs of stress do you experience?

Psychological Consequences

> Anyone who wishes to combine domestic responsibilities and paid employment with the least stress and most enjoyment might start by pondering this: the first step to better functioning is to stop blaming herself for not functioning well enough.
>
> —Faye J. Crosby (1991)

Though psychological effects of stress may seem less physically dangerous than some of the more obvious physical consequences, these effects may be equally destructive, particularly in an instance where a cycle begins with stress leading to depression or anxiety, which promotes further stress, and so on, until the individual finds himself or herself in a psychological state requiring professional treatment. Here we explore the most common psychological consequences of stress: anxiety, depression, and sleep disturbances.

> It pays to manage your stress as if your life depended upon the outcome—which, as we are finding more and more every day, it does.
>
> —John McNamany

ANXIETY   Although anxiety and stress are two completely different things, anxiety is one psychological manifestation of stress. **Anxiety** can be defined as an "anticipatory tension or vague dread persisting in the absence of a specific threat. In contrast to **fear,** which is a realistic reaction to actual danger, anxiety is generally related to an unconscious threat" (*Columbia Encyclopedia*, 2006). Anxiety and worry in small amounts can be motivating factors to deal with a concern or make a necessary change. While a small amount of anxiety can produce a beneficial amount of adrenaline, some individuals may experience a more long-term form of anxiety that is detrimental to productivity and general well-being. When anxiety fails to motivate, or becomes an inhibiting force, it has reached an unhealthy level.

A 2006 study (PRNewswire.com) of stress and anxiety found that persistent and excessive anxiety can contribute to unhealthy behavior patterns. Over 70 percent of men and women say that persistent and excessive stress or anxiety prompts them to avoid interacting with other people. Women are significantly more likely to say it precipitates overeating (54 versus 39 percent for men) and compulsive shopping (35 versus 17 percent for men), while men are more likely to abuse drugs or alcohol (31 versus 18 percent for women).

DEPRESSION   Depression appears to result from prolonged anxiety, and the two are closely related. Externally, depression seems to be a quiet state. However, according to Dr. Robert Sapolsky (2003), the helplessness of depression is actually active, twitching, draining, and energy-consuming. **Depression** is a condition characterized by feelings of persistent sadness, guilt, disinterest in previous activities or interests, and irritability. In a depressive disorders study (Lart & Wallace, 2002), researchers found that depression, which is a common response to stress, costs American business over $44 billion a year.

When employees are suffering from either anxiety or depression, it would help if management were more aware of the debilitating effects of these conditions. Engaging in depression-lifting activities like exercise, meditation, or even humor therapy may be beneficial.

SLEEP DISTURBANCES   Although adequate sleep is especially important during times of high stress, people often experience insomnia just before a stressful event, such as a major conference, an overbooking during the holidays, or an impending deadline. However, prolonged bouts of excessive stress will lead to chronic insomnia if the stress is not managed effectively.

People under tremendous stress are often unable to establish their biorhythm in relation to their sleeping times. This may be especially true in the hospitality industry where employees are needed around the clock and many may work swing shifts leading to abnormal sleep patterns. They do not sleep until late at night and as a result are unable to maintain wakefulness during the day when it is most required. Sleep deprivation has a negative effect on mood and performance. This will aggravate the stressful situation that causes the insomnia in the first place. Lack of sleep can lead to depression, errors in everyday tasks, and problems in memory recall. Managers need to recognize that stress at work may result in employee insomnia and be prepared to intervene and advise employees on successful insomnia-reducing strategies. These strategies may include the stress-reducing techniques found in this chapter, or adjusting work schedules to promote more regular sleep patterns for employees suffering from insomnia.

Behavioral Consequences

Behavioral consequences of excessive stress are the subtle and sometimes not-so-subtle ways behavior changes in response to the prolonged stress. The most common changes are increased smoking, alcohol and drug abuse, accident proneness, violent tendencies, and eating disorders.

INCREASED SMOKING   One of the most notable effects of stress on behavior is an increased tendency to smoke. Many tobacco users cite workplace stress as a reason for smoking. Ironically, smoking actually has the capacity to increase stress. The widespread use of cigarettes and other tobacco products is the single most significant and preventable cause of death in the United States. Every year, millions of workers die from heart attacks, cancer, strokes, and other devastating diseases directly caused by smoking (Quick et al., 1997).

ALCOHOL AND DRUG ABUSE   An increase in alcohol consumption and drug abuse is another behavioral consequence of an increase in stress. Workplace alcohol use and impairment directly affects an estimated 15 percent of the U.S. workforce, or 19.2 million workers, according to a recent study conducted at the University at Buffalo's Research Institute on Addictions (RIA, January 11, 2006). There are also reports of the widespread use of recreational drugs including marijuana and cocaine in the American workforce.

Using drugs or alcohol as coping strategies is ineffective and responsible for more stress in the long term. Also, this can escalate into substance abuse, resulting in costly employee health problems and accidents. In view of the social, economic, and health problems posed by alcoholism and drug abuse, it is important that managers be aware of whether employees are coping with stress through the use of drugs and alcohol.

Strategies for assisting employees in trouble need to be put in place. First, recognize that addiction may be a problem in a stressful workplace. Then, inform your employees that while consequences exist for inappropriate behavior, your company supports treatment and recovery for addiction problems. Finally, make it easy for employees to access support for their sobriety by offering employee assistance programs, and on-site counseling or support groups if the situation warrants that extent of intervention.

ACCIDENT PRONENESS   People under excessive stress also tend to be careless. Increased carelessness is due to the direct adverse effect which excessive stress has on people's decision-making ability and judgment, causing them to make hasty decisions and irrational judgments resulting in unfortunate accidents. Studies have indicated that not only does stress contribute significantly to the occurrence of accidents, but it also slows the recovery process and prolongs disability (Clark and Cooper, 2004).

VIOLENT TENDENCIES   Perhaps the most extreme manifestation of excessive stress is an act of violence by the highly stressed individual. There have been reports of overworked secretaries throwing ashtrays at their bosses and frustrated graduate students who pump bullets into their professors. Spouse and child abuse are also violent acts often precipitated by excessive stress. More recently, a phenomenon known as "desk rage" has emerged as a new manifestation of stress in the workplace. The Marlin Company of North Haven, Connecticut, released a study which revealed that 42 percent of office workers had jobs in an office where yelling and verbal abuse happened frequently (2001). The same article indicates the unwillingness of companies to acknowledge these problems as instances of worker confrontations causes them often to go unreported. Occupational experts and authorities on workplace stress, agree that the number and severity of incidents is rising.

It has been suggested that violence is a result of stress manifesting the "fight" portion of the "fight or flight" response associated with stress. The violence that results is sometimes displaced from the original source of stress and frustration, as painfully illustrated by road rage during the rush hour and violence in homes following stressful workdays.

EATING DISORDERS   Excessive stress may increase or decrease an individual's appetite. The loss of appetite is often a symptom of depression, one of the psychological consequences of stress. Overeating in response to excessive stress can often lead to obesity as well. Obesity, in turn, can lead to further health complications such as heart disease, cholesterol problems, and high blood pressure. Obesity as a health risk outstrips both cigarette and alcohol consumption in terms of health care costs. Health care providers generally agree that the more obese a person is, the more likely he or she is to develop health problems.

The incidence of obesity in the United States has grown at an alarming rate. Over 65 percent of adults over the age of 20 fall into the overweight and obese category according to the *Journal of the American Medical Association* (Hedley et al., 2004). Of those, more than 30 percent are classified as obese. Body weight is the result of genes, metabolism, and other factors, including behavior/environment. Stress as a product of environment is one of the most controllable aspects of weight gain and should therefore be addressed in the workplace. The connection between stress and eating disorders is becoming increasingly clearer. For example, both undereating and overeating can activate brain chemicals that produce feelings of peace and euphoria, which temporarily dispel depression. Some researchers believe that workers may be using comfort food to self-medicate painful feelings. These foods are high in sugar, fat, and calories and serve to calm the body's response to stress. It has also been suggested that there may be a link between today's fast-paced life and increasing rates of obesity.

Unfortunately, comfort food therapy leads to an unhealthy cycle where the stressed individual eats to relieve stress and gains weight; as a stress response the weight tends to cluster around one's middle; the social stress caused by the unattractive weight gain leads to further stress; and the cycle repeats eventually leading to obesity and all of the negative physical and psychological consequences associated with it. Overweight and obese people feel that workplace prejudice and discrimination are prevalent, causing further anxiety and stress.

At the other end of the spectrum we have the undereaters: people suffering from severe malnutrition, anorexia, or bulimia. Bulimic people in particular tend to suffer from high levels of anxiety and use the binge–purge cycle to relieve stress.

Do you have any behavioral responses to stress—either one of those mentioned, or any other?

STRESS IN INDIVIDUALS

Now that you know some of the causes of stress, it's time to look at how it affects individuals. Since you will be responsible for helping your employees to understand and manage their stress, the following sections focus on how you can become more aware of your own stress and manage it effectively.

How We Cause Our Own Stress

Your well-being is your responsibility, and there are many ways in which you can make yourself either healthy or unhealthy. While Western medicine has traditionally focused on *intervention* with regard to stress—that is, waiting until symptoms were evident and then intervening to reduce the effects—today's approach to stress is preventive. As we have seen, mental and physical well-being are key to employee satisfaction and productivity. General well-being is seen as a major responsibility of the individual; to a large extent you can either make yourself healthy or make yourself unhealthy.

One of the ways in which you control your own stress is through your cognitive response. For better or for worse, we know that stress is largely created in our minds. An individual interprets a given situation as either threatening and difficult or challenging and manageable, according to his or her perceptual filters. Past experiences, expectations, and personal beliefs all play an important role. When we imagine a stressful situation, our body behaves as if the event is really happening. Stress, then, can be increased by worrying and negative thinking, and reduced by positive thinking.

The importance of self-talk in reducing stress cannot be overestimated. There are a variety of ways in which we cause our own stress:

1. *Shoulds:* we tell ourselves what we "ought" to do.
2. *Criticism:* we are hard on ourselves.
3. *Blame:* we blame ourselves rather than solve the problem.
4. *Negative expectations:* we give up before we even begin.
5. *Can'ts:* we convince ourselves that we are going to fail before we try.

One of the most helpful ways to see the impact of individual perceptions on stress is to look at two options: You can take either the defensive path or the creative path. If you follow the defensive path, you deny the effects of stress and avoid reflecting about what you might to do reduce it. If, on the other hand, you choose the creative path, you use your skills of self-awareness and self-management to handle stress effectively, putting things into perspective to keep your life focused and balanced.

The Effects of Change and Uncertainty

Change is one of the major contributors to stress. Lifestyles and values are changing as individuals have more choices and are guided less by family and tradition. Many employees lack the codes of behavior and strong values that guided their parents.

Families are also changing. Nearly one-half of all marriages end in divorce and at least 40 percent of the children born in the twenty-first century will spend at least part of their childhood with only one parent. In addition, changing gender roles result in lack of clarity regarding acceptable behavior and role relationships. Increasing organizational diversity creates more effective organizations, but during the transition and adjustment phases any change brings with it a significant amount of stress for those involved.

The stress associated with change and uncertainty has been referred to as **decision stress.** There are too many alternatives and not enough information. Increasingly, employees are not simply asked to take risks regarding known variables—they are asked to make decisions without knowing exactly what the variables are or what the outcomes might be.

To make change as positive an experience as possible, you might consider some of the following guidelines:

1. change in small steps
2. change one thing at a time
3. have a clear, specific goal
4. find a support person
5. don't be discouraged by some degree of failure
6. use positive energy and self-talk.

Identify a specific change that created stress for you.

Individual Differences and Stress

How much stress is too much? There are striking individual differences in both the perception of stress and the degree to which individuals tolerate common stressors. Employees differ in their physiological resiliency, their psychological resiliency, and their social resiliency. Several factors determine how life situations will affect an individual. These include the degree of control the individual perceives he or she has over the situation, personality variables, and the individual's perceptual filters. The combination of these and other factors determines an individual's resiliency, or his or her ability to cope with stress.

Personality has been widely studied as it affects resiliency to stress. The degree of perceived control over a situation has been identified as a major variable in predicting stress levels. Researchers have identified what has commonly been referred to as "overcontrol personalities" and "undercontrol personalities."

BOX 7.1

Personalities and Stress

Overcontrol personalities	Undercontrol personalities
Take Charge Doer	Victim
Competitor	Worrier
Angry Demander	Avoider
Impatient	Creative Dreamer

Type A Personality and Stress

One of the most frequently explored relationships is between stress and the Type A personality. Generally, Type A personalities are impatient and "on edge" much of the time. They are competitive and tense. On the other hand, individuals who exhibit the opposite of Type A personality, labeled Type B, are generally relaxed, good listeners, and patient.

Recent studies indicate that in America, approximately 70 percent of men and 50 percent of women exhibit Type A personalities. Many Type A individuals attribute their more rapid career development to their personalities. Even though instances of many stress-related disorders are higher in Type A personalities, these individuals are unwilling to try to change that orientation because it has been their drive and intensity that has contributed to their success. Look closely at the characteristics of Type A personalities in Box 7.2 and see how many of these traits are typical of your personal style.

Take Responsibility for Reducing Your Stress

The amount of stress you experience is largely under your control. One of the most effective ways to manage stress is to develop the attitudes of an active stress manager. Our language influences the way that we think about stress; we say that "Joe contributes to my stress because he keeps missing deadlines," or that, "The Internet frustrates me because there are so many options," or "Meetings annoy me because they're often unproductive and take up a lot of time."

If you change things around a bit, you will find it easy to take more ownership of your stress. Suppose, instead of the statements above, you said: "I make myself stressed when Joe misses deadlines."

BOX 7.2

Characteristics of Type A Personality

Guilt when relaxing
Fast pace regardless of task
Attribute success to Type A behavior
Dynamic speech
Impatient when interrupted
Unaware of larger environment
Multi-tasker
Prefer "having" over "being"
Want to be focus of attention
Require measurable results from efforts
Strong need to win
Always in a hurry

Source: Adapted from Whetten and Cameron, 1984, p. 131

"I make myself frustrated when I spend so long online."

"I make myself annoyed when I know there's a meeting and I have a lot to do."

How does this change things? For one, it puts responsibility back on your shoulders. You can either become stressed or not—depending upon the way you think about the situation. In order to begin looking at things differently, your first step is to identify your most troublesome situations so that, when you allow yourself to become stressed by them, you'll be ready. Remember that the most productive way to respond to stress is in a creative or novel manner; you have the ability to reorganize and redefine stressful situations to make them more manageable.

THE IMPORTANCE OF MANAGING STRESS

After managers have learned to recognize the role of stress and have become aware of the consequences of excessive stress, the next logical step is to learn how to manage the level of stress in the workplace. In the following paragraphs we will discuss various techniques that experience reveals managers can use to manage stress effectively. The variety of techniques presented is designed to ensure that there is at least one technique that will appeal to each individual. We divide our discussions into internal control techniques and external control techniques, although there is some overlap.

Internal Control Techniques

One of the key techniques for internal control of stress is meditation. This involves a combination of physical relaxation and mental concentration. The mental concentration may focus on an object, an idea, or simply one's own breathing. Physical relaxation may take the form of motionless relaxation or a moving, stretching exercise such as yoga, tai chi, or a walking meditation. The following techniques are defined as **internal control techniques** because they are aimed at the inner functioning of the individual in an effort to reduce the amount of stress he or she experiences. The techniques discussed are the relaxation response, meditation, stress inoculation, and humor.

RELAXATION RESPONSE   For those who have never used relaxation techniques, the **relaxation response** is a good technique because it is simple and practicable by anyone. This term was coined by Dr. Herbert Bensen (1975). He is known for demystifying transcendental meditation and providing practical, everyday techniques for the reduction of stress through meditation. The technique proceeds in the following manner:

1. Sit or recline comfortably with your eyes closed.
2. Concentrate on your breathing, and repeat a word or phrase silently to yourself as you exhale.
3. As your mind wanders, gently bring your attention back to your breathing.
4. Practice for approximately 20 minutes every day.

Closely related to relaxation response is **progressive muscle relaxation.** This technique teaches you to relax your muscles through briefly tensing, and then releasing the tension on focused muscle groups. As you learn to recognize the feel of muscles relaxing, you can learn to induce physical muscular relaxation at the first signs of tension that accompany stress. This physical relaxation precedes mental calmness.

The time needed for completion of the exercise will become shorter with practice, and eventually, the individual can become relaxed in seconds under almost any circumstances. After mastering the relaxation response, proceed with the following steps:

1. Choose a time and place conducive to relaxation and meditation.
2. Employ your relaxation response technique.
3. Maintain your deep and controlled breathing throughout the exercise.
4. Shift your focus to the muscle groups in your arms. Tense them for five to seven seconds and then release the tension. Shift from simply recognizing the feeling of relaxation to deliberately relaxing the muscles even further. The relaxation portion should take less than a minute.
5. Repeat the muscle relaxation described above with face, neck, chest, abdomen, legs, and, finally, the feet.

MEDITATION   In addition to reducing stress and anxiety, **meditation** has been found to produce a variety of positive effects. For example, those who meditate regularly are likely to have a reduced heart rate, lowered oxygen consumption, and decreased systolic and diastolic blood pressure. They enjoy increased emotional control and alertness. In addition, meditation also increases creativity and intelligence, concentration, learning ability, and memory, thereby having a positive effect on work adjustment, performance, and job satisfaction. And, perhaps more important, meditation fosters individuals' resistance to stress. Therefore, with regular practice, meditation is an effective method managers can use both to prevent and to relieve stress.

Have you ever tried muscle relaxation or mediation to reduce your stress? How did these activities work?

STRESS INOCULATION   This form of cognitive behavior is similar to the relaxation response technique, but it involves an additional step of "pairing" a relaxed state to mental images that cause great stress.

The first part of this exercise is the same as the relaxation response with progressive muscle relaxation. The individual retires to a comfortable and quiet place for about half an hour. During this time, a deep and total relaxation of the body is initiated, with each muscle group slowly and deliberately relaxed. After the individual has achieved a state of deep relaxation, he or she can begin the inoculation phase. The individual initiates the inoculation phase by imagining a stress-producing mental image. For example, if an early morning public lecture is the stressor, then the mental image could begin from walking out of the house or walking into the lecture room. Progress through the mental scene should be slow. It is important for the individual to identify the specific issue that causes tensing up. When this happens, the imaging should be stopped and the individual must try to return to the relaxed state. He or she should continue only after the relaxed state is re-achieved.

The **stress inoculation** technique is useful for two reasons. First, the individual learns what, specifically, causes the stress and thus is able to anticipate his or her response. Second, the individual knows which muscle group usually tenses up and concentrates on relaxing it. This will enable the individual to relax in an inconspicuous manner whenever a stressful situation arises. Practice is essential to success, so one should incorporate stress inoculation as part of one's everyday routine.

HUMOR AS A STRESS RELIEVER

> Healing humor is the appreciation of incongruous elements in events or ideas that generate spontaneous pleasure. It is a sudden release from stress, that like a dammed-up river, overflows noisily and bubbling with the fullness of life.

> —Rudolf Klimes, Ph.D.

The nature of internal control centers on one's desire to rise above a stressful situation by virtue of a strong and appropriate response. One such response requires the ability to see the humor in an otherwise stressful situation. It does sometimes take an effort to rise above the immersion in a stressful situation to see it from a new and humorous perspective; but in so doing, one is able to dissipate the stress and focus more clearly on the situation at hand. The danger with this technique lies in the potential for using inappropriate humor, and making the situation worse.

The research into the therapeutic benefits of humor and laughter is still in its infancy, but it is generally recognized that laughter reduces the heart rate and blood pressure, relaxes muscles, and oxygenates the blood. In short, laughter reduces stress. In the long run, laughter has the potential to reduce pain as well as stress and enhance the immune system, thereby improving the overall well-being of the individual.

There are numerous strategies for maintaining a humorous outlook. Begin by maintaining a reservoir of humor in your working environment. Comic clippings or screensavers, funny calendars, jokes or humorous graphics attached to memos, or intentionally incongruous elements inserted into otherwise ordinary environments help to maintain a lighthearted atmosphere. The second line of defense would be a known place to turn to for uplift. This might take the form of a book or website, a coworker or friend who has the ability to find hilarity in situations, or you may call upon someone completely outside your work environment to mirror your situation back to you in a new and humorous light. The final step would be to actually learn humor strategies from a therapist or workshop, so that your internal defense could be enhanced in a more proactive manner.

Do you know someone who uses humor to reduce stress? Is it effective?

External Control Techniques

External control techniques are largely aimed at reducing the amount of stress experienced by managing more effectively the circumstances giving rise to stress. The external techniques discussed in the following sections are time management, exercise, diet, and nutrition.

TIME MANAGEMENT   **Time management** is an important issue with which managers must grapple. Because we discussed time management extensively in Chapter 6, it is sufficient to state here that the effective and efficient use of time is an essential method for the management of stress. As a first step toward the reduction of stress, it will be wise for the manager to begin organizing time to achieve the minimum amount of waste.

EXERCISE

> Training gives us an outlet for suppressed energies created by stress and thus tones the spirit just as exercise conditions the body.
>
> —Arnold Schwarzenegger

Physical activity can promote mental health in a variety of ways. It can relieve built-up tension in the body, and release endorphins, promoting a feeling of well-being. Exercise helps promote overall health which can also lessen your experience of stress. Some forms of exercise encourage social interaction, which also can reduce stress. It is common knowledge that regular exercise is crucial to ensuring good physical health and a sense of well-being. With regard to stress reduction, there are studies to indicate that exercise is also highly beneficial. There are a number of ways to explain the beneficial effects of exercise. Psychologically, it has been suggested that exercise allows the individual to overcome challenges, thus providing a sense of accomplishment that in turn affects confidence and the response to other stressful situations. Physiologically, stress decreases with regular exercise because there is increased circulation to the brain that facilitates greater availability of glucose and transportation of oxygen.

It is essential that an individual be cautious before he or she embarks on any type of exercise program. Unlike internal control techniques and other external control techniques, like time management, there is an element of risk in exercise, especially vigorous exercise, and this risk increases with age and the prior period of inactivity.

Individuals should consult a physician, ideally one who is skilled in preventive medicine, regarding the various aspects of an exercise program before embarking on a new program. After this step, there are some guidelines which managers should be aware of in terms of safety:

1. The implementation of an exercise program should be gradual. This is especially true for people who have been inactive for long periods of time. Walking and easy cycling are two of the safest ways to start.
2. There should be an exercise plan to guide progress. This is to ensure that there is proper muscle conditioning and warm-up and cool-down periods. It has been found that the people who suffer from adverse consequences in exercise are those who fail to note their own progress and limits.
3. A well-rounded exercise regime should include exercises that address muscle strength, muscle endurance, flexibility, weight control, and cardiovascular endurance.
4. The purpose of initiating an exercise program should be to provide enjoyment and physical relaxation, in addition to stress reduction benefits. It is important therefore that exercise is not turned into competition, thus perhaps generating more stress and tension than it relieves.

Physically Active Relaxation   Now that we have discussed the benefits of exercise, it would be useful to point out that an even greater benefit is available when you combine exercise with relaxation. In terms of physically active relaxation, we suggest investigating the forms of exercise which allow you to get into a meditative state. These would include yoga, tai chi, and walking or swimming combined with meditation. Taking a class after work or committing to an exercise program can greatly increase your potential for success in using these techniques.

DIET AND NUTRITION   One way individuals can achieve physical resiliency, or a state that helps humans cope with stress by virtue of a healthy physical condition, is by maintaining a nutritious diet. Certain foods may affect the human body's response to stress. For instance, high-sugar diets can stimulate the stress response. With this in mind, it is important to acknowledge the ways in which a person's diet can affect his or her ability to cope with stress.

The Food Pyramid has been revised in recent years and there are several variations to account for differing cultural interpretations of a proper diet. However, there are some basic principles that run throughout these recommendations:

1. Eat more fruits, vegetables, and whole grains.
2. Reduce intake of saturated fat, trans fat, and cholesterol.
3. Limit sweets and salt.
4. Drink alcoholic beverages in moderation, if at all.
5. Control portion sizes and the total number of calories you consume.
6. Include physical activity in your daily routine.

While you may know the proper way to eat, stress can motivate you to adopt a less than healthy diet that causes you to crave foods that are high in fat, sugar, and salt. In addition, stress or long work hours can affect one's ability to get enough sleep. Many turn to high caffeine beverages to enable themselves to maintain wakefulness. Overly stressed people are known to skip meals, eat randomly or mindlessly, rely on fast foods, or seek out comfort foods at the end of the day.

It is important to find ways to conscientiously maintain a healthy diet if you suffer from a stressful work environment. For example, reduce the amount of caffeine consumed by switching to a less caffeinated or caffeine-free drink. Fruit juice will supply energy without the negative side effects of caffeine. If caffeine is a necessity to start the day, stop consuming it by early afternoon to prevent sleep loss at night. Be certain adequate amounts of water replace the previously consumed beverages. Enhance your diet by planning ahead. Remove unhealthy foods from your home and workspace to reduce the temptation to snack. Replace them with healthy alternatives such as fruit or protein bars. Pack your lunch or plan for healthy meals, even if these meals must be brief.

How effective is your diet as a stress reducer? What foods should you add? Which might you reduce?

HOSPITALITY INDUSTRY INNOVATIONS

The importance of managing stress effectively is becoming clear because industry bears an increasingly heavy load of the direct and indirect costs of excessive stress. In response, a number of companies have come up with innovative ideas to help their executives and employees manage their stress. They have reasoned that, in the long run, the money spent on corporate stress management programs will have greater returns through decreased medical costs and lower absenteeism.

In the hospitality industry, client needs for stress reduction must also be considered, both as an aspect of customer service, which is at the heart of what we have always done, and as a response to the increasing demand from clients for these kinds of accommodations. This extends to all areas of the hospitality industry including hotels, restaurants, and hospitals.

Among the current corporate programs, the most innovative ones include a variety of wellness programs, such as humor consultation and lectures on feng shui (the Chinese practice of positioning objects such as furniture based on beliefs in the positive and negative effects of these placements).

Wellness Programs

Wellness programs are now commonplace in corporations across the country. The basic motives for wellness programs are threefold. First, physically and emotionally healthy workers are better workers. Second, healthy workers file fewer medical claims and have a lower rate of absenteeism and higher productivity. Third, hospitality workers under less stress themselves are more able to offer, not just competent, but compassionate service to those in their care. Because of these factors, successful wellness programs are saving companies more than they expend to implement the program and increasing the quality of the service they offer. For example, the Adolph Coors Company (Bailey, 1990) sees a return of $6.15 for every dollar spent on wellness.

Unfortunately, many wellness programs fail to meet their objective; the rate of participation from employees is low, high-risk workers remain unaffected, and the cost of health care continues to escalate.

Most companies with wellness programs typically offer aerobics and strength training classes at on-site facilities. Others such as Johnson & Johnson make health a top priority. Nearly 90 percent of their employees take advantage of the free health risk assessments and physical examinations. Employees can join free classes on topics such as weight management or nutrition. Some companies, like Coors, even go so far as to provide an entire center for wellness. Despite the difference in what individual programs offer, the basic aim for corporations is to help their employees lead healthy lives through education, incentives, and supervised programs. It is important for companies contemplating the implementation of a wellness program to note certain elements that are essential for the program's success. The following essential elements are identified by the Coors Company (1990), which boasts one of the most successful wellness programs:

> **Support and direction from the CEO is critical.** If upper management does not issue clear directives on the wellness program, it can remain a low priority with middle managers. Wellness must be a stated objective. By including wellness of employees as an objective in its value statement, a company is able to make clear to employees that it takes their physical and mental health seriously. Consequently, employees are encouraged to participate.

> **Employees should participate in development of wellness programs.** This is a commonsense approach because the wellness program is ultimately for the employees; their input is, therefore, critical. In addition, it also helps with planning logistics and scheduling classes. Perhaps the most important reason for employee input is the cultivation of support for the program; employees are much more likely to participate in a program which they have helped develop.

Ensure that wellness programs meet objectives. There should be in-house and external evaluations of programs to ensure that they are meeting their objectives. For example, smoking cessation classes should be reviewed on their success rates, noting which methods of instruction have been the most effective. External assessments are also important; wellness programs should be reviewed annually to determine whether they have been effective in helping companies curtail rising health costs.

Establish a separate budget for wellness programs. By having a separate budget for wellness programs, companies will be able to make clear to all managers that the program is considered a vital part of the organization. In addition, budgeting will ensure that expenses for the program will be controlled and monitored to prevent waste.

Wellness programs continue to increase in popularity. With the pressure of work increasing with time, the development of well-organized wellness programs is an excellent way for companies to offer individual opportunities for personal growth. Moreover, wellness programs help ensure that employees are healthy, mentally alert, and composed, leading to higher customer satisfaction, customer retention, compassionate service, and company growth.

It has become accepted knowledge that a good sense of humor is an extremely effective antidote to stress. Laughter can help decrease your blood pressure. The ability to laugh at tense situations diffuses stress, creating a positive atmosphere for you and for those around you. Humor consultation, as an aspect of wellness programs, is a relatively new trend in corporate efforts to help employees manage their stress. Innovative companies like Hewlett-Packard and Owens Corning have been among the first to hire humor consultants.

Training Management to Deal with Employee Stress

As mentioned previously, while the hospitality industry did not invent stress reduction, it has always been an integral part of customer service. Alleviating customer stress is inherent in pleasing the customer. A service provider automatically assumes responsibility for reducing or eliminating the stress of a frantic, distraught, or merely upset customer. In recent years, the hospitality industry has taken an even more clearly defined and proactive approach to the stress reduction aspect of customer service.

In the same way that other industries have recognized the need for stress management among their workforce, the hospitality industry has implemented courses to train managers to assist their staff in stress management. Managers who are not trained to deal effectively with stress can become part of the problem rather than part of the solution. Some of these courses are offered online to expedite the training with little lost work time. In addition, the industry offers stress-reducing services, not only for their customers, but also for their employees, with favorable results on all sides.

Hotel Spas

Contemporary upscale hotels offer a range of stress-reducing amenities and facilities. Everything from comprehensive concierge services to spas, fitness centers, and salons caters to the peaceful mindset of the client. Even middle-range hotels offer some of these amenities.

An exemplar of high-end attention to stress is the Four Seasons in Washington, DC. They offer seven different massage treatment options; five kinds of body treatments plus manicures, pedicures, and facials; a three-level 12,500 sq ft fitness facility including cardiovascular equipment, each with a television, DVD player, CD player, radio, and individual headset; strength training equipment with personal trainers available; an indoor lap pool; eucalyptus-scented steam room; as well as an aerobics studio offering yoga and spinning bikes; and complimentary fruit and fresh-squeezed juices.

Have you ever gone to a hotel spa? Why do you think an increasing number of hotels have added a spa to their facility?

Restaurant Offerings

An important aspect of stress reduction is healthy nutrition. Public awareness of these benefits in physical and emotional well-being has resulted in an increasing trend toward healthier offerings in restaurants of all types. Fast food restaurants are advertising reduced fat, reduced carbohydrates, higher protein, lower calorie dishes, along with a wider variety of offerings of salads, and yogurts, as well as milk, juice, and applesauce options for children's meals.

Many restaurants now publish the nutritional content of their menu items. It is not uncommon for restaurants to offer sections in their menus adapted for specific dietary preferences. Formal, mid-range, and budget restaurants including traditional as well as ethnic restaurants have adjusted their menus toward healthier offerings. However, recently the trend toward healthy fare has been compromised by a return to comfort foods. Various magazines have featured covers of luscious looking hamburgers, which are reportedly much healthier descendants of the original.

Hospital Stress Management and Stress Reduction for Patients and Staff

Hospital administrators and care providers are aware of the role that reduced stress plays in the acquisition and maintenance of health. In addition, they have recognized that hospital staffs are in a better position to make sound treatment decisions and administer compassionate care when their own stress levels are kept in check. The University of Virginia Hospital in Charlottesville, Virginia, has an outstanding program for helping stressed patients and employees.

A variety of programs and advice are provided for patients and their families. In-house programming—videos designed to help patients reduce and manage stress—are provided on the televisions in the patients' rooms. Classes are offered through the Family Medicine Center and online "healing stories" are provided to help others who are dealing with similar problems. In addition, The Women's Place offers classes in infant massage and pregnancy massage, expanding their concern for stress reduction for specific populations.

A program designed to assist both patients and staff with stress management and reduction at the hospital is called "The Mindfulness Center." This program is defined as "moment-to-moment, nonjudgmental awareness." It enhances the individuals' inner calm and peace, helping them to think more clearly and become more aware of their choices. The center offers short courses that help health care professionals take care of themselves so that they are able to be compassionate and empathic with their patients.

Specific hospitality segments, like the cruise lines, have recognized the increasing need for complete health care services. They offer speakers on wellness issues, full-service spas, healthy cuisine, and other services designed for an increasingly stressed, but proactive, market.

Summary

In this chapter we have seen that stress in the workplace has become a major concern that, indirectly and directly, costs industry billions of dollars annually. The hospitality industry is especially known for its stressful work schedules.

Stress is an external stimulus, which elicits a response from the body, commonly known as the "fight or flight" response. Stress in itself is not a problem; on the contrary, it is essential for growth, change, development, and performance. However, if excessive stress is not managed effectively, there will be adverse consequences.

There are three types of adverse consequences: physiological, psychological, and behavioral. Physiological consequences are the result of prolonged stress responses that the body has experienced. They are the most identifiable consequences because of their physical manifestations. Many examples exist, but the most prevalent ones are increased blood pressure, increased cholesterol levels, and formation of ulcers.

Psychological consequences of excessive stress are the result of interferences with the individual's thought and memory, and are often too subtle to be readily identified. Common examples are anxiety, depression, and sleep disturbances.

Behavioral consequences are the changes in the individual's behavior when he or she is under excessive stress. Common examples are increased smoking, alcohol, drug abuse, accident proneness, violent tendencies, appetite disorder, and withdrawal from social interaction.

Individuals have to recognize stress and take responsibility for dealing with it in productive ways. Understanding how we cause our own stress and how our personality and other individual factors contribute to our well-being is helpful in planning a positive course of action. A variety of stress management techniques exist. Both internal and external control techniques are targeted at helping the individual to reduce his or her stress levels and change to a more balanced and healthy lifestyle.

Finally, we discussed the latest corporate efforts in the management of employee stress. Some of these efforts are innovative, such as humor consultation, an attempt to lighten up embattled employees. However, the currently most common effort is the rapidly expanding wellness program, where corporations provide on-site exercise facilities with the latest in aerobic classes and nutrition education for both their staff and their customers.

Key Words

stress response *178*
fight or flight response *178*
stress *179*
eustress *179*
distress *180*
physiological consequences
  180
psychological consequences
  180

behavioral consequences
  180
weekend migraine *181*
anxiety *182*
fear *182*
depression *182*
decision stress *186*
internal control techniques *188*
relaxation response *188*

progressive muscle relaxation
  188
meditation *189*
stress inoculation *189*
external control techniques
  191
time management *191*
wellness programs *193*
SMART *197*

Exercises

Exercise 1   Recognizing Signs of Stress

Objectives:

- To reinforce the notion that stress can be reduced or eliminated
- To become more aware of personal reactions to stress
- To identify several personal stressors
- To generate ways to reduce or eliminate some of the most troublesome stressors
- To learn the SMART technique for stress relief

Group Size: 10–30

Time Frame: 30 minutes

Materials: A copy of the "Recognizing Signs of Stress Worksheet" for each participant

Procedure:

1. Review the material on stress and the problems associated with high stress.
2. Emphasize that individuals can learn to deal more effectively with stress and even eliminate some of the stress they may be experiencing.
3. Provide each participant with a copy of the Recognizing Signs of Stress Worksheet, and ask them to take 15 minutes and complete as much of it as they can.
4. Facilitate a whip of responses to the following:
   - One of my most common signs of stress is . . .
   - Just before encountering a stressful situation, I calm myself by . . .
   - During a stressful situation I calm myself by . . .
5. Ask the participants to form groups of four members each. Give participants the following instructions:
   - Provide an opportunity for each group member to share one of his or her personal stressors.
   - Provide an opportunity for each group member to share his or her methods of reducing or eliminating the stressor.
   - Ask group members to brainstorm additional ways in which the person's stress might be reduced.
   - Ask each group member to develop a SMART goal pertaining to the chosen stressor. The acronym **SMART** (Locke & Latham, 1990) stands for:

     Specific
     Measurable
     Acceptable
     Realistic
     Timely

     The SMART goal strategy is elaborated upon in Chapter 9.

6. Ask participants to confirm that each of them has developed one SMART goal pertaining to how one personal stressor might be eliminated or reduced.
7. Provide an opportunity for participants to make final comments or final questions.

***

Recognizing Signs of Stress Worksheet—Personal Stressors
What things in your professional life really bother you?
List at least four specific tasks or situations that cause you stress:

1.

2.

3.

4.

Are these stressors episodic or chronic?

Choose one of the stressors listed above that you find particularly problematic. How do you currently cope with this person or situation?

(continued)

(continued)

What are your signs of stress?

What do you do to calm yourself in the following situations?

1. Just before encountering a stressful situation
2. During a stressful situation
3. When you are feeling absolutely overwhelmed

What stress management techniques or assertive skills might you use to reduce or eliminate the specific stressors you identify above?

1.

2.

3.

4.

From what you have discovered about your stressors, clearly identify one SMART goal for yourself.

***

Exercise 2   Relaxation Techniques

Objective: To familiarize participants with relaxation techniques that might be beneficial to them in reducing stress

Group Size: 10–30 participants

Time Frame: 20 minutes

Materials: "Relaxation Techniques" sheets, one for each participant

Physical Setting:

1. Soft background music
2. Dim lights, if possible

Procedure:

1. Distribute the "Relaxation Techniques" sheets. Review the first two breathing exercises with participants. Ask if there are any questions.

2. Emphasize that the purpose of the exercise is not to achieve the result of relaxation, but rather to familiarize participants with a method that can help them relax if they commit themselves to an ongoing program of relaxation techniques.
3. Go through the first breathing exercise as explained on the "Relaxation Techniques" sheet.
4. Discuss its uses and potential impact on stress.
5. Follow the same procedure for each of the following exercises. Review the instructions with participants, make sure that no one has questions, and then follow the instructions in completing the exercise. After each exercise, discuss its usefulness as a stress management technique.

***

Relaxation Techniques

Below are examples of two relaxation techniques.

I. Deep breathing

1. You can become more aware of your breathing if you lie down on the floor. If this is not possible, then assume a relaxed posture in your chair. Place one hand on your abdomen and the other on your chest. Inhale slowly and deeply through your nose. You should be able to feel your abdomen move. Try to establish a pattern of deep breathing—in through your nose and out through your

(continued)

(continued)

mouth. Relax your tongue and jaw. Continue deep breathing for at least three minutes, concentrating on relaxing your entire body and on the rhythm of your breathing.

2. Stand with your hands on your hips. Inhale. Then, slowly exhale as you bend forward as far as you can. Inhale as you stand up straight again. Exhale and this time bend backward. Inhale as you come to an upright position again. Continue by bending forward, then back, then forward, then back. Exhale as you bend, and inhale as you return to an upright position.

II. Visualization

1. Close your eyes and put the palms of your hands over them. Try to block out all light and visualize just the color black. Use a mental image of something that you know is very black, and focus just on the color. Keep focusing on black for two to three minutes. Now, remove your hands and open your eyes very slowly. Notice how relaxed your eyes feel.

2. Close your eyes. Visualize an image that you associate with tension. Now, slowly replace it with an image you associate with relaxation. Allow yourself to experience the tension before you visualize your relaxing image. Remember to use all of your senses and to make both images as vivid as possible in your mind.

Examples might be:

1. A loud siren that changed into a music box.
2. A dark cave that opens into a green meadow.
3. A haunted house that turns into a summer cottage.

***

Exercise 3   Analyze the Characteristics of Stressful Situations

Objectives:

- To consider the important characteristics of the stressful situations that arise
- To identify ways of managing one important stressful situation

Group Size: 10–30 participants

Time Frame: 20 minutes

Materials:

1. A copy of "Characteristics of Stressful Situations" for each participant
2. A flip chart and markers

Procedure:

1. Allow five minutes for participants to make a list of three recent stressful situations that they've encountered on the job.
2. Ask participants to choose one of these situations—either the most stressful or a situation that is particularly troublesome to analyze.
3. Distribute the "Characteristics of Stressful Situations" sheets, one to each participant.

4. Allow five minutes for participants to individually respond in writing to each of the questions on the sheet.
5. Ask participants to form groups of three and to do the following:
   - Share two things that they became more aware of through this exercise.
   - Identify two ways in which they could deal more effectively with the particular stressful situation.
6. Record on a flip chart the participants' responses to the following questions:
   - How many people chose an ongoing source of pressure or stress?
   - How many people chose highly predictable situations?
   - How many people chose situations that they could influence?
7. Process the experience by discussing the following:
   - Why is it that we seldom fully prepare for predictable situations we know will be stressful?
   - What do you do when you can't influence or control a stressful situation?

***

Characteristics of Stressful Situations

Describe three recent situations that have caused you a significant amount of stress.

1.

2.

3.

Select one of these situations, and answer the questions below.

	little			great deal	
1. How much pressure did the situation place on me?	1	2	3	4	5

	episode			continuing	
2. Is the situation a single episode, or ongoing?	1	2	3	4	5

	predictable			unexpected	
3. To what degree could I have anticipated the event?	1	2	3	4	5

	no influence			high influence	
4. To what degree could I have changed or influenced the situation?	1	2	3	4	5

	active manager			passive victim	
5. To what degree did I respond like an effective stress manager?	1	2	3	4	5

***

Exercise 4   Mental Responses to Stress

Objectives:

- To increase participants' awareness of their attitudes toward stress
- To increase participants' awareness of their self-talk

Group Size: 10–30 participants

Time Frame: Approximately 30 minutes

Materials: "Mental Responses to Stress" worksheet

Procedure:

1. Review the importance of a positive attitude and positive self-talk in reducing stress.
2. Distribute copies of the "Mental Responses to Stress" worksheet to participants and ask them to complete each of the four questions. Allow approximately 10 minutes.

3. Lead participants in a discussion around the following questions:
   - What impact do your negative assumptions and self-talk have on your ability to deal effectively with a situation?
   - Why do you think so many people engage in negative self-talk?
   - What are some of the specific ways in which you can break ineffective habits and replace them with more positive methods of dealing with stressful situations?
   - Does anyone have an example of a stressful situation where positive self-talk might be particularly useful?
   - What types of situations are most influenced by your assumptions about yourself and your attitudes toward your abilities?

***

"Mental Response to Stress" Worksheet
List the four most persistent stressful situations that occur at work:

1.

2.

3.

4.

For each situation, list the things you assume, tell yourself, or expect:

1.

2.

3.

4.

For each situation, identify negative things that you assume about yourself in dealing with this situation:

1.

2.

3.

4.

What new things might you assume about yourself that would be more positive? What might you say to yourself the next time the stressful situation occurs?

1.

2.

3.

4.

***

Endnotes

Aboa-Éboulé, C., Brisson, C., Manusell, E., Mâsse, B., Vézina, M., Milot, A., et al. (2007). Job strain and risk of acute recurrent coronary heart disease events. *Journal of the American Medical Association, 298*(14), 1652–1659.

Atkinson, W. (2004). Stress: Risk management's most serious challenge? *Risk Management, 51*(6), 20.

Bailey, N. (1990). Wellness program that works. *Business and Health.*

Britt, C. (January 30, 2006). Heart disease linked to work stress. *Seattle Post-Intelligencer.*

Clarke, S. & Cooper, C. L. (2004). *Managing the Risk of Workplace Stress.* London: Routledge.

Costello, D. (2001). Stressed out: Can workplace stress get worse? *The Wall Street Journal*, B1.

Farren, C. (1999). Stress and productivity: What tips the scales? *Strategy and Leadership, 27*(1), 36.

Harris, E., Artis, A., Walters, J., & Licata, J. (2006). Role stressors, service worker job resourcefulness, and job outcomes: An empirical analysis. *Journal of Business Research, 59*(4), 407–412.

Lagasse, P., Goldman, L., Hobson, A., & Norton, S. R. (Eds.). (2006). *The Columbia Encyclopedia*. Sixth Edition. New York: Columbia University Press.

Lait, J. & Wallace, J. (2002). Stress at work: A study of organizational-professional conflict and unmet expectations. *Relations Industrielles, 57*(3), 463–488.

Levenstein, S. (1998). Stress and peptic ulcer: Life beyond helicobacter. *BMJ, 316*, 583–541.

Locke, E. A. & Latham, G. P. (1990). *A Theory of Goal Setting and Task Performance*. Englewood Cliffs, NJ: Prentice Hall.

Maitland, A. (April 19, 2005). Employees nurse the stress bug: Support in the workplace. *Financial Times*, 12.

Mazzolini, C. (February 26, 2005). Workplace stress takes its toll on individuals, company productivity. *Knight-Ridder Tribune Business News, 1*.

Quick, J. C., Quick, J. D., Nelson, D., & Hurrell, J. (1997). *Preventative Stress Management in Organizations*. Washington, DC: American Psychological Association.

Rosack, J. (2003). Depression most costly illness for employers. *Psychiatric News, 38*(14), 19.

Sapolsky, R. (2003). Taming stress. In *Scientific American* [On-line]. Available: http://www.sciam.com/article.cfm?articleID=00083A00–318C–1F30–9AD380A84189F2D7&pageNumber=7&catID=2

Thomas, G. (2000). *The Effect of Personality on Job-Related Stress Levels Among Human Service Workers*. Dissertation, Vol. 116, University of Sarasota.

Online Sources

http://www.reutershealth.com/wellconnected/doc14.html, 2002 study

http://www.mayoclinic.com/health/migraine-headache/DS00120/DSECTION=3

Faye J. Crosby (20th century), U.S. professor. Juggling, ch. 1 (1991).

Richard Hazard [rhazard@hazardandassociates.com]

http://www.mcmanweb.com/article-44.htm

http://sev.prnewswire.com/health-care-hospitals/20061109/DCTH01209112006-1.html

National Institutes of Health WebSite: http://www.nimh.nih.gov/publicat/depression.cfm#ptdep4

National Sleep Foundation, "Sleep is Important When Stress and Anxiety Increase, Says NSF." http://www.sleepfoundation.org/press/index.php?id=90, accessed September 24, 2005.

http://www.inova.org/inovapublic.srt/healthsource/workplacehealth/e-articles/oct05_02.jsp

Hedley A. A., et al. Prevalence of overweight and obesity among U.S. children, adolescents, and adults, 1999–2002. JAMA 2004:291: http://www.americanheart.org/downloadable/heart/1114880987205NationAtRisk.pdf

1238 JAMA, March 10, 2004—Vol 291, No. 10 (Reprinted) ©2004 American Medical Association. All rights reserved.

University at Buffalo (January 11, 2006). Journal of Studies on Alcohol. http://www.sciencedaily.com/releases/2006/01/060111073900.htm

Mary Dallman, (2003). http://www.anred.com/causes.html—What causes eating disorders? Proceedings of the National Academy of Sciences.

David N. Neubauer, M.D., (2006). Baltimore, MD. http://www.healthatoz.com/healthatoz/Atoz/common/standard/transform.jsp?requestURI=/healthatoz/Atoz/dc/caz/ment/eatd/edcauses.jsp.

http://mentalhealth.about.com/cs/stressmanagement/a/relresp.htm

http://www.guidetopsychology.com/pmr.htm

http://iml.jou.ufl.edu/projects/Spring05/Luft/benefits.htm

http://www.utahsafetycouncil.org/OFF%20THE%20JOB/rec%20safety/safe%20exercise.html

http://www.mayoclinic.com/health/healthy-diet/NU00190By Mayo Clinic Staff, January 11, 2006

http://stress.about.com/od/dietandsuppliments/a/goodnutrition.htm Updated: March 25, 2006

http://www.fourseasons.com/washington/fitness_facilities.html

http%3a//www.restaurantedge.com/index.phtml%3fcatid=418

http://www.virginia.edu/insideuva/2005/02/mindfulness.html

8

PROMOTING CREATIVITY

The intuitive mind is a sacred gift and the rational mind is a faithful servant. We have created a society that honors the servant and has forgotten the gift.

—Albert Einstein

Industry Perspective

In a corporate environment, the creative process is most important. The reward is improved profits, better employee benefits, higher return on investment, and further growth. However, if creativity is motivated by greed, then it is misdirected at the expense of shareholders, employees, and even communities in today's environment of leveraged buy-outs.

—Michael W. N. Chiu
President and Chairman
Prima Donna Development Corporation
Prima Hotels

CHAPTER OUTLINE

Introduction
    Definition of Creativity
    Importance of Alone Time
    Coming Up with Ideas

Tools of Creativity
    Keys and Glue
    Remindings
    Questions

Techniques for Improving Creativity Using Current Knowledge
    Free Association (Technique 1)
    Metaphors (Technique 2)
    SCAMPER (Technique 3)

Techniques for Improving Creativity Using Outside Sources
    Lists (Technique 4)
    Proverbs (Technique 5)
    The Fortune Cookie Meeting (Technique 6)
    Innovative Imitation (Technique 7)

Developing a Creative Group
    The Speech
    Discussion Formats
        Discussion format 1: *Group brainstorming*
        Discussion format 2: *The nominal group technique*
        Discussion format 3: *A combination—NGT–Storming*
        Discussion format 4: *Question questing*
    Choosing the Right Ideas
    Necessary Selection Criteria
    Desirable Selection Criteria
    The Rating Scheme

Blocks to Creativity and How to Eliminate Them

Summary

LEARNING OBJECTIVES

After reading this chapter, you will be able to do the following:

1. Define creativity.
2. Explain the importance of creativity to an organization.
3. Discuss the tools of creativity: keys, glue, remindings, and questions.
4. Describe how to use the free association creativity technique.
5. Explain each letter of the acronym SCAMPER and how this technique can be used to think creatively.
6. Define "innovative imitation" and discuss how it can be used to discover creative ideas.
7. List the steps that a manager takes when using the NGT–Storming discussion format.

8. Discuss the difference between necessary selection criteria and desirable selection criteria.

9. Explain two ways of thinking that may cause blocks in creativity and describe how these blocks can be eliminated.

Opening Scenario

Jim Martin, the GM of Harriot Hotels, was concerned that the hotel restaurant was losing customers. The restaurant was a moderately priced, family restaurant. He called together the executive team and told them that they would brainstorm for ideas to build the clientele of the restaurant. He went around the table and got the following ideas:

- The Director of Marketing suggested having happy hour with free hors d'oeuvres and drinks at half price.
- The VP of Finances suggested a clown to make balloon animals for the children.
- The Executive Housekeeper suggested that her brother-in-law, a magician, could perform magic tricks at each table.
- The F&B Director suggested that the restaurant have a cooking demonstration of the dinner special for the night.
- The Director of Sales suggested that they advertise a special children's menu and a baby-sitter so the parents could dine without the children.
- The GM suggested that a local jazz singer come to entertain.

The GM listed all the ideas and told the team to rank order from 1, the most favored, to 6, the least favored. He then went around the table and had each team member give their rankings for each item. Without encouraging the team to think creatively, they each came up with an idea that was relatively obvious. How could they have thought of more creative ideas?

INTRODUCTION

Why should managers be creative in the hospitality industry? This question could be answered with some fancy statistics that demonstrate the link between creativity and financial success, but we would rather let several creative leaders answer the question in their own words. Michael Leven, President and CEO of U.S. Franchise Systems, Inc., says, "Creativity is necessary for survival in today's environment. All hotels, once you get outside of the truly five-star hotels of the world, are the same; the product varies only in the color of the lobby. To survive, innovation is the key." William Eberhardt, who owns and operates Dining Associates, states, "Since my properties are extremely diverse in nature and service mainly repeat customers, I need to change and update them and inject fresh thought. For this reason, I am constantly generating new ideas, and I do not take the first idea, ever. Rather I always keep thinking." Charles Mund, CEO of Mega Management, says, "Profitability, growth, tapping new segments—these can only be achieved with creativity."

Their answers suggest that creativity leads not only to financial success but to a sense of personal fulfillment. Creativity makes work more fun and differentiates one organization from another. The message is clear: Your life in business environments will be more rewarding, more enjoyable, and more profitable if you can become more creative.

At a basic level, people who are creative put forward more ideas than people who are not creative. That's all there is to it. **Creativity** is not a mystical power. It is simply the ability to think up lots of ideas. They don't even have to be good ideas. If a manger invented the nuclear-powered salad bar, people would consider her creative even though they might not think the idea was good. With this in mind, this chapter is designed to teach, first, how to have lots of ideas and, second, how to tell which of those ideas are the good ones. Throughout our experience in teaching creativity, we have found that if people stick with these techniques until they generate *many* ideas, they almost always come up with at least one they really like. It is fine for a manager to come up with 100 bad ideas as long as he or she comes up with 101 ideas and the last one is creative.

> Do you consider yourself a creative person? Explain.

A Definition of Creativity

> Creativity is an end result of a combination of ingredients, including but not limited to inspiration, flexibility, instinct, adaptability, resourcefulness, original-ity and "adoptability," which is borrowing from someone else's ideas with appro-priate modifications. All of the above combined with a good dosage of risk-taking directly relate to the financial viability of a given business. In my mind creativity is a preamble to entrepreneurship.
>
> —Michael W. N. Chiu
> *President and Chairman*
> *Prima Donna Development Corporation*
> *Prima Hotels*

Creativity operates at an individual level, but can be stimulated by membership in a group and inspired by corporate culture. Research has demonstrated that many factors influence creativity in a work environment, including employees' knowledge of their job tasks, their education level, and their exposure to diverse situations. Support from both coworkers and nonwork associates, family, and friends can help to create an environment that stimulates creativity. Top executives are not the only people with creative potential, but these executives, like artists, thrive on their creativity. They also create environments around themselves that foster their creative potential. Other studies have suggested that, in fact, job dissatisfaction can stimulate creativity, but only if employees remain committed to staying with the offending organization.

The key, then, is to foster a climate in which new ideas are appreciated, and imple-mented, which empowers the expression of creative voice by dissatisfied team members who can contribute valuable suggestions. This is not to suggest that organizations strive to make their members unhappy in order to stimulate creativity; rather, it is to encourage the cultiva-tion of a corporate culture in which team members feel that their creative contributions will be valued.

Theorists suggest that there are different types of creativity depending upon the type of task at hand and the source of creative energy. For example, creativity that is a response to a known problem, **responsive creativity,** may operate differently than **proactive creativity,** defined as a voluntary contribution to resolve an issue not previously identified as problem-atic. Unsworth argues that the stimulation of different types of creativity demands different techniques—while responsive creativity may be facilitated by time pressure, that same pressure may stifle proactive creativity (Unsworth, 2001). For our purposes, this concept of the diversity of creativity will remain a sidelight; however, it is worth considering how different types of situations shape creativity.

Importance of Alone Time

Many creative leaders believe that if they can simply spend quiet time away from the office thinking, they are able to produce new ideas. Peter Yesawich, Chairman of Yesawich, Pepperdine, Brown and Russell, says, "The development of my creative ideas is a direct function of the extent to which I can withdraw from all the other things that are on my mind and focus my thinking." John Alexander, Chairman of the CBORD Group, Inc., states, "Creativity often requires that I leave town; my greatest creativity happens normally when I am on an airplane or in hotel rooms, where nobody knows where I am and no telephone can ring."

One of the best ways to promote clear thinking is to find some private time and space. Creative people know that it is usually not good enough to sit down and "just think about it" because people tend to have set patterns of thinking, whereas creativity depends upon pursuing as many patterns of thought as possible. The creativity techniques in this chapter are intended to help managers search for creative ideas in many more ways than "just thinking about it" would uncover.

> What do you do and where do you go when you need time alone?

Coming Up with Ideas

"Coming up with ideas" sounds easy; "being creative" sounds difficult. Why? People can usually come up with a few ideas about anything; but these ideas that come to mind immediately are almost never creative ideas—they are obvious ideas. Creative people think of the obvious ideas as well, but they don't stop there; they keep on thinking until they are out in the uncharted realm of *un*obvious ideas. It is these unobvious ideas that are creative.

For example, suppose we are trying to think of ways to serve salad at our restaurant. A few ideas will come to mind easily: in a bowl, in a salad bar, on a plate, in a sandwich. These four ideas are not considered creative because they've been done before. We just reached into our memories and took out these four ideas. But now we're stuck. We've used up the old ideas and now have to start thinking up some new ones. In other words, we have to be creative. What do we do now?

Let's look at what we came up with and how we came up with it:

- *Salad in a glass.* Whether or not this is a good idea, it is certainly a new one. We have never heard of a salad served in a glass. If we offered salad in a glass at our restaurant, people would consider us creative.

  Where did this idea come from? The process was simple; salad bowls are glass; glass . . . glasses!

- *Salad in a waffle.* This might not be too appetizing, but it *is* creative.

  Where did this idea come from? Glasses remind us of cut crystal. The cuts in the crystal look similar to the designs in waffles. Creativity depends upon one thing reminding of another, even though the logic of these remindings may not always be clear.

- *Salad in a garden.* Pick your own fresh vegetables in our backyard and we'll make a salad from them.

  This idea came from a more complex process than the preceding ones. Instead of just passively letting ourselves be reminded of things, we asked the question, "Where does salad come from?" The answer was "a garden," so "why not just leave the salad ingredients in the garden?" This time we came up with a creative answer to the initial question by asking a different question and seeing how it related.

- *Salad for Dessert.* This time we asked a question about the way in which salad is usually served and then considered some changes that could be made. Salad is usually served before the main course but what if we served it for dessert? Immediately visions of lettuce-flavored ice cream, jello molds with lettuce and carrots suspended inside, and salads with chocolate dressings come to mind.

- *Video Games and Vitamins Instead of Salad*

  Again, we changed the question. We asked the broader question, "What is the purpose of salad?" and decided that salad serves three important purposes:

  1. It is nutritious;
  2. It gives the customer something to do while the main course is being prepared;
  3. Eating a salad is fun.

  Then we decided that we did not need to serve salad in order to accomplish these three things. We could give the customers vitamin pills to take care of number 1, and we could let the customers play video games while waiting for the main course to take care of 2 and 3.

For the moment we aren't interested in whether any of these salad ideas is good, only that we can generate a lot of them. For managers to generate a large number of creative ideas, they have to ask a lot of questions and engage in some complex mental processes. Most of these will generate silly ideas. But if they stick with it for long enough, they will eventually find a useful and creative path of reasoning that no one has followed before. Sometimes, following 100 divergent paths is necessary before a good one is found.

The salad example is just an introduction to the sorts of mental processes that lead to creative ideas. In the upcoming sections of this chapter we will formally introduce multiple idea-generating techniques.

Perhaps the most famous practitioner of the philosophy of having a multitude of ideas was Thomas Edison. Edison said that, "invention is two percent inspiration and 98 percent perspiration." In order to get to the good ideas one has to work hard and test a lot of bad ideas. When looking for the right material to serve as a filament for the light bulb, Edison tested 749 different materials before he finally employed tungsten, which is used in light bulbs to this day. It is jokingly said of Edison's trial-and-error method that after inventing the light bulb the first thing he did was hold it up to his ear and say, "Hello, Watson, can you hear me?"

TOOLS OF CREATIVITY

Imagine that the human mind is an enormous room full of little boxes. In each box is one piece of information or one rule for understanding or operating in the world. In order to think, the brain is always opening the boxes and putting the contents of different boxes together to form new boxes. Creativity occurs whenever the brain unites the contents of two or more boxes that have never been united before in anyone's brain. For example, when Art Fry at the

3M Corporation combined his mental box containing note paper with his mental box for a new adhesive he had invented that would not stick permanently to anything, he introduced the Post-it pad—a creative and extremely useful idea.

Turning to the boxes that contain rules, if a hospitality manager combines the box that contains the rule, "people become happy when they win races" with the box that contains "the housekeeping staff is disgruntled," he may come up with the idea of raising the morale of the staff members by having them run a footrace against the portly executive at the company picnic. It may be a silly idea, but it is creative, and because creativity is, at least in part, a social process, increasing the social contact among members of different departments within the organization just might help diffuse conflicts and stimulate creativity (Perry-Smith and Shalley, 2003).

Notice that this definition of creativity suggests that you are creative whenever you come up with an idea that you think is new. It does not matter if it turns out later that someone else thought of it first. Of course, if the rest of the world is to think an idea is creative, it had better be something really new, because creativity is a socially defined assessment, based on the known ideas in a particular culture or context.

We apply four simple concepts to help explain the mental processes behind creative thought: keys, glue, remindings, and questions. If you understand these concepts, you will have a better understanding of what creative thought is, and will understand why the techniques in this chapter work.

In what specific ways would increasing your creativity be beneficial to you personally?

Keys and Glue

Using the model of the brain as a great room full of boxes of information, we will say that *keys* are what help open the mental boxes, while *glue* is what helps unite the contents of these boxes in potentially useful ways.

The brain already knows how to use keys and glue. Indeed, this theme is employed whenever one thinks; however, most of the time this occurs unconsciously. One doesn't think about which mental boxes to open—they just open if the brain decides to use that key. Similarly, one doesn't think about all the different ways of putting the contents of the boxes together—they just get put together in whatever order the brain decides to glue them.

Later in this chapter we discuss the creative use of keys and glue. Basically, this means consciously deciding to use the keys to open more boxes, particularly the unobvious boxes, and then gluing the contents of these boxes together in clever, unobvious ways.

Remindings

A thought never enters consciousness unless something puts it there. That is, you cannot just get the key to one of the boxes at random—something has to give you the key to that box. Often, people feel that an idea has popped into their head for no reason; however, there is always something (and it may be something unconscious) that was responsible for evoking that idea. For example, the thought of wombats does not just pop into someone's mind. There must have been something—a baseball *bat,* a previous thought that was related to wombats, a past experience that involved wombats—that served as a catalyst.

Thus, the basic currency of thinking is, in simplest terms, the process of one thought evoking another thought. Creative thinking depends upon making use of unobvious remindings.

This is because an unobvious reminding will generally give the key to an unobvious box or will suggest an unobvious way of gluing together the contents of two boxes.

Questions

The most powerful and ubiquitous tool for creativity is the question. In a sense, all creative thought depends upon questions. A key cannot be used until the brain knows which box to open next. Glue cannot be used until the brain knows which things to stick together. Again, this questioning process usually takes place unconsciously, but if a manager wants to become more creative, the most important thing he can do is to consciously ask more questions. If the manager learns to question everything—the big things, the small things, the relevant things, the irrelevant things, the possible things, and the impossible things—he will immediately become more creative.

Is it typical of you to ask a lot of questions? Explain.

TECHNIQUES FOR IMPROVING CREATIVITY USING CURRENT KNOWLEDGE

The following section introduces techniques that use only what you already know. In later sections, we will introduce techniques that require the use of other people and external stimuli as sources of ideas.

At the heart of the techniques in this chapter are two essential questions:

1. How does this problem or situation relate to other problems or situations I have encountered?
2. How can I change the way it is done now?

Free Association (Technique 1)

The **free association technique** of idea generation takes advantage of the remindings that occur when the mind wanders. When you use the free association technique, you start with something (a word, a question, a sketch, a smell, a feeling) that relates to the subject about which you are thinking. Let your mind wander and write down the intriguing boxes that it opens.

Suppose, for example, that a manager is thinking about what sort of entertainment he or she should use to attract guests to his or her bar on typically slow Wednesday nights. He or she started with the word "entertainment:"

Entertainment → Movies → Cybil Shephard →
     An article about Cybil Shephard → Magazines → Books →

Literary Classics → Sam Shepard → Acting and Writing →
     The Improvisational Comedy → Aha! Improvisational
     Comedy. Perfect!

This was a relatively logical reminding pattern. Usually, things are much more random. The randomness might seem like a hindrance, but if used correctly, it can turn out to be a source of especially creative ideas. The logical reminding pattern led to improvisational comedy which, although it is something the manager might not have thought of, is not enormously creative. Here is a much more "free" free association for solving the same problem:

Entertainment → *Movies* → **Raiders of the Lost Ark** → *Children* →
Bubble Gum → *Tooth Decay* → *Dental Floss*

Now, the manager faces a creative challenge. How can he or she relate dental floss and entertainment? He or she could offer a free dental X-ray with each drink purchased—nah. He or she could hire the local dentist to play the drums—nah. Drink discounts for dental technicians. A "best smile" competition. Drink discounts for people who have no cavities. Dental floss dispensers in the rest rooms. Sugarless drink specials.

Silly? Sure, but creative silliness might just be the ticket to a full bar on Wednesday nights.

Metaphors (Technique 2)

> Bug spray is like the walls
> We build around ourselves.
> And like these fragile walls,
> It never really works.

> —Kate Bergeron, age 14

This young poet saw a metaphorical similarity between bug spray and human defenses. Reading this poem, we learn something about the walls we build around ourselves and perhaps something about bug spray. The poet probably began by opening the "bug spray" box and then was reminded of the key to the "human walls" box. Then she found a way to glue the two together poetically. Figure 8.1 has a list of metaphors that are frequently used in business communications.

It makes sense that creativity and metaphor would be closely linked. **Metaphor** is, after all, the revealing of a relationship between two seemingly unrelated things. So if a manager needs some

---

Creative people use a lot of metaphors when they think and when they communicate. The lingo of business is replete with metaphors. Here are just a few of them:

Operational Nightmare
Emotional Rollercoaster
Competitive Dogfight
Advertising (Media) Blitz
Financial Drain
Corporate Marriage
Departmental Flagwaving
Cash Shortfall
Negotiation Marathon
Idea Wellspring
Transition Honeymoon

FIGURE 8.1   Metaphors in business communication

creative ideas, he or she should try to think of some creative metaphors. One should think about the metaphorical subject and see if anything he or she knows about it applies to the initial subject.

For example, suppose that a manager has the task of updating the computer system in his or her hotel. He or she may want some creative ideas about how to do this task well. He or she should think of a metaphor for the task, such as "updating a computer is like refinishing an old wooden table." Then, think about the metaphor and see if the metaphorical subject applies to the initial subject:

1. When refinishing an old table, you must repair the flaws in the wood before putting on the new finish. If the finish has already dried, it will be too late to do anything about it.
2. Between each coat of finish, a piece of steel wool should be used to rub it down.
3. Sometimes an old table is so rotten that it must be thrown out and a new one must be purchased.

These three observations are easily translatable to the computer-updating task:

Observation 1: Study the flaws in the old computer system and be certain that the updated system addresses those flaws.

Observation 2: Test and modify the updated system as it is being installed rather than waiting until it is all done.

Observation 3: Maybe an update is not enough—maybe it would be better to get a whole new system.

By constructing a metaphor with finishing a table, some good ideas were created about updating the computer system. Once again, if the metaphor provides the key to a mental box that is seemingly unrelated, a lot of silly ideas may arise, but there is also a greater chance that a creative idea will come to mind than through a more standard thought process.

SCAMPER (Technique 3)

Osborn (1953), a pioneer in the study of creative thinking, developed a list of action verbs that would lead to the generation of ideas about how to change something. Later, Eberle (1997) organized these action verbs into the acronym **SCAMPER:**

BOX 8.1

SCAMPER

S = Substitute
C = Combine
A = Adapt
M = Magnify, Minify
P = Put to other uses
E = Eliminate
R = Reverse, Rearrange

BOX 8.2

SCAMPER Technique

SUBSTITUTE:	Checkout by phone, by in-house television channel, by mail; allow checkout at breakfast.
COMBINE:	Combine check-out payment with check-in; offer breakfast food at check-out location; combine with services for ground transportation; combine with morning workout at hotel exercise facility.
ADAPT:	Adapt to the location of the guest; accept more credit cards; adapt to the times that guests want to checkout.
MAGNIFY:	Increase the number of people at check-out desk; make a big production out of checkout so that the guest enjoys it—have trumpets and encourage employees to weep as the guest leaves.
MINIFY:	Have all forms and bills prepared before the guest comes to checkout so that the least amount of time is required; cut some steps out of the current process; computerize to increase speed.
PUT TO OTHER USES:	While the guests are waiting to checkout, interview them about their stay and how the hotel could be improved; use check-out time as an opportunity to advertise specials that the hotel will be offering in the future.
ELIMINATE:	No checkout—the guest leaves a credit card or a large deposit with you upon arrival so that you don't have to collect money upon departure. Or, do not allow any guests to leave the hotel once they come in—this will significantly increase occupancy.
REVERSE:	Come to the guests' room and allow them to checkout there; have guests checkout when they arrive and check-in when they depart (we don't know, you figure it out).
REARRANGE:	Rearrange the check-out area; rearrange the procedure for checkout.

If a manager applies each of the SCAMPER verbs to a procedure or situation that needs to be changed, some creative ideas will evolve. Consider the traditional check-out procedure in a hotel. How can SCAMPER help generate ideas for improving the process? Box 8.2 provides an illustration.

TECHNIQUES FOR IMPROVING CREATIVITY USING OUTSIDE SOURCES

The techniques in this section will help to transcend personal and organizational boundaries in search of new ideas. Outside sources can be used to access new keys and boxes which lead to new, original ideas. We call these outside sources of ideas **locksmiths** because of their role in helping get the keys to the new boxes.

"Never, ever, think outside the box."

Notice that at the heart of all the techniques in this section is the question, "How could what I am learning from this locksmith relate to the idea I am looking for?" When you use one of the locksmiths, you are borrowing from another source and applying the idea to your own situation. Our interviews with innovative leaders confirm that businesses are filled with active borrowers.

Lists (Technique 4)

Lists can be used to grant easy access to a lot of unobvious connections. They take the place of the "let your mind wander" stage of free association (Technique 1). If the list chosen is not closely related to the subject at hand, it is more likely that one will find some truly creative ideas.

Suppose a mother is trying to think of a name for her baby. An obvious locksmith is a naming dictionary. She will not, however, find any creative names in a naming dictionary, because it only includes names that have been used before. A less obvious locksmith would be a nature encyclopedia, which will provide the keys to names such as "Platypus." A mathematical encyclopedia would be an even less obvious source of names. It would offer the keys to names such as "Rhombus," "Quadratic," "Slope," and Pythagoras." The child may never forgive her, but at least he or she will definitely have a creative name.

Proverbs (Technique 5)

In the definition of creativity provided, we suggested that one source of creative ideas is gluing the contents of a box that contains a rule for understanding and operating in the world to the contents of other boxes in original ways. For example, if the rule that says, "always eat the middle of an Oreo before eating the two cookies" is taken and applied to the box that contains peanut butter and jelly sandwiches, one may come up with a creative way of eating the peanut butter and jelly before eating the bread.

Schank (1988) suggests that proverbs are an excellent example of such rules for understanding or operating in the world. He refers to such rules as **explanation patterns,** or **XPs.** He maintains that proverbs not only reflect the tried and true wisdom of our culture, but also reflect the way our brains are organized. He has therefore developed the following technique of using proverbs as locksmiths.

Suppose a manager is trying to increase the number of repeat guests at his or her hotel. Using Schank's technique, the first step is to look in a book of proverbs under some of the headings that relate to this problem. The following proverbs are found under the headings of "hospitality," "repeating," "guests," and "friendship:"

1. Short visits make long friends.
2. The tree does not withdraw its shade even from the woodcutter.
3. Hospitality consists in a little fire, a little food, and an immense quiet.
4. In times of prosperity, friends will be plenty; in times of adversity, not one amongst 20.
5. Friendship is a plant which must often be watered.

Bonus! Fish and visitors smell in three days.

The next step in the process is to translate the proverb into neutral terms. Thus, the translated proverbs would read:

1. People enjoy short visits more than long visits.
2. It is important to be hospitable to everyone, even if they are not kind to you.
3. Peace and quiet are an important part of hospitality.
4. Friendships are easier to maintain when the friends are prosperous.
5. A friendship must be maintained if it is to grow.

Bonus! Manage your contacts and your food carefully!

The third step is to relate the sound advice in these proverbs to the situation at hand.

1. The first proverb might suggest that the manager should have short weekend specials and one-night specials. These will entice customers to come back again because they have not had time for the full experience.
2. The second proverb might suggest that the hotel staff is not sufficiently trained in dealing with difficult guests. Maybe if they learned to accommodate such guests, the guests would become repeat customers.
3. The third proverb suggests that the secret of encouraging people to return to the hotel is to create a placid atmosphere so that guests associate the hotel with relaxation and peace.
4. The fourth proverb suggests that part of the issue might be to convince guests that they are prosperous enough to deserve the hotel's services.
5. The final proverb might suggest that the manager needs to spend more time "watering" the friendships he or she has with customers. Maybe he or she should call them once a month just to see how they are doing. Maybe he or she should send Season's Greetings cards, birthday cards, or flowers.

One important thing to keep in mind when using proverbs as locksmiths is that the advice contained in them is not the law. In fact, for most proverbs there is another proverb that contradicts it. For every "too many cooks spoil the broth" there is a "two heads are better than one." Proverb number four in the list above is contradicted by "misery loves company." Proverbs one and five partially contradict each other.

Why is the tried and true wisdom in proverbs so full of contradictions? Well, proverbs became proverbs because they helped people deal with the difficult questions in life—the questions to which there are no right answers. This is why proverbs can be so beneficial to the creative process. Because they relate to questions for which there are no right answers, they lead to subjects where there is ample room for creativity. If there is no best answer, there is always a need to think of new and better answers.

The Fortune Cookie Meeting (Technique 6)

The fortune cookie meeting is a technique for an enjoyable and surprisingly effective creative meeting. Bring a bag of fortune cookies and pass a few cookies out to each person. Then, using Technique 5 (Proverbs), apply the fortunes in the cookies to the issue that is being discussed. Even when the fortune seems to be unrelated to the question at hand, find a way to relate it. Fortune cookies tend to contain proverbs and other "rules for dealing with the world" and, as such, serve as excellent proverbial locksmiths.

Innovative Imitation (Technique 7)

One of the best locksmiths available is another organization. Learn about organizations in other industries that have been successful in similar situations. Sometimes a manager will be able to import an idea in its entirety from one of these organizations. What is even better is when the manager can see a missing ingredient in the other organization's idea, which, if added to the idea, would be the key to the organization's success. Also, look at ideas that failed in other organizations. Failure is a crucial source of creative ideas. From learning about these failures, a manager not only can learn to avoid failure in his or her organization, but also might be able to see the missing ingredient that would turn that failure into a success.

There is nothing unethical about innovative imitation, and even though it involves "borrowing" other people's ideas, it is still creative because the idea can be refined for use in a new situation.

Creative imitation is not "innovation" in the sense in which the term is most commonly understood. The creative imitator does not invent a product or service; he perfects and positions it. In the form in which it has been introduced, it lacks something. It may be additional product features. It may be segmentation of product or services so that slightly different versions fit slightly different markets. It might be proper positioning of the product in the market. Or the creative imitation supplies something that is still lacking.

Who is the most creative person you know? In what ways is his or her creativity demonstrated?

DEVELOPING A CREATIVE GROUP

A great deal of the thinking and planning done by most organizations takes place in meetings. Thus, if an organization is to become more creative, it must promote creativity in groups. For some people, even job dissatisfaction can be a key to stimulating creativity—in order to improve working conditions—when coworkers give feedback, help, and support (Zhous and George, 2001). In this section, we will discuss the best ways of leading a group to a good idea.

One of the keys to developing creative groups is the inspiration of a team concept among the participants. Many innovative industry leaders expressed their beliefs that interaction with others stimulated the creative process.

Theoretically, a group should be extremely creative. The more people there are to think about something, the more boxes that can be opened and the more types of glue that can be supplied. In practice, however, groups often fail to live up to their creative potential. People in groups are embarrassed to share their bad ideas. They are afraid to share a bad idea for fear that others will think they are stupid. This fear is a serious hindrance to the group's creative process. Creating and maintaining good communication within the group and facilitating a social setting conducive to the flow of ideas is critical to the success of creativity, or "brainstorming," at the group level. Often, the best creative ideas stem from bad ideas. If people are not sharing their bad ideas, a crucial source of good ideas has been lost. Thus one of the important subjects discussed in this section concerns how to rid people of their inhibitions about sharing bad ideas.

The Speech

Before any group is asked to do something creative, it should be given a version of The Speech. The Speech is a way of ridding people of their inhibitions about sharing bad ideas. This is what The Speech should say:

> We are now going to try to (whatever the creative thing is you are trying to do). This is going to require some creative thought. I want to remind everyone that good creative ideas do not appear easily or quickly. They require a lot of thinking. So we are now going to try to generate a lot of ideas. Most of these ideas will be silly. That is *good*! We want silly ideas. Often the best creative ideas are the result of modifying a silly idea. So if you have a silly or foolish idea, share it! If you have a dumb question, ask it! We won't think that you are silly or foolish. We will think that you are making an essential contribution to the creative process.

Discussion Formats

Once the speech has been given, the discussion format is introduced. A discussion format is a procedure that the group will follow as it searches for ideas. The discussion formats that we will introduce are Group brainstorming, the nominal group technique (NGT), NGT–Storming, and question questing.

DISCUSSION FORMAT 1: *GROUP BRAINSTORMING*   In the *group brainstorming* discussion format, members of the group are encouraged to generate ideas in a rapid-fire, free-flowing manner. No one leads the discussion. The idea is to quickly get the keys to a lot of mental boxes. A fast note-taker should be used to keep a record of everything that comes up in the discussion, preferably on something large enough for all to see. Five rules must be followed:

- *No Judging.* No criticisms or judgments should be made about anything that anyone says. Never say: "Let's get down to earth" or "let's not be ridiculous" or "that's stupid."
- *Encourage Freewheeling.* As explained in The Speech, no idea is too absurd to mention. The general feeling should be that the wilder it is the better, because it will open up new paths of thought.
- *Go for Quantity.* As usual, the goal is to come up with as many ideas as possible. Do not allow any lulls in the conversation, keep the ideas flowing fast and furious (see rule 5).

- *Encourage Piggybacking.* If an interesting idea comes up, feel free to "piggyback" on it; modify it, pursue it further, or ask new questions about it.
- *Ask Questions.* The contributions to the brainstorming session should be both ideas and questions. When there is a lull in the discussion, a provocative question can be perfect for generating new discussion.

Once an extensive list of ideas and questions has been developed, the ban on judging is lifted and the group reviews the list. At this stage, the group should be more practical and try to converge upon a few ideas and questions it wants to consider more deeply.

There are no particularly good names in this brief transcript. Indeed, some of the ideas are horrible. For example, "Open Heart," with its suggestion of surgery, would be an embarrassing name for a restaurant that is supposed to be good for your heart. Still, no one passed judgment on the bad ideas. Instead, they concentrated on generating new ideas. Jane's group does not have the right name yet, but we can be confident that by the time they have thought of one hundred names they will have thought of at least one that they like.

BOX 8.3

Hypothetical Brainstorming Session

JANE:	Ok team, let's brainstorm names for our new fast-food restaurant that features low-sodium foods.
JILL:	Something that points out that the food will be good for your heart—Warm Heart, Sweet Hearts, Big Hearts . . .
TED:	Heart warming, Open Hearts, No Heart Breaker . . .
JANE:	No Salt Shaker, No Heart Breaker . . .
GLEN:	How about something using heart and hearth?
JILL:	The Warm Hearth, Hearth and Soul . . .
TED:	Food with Heart . . .
GLEN:	Hearty Food, Listen to Your Heart, An Affair of the Heart . . .
JILL:	The Hearty Hearth . . .
	(There is a brief lull in the conversation, Jane rekindles discussion with a question)
JANE:	Besides being good for your heart, what are the other benefits of low-sodium food?
JILL:	It isn't excessively salty, you can taste the other spices
GLEN:	Low Salt, High Taste, Saltaholics Anonymous . . .
TED:	Taste 'n Pepper
JANE:	The atomic symbol for Sodium is Na. How about NoNa?
JILL:	Low Na, BanaNa . . .
JANE:	We have the beginnings of some great names. How can we combine the three strengths: good for your heart, more interesting to taste, and fast service?
TED:	Great heart, Head Start, Taste Art . . .

Groups that are brainstorming can significantly increase the quantity and quality of their ideas if they use the techniques discussed in this chapter. The most effective techniques for group brainstorming are the following:

1. Free association
2. Locksmiths
3. SCAMPER.

First, let the brainstorming session take its natural course; then, when things slow down, utilize one of the techniques.

> Explain how evaluating ideas inhibits creativity.

DISCUSSION FORMAT 2: *THE NOMINAL GROUP TECHNIQUE*   The *nominal group technique* consists of six steps. The first three require divergent thinking (idea generation) and the last three require convergent thinking (idea selection).

Step 1   The group members work individually. For 5–20 minutes, each person works on generating a list of ideas and questions. If the subject for discussion has been introduced before the meeting, then people can be encouraged to come to the meeting with their lists already prepared. Participants should use the techniques previously discussed earlier in this chapter during Step 1 of the NGT.

Step 2   The participants begin to function as a group. The group leader goes around the table eliciting a single idea from each of the participants, while a recorder lists the idea on a large sheet of paper or chalkboard. After each person has contributed an idea, the leader again goes around the table taking a second idea from each participant. The leader keeps going around until everyone is out of ideas.

Step 3   The group discusses each idea that has been recorded. Questions may be asked, modifications may be suggested, problems with the idea may be pointed out, but no qualitative judgments such as "this idea is great" or "this idea is dumb" should be made.

Step 4   The participants individually rank the ideas. If there are 50 ideas, each participant's favorite idea would be ranked 1 and the least favorite idea would be ranked 50.

Step 5   An average ranking for each idea is tabulated.

Step 6   If there is a clear winner, go with that idea. Otherwise, take the top few ideas and try to get the group to agree on one of them.

DISCUSSION FORMAT 3: *A COMBINATION—NGT–STORMING*   *NGT–Storming,* a combination of the brainstorming format and the NGT format, is often the best group creativity format. This process includes the following six steps.

Step 1   Each individual compiles a list of ideas and questions. Again, the techniques from the previous sections should be used at this stage. This can be done before, or at the beginning of the meeting.

Step 2   A group brainstorming session begins. Group members both contribute entries from their lists and make up new ideas.

Step 3 When the brainstorming session concludes, people should contribute any ideas from their lists that have not yet come up in the discussion.

Step 4 The ideas are discussed.

Step 5 Participants are given some time to consider the ideas on their own. Sometimes it is wise to close the meeting at this stage so that people can go home and "sleep on it."

Step 6 The group tries to reach a consensus about which idea is best. If no consensus can be reached, the ranking system employed in NGT is used to select the "winning" idea.

DISCUSSION FORMAT 4: *QUESTION QUESTING* As we have frequently pointed out, the master tool for generating creative thoughts is a series of good questions. So, a particularly effective group discussion format we use is *Question questing*. The most creative meetings often begin with this technique. Question questing is basically a brainstorming session in which the sole objective is to produce lots of questions. The same rules that apply to group brainstorming apply to Question questing.

At certain times in a Question questing session, answering a question may be permitted. This applies particularly to informational questions that must be answered before a line of inquiry can be continued. When the leader of the group hears such a question being asked, he or she should say "Answer" and then provide the answer or allow a participant to respond. Once a lengthy list of questions has been developed, the group should go through the list, question by question, and attempt to provide creative answers.

BOX 8.4

Question Questing Session

FRED:	Should we build a new conference center?
JANE:	Why would we want to build a new conference center?
LIZA:	Who would we be serving in this conference center?
WILL:	What work is involved in building it?
JANE:	Do conference centers usually make money?
WILL:	Is there any competition?
LIZA:	Is the competition making money?
FRED:	Answer: There is a conference center 15 miles from here. They broke even last year. What would we do to beat the competition?
JANE:	Why do people go to conferences? What do they really want out of a conference center?
WILL:	Is there a service that our conference center could provide that no one has ever provided before?
LIZA:	Is there a more appealing name than "conference center?"
FRED:	What would happen if we opened up our conference center and then someone else opened up a better one?
WILL:	What does pond scum have to do with conference centers?
JANE:	Will we have to increase the water supply to the hotel?
LIZA:	What about parking?

(continued)

(continued)

FRED: In what ways is parking like stacking apples at a grocery store?

WILL: Where will we get the money?

LIZA: How is the local economy doing?

WILL: Is there a local business that would give us some money to start up if we would allow them to hold their conferences in our conference center?

LIZA: What color should it be? If we had unlimited time and money how would we do it? Where will this end?

(The question quest continues. Eventually there is a lull in the conversation so Fred steps in:)

FRED: Okay, any more questions?

WILL: Is there a way that we could build it closer to the airport?

JANE: Is there a way we could move the airport closer to the conference center?

FRED: What type of transportation do people prefer to take to an airport?

(The quest continues in this manner until Fred finally says:)

FRED: Who wants to break for coffee?

JANE: What is the meaning of coffee?

WILL: What would happen if instead of drinking coffee and smoking tobacco, people smoked coffee and drank tobacco?

(Two hours later . . .)

LIZA: If we build an inside-out, underwater, conference center, what color blimp would we use to transport our customers to the dark room?

When the question quest is over, the group would next pursue answers, perhaps by using one of the previous three discussion formats.

Which of the techniques just discussed do you find most promising? Identify a question or problem that could be addressed using that technique.

Choosing the Right Ideas

Before becoming too analytical, consider some easy scenarios that are likely to constitute the majority of cases.

Case 1: Harry, a manager at Warriot Hotels, has come up with an idea that is clearly superior to all others generated. It has caught the fancy of his colleagues as well. The majority agree that it is the idea to implement. In this case, Harry shouldn't overanalyze the situation, he should just go for the idea that everyone already agrees on.

Case 2: Another manager at Warriot Hotels, Mandy, faces a situation where she is attempting to increase breakfast sales. She has three choices: special prices, specialty items, and guaranteed quick service. It doesn't seem like a good idea to just try one, so she implements all three. Breakfast business began booming! Mandy wasn't able to determine what the impact of each idea was; however, the dining room is overflowing in the morning so determining the impact of each is the least of her concerns.

Case 3: Todd, another manager at Warriot Hotels, has several good ideas, but cannot combine them as Mandy did in Case 2 to produce a single "best" idea. His first idea has revenue-enhancing potential, the second might increase employee morale, and his third idea has the potential of improving service for the guests. It would be worthwhile for Todd to explore whether attributes of each idea could be combined to accomplish all three positive effects. In this case it is not necessary to determine which is the best idea for implementation.

The tough case arises when a group has generated five or six ideas that seem good, but only one or two can be selected. A clear choice is not evident, combining the ideas is not fruitful, and gut feel does not seem to be a good avenue to pursue.

The selection process consists of three elements:

- A list of "necessary" selection criteria;
- A list of "desirable" selection criteria weighted according to their relative importance;
- A rating scheme (e.g., a 1–10 scale where 1 is poor and 10 is excellent).

Necessary Selection Criteria

"Necessary" selection criteria, as the name suggests, are criteria that an idea must meet to be considered. If the idea fails to satisfy any of the "necessary" criteria, it cannot be considered for implementation in its present form. For example, the idea

1. Must have the potential to increase revenue;
2. Must not detract from the current level of customer service;
3. Must not adversely affect employee morale;
4. Must be in line with the company mission.

The first step, therefore, is to determine which ideas under consideration have fulfilled the "necessary" selection criteria. Second, if an idea fails to meet any of these criteria, you must drop or alter it in such a way as to bring it in line with the "necessary" conditions.

Desirable Selection Criteria

"Desirable" selection criteria are those which will be considered for choosing among the ideas that have survived Step 1. If the decision involves choosing a new item to include on the menu, the "desirable" criteria might include sales potential, cost, perceived quality of product, gross profit margin, compatibility with current menu, and availability from competitors. The better the idea satisfies the selection criteria, the better it should be rated for possible implementation.

The "desirable" selection criteria will not carry equal importance invariably. This relative importance of each criterion must be dealt with either explicitly or implicitly. The decision-maker may simply recognize that "sales potential" is very important and "availability from competitors" is far less important. On the other hand, the manager may choose to be considerably more precise in the decision making and attribute specific weights to these selection criteria. For example, the relatively important "sales potential" may carry 30 percent of the weight in the decision process, while the less important "availability from competitors" may carry only 5 percent of the weight.

All criteria important to the final decision should be included with some reasonable sense of their relative importance specified. This may seem like a very analytical, left-brain activity that any self-respecting, right-brain, divergent individual would find objectionable and, therefore, reject. However, everyone actually carries out such a process any time they make a choice among alternatives. A manager should have some bases in mind that range from "big-time" to "that-would-be-nice." The manager should then let his or her mental calculator make the necessary "soft" computations to reach a decision. The process is the same, only the level of formality differs. Next, we will take the slightly more formal approach with this decision process.

The Rating Scheme

The rating scheme is the final element of the decision process. This scheme enables you to rate each idea on each selection criterion. The rating range could be high, medium, and low; it could be excellent, good, fair, and poor; or it might be a 1–5 or 1–10 scale with the extremes representing least acceptable to most acceptable, respectively. Presumably, the various rating schemes will lead to the same choice if the scales are consistently applied. Terms such as high, low, excellent, and poor may have an appeal to the less quantitative individuals; however, the numeric ratings will force the decision process to be quite exact and will enable a manager to more carefully rank the alternatives.

We have now completely defined the three elements to our decision process:

- The "necessary" criteria have eliminated or caused the alteration of any ideas that violated any of these hurdles. For our purposes, assume five ideas have survived.
- The "desirable" criteria have defined the issues to be used to rate and select the ideas. Assume that each of the five criteria has been afforded equal weight. Because the weights must sum to 1 or 100 percent, each will have a weight of .2 or 20 percent in the decision process.
- The scale of 1 (low) to 10 (high) will be used to assess how well each idea fits each criterion.

The rating grid might appear as follows:

	Idea 1	Idea 2	Idea 3	Idea 4	Idea 5
Criterion 1 (.2)	8	9	7	8	7
Criterion 2 (.2)	6	8	7	5	9
Criterion 3 (.2)	7	9	6	8	5
Criterion 4 (.2)	5	7	8	9	8
Criterion 5 (.2)	8	6	6	7	9
Weighted Average	6.8	7.8	6.8	7.4	7.6

The weighted average for Idea 1 is calculated as follows:

$$W.A. = (8 \times .2) + (6 \times .2) + (7 \times .2) + (5 \times .2) + (8 \times .2)$$
$$= 1.6 + 1.2 + 1.4 + 1.0 + 1.6 = 6.8$$

The other weighted averages are computed in the same manner. According to these ratings, Idea 2 is the best, followed closely by Idea 5, then Idea 4.

Before selecting the best idea, however, ask yourself a couple of questions. Is the outcome consistent with what is anticipated? Does the outcome feel right? You might need to reconsider the weights assigned to the five criteria. Is it possible that a small change to these weights would result in a realignment of the ideas? For example, if Criterion 2 or Criterion 5 were weighted more heavily, Idea 5 would likely surpass Idea 2. Are the ratings as they should be? If Idea 4 were not rated quite so poorly on Criterion 2, or if Idea 5 had a bit better rating on Criterion 3, could they both surpass Idea 2?

Be careful, however, of becoming too taken by the apparent exactness of this methodology. Precision is nice but a wrong answer to three decimal places is still a wrong answer. Establishing the criterion weights and estimating the ratings is an inexact process that may give the illusion of correctness. If the numbers do not agree with what feels correct, rethink the process. The right side of the brain must be comfortable with what the left side of the brain is suggesting.

> Is it possible for a group to select an option or make a choice without establishing criteria?

BLOCKS TO CREATIVITY AND HOW TO ELIMINATE THEM

In the previous sections, we discussed how the creative process is supposed to work. Sometimes, however, the creative process does not work as well as it should. Sometimes the ideas simply don't flow. Sometimes they flow only in certain limited directions.

If you notice that ideas are not flowing with complete freedom, you may be experiencing a **creativity block.** A block is anything that prevents you from getting the keys to certain boxes or prevents the gluing of ideas in certain ways. Blocks can be imposed by other people, by the rules and values of society, or by your own mind.

Blocks must be eliminated so that the ideas can flow freely again. The tools that are used to eliminate blocks are called **sledgehammers.** The process of eliminating a block can be referred to as *smashing a block with a sledgehammer*. If you want to be creative, you must be vigilant in the search for blocks that may be inhibiting creativity. You must always carry the sledgehammers with which to smash the blocks.

The lyrics from Harry Chapin (Box 8.5) provide a poignant example of how blocks inhibit creativity. As you read them, try to think of some of the ways that you, your organization, and your society play the role of the first teacher in the song.

Success in business depends upon the ability to "paint a new and better flower" than the competition. There are very few businesses that can afford to coast along painting the same old red and green flowers.

We will discuss the six categories of blocks, and their six corresponding sledgehammers, in terms of ideas presented in *Flowers are Red* (Adams, 1979):

> Block 1: "There's no need to see flowers any other way than the way they've always been seen."

In business it is easy to adopt the attitude, "if it ain't broke, don't fix it." Red and green flowers are beautiful, so why change them? This attitude may have its place in some business situations, but it is never good for creativity. It is a block. It stops you from asking questions and considering alternatives. If you are not looking for ways to improve operations, then operations will not improve.

Ironically, organizations that became successful as a result of some highly creative ideas often began to suffer from Block 1 as soon as they become successful. This is because they are

BOX 8.5

The lyrics from Harry Chapin

Flowers are Red

The little boy went first day of school
He got some crayons and started to draw
He put colors all over the paper
For colors was what he saw
And the teacher said, "What you doing young man?"
"I'm painting flowers," he said.
She said, "It's not the time for art, young man,
And anyway flowers are green and red.
There's a time for everything, young man,
And a way it should be done.
You've got to show concern for everyone else
For you're not the only one."

And she said,
"Flowers are red, young man
Green leaves are green,
There's no need to see flowers any other way
Than they way they always have been seen."

But the little boy said,
"There are so many colors in the rainbow,
So many colors in the morning sun,
So many colors in the flower
And I see every one."

Well the teacher said, "You're sassy
There's ways that things should be,
And you'll paint flowers the way they are
So repeat after me,
'Flowers are red, young man,
And Green leaves are green
There's no need to see flowers any other way
Than they way they always have been seen.'"

But the little boy said,
"There are so many colors in the rainbow
So many colors in the morning sun
So many colors in the flower
And I see every one."

The teacher put him in a corner
She said, "It's for your own good.

(continued)

(continued)

And you won't come out, 'til you get it right
And are responding like you should."
Well finally he got lonely, frightened thoughts filled his head
So he went up to the teacher and this is what he said,
"Flowers are red,
Green leaves are green,
There's no need to see flowers any other way
Than the way they always have been seen."

Time went by like it always does
And they moved to another town,
And the little boy went to another school
And this is what he found,
The teacher there was smiling
She said, "Painting should be fun,
And there are so many colors in the rainbow,
So let's use every one."

But the little boy painted flowers
In neat rows of green and red
And when the teacher asked him why,
This is what he said,

"Flowers are red, green leaves are green
There's no need to see flowers any other way
Than the way they always have been seen."

—*Story Songs Ltd., 1978*

afraid to attempt risky new projects in which they may lose their prosperity. What such organizations fail to realize is that while they are resting on their laurels, other companies not suffering from Block 1 are out there trying to devise a way to put them out of business.

> Sledgehammer 1: "Look for new and better flowers. Try using some of the many colors in the rainbow, or in the morning sun . . ."

The sledgehammer that smashes Block 1 is to adopt the attitude, "Sure it ain't broke, but maybe it could be working even better." This concept applies not only to products and policies but also to ideas. Never accept an idea because it seems to be "the right idea." Assume that there are always two right ideas and that the one that hasn't been thought of yet is better than the current idea.

von Oech (1983) offers a good technique for encouraging people to wield Sledgehammer 1:

One technique for finding the second right answer is to change the questions you use to probe a problem. For example, how many times have you heard someone say, "What is the answer?" or "What is the meaning of this?" or "What is the result?" These people are looking for *the* answer and *the* meaning, and *the* result.

If you train yourself to ask, "What are the answers?" and "What are the meanings?" and "What are the results?" you will find that people will think a little more deeply and offer more than one idea (p. 25).

Block 2: "It's not the time for art, young man, and flowers aren't even my department."

An old hotel story describes a low-level employee returning home with the announcement that he had just been promoted to the position of Vice President in charge of Coffee. His wife, not believing such a position existed, phoned the hotel to check it out. When she asked the switchboard operator to connect her with the Vice President for Coffee, the operator replied, "Would that be regular or decaffeinated?"

Of course, a Vice President for Decaffeinated Coffee is a bit absurd, but specialization within the corporate structures is very much a reality. This kind of specialization is sometimes required to carry out the wide range of complex services that guests expect from a hospitality organization; handled incorrectly, however, it can be a block to creativity. An employee, devoted to a limited set of highly specialized activities, is unlikely to open a wide range of boxes or acquire the new boxes that growing and learning offer. Limited boxes result in limited creativity. If all a child has are red and green crayons, she will never draw anything but red and green flowers.

Sledgehammer 2: Cross the boundaries into new flower gardens; borrow other people's crayons.

If the person in charge of buffets does nothing except coordinate buffets, chances are those buffets will not be creative. Suppose, however, that this same person is encouraged

- To watch the way employees are motivated in the housekeeping department
- To observe how food is prepared so quickly in the snack bar
- To visit other hotels to see how they coordinate their buffets
- To read about rituals in other cultures for offering food to the gods.

Then this employee might return with some new ideas and approaches.

Even though an organization may require a high degree of specialization, it should keep open the borders between different departments. It should encourage cross-fertilization of ideas by sometimes inviting an accountant into an interior design meeting or a front desk manager into a food and beverage meeting.

Indeed, the creative manager of a large resort in the Southeast told us of the time he invited a chef to a marketing meeting. The chef was silent through the first hour of the meeting while the marketers were putting a new vacation package together. Then, when they thought they were finished and were about to close the meeting the chef said, "Wait, this package needs a garnish—something extra that will make it special." The marketers took his advice and added celebrity tennis tournaments to the package. Sales doubled.

Block 3: "I can only paint flowers in neat rows of red and green; I don't know how to use all the colors in the rainbow."

Block 3 is a lack of confidence in creative abilities. If you don't believe you have the ability to think creative thoughts, then you won't think creative thoughts. If you don't approach the world with an attitude that says, "I am going to have a great idea today," then you won't be looking for great ideas. If you don't look for great ideas, you won't find them.

> Sledgehammer 3: Use every crayon in the box.

Recognize that scientists have yet to discover, and probably never will discover, a gene that determines how creative a person will be. If a person is extremely creative, it is probably because that person has developed certain thinking habits that lead to creative ideas. He or she automatically uses many of the creativity techniques discussed in the earlier sections of this chapter. If a person seems to be extremely *un*creative it is probably because he or she has none of these habits, never questions anything, and never considers new ways of doing things. In neither case does the person's creativity level result from some inborn trait.

If creativity derives from mental habits rather than innate abilities, then becoming more creative is simply a matter of acquiring the right mental habits. We have never found an exception. You cannot help but be creative if you take the time to try.

> Block 4: "Painting should not be fun."

Some people take themselves and their jobs too seriously. When people start joking at a meeting they might say, "Let's get serious." When a discussion wanders off topic they might say, "Let's get back to business." But what is humor? Humor is looking at things in unusual ways, tampering with accepted ways of doing things, disregarding accepted values. The definition of humor sounds a lot like the definition of creativity.

There is a logical basis to the suggestion that humor and creativity naturally go together. The fear of failing, or of being wrong, foolish, or different can stifle creativity. Humor, however, encourages us to be foolish and to see things differently. In fact, when it comes to being humorous, the more foolish we are, the more successful we become. So the first benefit of humor is that it temporarily puts on hold the fears that inhibit creativity.

In addition, humor itself is often creative. Humor often results from connecting two concepts in a different and hopefully funny manner. The result is that an issue is seen in a different way. We find it funny when a comedian such as Steven Wright tells us that he accidentally inserted his ignition key in his apartment door; when he turned it, the apartment started up and he decided to drive it around for a while. Likewise, we are amused when he tells us that he mistakenly tried to turn his television on with his garage door opener; the TV screen rolled up exposing a tiny rake and lawn mower inside. Mixing functions of car and apartment keys or garage door openers and TV remote control units is the type of creative connection that we are seeking. Seeing items in a different way is the essence of creativity. The second benefit of humor, therefore, is to activate the mind to think in a creative way.

Finally, when you apply humor to a problem or opportunity in business, it helps you see the situation in a different way. Encourage employees to direct humor toward the salad bar, the check-in counter, the underused restaurant, or the over-booked rooms, and see what this humorous look might suggest. While the humor may not provide a direct solution, it will certainly get your employees thinking about the situation from a different angle, and that is the first step in reaching a creative solution.

Too often the environment in an organization is too somber and is not conducive to humor. When people feel that they must always be serious, they tend to limit their thoughts. They don't allow their minds to wander. This is a block to creativity.

Sledgehammer 4: Painting should be fun!

Smashing Block 4 is simple and fun—everyone should enjoy themselves. But joking and playing are useful for more than just icebreakers. They actually lead to good ideas.

Block 5: "There's a way things should be done" (Follow rules).

People like to make rules. Rules make life simpler. One of the ways rules do this is by keeping us from having to think. For example, most people do not decide for themselves whether or not to grow grass around their homes. It is just expected they will. However, they could instead think about the pros and cons, make a decision, and then be prepared to back up that decision. Some people have come up with creative alternatives, such as rocks, polished stones, sand, slate, artificial turf, or wood chips. These alternatives would not need to be watered, mowed, edged, or chemically treated. Why not plant tomatoes or corn in the front yard? The results would be both attractive and delicious, a very productive use of space. But most people do not bother to think about it—the convention of lawns has obviated the need to think. A lawn may be a good convention, but like all rules or conventions, it is a block to creativity.

Rules seem to be essential to the smooth functioning of families, businesses, schools, and societies. We have written rules and unwritten rules. We have rules that we follow without even knowing why we follow them. For example, you almost never stand with your back to a person to whom you are speaking. You are unwittingly following a rule that says, "Thou shalt face the person with whom thou art speaking."

Creativity depends upon breaking rules, doing something in a way that no one has done it before. Whenever rules are followed, things are being done the way everyone has done them before. The history of creative thought is a history of breaking rules. Copernicus broke the rule that the sun revolved around the earth when he advanced his theory of how the solar system really worked. Architect Isaiah Rogers broke with centuries of inn tradition in 1828 by building Boston's Tremont House, the world's first "modern" hotel. In this century, Portman (designer of "atrium" hotels) continued to revolutionize the physical shape of hotels, while Bill Marriott proved that a luxury hotel *could* be built in a rundown neighborhood like Times Square when he built the New York Marriott Marquis.

An organization that promotes the mentality that the rules must always be followed is suffering from a creative block.

Sledgehammer 5: Ask: "Why are flowers red and leaves green?" Create an organizational climate in which people are encouraged to break rules for creative purposes.

This is a two-part sledgehammer. The first part is always to question the rules. Ask, "Who says the sun revolves around the earth?" "Why is the front desk procedure this way?" "Why is there an unwritten rule that discourages us from singing during staff meetings?" Ask, "Why are the keys on a computer keyboard in that order?" As long as the rules are questioned, they will never hamper creativity.

Sometimes a manager will come to the conclusion that the rules are good rules and that thinking about them will simply increase everyone's understanding of them. Sometimes a manager will come to the conclusion that they are bad rules and that thinking about them will lead to creative improvement or innovation. Recognize that many people are averse to questioning and changing things. If a manager is always questioning things, he or she will probably have to endure the disapproval of uncreative people; but the rewards of being a freethinking creative person will make it worthwhile for both the individual and the organization.

The second part of this sledgehammer is to promote an organization in which the rules are flexible. Let people know that they are free to break or bend the rules as long as it is for creative purposes.

> Block 6: "But what if I make a black flower and no one likes it? What if it dies?"

A lot of people are afraid of their creative ideas. They think, "There must be a good reason why no one has ever tried it this way," or "What if I fail?" The fear of failure is a serious block to creativity. It is also a deeply ingrained block. From the earliest days of our schooling we are taught that there are right answers and wrong answers, and we are punished for offering the wrong answer.

People who are afraid of failing will not only be afraid to implement their creative ideas, but they will also tend to follow the thinking rules that have been used successfully in the past rather than trying to devise their own creative rules; therefore, they will have fewer creative ideas.

> Sledgehammer 6: Realize the benefits of failure.

Thomas J. Watson, the founder of IBM, once said, "The only way to succeed is to double your failure rate."

Carl Winston said, "If I'm not failing at least 25 percent of the time then I'm not being adventurous enough in my thinking." What these creative people are confirming is that failure is an essential part of the creative process. Creative ideas are often risky ideas. When an idea is implemented that no one has ever implemented before, new trails are being made and there are no rules to use for guidance. Creative people are willing to take risks. Edison was willing to fail 749 times before he found the right filament for his light bulb.

Another benefit of failure is that it often leads to new ideas that are successful. Columbus, after all, had been trying to sail to India. Popcorn was invented when Native American cornfields accidentally caught fire. Charles Goodyear discovered how to vulcanize rubber when he accidentally dropped a mixture of rubber, white lead, and sulfur onto a hot stove. Failure in one endeavor often leads directly or indirectly to success in another.

Looking back at all of the blocks to creativity that were covered, which one would you most enjoy smashing with your sledgehammer? Why?

Summary

This chapter's creativity philosophy should be looked at this way:

- Think up 101 ideas.
- Select a few good ones.
- Try one of them.
- If it fails, learn from the mistake.
- Try another idea.

We provided multiple techniques that will help a manager think creatively. Some of these techniques use the knowledge one already has; they just get the individual to use that knowledge in new ways. The other techniques that we discuss use locksmiths, or outside information, to help an individual find creative ideas.

In order to select a few good ideas from among many, apply the following three steps:

1. Create necessary selection criteria;
2. Create desirable selection criteria; and
3. Create a rating scheme.

Once you have selected a creative idea, implement it. However, you may face criticism from others who do not see the importance of creativity within organizations. Remember that failure is positive for a creative manager. Many creative thinkers had inventions that failed; however, their failure gave them new ideas and motivated them to keep working.

Key Words

creativity *206*
responsive creativity *206*
proactive creativity *206*
free association technique *210*
metaphor *211*

SCAMPER *212*
locksmiths *213*
explanation patterns, XPs *215*
creative imitation *216*

necessary selection criteria *222*
desirable selection criteria *222*
creativity block *224*
sledgehammers *224*

Exercises

Exercise 1   The Lines of Creativity

Without lifting your pencil from the paper, draw four straight lines which will go through all nine dots, but through each dot only once. After you have tried some different ways, ask yourself what restrictions you have set up for yourself in solving this problem.

***

Exercise 2   Matrix Analysis

Objective: To ensure that students open all of the boxes that are directly relevant to a problem

Procedure:

1. Split participants into groups of four to six people.
2. Read the following scenario to each group:

   Suppose that your hotel has a café which is extremely busy during meals, but is empty between meals. You cannot send the large staff home between meals; you are paying them to do nothing. So you want to think of something that will get people to use the café between meals.

3. Explain to participants that they will be filling out a matrix to help them think of ideas for getting more people into the café between meals. A matrix contains one series of related items along a vertical axis and another series of related items along a horizontal axis. Participants should fill in the matrix with ideas that relate the vertical items to the horizontal items. In this example, the vertical axis will contain different clientele groups and the horizontal axis will contain different slow periods during the day.

4. Allow participants 30 minutes to fill in the matrix with as many creative ideas as possible.
5. When the time limit is up, have all the groups convene and share their ideas for how to increase the café's business during between-meal periods.

GOAL: To increase business during between-meal periods

We have provided a few examples to better explain the purpose of the matrix. Fill in the rest of the matrix with as many creative ideas as possible.

	Breakfast-lunch	Lunch-dinner	Dinner-evening	Late night
Young Children	Morning snack and storytelling			
Students		Afternoon snack and study, student–teacher conferences		
Tourists			Regional desserts, local wine tasting	
Business People				A bar for "networking"
Theater Crowd			Discount drinks for people who went to really bad shows and walked out	
Senior Citizens		Snacks, early dinner, lectures, or discussions		

Source: Berger, F. & Ferguson, D. H. (1990). *Innovation: Creativity Techniques for Hospitality Managers.* New York: John Wiley & Sons, Inc.

Exercise 3   Promoting City Tourism

Objective: To encourage students to think creatively rather than purely analytical

Procedure:

1. Break participants into groups (about five people in each group).
2. Read the following scenario to the groups:

   Your company has been recruited to create an advertising promotion for the tourism industry of a city. The city is your choice and it may be located anywhere in the world you wish. With the costs of cable television programming going down, you have decided that you can afford a two minute mini "infomercial," rather than the 30-second spots you have used in the past. However, a creative approach is needed to make your new commercial attention getting and persuasive. You may make up any necessary details about your city—name, location, attractions, population.

3. Allow the groups to have 30 minutes to create their commercial. Let them know that they will be performing their commercial in front of the other groups.
4. After the 30 minutes has elapsed, have each group act out their commercial. Have everyone write down comments about the other groups' commercials. Everyone should vote for the commercial that they thought was the most creative; they cannot vote for their own. Have the participants vote individually, not as a group.
5. Each person should evaluate the groups according to how creative, attention-getting, and persuasive the commercial was.
6. Once the votes are in, discuss with the participants the aspects that made each commercial creative.

Exercise 4   SCAMPER

Objectives:

- To help students use the SCAMPER technique introduced in the chapter
- To encourage students to think more creatively

Procedure:

1. Divide participants into groups of four.
2. Have each group apply the SCAMPER technique to the traditional check-in process at a hotel.

   S = Substitute
   C = Combine

A = Adapt
M = Magnify, Minify
P = Put to other uses
E = Eliminate
R = Reverse, Rearrange

3. After a given period of time, 30 minutes should be sufficient, have the groups reconvene and present their ideas to the other groups.

4. Discuss with participants the difficulty of changing such a traditional process. Ask if it was difficult to think creatively. Ask if the SCAMPER technique helped them during the process.

Source: Osborn, A. (1953). *Applied Imagination: Principles and Procedures of Creative Problem Solving.* New York: Charles Scribner's Sons, 1953.

Exercise 5   My Hospitality Organization is Like . . .

Objective: To help participants find a way to glue together the contents of two seemingly unrelated boxes

Procedure:

1. On a flipchart or projection screen, display the following poem:

   Love is like a snowmobile.
   Cruising through the tundra.
   It flips over and pins you underneath.
   At night the ice weasels come.

2. Tell students: The meaning of this poem is not obvious. However, if you want to be creative you must learn to leap at any opportunity to explore the unobvious. This poem gives the keys to a lot of strange and seemingly unrelated boxes. If you can find a way to glue together the contents of these boxes, then you will have some creative ideas.

3. Have each participant take a few minutes to write down 10 conclusions about love that they derive from this poem. Encourage them to think beyond the obvious; the most creative ideas are the "far-fetched" ones.

4. Now display a different poem:

   My hospitality organization is like a snow-mobile.
   Cruising through the tundra.
   It flips over and pins me underneath.
   At night the ice weasels come.

5. Have each participant take a few minutes to come up with 10 conclusions about the hospitality organization that they derive from the poem. Encourage them to think about *whatever* the poem brings to mind.

6. Have participants share some of the conclusions they arrived at from the different poems.

Source: Berger, F. & Ferguson, D. H. (1990). *Innovation: Creativity Techniques for Hospitality Managers.* New York: John Wiley & Sons, Inc.

Endnotes

Adams, J. L. (1979). *Conceptual Blockbusting.* New York: W.W. Norton & Co., 13–82.

Archer, A. & Walczyk, D. (2006). Driving creativity and innovation through culture. *Design Management Review, 17*(3), 15–27.

Beagrie, S. (2006). How to be more creative. *Personnel Today,* 35–37.

Cooper, R. (2006). Group creativity: The effects of extrinsic, intrinsic, and obligation motivations. *Creativity Research Journal, 18*(2), 153–174.

Drucker, P. F. (1985). Entrepreneurial strategies. *California Management Review,* 9–25. (The term "creative imitation" was coined by Theodore Levitt of the Harvard Business School.)

Drucker, P. F. (1985). *Innovation and Entrepreneurship: Practices and Principles.* New York: Harper & Row, p. 206.

Eberle, B. (1997). *Scamper.* Austin, TX: Prufrock Press.

Ford, C. M. (2000). Creative developments in creativity theory. *Academy of Management Review, 25*(2), 284.

Gorgoglione, M. (2006). Supporting creative teams in organizations: An approach based on technology. *International Studies of Management and Organization, 36*(1), 8–15.

Hugos, M. (2006). How to get inspired: Leading innovation requires creativity. *CIO, 20*(2), 2.

Livermore, C. (2006). Creativity in virtual teams: Key components for success. *Journal of Global Information Technology, 9*(1), 69–72.

Madjar, N. O., Greg R., & Pratt, M. G. (2002). There's no place like home? The contributions of work and nonwork creativity support to employees' creativity performance. *Academy of Management Journal, 45*(4), 757–767.

Napier, N. & Nilsson, M. (2006). The development of creative capabilities in and out of creative organizations: Three case studies. *Creativity and Innovation Management, 15*(3), 268–281.

Osborn, A. (1953). *Applied Imagination: Principles and Procedures of Creative Problem Solving.* New York: Charles Scribner's Sons.

Perry-Smith, J. E. & Shalley, C. E. (2003). The social side of creativity: A static and dynamic social network perspective. *Academy of Management Review, 28*(1), 89–104.

Romero, E. & Cruthirds, K. (2006). The use of humor in the workplace. *The Academy of Management Perspectives, 20*(2), 58–71.

Schank, R. (1988). *The Creative Attitude.* New York: Macmillan Publishing Co. Chapter 8. pp. 222–250.

Schepers, P. & van den Berg, P. (2007). Social factors of work-environment creativity. *Journal of Business and Psychology, 21*(3), 407–429.

Secretan, L. (2007). Bold dreams. *Leadership Excellence, 24*(3), 7.

Taggar, S. (2002). Individual creativity and group ability to utilize individual creative resources: A multilevel model. *Academy of Management Journal, 45*(2), 315–330.

Tierney, P. & Farmer, S. M. (2002). Creative self-efficacy: Its potential antecedents and relationship to creative performance. *Academy of Management Journal, 45*(6), 1137–1148.

Unsworth, K. (2001). Unpacking creativity. *Academy of Management Review, 26*(2), 289–297.

Vandenbosch, B. & Saatcioglu, A. (2006). How managers generate ideas and why it matters. The *Journal of Business Strategy, 27*(6), 11–33.

Von Oech, R. (1983). *A Whack on the Side of the Head: How to Unlock Your Mind for Innovation.* New York: Warner Brothers, p. 25.

Zhous, J. & George, J. M. (2001). When job dissatisfaction leads to creativity: Encouraging the expression of voice. *Academy of Management Journal, 44*(4), 682–696.

9

SETTING PERSONAL AND PROFESSIONAL GOALS

Goals are the fuel in the furnace of achievement.

—Brian Tracy, *Eat that Frog*

Think you can or think you can't, either way you will be right.

—Henry Ford

CHAPTER OUTLINE

Introduction

Benefits of Goal Setting

Organizational Goal Setting
    Mission-Based Goals
    Individual Goals versus Organizational Goals
    Action Plans

Goal-Setting Theory
    Benefits of Setting Specific Goals
    Benefits of Setting Difficult Goals
    Cons of Setting Goals That are Too Difficult or Too Specific

Methods and Tools for Goal Setting
    SMART Goals
    Management by Objectives (MBO)
    360-Degree Goal Setting

Commitment to Goals
    Legitimate Authority and Peer Group—External Influences
    Participation and Competition—Interactive Factors
    Personal Goal, Self-Efficacy, and Internal Rewards—Internal Factors
    Adam's Equity Theory
    Difficult Goals
    Feedback

Achieving a Goal
    Using Visualization
    Setting Objectives
    Recording Progress
    Making a Gantt Chart
    Creating Goal Aids
    Evaluating Goals
        Selecting criteria for evaluating goal achievement
        Reevaluating goals
    Performance Evaluation
        Knowing When to Implement Goals

How to Avoid Goal Conflict

Group Development in the Goal-Setting Process
    The Beginning
    The Middle
    The End

Setting Personal Goals
    Establishing a Personal Goal
    Achieving a Personal Goal

Summary

LEARNING OBJECTIVES

After reading this chapter, you should be able to do the following:

1. Discuss the importance of setting specific and difficult goals, as described by the goal-setting theory.
2. Describe some of the problems hospitality industry managers face when setting specific and difficult goals.
3. List the meaning of each letter in the acronym SMART and describe what each means.
4. Compare and contrast the Management by Objectives and the 360-degree goal-setting tools.
5. Explain three of the benefits of setting goals.
6. Discuss the benefits of managers assigning goals to subordinates.
7. Describe the benefits of participatory goal setting.
8. Explain how managers can increase commitment to difficult goals.
9. Identify the processes one can take to increase the probability of achieving a goal.

Opening Scenario

Marlena was bright, energetic, and extroverted. She was an ideal hire. Although she was only an intern for the summer, the staff at Milton Hotel wanted to do their best to make her feel welcome, while providing Marlena with a solid learning experience. The staff of the Milton Hotel had to first set goals for the internship position. At an initial meeting the staff outlined the following goals:

1. The position would provide an excellent learning experience.
2. The student would not be assigned to a single department, but would instead have a chance to explore five different departments.
3. The student would have a weekly meeting with a staff mentor.
4. The student would have open access to company meetings and planning sessions, allowing him or her to participate as much as they wanted to.
5. When the summer was over, the student would write a detailed description with accomplishments.

The group also decided that the student would choose the first department that he or she wanted to work in, hoping that this would make the intern feel comfortable right from the start. Finally, there would be opportunities for the staff to evaluate the student and for the student to evaluate the placement.

The staff established evaluation criteria which they would use to evaluate the students:

1. Learning of technical skills.
2. Learning of human relations skills.
3. Creative contributions.

The student would be asked to develop his or her own criteria for the evaluation of each placement.

INTRODUCTION

The key to success for most hospitality entrepreneurs and senior-level managers is their ability not only to manage others, but also to discipline and manage themselves. This self-regulation empowers one to set realistic goals and objectives and determine the most efficient and effective way to achieve them. Continual goal setting and achievement leads to continued success.

Goal setting is the process of establishing desired results that guide and direct behavior. Initially, group members may each have their own individual goal in mind but, as the team develops, all members begin to create a shared vision of the desired outcome of their activities. An **achievement goal** directs a group toward a major outcome or product, while a **maintenance goal** maintains or strengthens the group itself. Goal-setting theory asserts that specific, difficult goals generate better performance than "do your best" goals or no goals at all (Gellatly and Meyer, 1992). Recent studies have clarified and expanded on this basic proposition.

In the first part of this chapter we will discuss goal setting in a professional environment. Organizational Goal Setting examines goal-setting theory, including the boundaries and inconsistencies that limit or eliminate its beneficial effects. Goal-Setting Theory is a discussion of formal goal-setting methods and tools. In Methods and Tools for Goal Setting we investigate goal commitment. Next, we discuss techniques that can be used when trying to achieve a goal. Then, we analyze the development of groups during the goal-setting process. You may find it useful to refer to the chapter on team building for further insight into group dynamics and the role of a team leader, or manager, in directing group efforts. In the final section of this chapter, we discuss personal goals that are set outside of the workplace. If you need an incentive to read further, remember that organizations that implement the goal-setting theory reap greater profits than organizations that do not (Terpstra and Rozell, 1994).

BENEFITS OF GOAL SETTING

Establishing a system of goals is a valuable tool that will enable managers to manage themselves and others in pursuit of larger organizational goals. Organizations that implement goal setting reap greater profits than organizations that do not. Merritt and Berger conducted a study on senior-level hospitality managers in 1998 to determine (1) whether the time and effort necessary for developing and implementing goals are well invested and (2) the extent to which goal setting contributes to a hospitality organization's success (bottom-line profit). All study participants stated that goal setting increases their organizations' bottom lines by at least 10 percent (Merritt and Berger, 1998). The study participants believed goals help managers translate general intentions into specific actions. David Chag, GM of the Country Club of Brookline, Massachusetts, stated: "Goals establish an end result, a direction of pursuit, a method of measurement, and foster teamwork and achievement. Goals help us perform beyond our capabilities and keep us focused when the going gets tough." Participants mentioned a variety of benefits that derive from goal setting. Some of the more notable advantages identified are as follows:

- *Directing attention and actions.* Goals give managers a target. They nurture an atmosphere that produces specific results within specific time periods.
- *Boosting performance toward peak levels.* Setting goals makes managers aware of the mental, emotional, and physical energy they will need for the task and encourages them to conserve and mobilize energy purposefully.

- *Bolstering persistence.* Goals exert the necessary pull to encourage people to overcome challenges.
- *Fostering development of innovative strategies.* Managers who set important goals will be surprised at how ingenious they can be in devising strategies to reach their goals.
- *Providing a short- and long-term game plan.* If set properly and realistically, managers can map out their future with their company, or effect plans to achieve other aspirations.
- *Preventing stress.* Comprehensive goals can help avoid burnout and produce positive feeling (Stallworth, 1990).

Individual goal setting must be aligned with organizational goals. It must support the goals and objectives of the organization. It is most effective to have goal setting occur at all levels of the organization, starting from the lowest level and progressing to the top executive team. The top executive team of the organization is responsible for making certain that the collected goals are aligned with the organization's goals.

ORGANIZATIONAL GOAL SETTING

Organizational goals are woven into the very fabric of an organization, superseding individual goals. Those who set goals must be aware of the impact these goals will have on the individuals affected by them. In turn, the employees must come to understand the integral roles they play in fulfilling the organizational goals that have been set.

Mission-Based Goals

The mission statement is a clear guideline for what an organization hopes to achieve and for the manner in which these achievements are to be accomplished. Organizational goals must always begin with the mission statement. In this way changes are made and problems are solved proactively rather than reactively. Mission-based organizational goals ensure that everyone is pulling in the same direction. For example, the finance department might try to establish a goal to incorporate the use of less expensive tableware and napkins to improve the bottom line. However, if that hotel's mission statement says that they hope to provide phenomenal dining experiences, cheap tableware isn't going to suffice. Look at some of the following mission statements. What kinds of goals might arise from statements such as these?

> Four Seasons is dedicated to perfecting the travel experience through continuous innovation and the highest standards of hospitality. From elegant surroundings of the finest quality, to caring, highly personalized 24-hour service, Four Seasons embodies a true home away from home for those who know and appreciate the best. The deeply instilled Four Seasons culture is personified in its employees—people who share a single focus and are inspired to offer great service.
>
> —Four Seasons Hotel

> At UVa Medical Center, we are a community with shared principles that shape the way we live and work:
> Mission . . .
> To provide excellence and innovation in the care of patients, the training of health professionals and the creation and sharing of health knowledge.

Vision . . .

In all that we do, we work to benefit human health and improve the quality of life. We will be:

- A community of caring people committed to our patients, our neighbors, and each other and committed to the professional development of our staff and faculty
- The provider of the best complex clinical care in Virginia and surrounding states, with national recognition in selected areas
- A highly effective organization which is committed to providing exceptional service to our patients
- A model of creative teaching and learning
- An organization dedicated to discovery and the application of innovative science.

Values . . .

This institution exists to serve others, and does so through the expression of our core values:

- Respect. To recognize the dignity of every person
- Integrity. To be honest, fair and trustworthy
- Stewardship. To manage resources responsibly
- Excellence. To work at the highest level of performance, with a commitment to continuous improvement

—University of Virginia Medical Center

Our mission is to be a growing restaurant company that achieves superior financial results by consistently exceeding our guests' expectations. Our commitment to and strong belief in the training, development and retention of performance-oriented team members will drive our success.

We are passionate about providing the "Logan's Roadhouse Experience" to each and every guest: Great food and drinks, fast! great prices; friendly, enthusiastic people; fun, casual, clean, upbeat atmosphere; great value.

We take great pride in the execution of our standards and the value of teamwork.

—Logan's Roadhouse®, Inc., headquartered in Nashville, Tennessee

Individual Goals versus Organizational Goals

One of the primary differences between individual goals and organizational goals is that the responsibility for development and implementation of these goals must be shared among at least several and sometimes many individuals. Group dynamics, issues of authority, and teamwork all come into play. Group brainstorming and other creative problem-solving methods are often employed. Priorities must be established when organizational goals and individual goals conflict.

Individual goals are similar to organizational goals in many ways. While few individuals write out a mission statement for their personal or professional lives, it is certainly a good idea to step back and look at the big picture. You may decide to establish a goal to take on more responsibility at work to advance your career and put your family in a better financial situation.

However, the extra time away from home might undermine another significant goal related to family well-being. In this case a compromise is obvious, but the awareness of the larger picture was required to realize that a compromise was necessary.

Action Plans

While all goals require some form of an action plan to ensure implementation, an organizational goal requires that a clearly defined plan of action which establishes set deadlines and names specific persons responsible for each aspect of the fulfillment of a goal be delineated. The goal must be made known to members of the organization through postings and discussions. The action plan must describe exactly what is to be done, in what steps, by whom, to what standard, during what period of time, and what measure will be used to gauge the success of the goal.

GOAL-SETTING THEORY

Benefits of Setting Specific Goals

Goal-setting theory contends that specific goals improve performance by producing higher levels of effort and planning than unclear or general goals. When groups pursue vague, unmeasurable goals, they can obtain satisfaction from even low levels of performance. In contrast, groups with specific goals strive for a measurable standard of success by increasing effort and attention. They work hard because they know what is expected of them, and they know that they will derive satisfaction from the specific goal attainment. The sense of mastery that comes from making progress toward and achieving a specific goal increases the group's intrinsic interest in the goal, motivating the group to work even harder.

Groups channel some of this extra effort into the development of appropriate plans. Studies show that groups with specific goals tend to plan and organize more effectively than groups with general goals. A specific goal directs a group's attention toward planning development that, in turn, creates a motivational effect to follow through with the plan.

Benefits of Setting Difficult Goals

Difficult goals create an anticipation of satisfaction that motivates extra intensity and duration on task performance; however, increased persistence and attention will not automatically lead to difficult goal attainment and improved performance. Groups also need to spend time choosing the most effective strategy for goal attainment. Groups with difficult goals are more likely to apply effective task strategies they learned indirectly, through practice, or directly through formal training methods. The development of better analytic strategies, in turn, improves the quality of decisions.

Difficult goals prompt more spontaneous planning, larger amounts of planning, and higher quality planning than do easy goals. Groups working toward a difficult goal engage in less preplanning than do groups working toward an easy goal because the difficult goal increases concern about making immediate progress on the task. Group members will cope with this concern by altering when they plan, rather than decrease how much they plan. Research has shown that certain incentives, such as putting pay at risk in achieving group goals, can also increase the level of spontaneous goal setting in which groups engage (Guthrie and Hollensbe, 2004).

However, planning may not always lead to improved performance. Weingart's (1992) study demonstrated that difficult goals can misdirect planning by leading groups to devote planning toward the most salient task characteristics, even though they are not necessarily the most important for accomplishing a task.

> Think of a difficult goal that you've set for yourself. Do you find it motivating or discouraging? Explain.

Cons of Setting Goals That are Too Difficult or Too Specific

While difficult and specific goals often enhance performance, they are not appropriate for every type of task or level of task performance. Earley et al.'s (1989) theoretical model explains the influence of goal setting on three levels of task performance. At the lowest level of task performance, when the group is simply carrying out the task, a group goal leads to improved performance through an increase in effort, diligence, and energy. At the second level of task performance, when groups are determining how to approach the task, goal setting helps limit the strategy domain to be searched. A specific goal is debilitating at the third level, where groups must choose between many available strategies where the best is not obvious.

Groups need to mold the specificity and difficulty of their goals toward the type of task that needs to be accomplished. "Goal setting works better on simple tasks than on complex tasks" (Kernan et al., 1994). The direct, motivational effects of goal setting—such as increased effort, attention, and persistence—improve performance on simple tasks. Complex tasks require more than simply an increase in effort; groups also need to learn how to do the task. A goal is therefore harder to achieve if the tasks to reach it are complex. When group members focus their attention on achieving the goal rather than on learning how to accomplish the tasks required to achieve it, performance is impaired. Researchers have not agreed on how complex tasks affect planning. Weingart's study suggests that complex tasks do not interfere with the quality of planning or the amount of in-process planning; however, Kernan's study found that the pressure and sense of urgency from complex tasks may inhibit planning, which may lower performance.

When a group works on a novel decision-making task, they will achieve better results with simple goals than with difficult goals. After the initial learning process, however, the introduction of specific, challenging goals can facilitate performance. The negative effect of specific, difficult goals is especially strong for inexperienced workers and groups working under time pressure. Groups that cannot retry a strategy should avoid difficult and specific goals.

METHODS AND TOOLS FOR GOAL SETTING

In this section, we discuss several methods and tools managers should use when setting goals for both their groups and themselves.

SMART Goals

Goals should be developed in a style consistent with what has been called a **SMART goal.** First, create a plan for how to accomplish the goal. Brainstorm to develop a list of possible alternatives—regardless of how impractical they appear. After recording possibilities, begin the culling process by considering the limitations of each alternative. Discard those that are unreasonable. The outcome of this process will be a goal that fits the requirements of a SMART goal, which includes:

Specific. Researchers have found that managers are more likely to succeed if their goals are specific and clear (O'Hair and Friedrich, 1992). Harry Waddington, former GM of the Piedmont Driving Club in Atlanta, said, "Focus is the key to my success. If I focus specifically on something long enough, I know that I probably can achieve it. If we properly plan a function and carefully focus on the details as it unfolds, we are likely to produce a huge success." It is not enough simply to set positive-sounding goals.

Measurable. Goals must be measurable because the resulting objectivity helps define goals in terms of actions that can readily be seen. Measurement can be as simple as an informal checklist, or it may be a complex and sophisticated evaluation form that measures performance in a variety of categories.

Acceptable. Even when goals are assigned by owners or upper management, those goals should not be imposed simply by fiat. When managers accept their goals and make a commitment to achieving them, goals have a much better chance of being realized. However, if the goal is more imposed than desired, the goal may be perceived as more difficult to attain, thereby resulting in frustration instead of a sense of accomplishment. The general manager of Grosse Pointe Yacht Club offered an insight regarding his past experience in a restaurant company: "Corporate set the

goals; the general managers were the enforcers. Department heads had very little say. Now that I am a manager, I try to involve everyone in the process, so our goals become more meaningful."

Realistic. Although goals should be challenging, they should also be set with regard to an individual's capabilities and limitations. Goals should not represent whatever levels of achievement a manager decides would be nice. For goals to serve as a tool for stretching an individual to achieve his or her full potential, those goals must be challenging but achievable. Likewise, before setting goals for themselves, managers should consider their capacity to stretch and honestly examine whether they have the requisite knowledge, skills, resources, and abilities. Thus, as they set goals, managers should consider what performance levels conditions realistically allow, what results will indicate success, and what an individual can accomplish when pushed. One manager explained how that approach works for him: "The process of lofty goal setting keeps everyone striving for improvement, rather than allowing the easier alternative. We want our managers continually stretching their limits."

Timely. The time dimension is a key issue. Goals should be temporally relevant; that is, appropriate for near-term concerns. For example, a 29-year-old manager would find a career development goal, such as obtaining industry certification, more salient than a goal of selecting a geographic location for retirement. "As the world evolves, circumstances change," says Mohammad Memar'Sadeghi, GM at Putnam Country Club in Mahopac, NY. "We can't just set and achieve goals in a vacuum. There are too many external variables such as weather, regulations, or economics affecting our business. We must be able to change, too—even if it means abandoning a goal altogether and creating a new one."

When goals are first established, they should be written down. Once written, goals will have more meaning and importance to the creator. Beverly Schlegel, manager of the Shenandoah Club in Roanoke, Virginia, remarked on this phenomenon: "I first became familiar with the importance of the goal-setting process in high school. Our journalism teacher pounded it into our heads at every opportunity." Schlegel uses a journalistic style format that covers the essential points, commonly known as "five Ws and an H:" who, what, when, where, why, and how. To this list, one should add a sixth W: who cares? Schlegel concluded, "To this day, I still ask those questions, not only when I write (my goals), but when I plan. This format is a major key to our success."

> Critique the system of SMART goals. Is the concept useful? What components, if any, are missing?

Management by Objectives (MBO)

The nurses in Hadley Hospital all appear to be doing similar work, but on questioning them, Sara, the head nurse gets a clear picture of her organization. Kelly says, "I am working." Greg says, "I am taking Mr. Cernebs' blood pressure." Juanita says, "I am helping people to get well." Of the three, Juanita demonstrates the mindset consistent with Management by Objectives.

Additional concepts from goal-setting theory have been incorporated into formal goal-setting methods, such as Management by Objectives (MBO), a highly used and successful method. Like goal-setting theory, MBO emphasizes specific goals and feedback; however, unlike goal-setting theory, MBO stresses the need for participation in goal setting. In the MBO process, supervisors meet periodically with subordinates to set goals and evaluate the extent to which previously set goals have been achieved. This process of review and revision includes a hierarchy of objectives and a time frame for completion. MBO will work only if it involves participation, feedback, and the widespread support of top management. Goal making is part of the feedback process, helping to break down communication barriers. Supervisors and subordinates can reduce tension through the goal-setting process.

Although the theory of MBO highlights feedback, in practice, the subordinate's feedback is often limited because supervisors assume the primary responsibility for setting goals in the organization. Subordinates may be hesitant to provide their superiors with complete feedback. Critics also argue that the results-oriented approach of MBO tends to focus responsibility at an individual level and on performance outcomes (Matthews et al., 1994).

360-Degree Goal Setting

The 360-degree goal-setting process has been designed in response to the drawbacks to MBO. In the MBO process, an employee or department is accountable to the manager. In the 360-degree format, they are accountable to the manager, as well as internal and external customers. By internal customers, we mean those inside the organization: supervisors, top managers, subordinates, coworkers, and representatives from other departments. External customers, on the other hand, are those outside the organization: clients and suppliers, for example. Goals presented using the 360-degree goal-setting process are stated in the customer's words, rather than the employee's. As a result, companies and their employees gather a precise and in-depth understanding of customer's expectations. An employee's performance can be specifically evaluated by customers in the employee's performance appraisal (goals precisely measured); furthermore, by linking 360-degree goals to appraisals, employees will be more accountable to their customers. Joint goal setting demands increased interaction among members of an organization, who thereby derive a much greater understanding of the roles people play. This interaction reduces the chances that they will set unrealistic expectations for other departments.

One of the drawbacks to the 360-degree process is that the feedback received from multiple customers can be confusing and conflicting. In order to make the process work, companies must be willing to expend the effort needed to gather input and output from various customers inside and outside the company (Milliman et al., 1995). The process can prove successful when it includes the participation of top management, extensive training, and pilot testing.

> What would you predict might be the most revealing type of information gathered through the 360-degree feedback?

COMMITMENT TO GOALS

Technology has engendered the following:

- Made it possible to accomplish tasks more quickly.
- The need for coordinated integration increases when technological advances impose requirements for individuals, or for groups, to work interdependently.
- Technological innovations often result in the boundaries between subunits becoming blurred and an organization's structure becoming less centralized.

Commitment transforms goal setting from words into action. A group demonstrates goal commitment through its determination toward reaching a goal—regardless of the goal's origin. In this rapidly changing world, filled with organizational upheaval, companies that want to compete need to understand goal commitment and the factors that promote and inhibit it. Locke (1988) summarized the determinants of goal commitment into the categories of **external influences, interactive factors,** and **internal factors.**

Legitimate Authority and Peer Group—External Influences

Peer groups influence goal commitment, sometimes to the detriment of the organization's goals. Employees will be more committed to goals supported by their peer group than by their manager. Usually, these goals are not as difficult as management would prefer. This **systematic soldiering** restricts output (Locke, 1988). The level of peer group cohesion will determine the extent of goal commitment.

One of the factors that determine goal commitment is legitimate authority. An employee is often willing to accept goals assigned by their superior because throughout their life they have been trained to listen to a person of authority. Most employees will listen to their supervisors because doing what one is told is part of the employment contract (Locke, 1988). Assigned goals can have beneficial outcomes, a fact that undoubtedly contributes to their continued use in organizations. Among their benefits are the following (Earley et al., 1987):

1. They afford a feeling of purpose, guidance, and explicitness concerning expectations.
2. They broaden individuals' beliefs regarding what they can accomplish.
3. They direct individuals toward developing high quality plans to realize their goals.

In the long term, specificity of intention embodied in an assigned goal can lead to persistence. When assigned goals are clear and fixed firmly in the minds of group members, the specificity of intention encourages follow-through.

Participation and Competition—Interactive Factors

Although assigned goals increase commitment, studies have not conclusively determined whether assigned goal setting or participatory goal setting produces greater commitment. Maier's research, which supports participatory goal setting, asserts that groups tend to set high goals—often higher goals than supervisors would dare to impose (Maier, 1967). Furthermore, groups tend to set highly realistic goals, even when they consider factors that are beyond their control. A group can set high goals and meet them because employees often know which factors are within their control and which are not.

Latham et al. (1991) have suggested that the key benefits of participation are not due to motivation (i.e., goal commitment) but rather due to cognition (i.e., task strategy development). Participatory goal setting increases self-efficacy, in turn, increasing motivation.

Studies have not yet proven how competition affects commitment. One study did show that people placed in a competitive environment tend to set higher goals and perform better than others in a noncompetitive environment (Locke, 1988).

Do you think competition helps with goal achievement under all circumstances?

Personal Goal, Self-Efficacy, and Internal Rewards—Internal Factors

Sasha had worked as a front desk assistant manager at Bonney Island Resort for three years. She loved the atmosphere and the clientele. She always received excellent ratings because she did everything she was asked to do, but lately her job satisfaction had fallen off a bit and her performance seemed rather lackluster as well. In a postevaluation interview she said, "It just seems like anybody could do my job. I've been doing the same work for years. It's not that I don't enjoy the people, it's just that I have no say in what I do." In response to this, Sasha's manager started to move her into the decision-making process. As she had more direct contact with the guests, she was able to establish goals for herself and for the desk in general that benefited the guests and the resort as well. She became more adept at the computer so that she could maintain eye contact with the guests instead of having "top of the head" syndrome. She worked on developing a plan so that each front desk staff member could walk the guest to the appropriate elevator rather than merely pointing the way. She began to develop a system so that at peak check-in and check-out times the reservationists who sit in the back could help the front desk staff to reduce the line of guests; this involved cross-training. In addition, Sasha found herself more interested and involved in the day-to-day goings-on around her.

Personal goals have direct effects on performance, as do **self-efficacy** judgments—the belief in one's task-relevant capabilities. Individuals are equally committed to self-set and participative-set goals. Self-set goals reflect personal or group expectations for task performance. Zander (1971) suggested that self-set goals of a group reflect the group's level of aspiration. Research supports personal goal setting over assigned goal setting, with findings that the aggregate of goals set by individuals in a group is higher than the one goal set for the group as a whole.

Unlike working individually on a goal, time and energy is required to coordinate members' ideas and efforts. Individuals will set higher goals for themselves than for other group members because they view themselves as more capable when they compare their skills and abilities. Individuals have lower expectations for others than for themselves. Group goal-setting methods (i.e., MBO) often include a discussion before reaching a consensus on a group goal. Researchers discovered that the discussion which takes place in a group before reaching consensus may lead to lowered expectations for the group's performance. Larey and Paulus (1995) explored a similar topic and found that participants who were asked to set a goal for a typical group member set roughly equivalent goals to participants asked to set goals for their own performance.

During the goal-setting process, individuals experience a normative shift that shapes their self-efficacy. When a group believes it can accomplish a task, members will push themselves. In contrast, incentives will not motivate a group with low self-efficacy. In other words, it would appear that self-efficacy can be more fundamental than rewards. Groups will not strive for rewards they believe are unattainable, but they will commit to goals they believe they can reach. Managers should pay close attention to changes in the group's self-efficacy, recognizing that groups are more likely to experience low self-efficacy in stressful situations, where anxiety replaces motivation. Participatory goal setting can channel anxiety into motivation and increase self-efficacy, leading to greater goal commitment than possible through assigned goals. Managers can raise group confidence and reduce anxiety by providing training, information about how to perform a task, process-oriented performance appraisal, and supportive supervisor behavior (Gellatly and Meyer, 1992).

Self-administered rewards are also essential to goal commitment. Hospitality industry managers can increase organizational commitment and performance by encouraging employees to engage in self-generated rewards and feedback. Goal setting plus self-generated feedback is more potent than goal setting plus feedback given by the supervisor because people are more likely to accept and derive meaning from self-generated feedback (Locke, 1988).

> Describe a situation where you have used a self-generated reward. Was it effective?

Adam's Equity Theory

Fairness is a key concept in all relationships and work environments. Adams (1963, 1965) proposed and developed the idea that inequity—or the perception of unfairness—can be an important motivator in organizations. When employees believe that they deserve more (or, in some cases, less) than what they have received, they experience tension and that tension, in turn, drives action.

Individuals come to hold a perception of inequity when they consider their personal contributions or effort and conclude that they have given more than they have received—that the outcomes are insufficient given their input. This input/outcome ratio is then compared with what they believe others in their situation are experiencing. Recall, for instance, your feelings when a friend got to use a new piece of equipment and you didn't, even though you helped to select it and she was on vacation during the process. Or, perhaps you've been working hard and coming in early so that you can take a few days off, but when you propose it to your supervisor, your request is refused. You know another employee whose performance is marginal got all four days off that he requested.

Perceptions of inequity can be related to almost any organizational variable—salary, vacation time, size of office, and other intangible factors. Complicating this issue are differences that may be due to cultural variables and other unanticipated and less well-understood personal factors and perceptions.

Individuals use a variety of methods in their attempts to remedy the inequity they experience. Adam's original theory proposed seven different strategies individuals can use to restore equity: (1) change the person's outcomes, (2) change the person's inputs, (3) change the outcomes of the comparison other, (4) change the inputs of the comparison other, (5) use different individuals for comparison purposes, (6) rationalize the inequity, and (7) make the individual leave the situation or even the organization.

In implementing the above strategies, an employee has any number of options: He or she may work harder, consult with his or her supervisor, seek legal counsel, or take any number of other actions. Adams warns that individuals who take measures to reduce their perceived inequity must be aware of the potential consequences of the specific actions they choose. Not all strategies are equally desirable or necessarily have long-term positive consequences.

Researchers building on equity theory have proposed that individuals differ in their preferences for equity or how strong their reaction is to perceived inequity. Three "types" have been identified:

(1) *Equity sensitives* seek balance as described in Adam's original theory. They are constantly aware of how their inputs and outcomes compare to those of their comparison group, and are upset when they perceive inequity.

(2) *Benevolents* are individuals who are able to tolerate inequity and who do not experience stress when their comparison others receive greater outcomes than they do. They are less concerned with external rewards and while they may recognize the lack of equity, they are not bothered by it.

(3) *Entitleds*, on the other hand, want and expect more than their comparison others. They feel "entitled" to more and better outcomes than their peers, as if they are "owed" preferential treatment.

While not everyone fits perfectly into one of these categories, you can use these concepts to better understand how equity theory translates into daily activities and how perceptions of equity can influence an individual's behavior.

> How is equity theory related to goal achievement?

Difficult Goals

Even though goal-setting theory extols the benefits of difficult goals, groups are more likely to accept easy goals that lead to low performance than hard goals that lead to high performance. Commitment declines as goals become more difficult. Managers need to gain high commitment when their groups are working on achieving a difficult goal. If people do not feel committed, they will give up their hard goals in favor of easier ones. When goals are not challenging, committed people may be inhibited about raising their goals and this inhibits performance, whereas people not committed to an easy goal may set higher goals because they want an additional challenge. However, culture may also play a role in this dynamic of goal commitment. A comparative study of American and Chinese workers has demonstrated that the American workers were motivated only by moderately difficult goals—goals that seemed too easy or too unattainable did not produce motivation to meet the goals. On the other hand, Chinese workers were increasingly motivated by increasingly difficult goals (Fang et al., 2004).

Managers can increase goal commitment by persuading groups that the goals are both attainable and important. This can best be accomplished when managers:

1. assert their legitimate authority;
2. convey normative information;
3. show that the goals provide opportunity for self-improvement;
4. challenge people to show what they can do;
5. are physically present at the work site;
6. are supportive and trustworthy;
7. provide a convincing rationale for the goal;
8. exert reasonable pressure for performance;
9. are knowledgeable about the task and job; and
10. serve as a role model for the behavior they desire in a subordinate (Latham and Locke, 1991).

Managers can increase commitment to difficult goals by making goals public rather than private. The public spotlight and pressure will motivate commitment. A study by Hollenbeck et al. (1989) found that groups are more likely to commit to difficult goals when the locus of control is internal. Also, it found that the commitment to difficult goals did not differ between self-set goals and assigned ones, except for individuals high in need of achievement who demonstrated higher commitment to self-set goals than did subjects low in need of achievement. Managers should not expect commitment from individuals who set low goals, even if they were allowed to participate in the goal setting or if they set their own goals because these individuals may not emphasize goal setting or accomplishments. A manager will need to offer potent external rewards or punishments to gain commitment toward difficult goals for this group. Linking pay to goal attainment may be one way of increasing commitment. Hollensbe and Guthrie (2000) have demonstrated that in group-pay plans, a higher, more frequent payout leads to higher commitment to goals. This type of motivator works best with small groups of five to eight people, in which the problem of **free riders**—people who exert minimum effort, but receive the same reward—is minimized.

> Have you ever made a personal goal public in the hope that it would help you accomplish it? Explain.

Feedback

The goal-setting theory explicitly states that feedback results in higher effort and performance than lack of feedback. Groups use feedback to adjust their goals and measure their performance. When groups receive negative feedback, they feel dissatisfied because their performance does not meet standards. If the group believes it can make its performance reach the standard, it will apply extra effort. Groups respond to negative feedback by setting higher goals than groups that receive positive feedback. The dissatisfaction from negative feedback prompts groups to develop more task strategies and spend more time in strategy sessions than groups that receive positive feedback.

In the short term, negative feedback positively affects goal setting, but at a certain point the dissatisfaction created by negative feedback can outweigh the benefits. High levels of dissatisfaction can lead to a decline in organizational citizenship behaviors and an increase in absenteeism and employee turnover. Even in the short term, negative feedback could be detrimental if the group does not believe its effort will ever result in positive feedback. Table 9.1 is a guide to help managers know when negative feedback will be beneficial to a group and when it could be detrimental.

Managers can use negative normative feedback to motivate group performance. Providing negative normative feedback will help managers impose higher performance standards. Managers who expect more from their subordinates often achieve better performance than those who demand less. If a manager plans to give negative feedback, he or she should be

TABLE 9.1 Negative Feedback	
When to use negative feedback	**When to avoid negative feedback**
Positive relationship with feedback source	Lack of organizational support
High-trust environment	Low trust
Support for goal accomplishment	Poor relationship with group leader
High task interdependence	Low task interdependence
High group efficacy	Low group efficacy

Source: Mesch, Farth, and Podsakoff, 1994.

sure that it is specific and nonevaluative. Even negative feedback needs to be delivered in a supportive way, avoiding the unattainable (and demotivating) expectation of perfection, so that employees feel motivated to take the risk of increasing their level of performance. Otherwise, negative feedback and excessively difficult goals for workers will not produce the desired result (Wilson, 1994; Fang et al., 2004).

ACHIEVING A GOAL

A written **goal statement** is a declaration of the outcome one plans to achieve. After a manager has developed a goal statement, he or she must consider how and when to accomplish the goal. The Merritt and Berger study reported two ways that their participants approached goal achievement: the cognitive approach (visualization) and the physical approach (setting objectives).

Using Visualization

Charles worked as the manager of The Salad Café, a bistro in a medium-sized city on the east coast. Though business was steady, many people walked past every day without ever giving his establishment a second glance. Charles decided to set a goal to bring in more of the foot traffic. He visualized people stopping on their usual trek and staring into his café. As he did so, he thought up a variety of creative ideas to entice people into his shop. In addition, he told his staff that people passing by were going to suddenly start noticing the shop. He repeated this mantra at every occasion and solicited ideas from his staff, and sometimes from his regular customers, asking how that vision could become a reality.

Changing the outward appearance might cause people to look twice, adding some kind of sound or music might also have that effect. He realized that these ideas were appealing to the senses and expanded the ideas further. When he ran out of ideas he would again visualize people stopping to notice his bistro and would picture what might make them do that.

Eventually he redecorated the front of his shop, adding an elaborate arched entryway. He tiled the area under his outdoor tables and a few feet beyond. so that passersby would feel as though they were already in the café. He kept fresh bread baking every day, displaying it in a front window, and using a small fan to push the aroma out onto the sidewalk. He created an artist's corner with an easel. Artists were invited to draw or paint there in full view of those passing by in return for free coffee or tea as they worked. At the opposite end of the café, a musician's corner was established with a similar arrangement.

Charles clung to the idea of attracting attention to his café tenaciously, until the vision became a reality.

As its name indicates, the cognitive approach takes place within the mind, through visualization. The fundamental premise behind visualization is that the subconscious mind cannot distinguish between an actual experience and one vividly (and repetitively) imagined. By concentrating on the goal and believing that it is attainable, one can engage one's subconscious mind to play a role in helping with goal achievement. Sherrie Laveroni, Executive VP of Operations at Loews Hotels, suggested the value of visualization: "When you set a goal, you set into motion 'possibility'—possibility for something better, greater. You immediately are activated to plan and imagine what could be . . . and how to make it happen."

Visualization involves first developing an enthusiastic and positive attitude and having confidence that the goal is attainable. The individual should be relaxed and not distracted while visualizing outcomes. The key step is to imagine accomplishment—success in detail. It's useful to focus repeatedly on a single situation in which you achieve your goal. Repetition is important in helping convince the subconscious that the success is real. Then, don't forget to come back to reality.

Setting Objectives

The physical approach involves doing and, in particular, setting objectives. **Objectives** are short-term milestones that enable managers to map out the conditions that must be met for goals to be reached. One manager finds setting interim objectives important, saying: "Our senior management team is ferocious about setting and achieving objectives. End-result goals would just be too complex to accomplish without interim objectives."

Steps in setting objectives include setting time limits for accomplishing the goal and evaluating how effectively time is spent on various activities. Interim goals constitute stepping stones that lead to accomplishment of the main goal. Also, interim successes will help reinforce those steps and inspire you to press onward. Throughout this process, regular deadlines act as powerful motivators in helping managers reach their goals. Deadlines help determine what must be accomplished and how it must be accomplished.

Recording Progress

An important facet of goal achievement is keeping accurate records of the progress made toward goal accomplishment. Precise records will document gradual progress toward a distant goal. Two basic methods for recording behavior are making a frequency count and recording time duration. Perhaps the easiest and most common method of assessment, a frequency count involves tallying the number of times a particular event occurs. For example, a manager may have a goal of improving food-service quality from 60 "good" or above ratings per 100 comment cards to 70 such ratings. A frequency count would include totaling the number of "good" or above ratings on 100 guest-service cards and comparing it to the benchmark of 60 (at the beginning of an improvement program) and to the goal of 70.

Making a Gantt Chart

Many times, achieving one goal first requires completing multiple steps or tasks. It is often difficult to organize these tasks; many get overwhelmed and completely abandon the goal they were trying to reach. A Gantt chart can help organize the tasks one needs to complete in order to reach a goal. A **Gantt chart** is a bar chart that records the progress of each task and shows when a task should be complete. One of the benefits of this chart is that it places all of the tasks that need to be completed on a single worksheet. A manager or group member can look at the worksheet and understand when to start working on a task or project, how long it should take, and how much work has already been completed. Figure 9.1 shows an example of a Gantt chart.

What type of tracking systems have you used to help record your progress toward meeting a particular goal? Did it work?

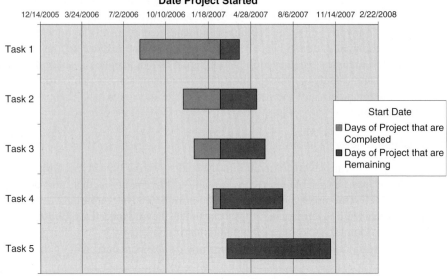

FIGURE 9.1   Gantt chart

Creating Goal Aids

Aids are used to help managers keep their goals before them at all times—ever-present but not intrusive. For example, a note to yourself reminding you of a goal is a **goal aid.** One club executive uses time spent in driving to work as quiet time for reviewing and emphasizing goal aspiration. A hotel general manager does daily step exercises to the accompaniment of "I *wish* to be a regional vice president, I *want* to be a regional vice president, I *will* be a regional vice president." This manager knows that wishing will not make it so, and this mantra reinforces his or her determination to achieve the goal.

Evaluating Goals

SELECTING CRITERIA FOR EVALUATING GOAL ACHIEVEMENT   Goals in the hospitality industry can be difficult to measure because often they are not tangible as are goals in manufacturing. A manufacturer can count the number of items produced, such as cars. In the hospitality industry the goals are often comprised of that ideal concept we call service. How does one measure service or the degree of customer satisfaction? It would seem to be a very subjective science. Feedback from our guests comes in many forms: comment cards, repeat business, informal comments made to direct contact employees, and the rise or decline of an establishment's reputation in a community. The criteria we use to evaluate our goals must be based on some measurable outcome we hope to achieve. One can measure the percentage of customers who are repeat business. One might also look for an increase in the covers in a restaurant, if the restaurant has the capacity to serve more customers. Industry ratings of your establishment are another indicator of goal achievement.

The criteria that you use must be related directly to the goals you have set. You might well achieve superior food by hiring an excellent chef, but if your goal was a clean and safe environment, an excellent rating for food tells you nothing about the cleanliness goal you established. You need to design a measurement instrument that directly reflects the purpose of your goal. This might be a survey or a checklist of observations that could be filled out by a staff member, a guest, or an outside consultant hired to help you see clearly to what extent you have achieved your goals.

The criteria should be established at the time you create the goal. Ask yourself: If this goal is realized, what would this look like? . . . what would it sound like? . . . what effect would it have on interactions among staff or between staff and guests?

REEVALUATING GOALS   Goals are likely to change with time. The decision to change goals should be both rational and conscious. For our purposes, reevaluation means rethinking the goal and making necessary adjustments. It does not mean quitting. A CEO of one northeastern resort offered his view on the reevaluation process: "We have to constantly rethink our interim goals and objectives. If we see that our guests' preferences are changing, we must determine how to best meet those needs—now and in the future. Often that means altering our goals and objectives to provide the level of service desired."

Performance Evaluation

Performance evaluation is evaluating the people who are responsible for implementing the goals. As with goal criteria, the evaluation must fit the task at hand. Specifications related to the goal must be spelled out, preferably in writing, so that each person responsible for the implementation of a goal understands the expectations to which they are being held. There ought to be scales that indicate how well a task is to be performed: how soon, how often, to what extent a thing must be done to be considered acceptable. In this way, performance evaluation is fair and equitable based on specific preassigned criteria. In an ideal case, the parameters of the assignment would be so clear that an employee could virtually evaluate oneself.

Knowing When to Implement Goals

Robby, newly hired at the Kick Back Lounge, was finding out how hectic a Friday night could be. He had graduated bartending school, but his best speed was only half as fast as Tyler who had been bartending for four years. Patrick, the manager, told him that he needed to pick up the pace if he intended to meet the bar's hourly goal for serving. Robby did try to go faster, but he became careless and confused. He couldn't remember where necessary items were kept, hurriedly put things back in the wrong place, and succeeded in slowing down both Tyler and himself. Finally Tyler said, "Why don't you go at a pace that is comfortable for you and I will pick up the slack." Robby gratefully slowed down just to a pace where he could concentrate and get things right. Between the two of them they were able to pick up the pace overall and finished out the evening successfully.

During the early stages of skill acquisition, performance goals may be distracting and, therefore, counterproductive. In the above scene, it was unrealistic of Patrick to expect Robby to perform at a speed similar to someone who had been doing the job for years. Different types of goals, including learning goals and performance goals, may be helpful during different phases of skill acquisition. Time lags between a goal being assigned and carried out can distract attention from reaching the desired performance level. Hospitality industry managers should give careful attention to when organizational goals are presented to employees, in order to establish focus on achievement at the appropriate time.

HOW TO AVOID GOAL CONFLICT

Groups pursuing multiple goals will devote more time and effort to one goal than another, often trading off between quantity and quality goals. Task difficulty and group interdependency will determine the goal selection and performance. If a group chooses difficult quality and quantity goals, it is often unable to improve the quality or quantity of their performance. As a result, they will trade off performance quality for performance quantity. Groups that are not highly confident of their task abilities will more likely de-emphasize quality for quantity goals. Managers should counter drops in quality performance for quantity by setting explicit goals for quality.

Managers need to avoid goal conflict. If a group is rewarded for a quantity goal while being asked to make a quality goal a top priority, they will commit less to both the quantity and quality goals, or lower commitment at the expense of the other. Goals need to be managed carefully, in terms of their number and priority. Groups should focus on a limited number of goals, not more than eight at a time, and these goals should be prioritized clearly by urgency and significance (Curtis, 1994).

Sometimes conflict arises between individual and group goals. When people work on a task interdependently, they set goals for the group as well as for each individual within the group. To avoid goal conflict, managers should set the individual goal so that its attainment facilitates the attainment of the group goal. It is critical to reduce the conflict between the individual and group goal by explicitly stating which goal is more important. Managers can gain greater goal acceptance and performance by setting group goals in addition to members' individual goals. When people only set individual goals, they tend to be more competitive and less cooperative than those with a group goal, or a group goal plus an individual goal (Bettenhausen and Murnighan, 1991).

Studies have not definitely determined whether interdependent groups focus more on maintenance goals or on achievement goals. Although Hackman (1991) argues that interdependent groups will focus on maintenance goals, Matthews et al. (1994) found that introducing an interdependent group process, as well as task complexity, causes groups to select achievement goals due to problems in monitoring and measuring individual input or process.

> What motivates you to accomplish difficult but important goals?

GROUP DEVELOPMENT IN THE GOAL-SETTING PROCESS

Whether you intend to lead or just participate as a group member, it is helpful to understand the various phases of development your group will experience as it evolves. Simply stated, group development is the path a group takes over its life span toward the accomplishment of its main tasks.

Over the years, researchers studying theories about the life cycle phases of groups generally agree. Few breakthroughs have emerged since Tuckman's pioneering work in the mid-1960s. Not surprisingly, many research studies conclude that group phases fall generally into one of three broad categories or stages: beginning, middle, and end.

The Beginning

Budding group relationships are exciting times filled with positive expectations. It is during these early stages of development that groups begin to generate plans, formulate ideas, and set goals. The outlook is positive. Tuckman (1965) concluded that this is the *forming* phase in which group members test and feel their way along. It's likely that you will experience similar feelings as you become oriented to the task at hand and seek to understand the group mission.

Unfortunately, such periods are also punctuated by fears, anxieties, and dissatisfaction that can lead to hostility and conflict between the subgroups. Lewin (1951) assumed that groups experience turbulent conditions, especially when ongoing change is present. Tuckman (1965) uses the term **storming** to describe intragroup (inside the group) conflict—the seemingly requisite amount of overt elbowing and covert backbiting that occurs as frustration sets in and teammates express an emotional response to their task's demands. Team members are uncertain of themselves and their relationships with other group members and often exhibit guardedness, as well as a mixture of curiosity and confusion. Moreover, during this early stage, members develop a dependence on each other.

Do not despair, but be aware. Confusion is a normal part of group development. By understanding that the early part of the group development process lacks structure, you will be better equipped to deal with the issues more effectively and help your team evolve to a more productive and satisfying level.

The Middle

The middle stage ushers in a period of dynamic growth and group interaction. This is the time to resolve conflicts and develop group norms. Such an ability to repair boundaries and move as a whole to meet oncoming challenges and periods of nonequilibrium characterize the middle period. Members align and work together toward a realistic appraisal of what they can accomplish.

A settling down and maturity develops as members become more comfortable with themselves, their teammates, and the defined mission. This is the phase in which interdependency and trust form. Such interaction fosters cohesion. Tuckman refers to the middle stage as the time for **norming,** and **performing.**

The process of norming is the time when alternatives are chosen and agreed upon, policies set, and goals established. An awareness of deep structure in terms of shared values and vision ensues during this time. Members develop new skills and accept their appropriate roles within the group. Communication transforms from discussion into dialogue as an open exchange of relevant interpretations of the task problem emerges.

Over time an increasing sense of togetherness and alignment help move the group closer to their common goal. *Performing* categorizes functional role relatedness as solutions develop and members carry out the work. Members become like spokes in a wheel—each playing a vital role in contributing to the overall team's success—through aligned individual effort and thereby toward group effort. Such alignment emulates a Zen-like phenomenon known as synergy. The concept asserts that the whole (result) is greater (better) than the sum of its parts (each group member's individual effort). Groups become synergistic or, in a sense, $1 + 1 = 3$.

The End

The end is the period of disengagement and adjournment (Tuckman, 1965). It is a time concerned with sadness, good-byes, and self-evaluation. This final phase can be a difficult and emotional period for team members, inducing feelings of anxiety as members begin to think about life outside the group in this distinct stage.

Moreover, the final phase can produce positive effects as well, including those such as self-satisfaction for a job well done. Feelings such as these go far beyond monetary or other external rewards. Furthermore, team members can develop positive feelings for the leader, especially when the group process is successful and the project task goes well.

> What, specifically, can a manager do to recognize employees for accomplishing a goal?

SETTING PERSONAL GOALS

So far, we have discussed goal setting in a professional setting, providing a framework for managers and groups to set and achieve goals within their organization. However, setting professional goals is often not the same as setting individual goals. The goal setting that we discuss here reflects your personal needs and desires. If you assume that the company goals and objectives are enough, you will always be achieving what the company expects, but will take little notice of your own personal needs. Ten years from now you may reflect and realize that you have not achieved what *you* have wanted or expected from yourself.

Make sure that the goals you set are realistic and attainable. Though it may take a lot of determination and hard work to achieve goals, it will be far more rewarding than those goals that can be achieved "overnight." On the other hand, do not set goals that will be impossible for you to achieve. In this situation, you are setting yourself up for failure, and when you do fail, you will be less apt to set goals in the future. Before you begin goal-setting procedures, make sure that you are willing and able to work on and eventually achieve the goals you have chosen.

Set time aside to think about and choose your goals. Do this away from the workplace, in a peaceful and relaxing environment. Once you have chosen your goal or goals, continue to set time aside for reflection and reinforcement. A good time for this may be in the shower each morning or during a brisk walk each evening.

Establishing a Personal Goal

1. *Brainstorming*. On a piece of paper, write everything you have ever desired to have, to do, or to be. Lay aside all inhibitions and just dream. Do not yet conclude whether these dreams are practical, logical, or possible.
2. *Ranking*. Next, determine which of these are your strongest desires. Select number one as the goal you really care about attaining. Unless you are working toward something you really want, you will not expend sufficient effort to attain it.
3. *Identify Methods of Achievement*. Brainstorm again, and list every possible alternative means of achieving your goal that you can think of regardless of how impractical or foolish it may appear to be.

4. *Consider Limitations.* Now is the time to forsake the unreasonable. All goals have certain specific criteria that they must meet before they are acceptable and can be accomplished. Goals should be specific (something to aim toward), realistic (within reach), and clear (to avoid misinterpretation).

5. *Identify Risks.* After you have considered your limitations, think carefully about the risks and undesirable aspects connected with accomplishing the goal. Risks refer to what you might lose by pursuing your goal via each alternative. Include such things as undesirable aspects as well as material items. These will exist to some degree in every goal-setting situation. Moreover, in order to accomplish this specific goal, you have to consider the rewards and accept the unpleasantness of sacrificing momentary pleasures that go along with accomplishing the goal.

Goal selection and establishment are the first, and perhaps the most important steps in accomplishing what you want to do. At this time, your goal should be specific and realistic. It should be measurable. You should have considered your personal capabilities, environmental limitations, and the risks involved. If you deem your personal goal reasonable and acceptable, you can progress to the physical and cognitive steps toward achievement.

It is also important that you have a written goal statement. Once written, the goal will have more meaning and importance. You may also want to write down what you believe are the steps necessary to achieve your goal. Keep in mind what has been mentioned beforehand, that the steps you take must also be logical, reasonable, and within reach. Make sure to include a deadline in your written statement. Without a deadline, there is less urgency, resulting in laxness and the risk of dissipation of interest. The deadline you envision should also be reasonable and attainable.

Create one personal goal statement. Make sure the goal is achievable and important.

Achieving a Personal Goal

At this point you should have your established documented goal. This goal statement is a declaration of the outcome you plan to accomplish. Now you must consider how you will accomplish your goal:

1. *Develop a positive attitude and enthusiasm.* First you should possess a positive attitude and a certain degree of enthusiasm. If you do not have the confidence that your goal is attainable, no amount of work will be able to overcome that.

2. *Allow yourself to relax.* Sit back, lie down, whatever is most comfortable for you. Allow your entire body to unwind and let go. Close your eyes and breathe easily, slowly, and deeply.

3. *Imagine accomplishment.* Now let yourself see the success. Fill your mind with thoughts of your achievement. Allow yourself to see everything vividly and in detail. Give yourself time to dwell on these positive thoughts—enjoy the pleasant feeling of accomplishment. Make these images as vivid as possible. Use your imagination to increase familiarity with the scene. Now concentrate on a single situation in which you achieve your goal. Visualize success and "winning" time and time again. Tell yourself that you are entitled to the best, and convince yourself that the imagined scenario exists. Although this may sound repetitive, repetition is of major importance in order to convince the subconscious that the success is real.

4. *Reorientation.* After an intense session of the visualization process, clear your mind and relax. Allow time to reorient yourself with your surroundings and resume your daily activities. This may be important in order to avoid any possible obsession or loss of touch with reality regarding the goal.

After you have visualized *how* you are going to accomplish your goal, the next step involves taking physical action. The main thing that you need to do to accomplish your personal goal is to set objectives:

1. *State requirements and methods.* Ask yourself what must be done—brainstorm. How can it be accomplished and what is the most effective method?

2. *Set up a time frame.* Your next step is to establish a time frame during which you plan to accomplish your goal. Evaluate how your time is spent. Organize your activities so that you are able to spend more time achieving your goals. Next, determine whether you are using your time effectively. Sort out activities that hinder your progress toward your goal. Decide on how to eliminate or spend less time on these activities. This will give you more time for goal-achieving activities.

3. *Break down.* Break down your goals and set attainable and less ambitious goals that will lead you to accomplishment. When goals are broken down into smaller units, the goal becomes more manageable and less overwhelming. Your first goal should be set only slightly higher than your present level of operation. You can use the analogy of stepping up a ladder. As you move up each rung of the ladder, you become a step closer to your goal. It also becomes more difficult to move higher up, giving you more of a challenge and more incentive to take the next step. Your small successes will be reinforcement as they inspire you to sustain your determination.

4. *Deadlines.* A regular series of deadlines act as a powerful motivation in helping you meet your goals. Deadlines help determine what must be accomplished and how it must be accomplished. You should check your progress on a scheduled basis and write exactly what you need to accomplish by the end of your goal. Be as specific as possible. Set periodic checks to determine how close you are to achieving your goal and reassess your progress. At each checkpoint evaluate your progress. Determine if you have met, exceeded, or fallen short of your goals. If you have fallen short of your goals, make plans to compensate for lost ground. Be sure to notice what you have accomplished and determine your progress considering the conditions.

5. *Reevaluate and set new deadlines.* Your original goals may change as time passes. There is nothing wrong with that. However, the decision to change your goals should be a rational and conscious choice. If you have underestimated what you have accomplished, you may want to set higher goals for yourself. Reevaluate. Have you maximized your efforts? Was your goal attainable and realistic within the established time period? Is your original goal no longer possible? Reevaluation means restructuring and reorganizing; it doesn't mean quitting so don't give up too soon. Review what you have been doing and what you plan to accomplish. You may need to set new deadlines or revise your goals.

These guidelines should aid you when setting/creating and accomplishing personal goals. Remember, it is important to set and achieve goals within the workplace, but it would detrimental for you to ignore your own personal goals.

Using the personal goal you have just set for yourself, go through as many of the steps above as possible.

Summary

In this chapter we discuss the process of setting effective, achievable goals. The goal-setting theory states that a goal should be both specific and difficult. Specific goals allow individuals or groups to measure their performance and generally increase their productivity. Difficult and challenging goals provide individuals or groups motivation to achieve. However, the goal-setting theory also warns against setting too specific and/or too difficult goals; if individuals feel that their goal is unattainable, they will give up immediately.

There are multiple methods and tools individuals and groups can use to set goals. We emphasize the importance of setting a SMART goal. The SMART guidelines call for a goal to be *Specific*, *Measurable*, *Acceptable*, *Realistic*, and *Timely*. We also discuss tools such as MBO and 360-degree goal setting. MBO stresses that every one who works toward achieving a particular goal should be involved in setting that goal. The 360-degree goal setting suggests that groups within an organization should request feedback from both their internal and external customers before setting a goal, which ensures that the goal fits with the organization's overall strategy.

Once a hospitality organization learns how to set effective goals, it will see that goal setting has many benefits. These include (1) directing attention and actions, (2) boosting performance toward peak levels, (3) bolstering persistence, (4) fostering development of innovative strategies, (5) providing a short- and long-term game plan, and (6) reducing stress.

Goals are often difficult to achieve without everyone's commitment. In this chapter we discuss several factors that affect an individual's commitment to a goal and suggest several actions a manager can take to increase the commitment one has toward achieving a goal. Once everyone in a group is committed to a goal, we emphasize several procedures that will help them achieve the goal. We suggest (1) using visualization, (2) setting objectives, (3) recording progress, (4) making a Gantt chart, (5) creating goal aids, (6) reevaluating goals, and (7) knowing the best time to implement goals. We also suggest that groups ensure that individual and group goals do not directly conflict.

We then discuss a group's development during the goal-setting process. A group goes through stages of *forming*, *norming*, *storming*, and *performing*. Groups have a difficult time during the beginning, but as they become more acquainted and comfortable with each other, the group can begin the process of setting and achieving goals. Finally, we discuss the importance of establishing and accomplishing personal goals in addition to professional goals. We provide guidelines for individuals to follow when they are both setting goals and attempting to achieve them.

Key Words

achievement goal *239*
maintenance goal *239*
SMART goal *244*
external influences *247*
interactive factors *247*
internal factors *247*

systematic soldiering *247*
self-efficacy *248*
free riders *251*
goal statement *252*
objective *253*

Gantt chart *253*
goal aid *254*
storming *257*
norming *257*
performing *257*

Exercises

Exercise 1 How to Enhance Goal-Setting Ability

Objective: To ensure that managers and employees examine their goal-setting process

Procedure:

1. Have individuals fill out the "Goal-Setting Ranking Worksheet."
2. Have everyone share their results from the "Goal-Setting Ranking Worksheet."

***

Goal-Setting Ranking Worksheet
Put yourself in the role of a manager as you complete this worksheet

I set goals with my employees once a year   1 2 3 4 5   I set goals with employees every six months

I do not bother to define goal-attainment success   1 2 3 4 5   I always ensure goal-attainment success is defined

I ensure that at least three goals are considered   1 2 3 4 5   I ensure that three to seven goals are considered

Only the goals of subordinates are discussed   1 2 3 4 5   I always include a discussion of my own goals, along with my subordinates

I rarely check the alignment of personal goals to organizational goals   1 2 3 4 5   I always check the alignment of personal goals to organizational goals

Once defined, my goals are never changed   1 2 3 4 5   My goals are always subject to change, as the environment changes

***

Exercise 2   Setting SMART Goals

Objective: Obtain practice writing "SMART" goals
Procedure:

1. Have individuals write three goals they would like to achieve using the techniques taught in the chapter.

2. Give individuals 5–10 minutes to complete their goals.
3. Group students into pairs.
4. Have everyone judge their partner's goals using the "SMART" checklist provided.

***

"SMART" CHECKLIST FOR SETTING GOALS

Goal 1: SMART CHARACTERISTICS   **SUGGESTIONS**

SPECIFIC: Was the goal specific?

MEASURABLE: Was the goal measurable?

ACCEPTABLE: Was the goal acceptable/attainable?

REALISTIC: Was the goal realistic?

TIMELY: Can the goal be completed in a timely manner?

***

Goal 2: SMART CHARACTERISTICS   **SUGGESTIONS**

SPECIFIC: Was the goal specific?

MEASURABLE: Was the goal measurable?

ACCEPTABLE: Was the goal acceptable/attainable?

REALISTIC: Was the goal realistic?

TIMELY: Can the goal be completed in a timely manner?

***

Goal 3: SMART CHARACTERISTICS   **SUGGESTIONS**

SPECIFIC: Was the goal specific?

MEASURABLE: Was the goal measurable?

ACCEPTABLE: Was the goal acceptable/attainable?

REALISTIC: Was the goal realistic?

TIMELY: Can the goal be completed in a timely manner?

***

Exercise 3 Troubles at Milton Hotel Company

Objective: To show that not everyone in a group will agree on the particular manner in which to achieve a goal

Procedure:

1. Divide participants into three groups: Group 1—Managers of Milton Hotels; Group 2—Subordinates/frontline employees at Milton Hotels; Group 3—Observers.

   Variation: If there are a lot of participants, have multiple sets of groups, where there are approximately three to five participants in each group.

2. Explain to all the groups that Milton Hotels is experiencing financial difficulty and the CEO, Robert Harnan, has set two goals for the company that he would like to see accomplished within the next year. **Goal 1:** Increase revenues; **Goal 2:** Decrease expenses.

3. Separate Groups 1 and 2 into two different corners of the room. Have half of the observers sit with Group 1 (managers) and the other half of observers sit with Group 2 (subordinates).

4. Tell both Group 1 and Group 2 that they need to come up with a list of four ways that the company can increase revenues and four ways that the company can decrease expenses. (Give participants about 10 minutes to do this.)

5. Have Group 3 (observers) merely sit with the groups during this time; they will be keeping notes in the next step.

6. After about 10 minutes, tell the groups to reconvene in the center of the room, sitting opposite of each other (i.e., the managers on one side facing their subordinates on the other side).

7. Get Group 1 and Group 2 to present their ideas to each other and explain to them that they need to come to an agreement on the steps that need to be taken to reach CEO Robert Harnan's goals (four things the company can do to increase revenues and four things it can do to decrease expenses).

8. Have the observers keep notes on the attitudes they notice during the conversation, the methods both Group 1 and Group 2 used as they were trying to get their ideas accepted (allow 30 minutes).

9. At the end of 30 minutes, tell the groups that they are out of time. Explain that in the workplace, members of a group cannot spend a significant amount of time trying to reach an agreement on *how* to go about accomplishing a goal; if they do, they will never have time to begin working toward *achieving* that goal.

Exercise 4 Improve Your Service

Objectives:

- To give participants experience working toward achieving a goal in a real-world situation
- To give participants practice providing feedback on others' goals and how well they are achieving them

Procedure:

1. Divide participants into groups of three.
2. Have each individual write down three components of service that they would like to enhance (e.g., smile more, remember names of regular customers/clients).
3. Tell groups that they will be participating in a role play. Have groups decide who will be person A, person B, and person C.
4. Have person A act as an angry customer. Person A has been staying at this boutique hotel for several nights. He or she went out to dinner and after returning could no longer find an available parking space. Person A comes in to the hotel ranting about the lack of parking spaces and goes to the front desk where he or she encounters person B. Tell person B that as he or she deals with this upset customer to focus on the three components of service that he or she wished to improve. Have person C serve as an observer, keeping note on how well person B achieved his or her goal of improving the three components of service previously stated.

5. After each role play, have person C give person B feedback on the service experience and possible ways that he or she could improve the three components of service that he or she has written down.

6. The participants should have the opportunity to role-play as person A, person B, and person C.

7. After everyone has role-played as person B, lead the class in a discussion.

   - Ask what each person noticed as an observer. Was person B able to successfully achieve the goal of improving his or her three components of service?
   - Ask participants if it was easy to remember their goals as they were dealing with the difficult customer.

Exercise 5 Brainstorming, Ranking, and Mapping Goals

Objective: To acquaint managers with three important functions of the goal-setting process

Procedure:

1. Introduce the fact that successfully created goals and objectives develop from a well thought out and carefully implemented process. Goal setting is hard work!
2. Divide the group into small groups of three to five participants.
3. Read, project, or hand out the mini scenario.

As a first step toward goal setting, specify exactly what is to be accomplished: the job, assignment, or responsibility. Participants can use brainstorming methods to assist in identifying problems and then rank the ideas that emerge.

BRAINSTORMING

Create a list of wants or desires as they relate to the job, assignment, or responsibility. Try to put aside inhibitions and be creative—in a dreamlike state. This is the time to catalog all options. Resist the temptation to evaluate whether or not these dreams are practical, logical, or even possible.

RANKING

Next, prioritize to determine which of these desires is most important. Select the most important option as the goal.

MAPPING A STRATEGY

Create a plan for how to accomplish the goal. Brainstorm to develop a list of possible alternatives—regardless of how impractical they appear. After recording possibilities, begin the culling process by considering the limitations of each alternative. Discard those that are unreasonable.

Time: Minimum of 20 minutes. Time spent is contingent on the number of small groups and amount of discussion.

Mini Scenario: Dutton Crowfield, 40 years old, is the executive assistant manager at Deep Forest Resort. While she "grew up" in the hospitality industry, she has no formal education beyond high school. She has decided that she wants to obtain a bachelor's degree in hospitality or business within five years.

In checking possibilities, she has discovered the following options:

1. Flossmore College of Vocational Studies offers credit for life experience and "hotel–motel management degrees within six months." The school is not accredited; they have a post office box address, and an 800 number. After sending for information, she received mailings from three similar schools with the same post office box in Hackensack, New Jersey.
2. Eastern Louisiana Community College (five miles away) offers an associate's degree in hospitality management and evening classes. There are three other community colleges within 20 miles of the resort that offer two-year business degrees.
3. University of Alabama offers an external degree program (BS) in business administration entirely via the Internet.
4. University of Orleans (75 miles away) offers evening and weekend classes leading to a bachelor's degree in hospitality management. Dutton has pretty much written off this option since it is so expensive.
5. UNLV says they will accept her as a full-time undergraduate student in their hospitality program. Dutton has found that other "traditional" universities are interested in her, too, due to her years of experience in the industry.

Materials:

1. A room with movable chairs or table and chair setting.
2. One flip chart with marking pens for each small group.

Questions:

1. How would you complete the brainstorming process if you were Dutton? Has she cataloged all options? Has she made any errors in the process so far?
2. How would you prioritize the list of alternatives?
3. Make a choice and begin to map a strategy for how to accomplish the goal.
4. How would you deal with some of the limitations of the alternatives?
5. Which limitations cause you to discard the alternative as a possibility?
6. Which limitations can be mitigated?
7. What would you do?

Endnotes

Adams, J. S. (1963). Toward an understanding of inequity. *Journal of Abnormal and Social Psychology, 67*, 422–436.

Adams, J. S. (1965). Inequity in social exchange. In L. Berkowitz (Ed.). *Advances in Experimental Social Psychology*, Vol. 2. New York: Academic Press. pp. 267–299.

Bettenhausen, K. L. & Murnighan, K. (1991). The development of an intragroup norm and the effects of interpersonal and structural challenges. *Administrative Science Quarterly, 36*(1), 20–35.

Chesney, A. A. & Locke, E. A. (1991). Relationships among goal difficulty, business strategies, and performance on a complex management simulation task. *The Academy of Management Journal, 34*(2), 400–424.

Curtis, K. (1994). *From Management Goal Setting to Organizational Results: Transforming Strategies into Action*. Westport, CT: Quorum Books.

Earley, P. C., Prest, W., & Wojnaroski, P. (1987). Task planning and energy expended: Exploration of how goals influence performance. *Journal of Applied Psychology, 72*(1), 107–114.

Earley, P. C., Connolly, T., & Ekegren, G. (1989). Goals, strategy development, and task performance: Some limits on the efficacy of goal setting. *Journal of Applied Psychology, 74*, 24–33.

Fang, E., Pamatier, R. W., & Evans, K. R. (2004). Goal setting paradoxes? Trade-offs between working hard and working smart: The US versus China. *Journal of the Academy of Marketing Science, 32*(2), 188–202.

Gellatly, I. R. & Meyer, J. P. (1992). The effects of goal difficulty on physiological arousal, cognition, and task performance. *Journal of Applied Psychology, 77*(5), 694–704.

Gersick, C. J. G. (1988). Time and transition in work teams: Toward a new model of group development. *Academy of Management Journal, 31*(1), 9–41.

Gibbard, G. S. & Hartmann, J. J. (1973). Relationship patterns in self-analytic groups: A clinical and empirical study. *Behavioral Science, 18*(5), 335–353.

Gilliland, S. W. & Lamis, R. S. (1992). Quality and quantity goals in a complex decision task: Strategies and outcomes. *Journal of Applied Psychology, 77*(5), 672–681.

Guthrie, J. P. & Hollensbe, E. C. (2004). Group incentives and performance: A study of spontaneous goal setting, goal choice, and commitment. *Journal of Management, 30*(2), 263–84.

Hackman, J. R. (2002). *Leading Teams: Setting the Stage for Great Performances*. First Edition. Boston, MA: Harvard Business School Press.

Hare, A. P. (1976). *Handbook of Small Group Research*. Second Edition. New York: The Free Press.

Hollenbeck, J., Williams, C., & Klein, H. (1989). An empirical examination of antecedents commitment to difficult goals. *Journal of Applied Psychology, 74*, 18–23.

Hollensbe, E. C. & Guthrie, J. P. (2000). Group pay-for-performance plans: The role of spontaneous goal setting. *Academy of Management Review, 25*(4), 864–872.

Huseman, R. C., Hartfield, J. D., & Miles, E. A. (1987). A new perspective on equity theory: The equity sensitivity construct. *Academy of Management Review, 12*, 222–234.

Kernan, M. C., Bruning, M. S., & Miller-Guhde, L. (1994). Individual and group performance: Effects of task complexity and information. *Human Performance, 7*, 273–289.

Lacoursiere, R. B. (1980). *The Life Cycle of Groups: Group Developmental Stage Theory*. New York: Human Sciences.

Larey, T. S. & Paulus, P. B. (1995). Social comparison and goal setting in brainstorming groups. *Journal of Applied Social Psychology, 25*(18), 1579–1596.

Latham, G. P. & Locke, E. A. (1991). Self-regulation through goal setting. *Organizational Behavior and Human Decision Processes, 50*(2), 212–247.

Latham, G., Locke E., & Winters, D. (1994) Cognitive and motivational effects of participation: A mediator study. *Journal of Organizational Behavior, 15*(1). 49–63.

Lewin, K. D. (1951) [Cartwright (Ed.)]. *Field Theory in Social Science; Selected Theoretical Papers*. New York: Harper & Row.

Locke, E. A. (1988). The determinants of goal commitment. *Academy of Management Review, 13*(1), 23–39.

Maier, N. R. F. (1967). Assets and liabilities in group problem solving: The need for an integrative function. *Psychological Review, 74*(4), 233–249.

Matthews, L. M., Mitchell, T. R., George-Flavy, J., & Wood, R. E. (1994). Goal selection in a simulated managerial environment. *Group and Organization Management, 19*(4), 425–449.

McGrath, J. E. (1984). Time, interaction, and performance (TIP): A theory of groups. *Small Group Research, 22*(2), 147–174.

Merritt, E. A. & Berger, F. (1998) The value of setting goals. *Cornell Hotel and Restaurant Administration Quarterly, 39*(1), 40–50.

Mesch, D. J., Farh, J., & Podsakoff, P. M. (1994). Effects of feedback signs on group goal setting, strategies, and performance. *Group and Organization Management, 19*(3), 309–333.

Milliman, J. F., Zawacki, R. A., Schulz, B., & Wiggins, S. (1995). Customer service drives 360-degree goal setting. *Personnel Journal, 74*(6), 136–144.

Mitchell, T. R. & Silver, W. S. (1990). Individual and group goals when workers are independent: Effects on task strategies and performance. *Journal of Applied Psychology, 73*(2), 185–193.

O'Hair, D. & Friedrich, G. W. (1992). *Strategic Communication in Business and the Professions.* Boston: Houghton Mifflin Company.

Shalley, C. E. (1991). Effects of productivity goals, creative goals, and personal discretion on individual creativity. *Journal of Applied Psychology, 76,* 179–185.

Spitz, H. & Sadock, B. J. (1973). Small interactional groups in the psychiatric training of graduate nursing students. *Journal of Nursing Education, 12*(2), 6–13.

Stallworth, H. (1990). Realistic goals help avoid burnout. *HR Magazine, 35*(6), 171.

Terpstra, D. E. & Rozell, E. J. (1994). The relationship of goal setting to organizational profitability. *Group and Organization Management, 19*(3), 285–294.

Thompson, Jr., A. A. & Strickland, III, A. J. (1995). *Strategic Management Concepts and Cases.* Burr-Ridge, IL: Richard D. Irwin, Inc. p. 34.

Tuckman, B. (1965). Developmental sequence in small groups. *Psychological Bulletin, 63,* 384–399.

Weick, K. E., Bougon, M. C., & Maruyama, G. (1976). The equity context. *Organizational Behavior and Human Performance, 15,* 32–65.

Weingart, L. R. (1992). The impact of group goals, task component complexity, effort, and planning on group performance. *Journal of Applied Psychology, 77*(5), 682–693.

Wilson, S. B. (1994). *Goal Setting.* New York: Academy of Management Association.

Zander, A. (1971). *Motives and Goals in Groups.* London: Academic Press.

10

MANAGING CONFLICT

Great ideas often receive violent opposition from mediocre minds.

—Albert Einstein

CHAPTER OUTLINE

Introduction

The Nature of Organizational Conflict
    Stages of Conflict Development
        Anticipation
        Unexpressed concerns
        Discussion
        Open dispute
        Open conflict
    Categories of Conflict
        Interpersonal conflicts
        Interdepartmental conflicts
        Organizational conflicts

Managing Conflict
    Importance of Managing Conflict
    Diagnosing Conflict
        Collection of data
        Uncovering issues
        Understanding relationships
        Analyzing costs
        Assessing timing

Conflict Management Styles
    Competing
    Accommodating
    Avoiding
    Compromising
    Collaborating

Methods for Preventing Conflict
    Focus on Common Goals
    Encourage Cross-Training
    Improve Communication
    Expand Resources
    Clarify Procedures and Policies

The Manager as Mediator and Negotiator
    Requirements for Mediation and Negotiation
    Guidelines for Mediation
        Create a nonthreatening environment
        Remain impartial
        Allow equal airtime
        Focus on the problem
        View the situation from multiple perspectives
        Consider the options
    Best Practices for Negotiation
        Be prepared
        Diagnose the fundamental structure of the negotiation

Identify the best alternative to the negotiated agreement
Be willing to walk away
Master paradoxes
Remember the intangibles
Actively manage coalitions
Protect your reputation
Practice persuasiveness
Remember that rationality and fairness are relative
Continue to learn from the experience

Dealing with Difficult People
Overbearing Behavior
Shrinking Violets
Cynics
Nonconformists
Passive-Aggressive Behavior
Tips for Thwarting Negative Behaviors and Encouraging Positive Behaviors

Functional Conflict
Devil's Advocacy
Dialectic Model

Summary

LEARNING OBJECTIVES

After reading this chapter, you will be able to do the following:

1. Explain the sources of conflict.
2. Describe the stages in which conflict develops.
3. Define the three categories of conflict.
4. Discuss the importance of managing conflict.
5. Identify and define each style of conflict management.
6. Understand the differences between mediation and negotiation.
7. Describe how managers should deal with problematic behavior.
8. Discuss how the devil's advocacy technique and the dialectic model encourage functional conflict.

Scenario: Allison's Altercations

Allison leaned back in her chair to enjoy the momentary solitude of her office. She had worked for Meriwether Hotels for 15 years and had a superb track record. For the past five years she had been general manager of the Chicago Meriwether, which was profitable. Although each department seemed to be operating smoothly, Allison was concerned about the high level of personal conflict in the hotel. As she looked out her office window, she reviewed the morning's events.

It all began with the food and beverage profit-and-loss statement. Recently the food and beverage department had installed a new point-of-sale system, and Allison

(continued)

(continued)

expected a detailed sales analysis of each item. But as she scanned the statement she noticed that the largest beverage item sold was listed as "miscellaneous goods." The director of Management Information Systems (MIS) explained that the beverage manager was resisting the new system and had not informed MIS of the new wine list recently introduced. Consequently, the last month of wine sales had been inaccurately recorded.

During her morning tour of the hotel, Allison noticed that Ralph, the assistant manager, and Karl, one of the maintenance personnel, were standing by the door to the food and beverage office. When she asked what was wrong, Ralph explained that Edward, the food and beverage manager, had rekeyed the door lock. She knew that Ralph often used the extra desk in Edward's office and that he and Edward didn't get along very well; she tried not to jump to the conclusion that this was a hostile act on Edward's part.

As Allison continued her tour of the hotel, Robert, the rooms division manager, informed her of an incident that had occurred the previous afternoon. Robert had been walking through the banquet room at 2:00 p.m. and found Sally, the assistant food and beverage manager, talking to a few employees, all of whom were intoxicated. When Robert asked Sally if she had told these employees to leave the premises, she became hostile and began yelling at him. Robert quietly withdrew.

As Allison and Robert discussed this incident, they neared the café and heard raised voices coming from the kitchen. The head chef and a waiter were arguing so loudly that their voices were carrying into the crowded dining room and into the lobby. What's more, service had come to a dead halt and the hushed guests looked uncomfortable and concerned.

Allison reflected on the implications of these situations. Although she had always done her best to prevent conflicts among the staff, they continued to arise, wasting enormous amounts of time and energy. She leaned back in her chair and wondered what course of action she should take to resolve the latest in a never-ending series of conflicts at the Meriwether.

INTRODUCTION

A conflict is a disagreement. It is commonplace to find professional disagreements in all types of hospitality organizations. **Conflict management** is the process of diagnosing a situation and then selecting and implementing an appropriate intervention strategy. While some forms of conflict require the aid of an external agent, this section focuses on situations that managers can handle in the course of daily operations. After exploring the nature of conflict, we will present diagnostic and intervention techniques that can be utilized to enhance successful conflict management in hospitality organizations. On any given day hospitality organizations are riddled with various types and degrees of conflict. In fact, some types of conflict are so common that they have become an industry tradition. The head chef's first argument with one of the wait staff is considered a "rite of passage;" the front desk clerk's first quarrel with a housekeeper is part of the "socialization process" characteristic of the industry. Whatever form it takes, dysfunctional conflict can hamper operations and consume a great deal of a manager's time as he or she not only manages the actual conflict situation but also continues to feel its consequences. It should be obvious that, because conflict occupies so much of a manager's time and energy, the ability to manage conflict skillfully is key to managerial success.

THE NATURE OF ORGANIZATIONAL CONFLICT

Conflict, which is not uncommon in the life of organizations, seems to be inevitable in hospitality organizations. The structure of complex organizations places individuals with different perspectives, objectives, and value systems in interdependent relationships. **Conflicts** can arise due to personal differences that result in conflicting perceptions and expectations. Employees within an organization may also have different objectives with incompatible goals. One must remember that not all conflict is negative. Functional conflict is useful in spurring an organization forward to navigate inevitable change and to rise from complacency to new challenges. We will discuss this aspect of conflict later in this chapter, but as we address concerns related to conflict, one must not develop a tendency to avoid conflict in general.

Communication problems, such as faulty communication and informational deficiency, are also a common source of conflict. Faulty communication occurs when individuals communicate in a way that unintentionally angers or annoys others. Informational deficiency can result when individuals use different sources of information that do not agree or that are interpreted differently. Another source of organizational conflict is competition over scarce resources, such as the distribution of space, money, equipment and/or personnel, as

"We may as well go home. It's obvious that this meeting isn't going to settle anything."

well as the stress that results from the inherent uncertainties involved in a dynamic work environment. Interdependence of various groups and individuals upon one another in order to perform their job responsibilities can also cause conflict when dependent tasks are performed late or inadequately. Finally, conflicts can arise when employees perceive reward systems as unfair, or when they are resistant to proposed organizational changes.

Describe a conflict that you were unable to resolve. What happened?

Stages of Conflict Development

Many conflicts within an organization develop in five stages. These five stages are the following: (1) anticipation; (2) unexpressed concerns; (3) discussion; (4) open dispute; and (5) open conflict.

ANTICIPATION   Employees and managers may begin to see the potential for conflict before it arises. For example, if a manager notices that it is difficult to communicate with a certain employee, he or she may begin to anticipate a potential conflict due to their lack of communication.

UNEXPRESSED CONCERNS   After an employee or manager realizes that there is a potential for conflict, he or she may begin to watch that person for signs of trouble. If the uncommunicative person makes an error, the manager may not feel comfortable addressing the employee about his or her shortcomings, because they do not have a previous relationship.

DISCUSSION   Differences of opinion begin to emerge in the third stage of conflict development. People feel more comfortable discussing differences and potential areas of conflict once they have received reassurance from trusted friends.

OPEN DISPUTE   The differences of opinion that emerge during the discussion stage become clearly defined during the fourth stage of conflict development. Each person defines his or her point of view and clearly expresses it to the other.

OPEN CONFLICT   During the final stage of conflict development, individuals commit themselves to a specific viewpoint and feel personally attacked if that point of view is criticized. Once conflict reaches this stage, it is often difficult to separate the individual from his or her position.

Categories of Conflict

One way of conceptualizing conflict is to determine whether the conflict was interpersonal, interdepartmental, or organizational. Later in this chapter we will discuss the fact that conflict is not necessarily bad. Obviously, if there were no forms of conflict there would be no impetus for change or growth. Although we will continue to examine dysfunctional conflict at this time, there are several types of conflict that can be beneficial to the organization.

INTERPERSONAL CONFLICTS   Interpersonal conflicts include disputes among employees, or between employees and their supervisors. Such conflicts occur frequently and individuals must determine whether or not the conflict is important enough to pursue.

Often, however, unresolved conflicts create tensions that interfere with productivity and create stress for both parties. In the opening scenario, Ralph and Edward were having an interpersonal conflict.

Think of all the interpersonal conflicts that arise daily in the hospitality workplace. It might be two assistant managers who both believe they should be promoted, or employees who don't get along. Perhaps an administrative assistant is slow and so others are called upon to pick up additional work. In addition, conflicts with guests are an unavoidable part of the service delivery process. An employee who understands conflict situations and knows how to approach them productively is a tremendous asset to a hospitality organization.

Conflicts become particularly difficult and stressful when one party has more authority and uses his or her power in inappropriate ways. When you disagree with or have a conflict with your supervisor, it becomes much more difficult to resolve the issue. In such cases, it is particularly important to consider all aspects of the situation ahead of time and to understand the principles discussed in this chapter. Your ability to analyze interpersonal situations and to consider the options you have in responding will help to ensure your mental health and personal effectiveness.

Describe a recent interpersonal conflict you've experienced.

INTERDEPARTMENTAL CONFLICTS   Conflicts that are interdepartmental usually have to do with unequal resource allocations. A classic source of conflict in hospitality organizations is that often the marketing department sits on the main floor or mezzanine with plush offices while human resources is in the basement. In the opening scenario, the information systems department was in conflict with the food and beverage department.

Often, too, lack of understanding and respect for the contributions made by other units within the organization result in hard feelings and rigidity. Efforts to share information freely through meetings, memos, and other announcements can be helpful. HR practices, such as job rotation, can also create a healthier work environment.

ORGANIZATIONAL CONFLICTS   You may not even be aware of conflict at the organizational level, but the outcomes can significantly affect your experience as an employee. If your hospitality organization is not performing well and is seen by corporate executives as "floundering," morale and productivity often decrease. Likewise, disagreements about the organization's vision and mission can derail the hotel, restaurant, or club still further. It is particularly important, then, to understand conflict-resolution techniques and to recognize conflict at this level since it affects—either directly or indirectly—almost everyone in the organization.

MANAGING CONFLICT

Many of the employees Suzanne supervised felt that Monica was the most difficult person in the team. She would walk behind you deferentially, all the while kicking you in the butt. Her behavior was having a negative effect on the team. Suzanne thought about her options. She could immediately list four of them.

Option 1: She could transfer Monica to another group.

Option 2: She could sit down with Monica and give her some examples of her negativity.

Option 3: She could document Monica's behavior with the goal of firing her.

Option 4: She could ignore the behavior, saying to herself, "There's one like Monica in every group."

Suzanne decided to speak with her manager, Phil, about the four options.

Phil said, "Several of your options are good, but let's eliminate number four. If you allow Monica to continue because 'there is one in every group', soon you will have far more than one in every group. An attitude like that tends to multiply among workers. Your remaining strategies are a little weak individually. I would recommend you combine them to combat the problem from a variety of aspects all at once. Speak with Monica about her negative behavior. Explain to her that she will be moved to a new group to give her a fresh start. Then document her progress so that if she improves you can reward her, and if she fails to improve, you have the option of letting her go."

Managers are in an important position to influence conflicts and thereby make significant contributions to a healthy work environment. The reasons for this are that managers have responsibility for other people's needs, are in a coordinating, team-facilitating role, are close enough to their team members to observe what is going on, and are responsible for the quality of work and service. The challenge for management is to design systems that can effectively deal with conflict, both negative and positive. To do this there has to be a clear understanding that there are different types and levels of severity of conflict.

Importance of Managing Conflict

Although conflicts are indigenous to all organizations, they are often suppressed by managerial passivity, with the hope that they will dissipate as naturally as they arose. Avoiding conflict in order to maintain a harmonious work environment impairs the flow of information and ideas throughout the organization. Suppressed conflict can cause loss of morale and motivation, miscommunication, blurring of the original problem, strained interpersonal relationships, decreased productivity, focus away from organizational goals and objectives, and impoverished customer service.

In a hotel scenario, conflict situations may arise and continue for days without any course of action. For example, an assistant manager and the food and beverage manager are in disagreement over staffing levels in the dinning room and the incident is now three days old. While each of the parties maintains the outward appearance of genteel working realties, they avoid taking an active role in handling the staffing situation. Instead, they begin to engage in organizational "guerilla warfare." This may involve withholding information from one another and office lockouts. By passively avoiding conflict rather than actively managing their discordant viewpoints, the situation will escalate to the point where time and energy are directed away from organizational concerns.

Effective conflict management requires an ability to understand the limitations and opportunities in any given conflict situation and to implement a course of action that benefits both the hospitality industry organization and its members. Realizing that organizational conflict is a natural occurrence that can have favorable outcomes is the first step in harnessing the energy of this dynamic force. Nonetheless, encouraging functional conflict and working with dysfunctional conflict involves actively managing the process. This requires diagnosing and then using suitable intervention methods in each conflict situation (Rahim, 1986).

> What are the specific consequences you've experienced of unresolved conflict?

Diagnosing Conflict

Diagnosing can be a difficult task since symptoms often masquerade as problems and effectively obscure the cause of a conflict. Differences in personal opinions, needs, and goals can cause friction. Pressures that are external to the workplace such as family or financial problems are imported into the organization and can engender irresponsible or temperamental behavior. Perceptions of inequity can cause competition or bad feelings among workers, and incompatible personalities can result in the development of factions.

In order to separate symptoms from problems and properly diagnose conflict, five factors should be examined:

1. Collection of data;
2. Uncovering issues;
3. Understanding relationships;
4. Analyzing costs; and
5. Assessing timing.

These factors will not only help to uncover the root of the problem they will also provide guidelines for selecting an appropriate intervention strategy. Conflict situations which are critically impeding service or operations preclude lengthy diagnosis. These five factors can be used as a mental checklist for quickly assessing the situation and for determining a suitable course of action.

COLLECTION OF DATA   Most conflicts can be successfully managed only after sufficient amounts of data have been obtained. Through discussions with each of the parties, the manager can begin to sift through feelings, perceptions, and emotions in order to uncover the true source of conflict. Understanding personal needs and priorities will also delineate potential causes of the conflict as well as indicate possible resolutions.

The symptoms that make a given conflict apparent are often the culmination of a prolonged series of events. Therefore the actions and reactions that preceded a given episode should be explored. In order to discover factors that have influenced the current situation, information should be obtained about the parties' previous interactions and their personal and professional concerns. In addition, factors external to the workplace that might significantly impact the situation should be considered. This background information will help place the conflict in its proper perspective.

UNCOVERING ISSUES   Through the information-gathering process, one begins to uncover the root of a problem: the actual issues involved. At the Meriwether, the lock-out episode that Allison encountered stemmed from a staffing dispute. When the conflict was traced back to its origin, it was discovered that the food and beverage manager believed that the assistant manager had engaged in unethical business practices. As is often the case, the issue which precipitated the dispute was preceded by a long series of actions and reactions.

The issue involved affects the degree of difficulty that will be encountered in managing the conflict. In our example, the managers' dispute revolved around both ethics and personal perceptions. In the case of ethics, it would be difficult for these individuals to find a common working basis. By definition, values and ethics are principles which cannot be sacrificed. Thus, a compromise or even a slight alteration in either of their positions would constitute a violation of their basic integrity (Greenhalgh, 1986).

In contrast to conflict stemming from value-laden issues, disputes caused by less significant issues such as misunderstanding or miscommunication are easier to resolve. A common example is when a valued employee unexpectedly gives notice. The manager may first assume the cause to be a personal problem between employee and supervisor. Further information may reveal that the employee had worked every weekend for nine months and then was denied one weekend off for a family event. If this was a case of mis-scheduling due to miscommunication, misinformation, or negligence, what initially appeared as a deep-rooted conflict becomes relatively simple to resolve. Once the fundamental issue has surfaced, solutions acceptable to all parties involved can be readily achieved.

UNDERSTANDING RELATIONSHIPS   Organizations place individuals in a series of inter-dependent relationships. How long the parties anticipate that their working relationship will continue, and their degree of dependence on each other, will affect the conflict management process. If individuals anticipate working together for a long period of time, they will be inclined to discuss their differences and to try to arrive at mutually beneficial solutions. By contrast, when the relationship is temporary (such as with seasonal employees), there will be a lower level of commitment to conflict management and its outcomes.

Another important consideration concerning relationships in conflict is the power structure between the parties involved. The subordinate who is candid with coworkers may be close-mouthed in the presence of the supervisor. The subordinate might naturally assume that whatever the source of conflict—incompatibility of values, opinions, or personalities—it will be resolved in the supervisor's favor. The supervisor, on the other hand, may not be comfortable interacting in a problem-solving mode with his or her subordinates. Thus the fears and inhibitions consequent to an imbalance of power will tend to increase the difficulty of managing the conflict.

ANALYZING COSTS   When individuals believe that they are likely to lose something of great value, they will desperately cling to their positions (Greenhalgh, 1986). If, for instance, the beverage manager at the Meriwether believes that she is being replaced by a computer, and if the director of MIS believes that his position is in jeopardy unless the beverage manager implements the new system, the parties will be reluctant to settle their dispute. Regardless of whether or not their perceptions are accurate, each party believes that the costs they would incur outweigh the benefits of altering the status quo. Thus they will be hesitant to work through the conflict.

While it is important to consider the personal stakes in a conflict, the costs incurred by the organization should also be evaluated. These include both financial and non-monetary costs, since it is likely that some outcomes may result in the loss of money, time, and human resources.

ASSESSING TIMING   The timing of an intervention is as critical as the selection of the inter-vention method itself. Timing involves three distinct considerations. The first consideration is whether or not adequate information has been obtained. While a situation may seem to warrant immediate attention, it may be more effective to postpone intervention attempts until all of the variables have surfaced and are understood.

Second, an intervention's timing should be considered relative to its impact on operations. In an emergency situation immediate action is required. By contrast, acting too hastily can have a negative impact on operations. When the Meriwether's assistant food and beverage manager confronted the rooms division manager, the latter could have attempted to take decisive action. Yet, if he had engaged in an argument or tried to force the issue, she may have walked out or developed a negative attitude which, in turn, would have impacted the remaining functions scheduled for that day.

Finally, the emotional states of all the parties involved must be considered in the conflict intervention process. When the disputants are engaged in heated argument and emotional levels are soaring, intervention may be ineffective or, at best, temporary in duration. Conflict intervention is also influenced by the intervener's state of mind. If the intervener has a personal stake in the outcome, or is simply upset at the individuals involved, it may be difficult to remain objective.

How does emotion influence your behavior in conflict situations?

CONFLICT MANAGEMENT STYLES

Successful conflict management requires implementing an intervention strategy suited to the specific situation. Most agree that the five strategies identified by Thomas and Killman provide the most useful framework:

1. Competing
2. Accommodating
3. Avoiding
4. Compromising
5. Collaborating

These five strategies, shown in Figure 10.1, can be plotted on a graph based on how assertive and cooperative a manager is (Jones, 1976).

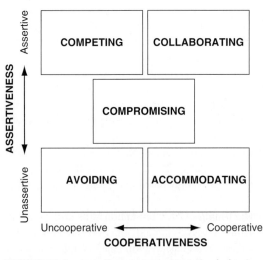

FIGURE 10.1 Assertive versus cooperative behavior

While one style may be more comfortable or intuitive than another, gaining familiarity with a range of techniques creates opinions for tailoring the intervention to the circumstances at hand.

Competing

With the **competing** conflict management style, the individual attempts to resolve the conflict by using aggressive behavior through the forceful use of authority and intimidation. The advantage of this approach is that, assuming that the manager's judgment is correct, the decision might be better than a decision reached through compromise. However, use of this style may lead to hostility and resentment among employees.

Accommodating

Accommodating refers to situations in which the manager appeases the need of one of the parties without attending to the other's concerns and desires. This intervention style is appropriate when harmonious relations are important or when the situation is personally inconsequential.

Accommodating is the single most important strategy in many customer interactions. When a customer becomes irate about some aspect of a hospitality organization's service, there is no time to ask for the customer's understanding or to set up an appointment so that an equitable solution can be achieved. The customer's needs must be addressed immediately.

Avoiding

Avoiding a conflict refers to reflecting the situation away without dealing with the causes of the conflict. It should not be used as a sole intervention strategy, since storing conflict away usually results in its later reemergence with greater intensity. As incidents occur and are avoided, they become like a growing stockpile of dynamite. All it takes is a casual comment or gesture taken the wrong way to spark the explosive reaction.

However, avoiding can be used effectively in certain circumstances. For example, when the timing of a situation is inappropriate or when information is insufficient, avoidance may be the most viable course of action. If an assistant food and beverage manager began causing a scene in a public part of the hotel, the rooms division manager would strategically withdraw and avoid further conflict. To attempt to work it through when tempers are flaring and employees are present is counterproductive for the hotel. By temporarily avoiding the conflict, the rooms division manager prevents the situation from deteriorating and saves embarrassment for everyone concerned.

Compromising

In conflict situations, **compromising** is frequently associated with collective bargaining between labor and management. Yet this intervention style also can be implemented when working with the conflicts that arise in the course of daily operations. Successful bargaining requires sufficient time and an awareness and understanding of the needs of each party. The parties must also be at a point where they are willing to negotiate. Although a compromise provides a resolution to a conflict, it also has many negative side effects. When a compromise is made, each party gives up something of value. This can result in negative feelings since none of the parties is fully satisfied.

TABLE 10.1 Comparison of Five Conflict Management Approaches

Approach	Objective	Rationale	Likely outcome
Avoiding	Avoid dealing with conflict	"I'm not involved."	Problem unresolved.
Competing	Get your way	"I know what's right."	You feel like a winner but the other person feels like a loser.
Accommodating	Don't upset the other person	"How can I make you feel better?"	Other party will take advantage.
Compromising	Reach an agreement	"Let's find a solution so we can get on to something else."	Solution may not be effective.
Collaborating	Solve the problem	"This is my position; what is yours?"	Problem likely to be resolved; both parties treated fairly.

Collaborating

Collaboration as a conflict management style views individuals as partners who can each satisfy their personal needs. By working together and exchanging ideas, information, feelings, and beliefs, individuals may discover a wide range of solutions that fully satisfy their mutual concerns.

In the case of the conflict between the MIS department and the beverage manager, a collaborative approach would be appropriate. Although the situation is taking its toll on the organization, further diagnosis is required since the fundamental issues involved are still unknown. Fortunately, the situation does not require rapid intervention, so there is adequate time available to gather the necessary information. The parties must continue to work together. Table 10.1 illustrates the comparison of the conflict management approaches.

If the general manager simply reprimanded the beverage manager for not complying with the new system, she would probably be addressing symptoms rather than the actual problem. However, devoting energy to gathering information and to bringing the parties together may help them to generate joint win-win solutions that will benefit them both.

> Which conflict style feels most comfortable to you? Give an example of when you have approached a conflict in each of the five ways.

METHODS FOR PREVENTING CONFLICT

Throughout this chapter, we have focused on techniques that managers can use to approach a resolution in the event of a conflict. Managers must bear in mind that not all conflicts are counterproductive. Some conflict is beneficial for raising necessary concerns, initiating positive change, or exposing situations that have been submerged. Conflict management also requires analyzing a situation and searching for ways to prevent conflict that is not productive. In this section, we will explore five structural changes that managers can make to prevent conflict: focus on common goals, encourage cross-training, improve communication, expand resources, and clarify procedures and policies (McShane and Von Glinow, 2000).

Focus on Common Goals

A hospitality industry manager can reduce conflict by encouraging all departments of the organization to focus on a common goal. If two departments disagree on something, it will be easier to solve if both parties are directed by the same goal, rather than an individual department's goals. For example, if the waitress and the cook described at the beginning of the chapter were both focused on providing phenomenal customer service, then they would have set their conflict aside to serve the customers in the dining room.

Encourage Cross-Training

Conflict can be reduced if management encourages cross-training throughout the organization. If individuals train in multiple departments, they will have a better understanding of what each department's role is within the hospitality organization. With this better understanding, employees will have an easier time comprehending the actions of their fellow employees in different departments. For example, at the beginning of the chapter, we described the conflict between the director of MIS and the beverage manager. If the beverage manager had trained in the MIS department, he would understand the importance of accounting for all inventories.

Improve Communication

Managers can reduce conflict by encouraging communication within their organization. When managers and employees do not effectively communicate, misunderstandings can easily turn into large conflicts. For example, at the beginning of this chapter, Ralph was upset that Edward had rekeyed the lock to the office they both shared. If Ralph and Edward had effectively communicated, then Ralph would have known that Edward believed Ralph had been participating in unethical behavior. If Ralph knew that Edward felt this way, he could have explained his behaviors and they may have been able to settle the situation.

Expand Resources

Managers can reduce conflict within their organization by expanding the amount of resources and the quality of resources available to employees. Although expanding resources requires additional funds, conflict can also be costly. Managers should compare these costs to see if expanding resources will be cost-effective for their organization.

Clarify Procedures and Policies

Clarifying procedures, rules, and policies will help managers avoid conflict within their organization. Employees may unintentionally violate a procedure if management has not clearly articulated all organizational rules and policies. Once a policy is implemented, it is important for management to reinforce that policy; otherwise, it will soon be forgotten and violated.

Are there other ways in which managers can try to prevent or reduce potentially disruptive conflicts?

THE MANAGER: MEDIATOR AND NEGOTIATOR

When conflict is viewed as opportunity, it becomes possible to establish an environment for developing creative solutions, which are satisfying to everyone. This requires that all of the individuals involved in a dispute collectively work through their differences. Collaboration, when used as a conflict management technique, provides a means for conflicting parties to work together to satisfy both individual and organizational goals.

When conflicts first surface, they often demand a more immediate form of intervention for the sake of a smooth operation. Whereas alternate styles produce rapid results and address the needs of the situation, they do not attend to the source of conflict as collaboration does. In cases where compromising, competing, avoiding, and accommodating have been employed, collaboration should be introduced as a reinforcement technique.

Whether used as a primary or secondary intervention measure, collaboration requires that managers act as mediators and negotiators. In the case of mediation, the manager serves as an impartial third party who brings individuals together and helps promote the discussion of feelings, perceptions, and beliefs so that mutually satisfying solutions may be found. Similar to mediation, negotiation involves exchanging ideas, information, feelings, and perceptions and aims at solutions that both benefit the hospitality organization and satisfy the disputants.

Requirements for Mediation and Negotiation

There are five characteristics that are common to all mediation and negotiation situations: (1) There must be two or more parties; (2) There must be a conflict between two or more parties; (3) The parties must come together by choice, not by force; (4) Both parties should possess a "give-and-take" attitude; (5) Both parties must want to find an agreement (Lewicki et al., 2007).

If a manager finds that a conflict meets the above criteria, he or she may proceed with either mediation or negotiation. If the dispute is between two employees, he or she would serve as a mediator. However, if he or she is involved in the dispute, then a negotiation is necessary. The following sections provide guidelines for practicing both mediation and negotiation.

Guidelines for Mediation

When acting as a mediator, a manager should use the information and understanding that has been gained through the process of diagnosing conflict. Remember that this includes considerations related to pertinent data, relative issues, relationship among participants, potential costs, and appropriate timing. The following guidelines provide a framework for using mediation to manage conflict.

CREATE A NON-THREATENING ENVIRONMENT A non-threatening environment is not something one creates at a particular moment when a conflict arises that must be solved. A quality manager maintains this environment on a day to day basis by listening to and addressing employee concerns in a timely manner, withholding judgment in difficult situations, and establishing a reputation as a fair and reasonable manager in all situations. At the problem-solving session, the parties need to be put at ease. Hold the meeting on neutral ground. For example, if the conflict were between a housekeeper and her supervisor, they would not meet in that supervisor's office. The manager should state at the outset why the meeting was convened. Describe the conflict in terms which are not accusatory. Establish the focus of the meeting on the successful resolution of the conflict, outlining the boundaries within which the resolution can occur.

Describe what the physical situation would look like if you were responsible for creating a non-threatening environment.

REMAIN IMPARTIAL   Managing conflict involves far more than simply what is said orally. Judgmental comments and body language can easily dissuade individuals from conducting an open exchange of thoughts and feelings. A professional, unemotional distance, especially on the part of the manager, is imperative. Too often, those most closely involved in the conflict are emotionally enmeshed, preventing clear and logical thinking. This is exacerbated if there is a perception that the manager, as mediator, has preconceived biases related to either the employee or the issues. Those involved must be assured that the primary motivation on the part of the manager is merely the fair and successful resolution of the problem at hand. If a manager has personal involvement in the conflict, it is important to maintain an open mind.

ALLOW EQUAL AIRTIME   A problem-solving session is an exchange; therefore, one party should not dominate the conversation. As a manager, there are several techniques that may be employed to avoid this situation. Sometimes a timer may be used so that each person has three minutes to speak on a rotating basis. Persons involved may also be asked to come prepared with a short summary of their perspective on the situation and ideas for resolution. At the end of the mediation session, each person should have the opportunity to review their summary of the situation based on new insights gained in the process of the meeting. When using the timer strategy, the manager must hold firmly to the guidelines established at the outset of the meeting.

FOCUS ON THE PROBLEM   The manager is responsible for maintaining group focus on the resolution of the problem. It is easy to become sidetracked by the emotional content that conflict resolution is likely to raise. Don't dwell on the thoughts and feelings of individuals. While emotions have their place and are likely to emerge, the meeting should concentrate on the issues. The focus should include issues related to the problem. Participants should examine the effects of the conflict on the employees' ability to work effectively, on the quality of the service offered to customers, and on the hospitality organization itself.

VIEW THE SITUATION FROM MULTIPLE PERSPECTIVES   Finding mutually satisfying solutions often requires seeing the situation from a different perspective. Relevant perspectives include those of the involved parties, the organization's point of view, or even an outside point of view. Giving involved parties the opportunity to share their perspectives with one another in a protected environment. A manager can research how other organizations in the hospitality industry have resolved similar problems. Sometimes a consultant can be brought in to help people see things in a new light. A perspective from someone not emotionally involved in the problem may be welcomed.

CONSIDER THE OPTIONS   Encourage new ideas, find areas of agreement, and look for solutions that satisfy individual and organizational needs. If a problem has become a conflict, it is likely that the most obvious solutions have proved ineffective for some reason. Many times people are so committed to seeing their solution put into practice (or in preventing an opponent's solution) that they fail to even consider alternative solutions. A brainstorming session to develop a variety of potential solutions can be effective. A manager may come to the mediation meeting with several suggestions of possible solutions to help get people thinking. Often an unsatisfactory solution can be worked into a viable solution, if given enough consideration.

Best practices for negotiation

The following 11 guidelines (Lewicki et al., 2007) provide a framework for managers to use during negotiations as they are managing conflict within their organization.

BE PREPARED   As with everything in life, being prepared is essential. Preparation allows a manager to both develop a clear idea of his or her goals and better articulate these goals to the other party.

DIAGNOSE THE FUNDAMENTAL STRUCTURE OF THE NEGOTIATION   After a manager has finished preparing, Lewicki suggests diagnosing the fundamental structure of the negotiation.

IDENTIFY THE BEST ALTERNATIVE TO THE NEGOTIATED AGREEMENT   It is important for the manager who is negotiating to know the best alternative to the negotiated agreement—**BATNA.** Understanding the BATNA is important because it allows the manager to evaluate the offer from the opposing party by comparing it to the best alternative.

BE WILLING TO WALK AWAY   If an offer presented by the other party is not better than the manager's BATNA, the manager must be willing to walk away from the negotiation. If the manager does not walk away, he or she may enter an agreement with the opposing party that is viewed as unfair.

MASTER PARADOXES   In most negotiations, managers are required to make decisions between two contradicting options. For example, the manager must know when to yield to the other party and when to stick to his or her principles. A manager may also need to decide whether to stick with a previous strategy or pursue new options.

REMEMBER THE INTANGIBLES   If the other party is especially adamant about a particular issue, the manager should understand that **intangible factors** are most likely influencing this behavior. For example, an employee may avoid making an agreement if he or she believes the manager will perceive it as a sign of weakness. If the manager understands this intangible factor, then he or she can try to convince the employee that agreement does not show weakness.

ACTIVELY MANAGE COALITIONS   Understanding relationships is important during negotiations. Negotiating with a group of employees who want to cooperate and build a relationship with management will be quite different from negotiating with a group of employees who are uncooperative.

PROTECT YOUR REPUTATION   No matter what the situation, managers should always protect their reputation. Once a manager has built a certain reputation, it is often difficult to change.

PRACTICE PERSUASIVENESS   Persuasiveness involves convincing employees to act on your information or recommendation. To do this you must learn to interpret the other person's point of view and gradually bring them around to your own. Recognize when to push forward and when to back off. You may need to help someone see that they are caught in a paradigm that is no longer useful. Your own reputation can be persuasive as can be the opinion of experts or the opinion of other like-minded individuals within your own organization. Persuasion is an art, with the above mentioned strategies as your palette. Different individuals will react differently to various persuasion methods. Practice role playing these techniques with a colleague to help develop your skills at persuasion.

REMEMBER THAT RATIONALITY AND FAIRNESS ARE RELATIVE   Managers should communicate with the other party to ensure that both parties feel the agreement is fair. A manager may leave a negotiation feeling that the results were equitable. However, the other party may leave feeling that the results were not equitable. In such a situation, the manager may not be aware that his reputation has been damaged.

CONTINUE TO LEARN FROM THE EXPERIENCE   Each negotiation will have strengths and weaknesses in terms of the manager's success in resolving the conflict. Understand the techniques that worked well and make a list of areas that could be improved upon for the next negotiation. Managers must use each encounter to further understanding and skill in resolving conflict.

> Have you been involved in a negotiation situation? If so, describe the issue and the outcome. Would you do anything differently if you were to engage in this activity again?

DEALING WITH DIFFICULT PEOPLE

As humans, we all can be difficult at times. In certain individuals, these difficult behaviors can develop into a recognizable pattern of behavior that can affect customer service, employee morale, and the success of a hospitality organization. The more capable a manager is at thwarting destructive patterns of behavior, the more successful he or she will be at establishing a pleasant working atmosphere for everyone.

The following are a few examples of the patterns of behavior one may encounter in the hospitality workplace. Bear in mind that any individual may have a bad day, and one should not be too quick to jump to conclusions about employees' shortcomings based on one or two exchanges. Difficult people are a challenge for a facilitator. There are various strategies for dealing with some of the more common types of difficult people.

Overbearing Behavior

Derek was more than proud of his position as head chef. He felt he ran a tight ship—but his crew was always on the verge of mutiny. He never asked for anything to be done, he demanded. He insisted on being treated with the utmost respect, but seldom treated anyone else in that way. He was effective in his position, but he bullied his staff and even his supervisors. He took absolute credit for every success and found a scapegoat for every failure. When he left our organization, he had a stellar resume, but I can't imagine who gave him a character reference, probably someone who felt coerced into doing so . . .

Employees who exhibit overbearing behavior can be a source of conflict and intimidation within an organization. They desire opportunities for influence, dominance, challenges, and recognition. Managers should recognize their need for approval by encouraging them to earn people's respect rather than demand it. Give them lots of work and make sure it is well done. Listen to what they have to say, but avoid arguments. For example, in a meeting when the discussion seems to be moving into something personal or counterproductive, then summarize what was said and turn to another person saying, "How do the rest of you feel about that?"

Shrinking Violets

Our children were swimming in the hotel pool. Some rowdy teenagers were carrying on to the extent that our children and other guests were made to feel very uncomfortable. I understand that there was no lifeguard, but there was an outdoor café attached to the hotel with a manager on duty. I thought she would say something to these kids. They were loud enough to attract the attention of the people dining, but she pointedly ignored them.

Finally, my husband spoke to her about the situation. She glanced over timidly and mumbled something like 'boys will be boys'. When pressed she said, 'Just a minute . . .' and disappeared into the hotel, never to be seen again. Eventually another guest retrieved a different manager from within the hotel and he spoke to the kids and they modified their behavior. Of course, this was after most of the other guests had given up on the situation and left. We would have had an entirely different experience if that first manager had just addressed the loud teenagers as soon as it was obvious there was a problem.

These employees, often new hires, may not understand their job description and fail to live up to expectations. They show no initiative. Often a straightforward communication such as, "This is what we hired you to do. Please do it," is all that is needed to get the employee up to standard. Help these employees to gain self confidence by making sure they carry the task through to completion. If employees are shy, help them to start to feel more comfortable by asking for their opinion on topics that are relatively benign. If the employee is noncommunicative and passive, elicit a response by employing attending behaviors such as leaning forward to show interest in the employee.

Cynics

Patricia was always the most often heard at our staff meetings. Even when she wasn't making snide remarks about the items on the agenda you could hear her loud sighs and see her rolling her eyes. Sometimes her sarcastic remarks were actually quite funny, so she wasn't as unpleasant as I am making her sound. However, she had been around for quite some time and was resistant to new managers and the new ideas that came with them. One time we started a plan of strategic improvement. Patricia judged every new idea as impossible, absurd, or bound to fail until we were all afraid to make any more suggestions. When Molly, our supervisor, tried to talk to Patricia about her negative behavior she became defensive, almost hostile.

Cynics are usually highly competent members of teams who have developed a negative attitude over a long period of time. Due to their negative viewpoint, they constantly suspect ulterior motives behind the manager's actions. Because of their experience and their usual powerful placement in an informal network, they can influence others, placing doubts in the heads of other employees. When the cynic's remarks are taken as a fact, a drop in morale can create a drop in customer service. Managers can deal with this problem by confronting the cynic directly, focusing on the effects of the cynic's behavior on customer service. You will need documentation of specific examples to convince the cynic. Arm yourself with substantiated facts to counter the cynic's typically grand condemnations. During the confrontation, do not let personality become an issue. Focus on the effect the cynic has on other employees and customer service.

Nonconformists

I don't know why we hired Daisy. We have a very conservative clientele, and strict rules of dress and behavior. But Daisy is one of those people who feel that rules just don't apply to her. She seems to enjoy conflict. Even when you agree with her, she finds something contrary to say in reply. You might say she doesn't know how to take "yes" for an answer! When reminded of some transgression she will argue that it doesn't interfere with her ability to perform her job, or that the customers prefer it when she is less formal with them. She knew the regulations when she was hired, but feels as though every point is up for debate. She just doesn't understand that we have an image to maintain.

Nonconformists do not like to follow rules. To deal with nonconformists, it is necessary to clarify the parameters of their behavior in relation to the expected performance level of the job. Nonconformists should be given the opportunity to let meaning be derived from their own behavior; they should express how their behavior is affecting the performance of the group. At the same time, be sure not to stifle their creativity. Rather, put their creativity to use by giving them work where there is an opportunity for real achievement.

Passive-Aggressive Behavior

Gillian is so nice to everyone; you'd never guess what a pill she is to work with. She happily hands off her work to others, and spends time talking to friends on the phone when she is supposed to be taking customer calls. During meetings she taps her foot and her pencil, looks out the window, acting completely bored. She drains energy from the rest of the group. If Gillian doesn't want to do something, she doesn't refuse directly, she just dodges the task until someone else gives up and does it for her. She talks the talk. To listen to her, you'd swear she does 90% of the work around here and that she'd love to do more, if only. . . .

Passive-aggressive people exhibit a negative reaction to authority. Instead of releasing their aggression or dealing with it in another manner, they channel their anger into passive behavior that slows and blocks the efforts of others. Passive-aggressive employees are not easy to spot, as they can be charming and have many friends. There are, however, certain signs that indicate a person has passive-aggressive tendencies. For example, when they are assigned an easy task, they demonstrate helplessness. They may also tend to put others on the defensive when interacting with them. Without action taken to stop them, passive-aggressive employees can undermine group morale.

Avoid arguments. When you confront an employee, do so without defensiveness and acrimony. Retain control of the meeting and make it clear that you are not interested in anything other than constructive examples.

> Which of the personalities described above do you personally find most difficult to work with? Explain.

Tips for Thwarting Negative Behaviors and Encouraging Positive Behaviors

The best way to address behavior concerns is to create a work environment that prevents or minimizes undesirable behaviors while encouraging the development of team-oriented behaviors. The following tips will help you to do this:

1. Provide orientation that talks about the specifics of the job and sets performance standards.
2. State goals clearly for each member of your team and for the entire team.
3. Coach employees so that they work up to their greatest potential.
4. Use active listening with all of your employees.
5. Provide sensitive and thoughtful problem-solving help for your employees.
6. Communicate respect toward all of your employees.
7. Use your managerial position and skills to energize and actualize a vital and high performance team.

FUNCTIONAL CONFLICT

The word "conflict" generally connotes a negative event or situation. Most people envision social conflict in terms of warfare, dissension, and hostility. Conflict is regarded as a destructive force that should be avoided, or at least reduced and eliminated as expeditiously as possible.

Functional conflict is the positive variety of conflict. Conflict frequently arises due to differences within an organization. From the organizational perspective, the very nature of differences, and constructive use of these differences, can foster organizational excellence. Effective organizations take advantage of employees' differences to create synergy, thereby making the team of employees more valuable than the sum of individual contributions. Organizations that attempt to remove all sources of conflict will diminish their potential. Conflict has the potential to stimulate new ideas, encourage creativity, introduce alternative perspectives, lead to an awareness of underlying organizational problems, serve as a catalyst for altering the status quo, and enhance teamwork through mutual problem solving. There are two primary ways that managers can stimulate functional conflict. These methods are devil's advocacy and the dialectic model.

Devil's Advocacy

The **devil's advocacy technique** requires an individual to take the opposing perspective from the rest of the group. The adoption of the devil's advocacy model may prevent what is known as *groupthink*. Groupthink occurs when individuals in a group agree on an idea simply to reduce conflict and come to a unanimous decision. As a result, the group fails to thoroughly evaluate the idea and test it for real-world application. A devil's advocate will ask questions and encourage the group to think about possible problems that may arise during the implementation of the idea.

Do you often play devil's advocate? What has been your experience with this technique in the groups in which you have participated?

Dialectic Model

The **dialectic model** is based on traditional ideas about debate. It requires individuals in a group to discuss alternative options to a proposed idea, rather than criticizing an idea as a devil's advocate would. Two groups are formed and charged with seeking the merits of two different ideas. The manager would oversee the ensuing debate. Decisions would be made based on the points raised in the debate. The decision might include a compromise of the two original ideas. A manager using the dialectic model must encourage his or her group members to evaluate all proposed ideas based on facts relevant to the solution.

> *Northern University relies a great deal on student workers for their food service organization. In the summer, the Student Center hosts a series of conventions, everything from the Regional Convention of Methodists to the Annual Goat Farmer's Collective. There are also a variety of summer camps and instructional workshops that use the dormitories and require that those food service providers are staffed. The problem is that most of the student workers go home in the summer. The full time food service employees must cover shifts all week, including the weekends.*
>
> *The proposed solution is to offer longer shifts and swing shifts to workers to cover the needed times. The Director of Food Service organized a team of employees that included food service managers, cooks, and kitchen staff to debate the problem. Rather than seeking the pros and cons of the longer shifts/swing shifts proposal (which were obvious to everyone concerned), the team was tasked with establishing one or two other viable alternatives. One alternative they came up with was to hire temporary employees. Another was to transfer university employees with less summer work to food service to help cover the shortage. The team was then divided into three groups—one for each proposed solution. Each team had to research the viability and benefits of their assigned option and to be ready to refute any negative aspects associated with it.*
>
> *On an appointed day, they came together and enjoyed a rousing debate. The alternatives had been thoroughly considered, The Director of Food Service mediated the debate, and when a solution was agreed upon, all felt they had had adequate input.*

Summary

In this chapter we discuss the management of conflict. Conflict management is the process of diagnosing a situation and then selecting and implementing an appropriate intervention strategy. Conflict may arise for a number of reasons, including faulty communication, informational deficiency, competition over scarce resources, interdependence of various groups and individuals, perceived unfair reward systems, and resistance to proposed organizational changes. Conflict within an organization develops in five stages: anticipation, unexpressed discomfort, discussion, open dispute, and open conflict. Once conflict emerges, it can be divided into three categories: interpersonal, interdepartmental, and organizational.

It is important to manage conflict because it can build up or break down an organization. A manager must diagnose a conflict before attempting to solve it. To properly diagnose a conflict, we suggest taking five steps: collect the data, uncover the issues, understand the relationships, analyze the cost, and assess the time.

Once you have diagnosed a conflict, there are five management styles to choose from: competing, accommodating, avoiding, compromising, and collaborating. When using the collaborative approach, managers often take on the role of either a mediator or negotiator, depending on the diagnosis. We provide guidelines for hospitality managers to use in both mediation and negotiation situations.

We identify several types of behaviors: overbearing, shrinking violets, cynics, nonconformists, and passive-aggressive. We discuss the ways a manager should handle these behaviors. Finally, we provide a list of tips for managers to use to thwart the behaviors of problem employees.

Key Words

conflict management *276*
conflict *277*
competing conflict
   management style *284*
accommodating conflict
   management style *284*

avoiding conflict
   management style *284*
compromising conflict
   management style *284*
collaborating conflict
   management style *285*

BATNA *289*
intangible factors *289*
functional conflict *293*
devil's advocacy
   technique *294*
dialectic model *294*

Exercises

Exercise 1   Are You Convinced?

Category: Conflict Management/Negotiation

Objective: To enhance one's persuasive abilities through participation in minidebates concerning job-specific conflict

Number of participants: Two participants for each topic and unlimited observers

Time Frame: Five minutes per topic

Materials: "Key Persuasion Techniques." Handout of topics.

Procedure:

Preparation: Create a list of debatable topics that are relevant to your organization, and have it ready as a handout. Below is a sampling of hospitality-specific topics:

- The negative effects on guests and staff from overbooking reservations outweigh the benefits received from this procedure.
- Hotels should use unannounced surveillance to ensure that room attendants are not pilfering from guest rooms.
- The executive chef should devote an equal amount of time planning menus for employee dining as he or she does for creating menus for the hotel's restaurants and banquet events.
- Random drug testing is an effective method to help ensure a safe work environment.
- Department heads should hold supervisors accountable for the mistakes of the line-level employees the supervisors oversee.

- In restaurants, guests' complaints are more often due to errors made by the back-of-the-house staff than from mistakes made by the front-of-the-house staff.

1. Using "Key Persuasion Techniques," explain the effective persuasion behaviors.
2. Distribute the scenario handout. Ask participants to form pairs and chose a topic. Make sure there are enough topics for each pair, or have the pairs come up with original topics.
3. Pairs will spend 10 minutes planning their persuasive argument.
4. The objective is for each pair to persuade the audience on the topic chosen. The audience will listen to the persuasive argument and decide if they were convinced or not.
5. Ask each pair to present their argument and have the audience determine whether or not they are convinced.

KEY PERSUASION TECHNIQUES

1. Use positive, tactful tone of voice.
2. Present one idea at a time.
3. Give strong supportive evidence.
4. Appeal to self-interest.
5. Make a logical argument.

Variation: Participants can split off into two groups to conduct the debates, thus increasing the level of each person's participation. This variation also relieves some anxiety from participants to "perform" in front of the group.

Exercise 2   Yes, and . . .

Category: Conflict Resolutions

Objective: To help participants acknowledge the benefits of nonconfrontational responses in a conflict situation

Number of Participants: Any number

Time Frame: 20 minutes

Materials: A list of topics for each pair

Procedure:

Prepare a list of topics on which participants may debate. Examples may be

- Closing the main dining restaurant for breakfast.
- Upgrading the desks in the guestrooms.

- Increasing the rack rate by 10 percent.
- Introducing discount rate for senior citizens.
- Hiring an additional part-time administrative assistant for General Manager.
- Hiring a consultant to conduct "time management" training course.

1. Divide participants into pairs, and assign a topic to each group.
2. Ask one person in each pair to take a positive position to argue in favor of the topic, and the second to take the negative position not in favor of the topic. The first person in favor of the topic should try and persuade the second person to change his or her position.

3. In the dialogue, each response should start with one of the following:
   - Yes, . . . and
   - I appreciate, . . . and
   - I agree, . . . and
   - I respect, . . . and
   - I understand, . . . and

Do not use the word "but."

4. After five minutes, the facilitator should ask the pairs to switch roles and argue the other position.
5. After another five minutes, debrief as a class by asking the following questions:

- Were you able to persuade your partner?
- How effective were you in your persuasion?
- How did you feel when you responded using supportive sentences?
- What are the benefits of nonconfrontational response?
- How did you feel when you switched roles and started arguing for an opposite point of view?
- Discuss how the use of supportive sentences influences one person's attitude toward the person with an opposite view.

Endnotes

Aritzeta, A., Ayestaran, S., & Swailes, S. (2005). Team role preference and conflict management styles. *International Journal of Conflict Management, 16*(2), 157–179.

Blackard, K. (1999). How to make the most of the employment ADR process. *Dispute Resolution Journal,* New York.

Cottringer, W. (2006). Resolving workplace conflict. *Security Management, 50*(7), 42–46.

DeReuver, R. (2006). The influence of organizational power on conflict dynamics. *Personnel Review, 35*(5), 589–594.

Desivilya, S. (1988). Using conflict in organizations. *International Journal of Conflict Management,* Bowling Green.

Donais, B. (2007). Training managers in handling conflict. *Canadian HR Reporter, 20*(5), 13–16.

Dreachslin, J. & Kiddy, D. (2006). From conflict to consensus: Managing competing interests in your organization. *Healthcare Executive, 21*(6), 9–15.

Greenhalgh, L. (1986). SM Forum: Managing conflict. *Sloan Management Review,* 46.

Heames, J. & Harvey, M. (2006). Workplace bullying: A cross-level assessment. *Management Decision, 44*(9), 12–14–1221.

Hede, A. (2007). The shadow group; Towards an explanation of interpersonal conflict in work groups. *Journal of Managerial Psychology, 22*(1), 25–43.

Humphrey, R. (2006). Promising research opportunities in emotions and coping with conflict. *Journal of Management and Organization, 12*(2), 179–188.

Inderst, R., Muller, H., & Wameryd, K. (2007). Distributional conflict in organizations. *European Economic Review, 51*(2), 385–397.

Jones, J. (1976). The Thomas-Kilmann Conflict Mode Instrument. *Group & Organization Studies, 1*(2), 249–251.

Lee, V. B. (2007). *Measuring Social Stressors in Organizations: The Development of the Interpersonal Conflict in Organizations Scale.* University of South Florida, Dissertation, 115 p AAT 3248288.

Lewicki, R. J., Barry, B., & Saunders, D. M. (2007). *Essentials of Negotiation,* New York: McGraw-Hill Irwin. pp. 6–8, 256–264.

Meyer, S. (2004). Organizational response to conflict: Future conflict and work outcomes. *Social Work Research, 28*(3), 183–191.

McShane, S. & Von Glinow, M. A. (2000). *Organizational Behavior,* New York: McGraw-Hill Irwin. pp. 412–415.

Piper, L. E. (2006). A theoretical model to address organizational human conflict and disruptive behavior in health care organizations. *The Health Care Manager, 25*(4), 315–322.

Rahim, A. M. (1986). *Managing Conflict in Organizations.* New York: Praeger Publishers. pp. 24–37.

Sizoo, S. (2007). The effect of intercultural sensitivity on cross cultural service encounters in selected markets. *Journal of Applied Management and Entrepreneurship, 12*(1), 47–67.

Webb, K. & Lambe, C. J. (2007). Internal multichannel conflict: An exploratory investigation and conceptual framework, *36*(1), 29–42.

11

MOTIVATING EMPLOYEES

Desire is the key to motivation, but it's determination and commitment to an unrelenting pursuit of your goal—a commitment to excellence—that will enable you to attain the success you seek.

—Mario Andretti

What you have to do and the way you have to do it is incredibly simple. Whether you are willing to do it, that's another matter.

—Peter F. Drucker

CHAPTER OUTLINE

Introduction

Sources of Motivation
   Communication
   Confidence
   Connection

Need Hierarchy Theories
   Maslow's Hierarchy of Needs Theory
      Identification of need hierarchy
      Application of Maslow's theory
   Herzberg's Hygiene–Motivation Model
      Hygiene factors
      Motivational factors
   Alderfer's Theory of Existence, Relatedness, and Growth

Operant Conditioning Theory
   Positive Reinforcement
   Extinction
   Punishment
   Avoidance Learning
   Applications of Operant Conditioning Theory

Expectancy/Valence Theory
   Applications of Expectancy/Valence Theory

Summary

LEARNING OBJECTIVES

After reading this chapter, you will be able to do the following:

1. Identify three sources of motivation.
2. Discuss each of the needs in order within Maslow's Need Hierarchy Theory.
3. Describe the difference between Herzberg's hygiene factors and motivational factors.
4. Explain Alderfer's theory of existence, relatedness, and growth.
5. Identify the differences between Maslow's, Herzberg's, and Alderfer's Need Hierarchy Theories.
6. Discuss the four components of the Operant Conditioning Theory.
7. Explain how a manager can use the expectancy/valence Theory to motivate employees.

Scenario: What Does Sonia Want?

Sonia knew that her coworkers were talking about her. Not long ago she was one of the most productive members of the sales team. Now, whenever she got a chance, she would take off early and head immediately to see her daughter and grandson. Her performance review had gone fairly well, but even the small salary increase

(continued)

(continued)

couldn't keep her from watching the clock. What did a little more money matter when her grandson was growing every day and when her late hours prevented her from seeing him as often as she wanted? After 20 years with the hotel, she had all the financial security she needed. What she didn't have was the ability to do the things that were most important to her without creating resentment and hard feelings among her team members.

It wasn't that her manager didn't try to figure out how to remedy the situation, but at 28—what did he know? He was forced to call her in on several occasions because of complaints from her colleagues. When he asked if there was a problem, she just said, "No, I'm fine. I'm fine." He would shrug his shoulders and say something like, "You could be earning so much more than you are if you would just put a bit more effort into your work." Just what she needed! More work!

In this chapter you will discover several ways in which Sonia's supervisor could have solved her motivation problem. By treating her like all other employees and not addressing her individual needs, Sonia remained unhappy and unproductive. Understanding motivation will enable you to keep your employees focused and productive.

INTRODUCTION

Motivating employees is a basic key to effective management. If employees are motivated, they will work their hardest, thereby increasing output both quantitatively and qualitatively. If, however, employees are not motivated, absenteeism and job turnover will increase, performance will decline, and the efficiency of the organization will be impaired. An insightful manager can maintain a high degree of productivity by designing jobs that engender and maintain the motivation of employees at all levels of the organization. To do this, however, the manager must understand the factors that influence motivation, the relationship between motivation and behavior, and the application of motivation concepts within the organizational work setting.

Researchers have developed theories that attempt to organize motivational concepts into a manageable system and establish guidelines for the implementation of motivation-increasing techniques. A good motivation theory provides managers with a worthwhile schematic representation, but managers must take the individual differences of employees and the dynamics of the environment into account before applying any model to a specific case.

In this chapter we outline the basic concepts of employee motivation and present three fundamental models: need theories, operant conditioning techniques, and the expectancy/valence theory. Need hierarchy theory states that **motivation** stems from an individual's desire to satisfy specific personal and relationship needs. **Operant conditioning** theory suggests that individuals are motivated to perform well only if they believe that such behavior will bring about rewards. Expectancy/valence theory holds that one's motivation to behave in a specific manner is influenced by the belief that effort will produce the desired behavior and that this behavior will bring about attractive outcomes.

These theories have many similarities, and each provides a valuable model for conceptualizing employee motivation. No one theory is necessarily "better" than the others; all three are useful tools that will support your efforts to enhance employee motivation. If you understand which aspects of the work environment motivate employees, you will be better equipped to design and implement programs aimed at increasing motivation. Remember, the theories are not "the rule;" rather, they are presented in the hope that they will elucidate potentially useful concepts of employee motivation. It is crucial to remember that both individuals and the environment are variable; hence, you need to be cautious when adapting these theoretical models to real-life situations.

Both human and environmental factors influence motivation. The organizational environment presents individuals with various challenges and reward systems, all of which have a direct impact on employee behavior. In addition, each employee possesses a unique set of psychological characteristics that spring from the individual's innate disposition and are tempered by his or her experiences. Hence, each employee will react differently to the variable stimuli inherent in the organizational environment.

Why is it that some employees seem motivated to do their best in all aspects of their job while others grumble about almost everything? Why do some tasks seem especially appealing to us while others appear particularly distasteful? What are the forces that motivate a person to work hard?

> In the context of your own work experience, what factors tend to elicit a high degree of personal motivation? What types of questions do you ask yourself? What subconscious decisions do you make before you dedicate your heart and soul to a project?

SOURCES OF MOTIVATION

Certainly, the "What's in it for me?" question plays a major role in motivating individuals. Self-interest is the most ubiquitous and powerful of all motivating forces. Individuals ask themselves this question in numerous situations; however, the answer is usually different in every circumstance. In some instances individuals have a specific need in mind—a promotion, for example—and seek out the tasks that they believe will lead to need satisfaction. In other cases, they are looking for something less tangible yet equally important. Examples of intangible yet motivating needs include such goals as appreciation from superiors or the opportunity to demonstrate creativity. Many individuals find that the tasks which are the most enticing are those which promise to fulfill both personal and organizational goals. Indeed, whenever individuals find some way of relating the organizational "big picture" to personal needs, their motivation levels soar.

Issues of motivation can be acutely felt in the hospitality industry where so many of the workers are low to semiskilled, and a large number of the employees come from economically and culturally diverse backgrounds. Many times, the workers providing the service have never been in a position to receive the level of service they are expected to provide. Managers should help these employees develop a plan for career advancement. They should be assigned to a mentor who would help them to articulate their goals and suggest a plan for reaching both their personal and career goals.

Of course, it is impossible to engineer an organization such that the goals and values of each employee are in perpetual harmony with those of the institution. That would be motivational nirvana! In the real world, individuals need change constantly. Similarly, in a dynamic organization new ideas and projects are proposed every day. The trick to harnessing the full motivational potential of employees is to match the right people to the right jobs. At any one time, each employee has a unique set of goals that will set his or her motivational wheels in motion. It is the manager's job to provide each employee with the opportunity to strive toward fulfillment of his or her goals within the broader organizational context.

Communication

Determining exactly what is necessary to provide the motivational spark is not an easy chore. All too often, managers are not in touch with employees' needs. This communication block drastically impairs motivation. How can a manager possibly hope to motivate employees if he or she has no idea what they want? It is absolutely crucial to understand what the employees value. Only when the manager knows what is important to employees can he or she offer them a chance to fulfill these needs.

Communication is vital. Yet, it is often tangled in a web of misperceptions. In many organizations, employees have little chance to voice their needs or, even if they do, they may feel uncomfortable about saying how they really feel. Although they may complain behind their manager's back, when it comes time to admit that they are concerned with personal goals they may be afraid of sounding selfish. The most effective managers encourage employees to express their needs clearly and work with them to reach their goals. Managers must help employees to see the connection between their own goals and those of the company. If employees believe that they are helping the company as they help themselves, they will be proud of their intentions and be more honest about what they need.

Confidence

When employees are given a choice of actions, they will perform those tasks that they believe are most likely to bring about the results and subsequent rewards they desire. Employees who are unsure that they are capable of achieving the results needed to elicit

rewards will be hesitant workers. Why should employees devote themselves to a project that is likely to fail? It seems logical to guard one's time and effort until there is a likelihood of success.

Often a lack of motivation is really just a lack of confidence. An individual may feel that he or she is not qualified to meet the challenges presented by the job. If this is true, the manager should not have chosen that person in the first place since failure will only reinforce that person's lack of self-efficacy. If, however, the person does have the necessary skills, but is nevertheless plagued by self-doubt, managers must provide reassurance. Emphasizing that the person was chosen because of his or her special talents and pointing out those personal qualities that are particularly suited to the task at hand is often effective. Furthermore, managers can assure the employee that the path is clear—the organization supports the project and will do its best to aid in its completion. The more confidence employees have in their ability to achieve, the more motivated they will be to work hard.

> What have managers (or others) done in the past to increase your self-confidence as it relates to a job you have been asked to perform?

Connection

Once employees have communicated their goals and have increased their self-efficacy, motivation will be heightened. Right? Wrong! A final step is necessary to ensure that employees will be motivated to perform the tasks for which they have been selected. This is the idea of connection. Employees must believe that their success is related to realizing the rewards they desire.

Employees must trust their managers and believe that hard work and success will pay off. Human nature dictates that the bottom line in most motivational situations is "me." "Will I get what I want?" "How can I be sure?" Managers must explain that the organization cares about its employees and must promise that excellence will be rewarded. Of course, as in most situations, actions speak louder than words. Employees who can see the connection between results and rewards will be motivated to give their best performance.

The premise of this section is that individuals will be motivated when effective performance guarantees outcomes that each individual values. Therefore, managers must create a work environment in which this situation exists. Keeping these ideas in mind, let us now discuss three theories of motivation.

NEED HIERARCHY THEORIES

Maslow's Hierarchy of Needs Theory

Need hierarchy theory, developed by Abraham Maslow in the 1940s and 1950s, has been embraced by many scholars and practitioners. The fundamental concepts of Maslow's theory are particularly useful in analyzing motivation within the work environment.

Maslow's model postulates that individuals are motivated by the desire to satisfy specific needs. In addition, Maslow argues that the needs individuals pursue are similar among most populations and that they are arranged in a hierarchical progression. In other words, individuals attempt to satisfy the lower needs first. Once these are satisfied, individuals move up the hierarchy one step at a time, attempting to satisfy the next successively higher-order needs.

IDENTIFICATION OF NEED HIERARCHY   The needs categories identified by Maslow are arranged from low order to high order in a pyramid.

According to this theory, individuals' most basic concern is for fulfilling their physiological needs, such as food and clothing. If these needs are not met, then individuals will expend all of their motivational energy toward resolving them. Since the pursuit of needs progresses in a strict hierarchical fashion, individuals will be concerned solely with these physiological needs, and will not be aware of the other four needs groups. For instance, a hungry person may lack a sense of safety (need 2) and may have a low degree of self-esteem (need 4), but these higher-order needs have no potency until the lowest-order needs have been fulfilled. Once a need has been satisfied, it ceases to function as a motivating force and individuals become concerned with fulfilling the next higher-order need. As each need is satisfied, it becomes less important, while the adjacent hierarchical need becomes more important.

1. *Physiological Needs.* There are myriad examples of each need hierarchy in everyday life (Figure 11.1). Suppose, for example, that you have not eaten in 24 hours. You would certainly be hungry and, after a while, you would probably be unable to concentrate on anything else, even if there were other problems and inconveniences in your life at the time. Even though you may be dealing with an angry and unreasonable guest, you push that problem to the back of your mind and all you think about is getting a sandwich at the employee cafeteria. Now suppose you ate a sandwich. You would feel much better and your hunger need would become less urgent. If you ate a second sandwich, you would be even more satisfied and, most likely, you would lose the motivation to search for more food. If you ate a third sandwich, you would be quite full, and as you sat back to pat your stomach, it would suddenly occur to you that you had not paid attention to the guest's needs. You would rush to make sure that the guest had been appeased, and then make a service recovery by sending chocolate truffles to his room. As your lower-order need became satisfied, the higher-order concern became more pressing.

2. *Safety Needs.* The previous situation is clearly a simplification of Maslow's theory, yet it helps to demonstrate the dynamics of the proposed hierarchical progression. Maslow's need hierarchy model deals with a series of complex emotional needs. Once basic physiological needs have been satisfied, individuals become concerned with their safety needs. Maslow explains that in a civilized society, most individuals are reasonably

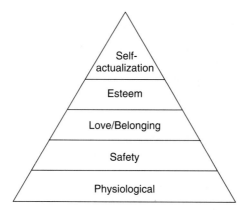

FIGURE 11.1   Maslow's hierarchy

protected from the forces of nature that threatened primitive men. Therefore, instead of a literal interpretation, the safety needs are manifested in the common preference for a job with tenure and protection, the desire for a savings account, and for various types of insurance (Maslow, 1943). The move by many progressive organizations to more flexible and individualized benefits is another example of how safety needs are expressed in the workplace.

3. ***Love and Belongingness Needs.*** Once the physiological and safety needs are satisfied, individuals then become concerned with the love and belongingness. During this stage, a person will notice the absence of friends, a spouse, or children. The individual will long for relationships with other people and will desire to have a place in a group. Since the person at love and belongingness stage has already met physiological and safety needs, this will be the main priority. They will strive to reach this goal with great intensity, forgetting that when they were hungry they didn't think about love at all. Individuals at this stage in their need hierarchy will be especially concerned with establishing and maintaining friendly relationships with coworkers.

4. ***Esteem Needs.*** Maslow's fourth hierarchical category is the need for esteem. According to Maslow these needs can be divided into two stages. First, individuals feel the desire for achievement and independence; second, they need to establish a reputation or prestige in the eyes of others. Maslow believed that once an individual satisfied the need for self-esteem, he or she would have an increase in self-confidence and feelings of self-worth. An individual who ignores these needs for self-esteem, on the other hand, is likely to feel helpless and inferior.

5. ***Self-Actualization Needs.*** The need for self-actualization is the final step in Maslow's hierarchy. Self-actualization is the need to strive for ultimate fulfillment of one's potential in all endeavors. For example, Nikki has spent two years taking Internet courses and gone to night school to get her master's degree. She now feels she is ready to move up from her current position as Director of Human Resources. Maslow writes, "A musician must make music, an artist must paint, a poet must write, if he is to be ultimately happy" (Maslow, 1943). Maslow believes that the need for self-actualization will become apparent only when the four lower-order needs have been satisfied. He said that the people who achieve self-actualization could be expected to be the healthiest and most creative individuals. We know relatively little about self-actualization because many people do not achieve it. While they may satisfy their other four needs, not everyone you know strives to satisfy the fifth and final need of self-actualization.

Describe a situation where you were very aware of the type of need that was motivating your behavior.

APPLICATION OF MASLOW'S THEORY

Kelly had had a busy day. She skipped lunch and was hungry and as a result was tired. She had not made plans for dinner. When she arrived at her hotel, she wandered into the bar where peanuts and cheese were available. The air conditioning in the room was a welcome relief after a sweltering day. The television was on and a couple of individuals were discussing a strange news story. The bartender asked Kelly her opinion on the story and drew her into the conversation. She expressed a unique insight much appreciated by the others.

This anecdote illustrates clearly the relationship between the hospitality industry and the satisfaction of needs. Kelly is ushered through the first four stages within a matter of minutes. We are in the business of satisfying human needs and it helps to understand the hierarchy. Had Kelly not been able to satisfy her hunger first, or had the room felt uncomfortable or unsafe, she might not have been able to focus on the conversation. Had the bartender not drawn her into the conversation, she might have felt alone or left out.

Clearly, as hospitality managers, we must be aware of our guests needs, but equally important are the needs of our staff. Much of Maslow's later work focused specifically on the motivational problems of employees in work settings. According to Maslow, managers have the responsibility to create a climate that encourages employees to rise to their fullest potential. Managers can increase opportunities for need satisfaction by expanding autonomy, variety, and responsibility. If managers fail to provide such a climate, they risk increased employee frustration, poorer performance, lower job satisfaction, and increased withdrawal from the organization.

Need hierarchy theory urges managers to give employees the benefit of the doubt with regard to motivation appraisal. The fundamental premise of the theory holds that individuals are eager to strive toward self-improvement. Many employees who have succeeded in fulfilling their present need level wish to be challenged further so that they might advance another level in their hierarchy. All too often, however, employees are not rewarded for the minimal demands of their job. If this happens, they may become timid and withdrawn. A good manager recognizes healthy motivation and nurtures it by providing opportunities for employees to meet challenging demands.

Of course, a precise, literal interpretation of need hierarchy theory rarely will be applicable to a particular organization. Even the most empathic of managers can do little to fulfill the love and belonging needs of an individual. These patterns are established early in life and are maintained primarily by each person's family and friends, not by the company manager. Similarly, it is not within the realm of responsibility of the organization to further the development of an employee's artistic talent in order to heighten his or her degree of self-actualization. However, concepts of need hierarchy are indeed useful if managers learn to adapt the theory to realistic organizational situations.

Each of the five needs proposed by Maslow has an important analog in corporations. The basic physiological needs may be translated into the need for an adequate salary, while safety needs may be apparent as the desire for job security or retirement benefits. Love needs can be thought of as the need for satisfying collegial relationships, and esteem needs may be expressed as the desire to be appreciated as a team member. Finally, the need for self-actualization may be manifested as an employee's need to reach his or her potential in all facets of the job and to demonstrate his or her creativity while making a unique and memorable contribution to the organization.

It is important to remember that there is not one specific ordering system that is the universal rule for all employees. While one employee may view a high salary as his or her most important need, another may be more in need of recognition, and a third may be primarily concerned with peer relationships. A manager must realize that each employee may be at a different level in the hierarchy, and that employees progress along their need hierarchies at different rates. Hence, what is important to one employee at a specific time may not be motivating to other employees. If managers understand these crucial facts, need theory becomes a valuable guide for the design of reward systems. Managers should also realize that employees can cycle through priorities during different phases of their lives. That is, employees' life circumstances bring about shifts in their needs, in terms of financial reward and need for recognition. These stages are not necessarily levels irreversibly attained, but remain in flux based on changing conditions (Rottier, 2001).

> *Cheryl, the head housekeeper for Hotel Buena Vista, was frustrated. "I hired Maria and Leon at the same time, about 3 years ago. They are both good house-keepers, but could be better. I've been working with them, and Leon is responding well. Maria just doesn't seem to put in the effort. Leon seems to get along well with everybody, but Maria seems withdrawn. I have treated these employees equally, praising them and offering recognition for good performance. Leon is striving to become Employee of the Month. Maria just doesn't seem to care. She does what she has to, and she complains about her salary. Maybe she should do more to earn it!"*

Maria and Leon both have the same needs related to their work in the organization. However, the employees differ with respect to the order in which they value these needs. In addition, they have progressed to different levels along their need hierarchies (Figure 11.2) For example, the need that is motivating Maria is the need for a salary increase because she is a single mother and currently has a son in college. Maslow's theory would maintain that Maria is concerned solely with satisfying this need and that the possible fulfillment of other needs will not be motivating at this time. Leon, on the other hand, has no children and feels a less urgent need for a high salary. Since his salary need is satisfied, he has progressed along his need hierarchy through the need for job security and building a satisfying relationship with his peers to the need for recognition from his supervisors.

Although Maria has a need for recognition from supervisors, she will be unable to concern herself with fulfilling this need until her need for a high salary has been met. In other words, need

Employee A: Maria		Employee B: Leon	
Challenge and Feeling of Worth = *Self-actualization*	This need is not yet vital for Employee A	**Challenge and Feeling of Worth** = *Self-actualization*	This need is not yet vital for Employee B
Recognition from Supervisors = *Esteem Needs*	This need is not yet vital for Employee A	**Recognition from Supervisors** = *Esteem Needs*	All of Employee B's motivation is focused here
Satisfying Relationships with Peers = *Need for Belongingness*	This need is not yet vital for Employee A	**Satisfying Relationships with Peers** = *Need for Belongingness*	Employee B has already satisfied this need
Job Security = *Safety Needs*	This need is not yet vital for Employee A	**Job Security** = *Safety Needs*	Employee B has already satisfied this need
Adequate Salary = *Physiological Needs*	All of Employee A's motivation is focused here	**Adequate Salary** = *Physiological Needs*	Employee B has already satisfied this need

FIGURE 11.2   Example of differing need hierarchies

theory predicts that verbal praise from a supervisor, or an employee-of-the-month-certificate, would be a satisfying reward for Leon, but that Maria would not appreciate such recognition at this time.

Need hierarchy theory provides both an explanation and a solution for the problem of low employee motivation. If an employee demonstrates a sudden lack of motivation, it could mean that he or she has shifted along the need hierarchy, but his or her job has not accounted for the fact that a different need has become dominant. The job may be providing rewards for a former need and may not have accommodated the employee's recent transition to a new need. Need hierarchy theory prescribes that the manager must determine what need is the current motivating force and then must redesign the reward system so that it offers incentives which meet this need. A manager who understands the principles of need hierarchy theory and is sensitive to the changing needs of employees will be able to redesign jobs so that employees remain motivated.

If you were a manager, how would you go about determining individual employee needs?

Herzberg's Hygiene–Motivation Model

In the late 1950s, Herzberg (1959) proposed a two-factor theory of hygiene and motivation. By asking employees to list those incidents at work which they found satisfying and those incidents which led to their dissatisfaction, Herzberg identified two sets of factors which are needed for employee motivation.

HYGIENE FACTORS The first set, which he calls hygiene factors, are related to the work environment. Box 11.1 provides a list of some of the more common.

In Herzberg's model, hygiene factors cannot be used to increase motivation. The most that can be done with hygiene factors is to maintain them at a level where they will have no negative effects. Neglected hygiene needs engender employee dissatisfaction. In order to set the stage for the development of motivation, these environmental factors must be "cleaned up."

BOX 11.1

Common Hygiene Factors

1. Company Policy and Administration
2. Technical Supervision
3. Interpersonal Relations with Supervisors
4. Interpersonal Relations with Peers
5. Interpersonal Relations with Subordinates
6. Salary
7. Job Security
8. Personal Life
9. Working Conditions
10. Status

MOTIVATIONAL FACTORS   Once the environment has been cleared of all external hygiene problems, Herzberg's second group of factors—the motivational characteristics—come into play. These factors are directly related to the individual's job (see Box 11.2).

Herzberg contends that these six factors have a significant influence on employee motivation. Simply adjusting the environment (hygiene) will not increase motivation; concentrating on the job itself (motivation) will.

The needs outlined in Herzberg's model are closely related to those in Maslow's theory. Salary, personal life, and working conditions fall under the category of Maslow's basic physiological needs. Job security and company policy and administration are organizational adaptations of Maslow's safety needs. Interpersonal relations and technical supervision are expressions of the need for social belongingness. Status recognition and advancement are literal interpretations of Maslow's concept of esteem needs. Finally, Maslow's need for self-actualization is translated in the Herzberg model to encompass achievement, responsibility, the work itself, and the possibility of personal growth.

Perhaps the most fundamental difference between the two theories is that Maslow states that as an individual advances along the personal need hierarchy, each need in succession has the power to serve as a motivating factor. Herzberg, on the other hand, maintains that hygiene needs do not have the potential to motivate employees; they must only be maintained to allow the true motivational factors at the top of the list to take effect.

Do you agree with Herzberg's motivational factors? Explain. Has anything been left out of his model?

Alderfer's Theory of Existence, Relatedness, and Growth

Alderfer (1972) added yet another twist to need hierarchy theory. Alderfer grouped human needs into three basic categories: existence needs, relatedness needs, and growth needs. Existence needs are necessary to sustain human life and are analogous to Maslow's physiological and safety needs. In the work environment, existence needs include salary, fringe benefits, and working conditions. Relatedness needs involve relationships with other people and include Maslow's needs for social belongingness and admiration from others. Growth needs encompass the desire for creative expression and intellectual challenge. These needs are related to Maslow's concepts of self-esteem and self-actualization.

BOX 11.2

Common Motivational Factors

1. Achievement
2. Recognition of Achievement
3. Advancement
4. The Work Itself
5. The Possibility of Personal Growth
6. Responsibility

Like Herzberg's model, Alderfer's theory designates specific needs that are rearrangements of Maslow's original needs. However, Alderfer differs from Herzberg with respect to rules that govern the motivational characteristics of individuals. While Maslow maintains that only one need can be dominant at any one time, Alderfer believes that motivation can be inspired by several needs operating at the same time. Furthermore, Alderfer's model allows for movement in either direction along the need hierarchy. The existence–relatedness–growth (ERG) theory suggests that one unfulfilled need will sharpen the individual's awareness of other unsatisfied desires.

The novel idea in Alderfer's theory is that an unsatisfied need not only motivates individuals to strive for its satisfaction, but also increases their preoccupation with the need one step below on the ladder. For example, an individual with unsatisfied relatedness needs will be concerned with fulfilling both relatedness and existence needs at the same time. Similarly, for an individual with unsatisfied growth needs, both growth and relatedness needs will be salient. This concept leads to Alderfer's proposal of the frustration–regression phenomenon. If a person is repeatedly frustrated in his or her desire to satisfy a need, he or she will "give up" and slide down the hierarchy to the next-lower need. Hence, a need that appears unattainable will cease to be a motivational force. Instead, the need directly beneath it will reappear as a potent source of motivation.

The frustration–regression model may help to explain puzzling employee behavior. An employee whose attempts at creativity have been continually ignored will fall down a step in the hierarchy and become overly concerned with building closer relationships. This behavior may be confusing to coworkers. Why has this previously independent, free-spirited individual suddenly become effusively friendly and group oriented? Alderfer's ERG theory and the concept of frustration–regression provide a viable explanation for such behavior.

> Critique Alderfer's motivational theory. Where do you agree with his ideas? On what specific points do you disagree?

OPERANT CONDITIONING THEORY

Techniques of operant conditioning, developed by Skinner in the 1950s, helped to lay the foundation for the field of behavioral psychology. Within the last decade, increased attention has been paid to application of these principles to organizational settings. The following sections discuss four fundamental components of operant conditioning theory: positive reinforcement, extinction, punishment, and avoidance.

Operant conditioning theory is based on the belief that managers can control employee behavior through the strategic manipulation of reward systems. Operant conditioning differs from Pavlovian conditioning in a number of ways. **Pavlovian conditioning** involves "training" an individual to perform a specific behavior in response to a specific stimulus. The familiar example of the salivating dog illustrates this idea. A dog will salivate when it sees food. If, in a large number of trials, a bell is rung at the same time that food is presented, the dog becomes conditioned to salivate at the sound of the bell alone.

In Pavlovian conditioning, the individual cannot control when the stimulus is presented. The ringing of the bell is controlled by the experimenter. In operant conditioning, however, the individual can control whether a stimulus is released or withheld. The individual does this by displaying the behavior which he or she has learned is associated with particular rewards or punishments. Operant conditioning derives its name from the fact that individuals operate actively upon their environment in order to elicit the stimuli they desire. Through the conscious modification of their behavior, employees, theoretically, have the power to control the allocation of rewards and punishments.

Operant conditioning has several manifestations. It can be used to elicit a desired behavior pattern or it can be used to eliminate unwanted behavior. Positive reinforcement and avoidance are examples of techniques that help to establish behavior patterns, while extinction and punishment serve to eliminate behavior patterns. However, as we shall see, sometimes these signals can get crossed. A manager might end up discouraging good performance and establishing unwanted behavior. The manager must make certain that the correct operant conditioning techniques are applied to the appropriate behaviors.

Positive Reinforcement

Myriad examples of positive reinforcement are encountered in everyday life. For instance, let us take the case of a child who has a chronically untidy room. Since the child has no motivation to clean up the room, her parents must remind her incessantly to make her bed and pick up her clothes. There is no hope that the child will be motivated to do it soon her own, and the parents are faced with the burdensome task of constantly pestering the child. The child's lack of motivation to engage in room-cleaning behavior is likely to continue indefinitely unless a positive reinforcer-an activity the child enjoys-is introduced. Let us suppose that one day both parents remind her to clean her room, and that after she does so she is rewarded with a trip to the zoo. This greatly increases the likelihood that the child will clean her room the next day without being told, with the hope of another enjoyable activity.

If someone were to give you positive reinforcement, what would you like it to be? What "positive feedback" is most meaningful to you in a workplace setting?

Extinction

Of course, most parents have neither the time nor the desire to spend every day at the zoo. Yet if the child cleans up her room for several consecutive days and her parents do not take her to the zoo, then the positive reinforcer will lose its influence and the child will probably slip back to her old habits. The child will not be motivated to clean her room because the trip to the zoo is no longer a consequence of room-cleaning behavior. This phenomenon is known as "extinction." When the parents failed to uphold the positive reinforcement, the child ceased to be motivated to engage in proper behavior. Of course, it is unreasonable for the child to expect that she will be taken to the zoo every day, but the parents might take her there often enough that she will be motivated to continue her room-cleaning behavior. A manager should be careful not to let extinction techniques creep in on desired behavior. The trick to establishing an effective schedule of positive reinforcement is to reward often enough to prevent the extinction of desired behavior.

Since extinction is an effective method of eliminating behavior, it provides a valuable technique for terminating unwanted behavior. When positive reinforcement is withheld, the individual will perform the undesirable behavior for some time, assuming that the reward is impending but just slightly overdue. If, however, the positive reinforcement is restricted for a long enough period of time, the employee will realize that the behavior is no longer bringing about positive consequences. When this happens, the employee will stop performing the undesirable activity.

Punishment

Undesirable behavior may also be terminated through the use of "punishment" techniques. This method involves introducing an unpleasant consequence or discontinuing a positive consequence every time that an individual engages in unwanted behavior. This idea is equivalent to the tactics employed in the discipline of children: "If you keep punching your sister, you will stay in your room!" (introduction of adverse consequences in order to punish unwanted behavior), or "If you don't stop throwing your food you will get no dessert!" (removal of positive consequences in order to punish unwanted behavior).

Although punishment can often be an effective method of shaping behavior, as a general rule managers should direct their efforts toward the rewarding of desired behavior rather than to the punishment of unwanted behavior.

What are some of the relationship risks involved in using punishment for performance management?

Avoidance Learning

A fourth application of operant conditioning is "avoidance learning." This method, like positive reinforcement, helps to increase the occurrence of desired behavior. This technique involves presenting an unpleasant stimulus that the individual can remove by engaging in the appropriate behavior. For example, a child who is reprimanded every time he throws his food on the floor will modify his behavior in order to avoid the consequences of a reprimand. In order to avoid the unpleasant stimulus of a reprimand, the child will learn the desired behavior of appropriate table manners.

Applications of Operant Conditioning Theory

It is easy to see how the technique of operant conditioning can be applied to situations in hospitality organizations. Salary increases, promotions, and even nonmonetary recognition such as "employee-of-the-week" awards provide excellent examples of positive reinforcement. By providing such incentives, the organization increases the likelihood that employees will be motivated to perform as the company desires. By the same token, however, managers who fail to reward desired performance risk extinguishing this behavior. Managers must be certain to reward the good behavior of their employees; otherwise, operant conditioning theory predicts that these individuals will lose the motivation to perform.

In addition to positive reinforcement and extinction, avoidance learning can also be used. For example, a restaurant hostess who has had several embarrassing experiences of having to relocate a party to a different table due to complaints of nearby cigarette smoke will learn to ask a party if they prefer a nonsmoking area before seating them. The hostess will modify her behavior to avoid similar embarrassing situations in the future.

It is important to realize that the principles of positive reinforcement, extinction, punishment, and avoidance learning can have unintended side effects—both positive and negative. Suppose a new porter begins his first day on the job by carelessly banging luggage into the elevator door, placing suitcases on the floor instead of on the luggage stand, neglecting to open the curtains, and forgetting to demonstrate the heat and air conditioning panel. Suppose, furthermore, that the first guest encountered by the porter provides him with a generous tip despite his poor performance. This reward will serve as positive reinforcement for behavior that is certainly not desired by the organization. If other generous guests continue to tip the porter, the poor behavior will not be extinguished. A manager must recognize that operant conditioning is in perpetual undercover operation and that unintended rewards and punishment inherent in the organization often have a strong influence on employee behavior.

A manager familiar with operant conditioning can use this theory both to encourage positive behavior and to eliminate poor performance. Hammer (1971) outlines several rules regarding the application of operant conditioning. He cautions that although these rules seem simple and logical, managers who do not realize the potency of operant conditioning often violate them.

Rule 1: Don't reward all people the same

In other words, rewards should be differentiated on the basis of performance with respect to a defined objective or standard. Employees compare their own performance with that of their peers to determine how well they are doing and they compare their rewards to the rewards of their peers in order to determine how to evaluate their rewards. While some managers seem to think that the fairest system of compensation is one in which everyone in the same job classification gets the same pay, employees want differentiation so that they know their importance to the organization. It can be argued that managers who reward all people the same are encouraging, at best, only average performance. The behavior of high-performance workers is being ignored and therefore extinguished, while the behavior of average performance and poor performance workers is being strengthened by positive reinforcement.

Rule 2: Failure to respond has reinforcing consequences

Managers who find the job of differentiating among workers so unpleasant that they fail to respond must recognize that failure to respond modifies behavior. Managers must be careful that they examine the performance consequences of their nonaction as well as their action. For example, if a manager fails to reward an employee who has performed excellently, the employee's motivation to strive for excellent performance will be extinguished.

> Do you think your behavior and motivation would be negatively affected if you were not recognized for your accomplishments? Explain.

Rule 3: Be sure to tell an employee what he or she can do to obtain reinforcement

By making the contingencies of reinforcement clear to the employee, a manager actually may be increasing the individual freedom of the employee. The employee who has a standard against which to measure his or her job will have a built-in feedback system which allows him to make judgments about his or her own work. If an employee's goal is specified, then he or she will associate rewards with his or her performance and not with the biases of the supervisor. If the supervisor fails to rate accurately or administer rewards based on performance, then the stated goals for the employee will lose stimulus control, and the employee will be forced to search for the "true" contingencies (i.e., what behavior he or she should perform instead in order to get rewarded).

Although research has demonstrated that cash incentives can produce strong positive feedback on performance (Stajkovic, 2001), the rewards offered do not necessarily have to be cash incentives in order to increase motivation. For example, a points system to earn rewards can increase motivation. Some employees may also respond positively to public recognition although this strategy must be utilized with careful regard to cultural standards of praise (Wiscombe, 2002).

Rule 4: Be sure to tell a person what he or she is doing wrong

As a general rule, few people find the act of failing rewarding. A supervisor should never use extinction or punishment as a sole method for modifying behavior, but if used together with methods of positive reinforcement (Rule 3), such combined procedures can hasten the change process. If the supervisor fails to specify why a reward is being withheld, the employee may associate it with past desired behavior instead of with the undesired behavior that the supervisor is trying to extinguish. In other words, if a manager withholds a reward or dispenses a punishment without clarifying the reasons for such an action, the manager may be extinguishing good performance while having no effect on undesired behavior.

Rule 5: Don't reprimand in front of others

The reason for this rule is quite simple. The reprimand should be enough to extinguish the undesired behavior. By administering the reprimand in front of the work group, the employee receives double punishment. This additional punishment may lead to negative side effects in three ways. First, the employee whose self-image is damaged may feel that he or she must retaliate in order to protect himself or herself. Therefore, the supervisor has actually increased undesired responses. Second, others in the work group may misunderstand the reason for the punishment and through "avoidance learning" may modify their own behavior in ways not intended by the supervisor. Third, the entire work group is also being punished in the sense that observing a member of their team being reprimanded has noxious or aversive properties for most people. This may result in a decrease in the performance of the total work group.

Rule 6: Make the consequences equal to the behavior

In other words, be fair. Don't cheat employees out of their just rewards. Tell good employees what they are doing right. Many supervisors find it difficult to praise an employee. Others find it difficult to counsel an employee about what he or she is doing wrong. When managers fail to use these reinforcement tools, they are actually reducing their effectiveness. When a worker is overrewarded, he or she may feel guilty. If his or her performance level is less than the others who get the same reward, he or she has no reason to work harder, but can feel content to remain a free rider. On the other hand, when a worker is underrewarded, he or she becomes angry with the system. His or her good behavior is being extinguished, and the company may be forcing the good employee (underrewarded) to seek employment elsewhere while encouraging the poor employee (overrewarded) to stay.

Operant conditioning should not be applied blindly to all situations. The methods of positive reinforcement, extinction, punishment, and avoidance learning are certainly valuable conditioning tools, but managers must use them with discretion. It is crucial to realize that adult employees are not easily conditioned. Employees are creative, rational beings and they should be treated as such. Most individuals will be extremely resentful if they feel that the organization is attempting to "control" them. Similarly, management by slogan, especially when problems lie with the structure of the system, rather than with workers, can lead to resentment and cynicism among employees. The ethical issues concerning the manipulation of employees' behavior are profound, so managers should use caution before applying operant conditioning techniques.

We do not advocate that operant conditioning theory be interpreted literally and applied verbatim. Rather, operant conditioning techniques are best used as a tool to help managers understand the sources of employee motivation and the reasons for employee behavior. Managers who discover the positive reinforcers and the unpleasant stimuli present in the organizational environment will be able to arrange these forces so that they lead to an increase in employee motivation, performance, and satisfaction.

EXPECTANCY/VALENCE THEORY

In the previous discussion of motivation, we maintained that employees engage in behaviors in order to satisfy their needs. Often, however, individuals are faced with more than one potentially need-satisfying behavior. The expectancy/**valence** theory, developed by Hackman and Lawler (1971), provides an explanation of how employees choose from among a large set of alternative behaviors.

The expectancy/valence model is based on the theory that individuals behave according to their perceptions about how well they will be able to perform, what will happen if they perform at that level, and how strongly they desire the rewards they will receive for this behavior. The theory purports that as individuals contemplate engaging in a behavior, they ask themselves three questions:

1. "Can I perform at that level if I try?"
2. "If I perform at that level what will happen?"
3. "How do I feel about those things that will happen?"

The first of these questions involves the individual's assessment of the probability that his or her effort will enable him or her to attain the required level of performance. This is called the effort to performance (E→P) expectancy. The second question involves the individual's assessment of the likelihood that the required performance will lead to specific outcomes. This perceived probability is labeled the performance to outcome (P→O) expectancy. The third question deals with the individual's perception of the attractiveness of each of the outcomes. The measure of desirability that an employee implicitly assigns to a particular outcome is called the valence (V) of the outcome (see Box 11.3)

The E→P expectancy and the P→O expectancy can take on a mathematical value from zero to positive one. A zero value indicates that the employee has no belief that his or her efforts will lead to a particular performance (or that a performance will lead to a specific outcome), and a value of one means that the employee is certain that the performance (or outcome) will occur. Most expectancy values fall between these two extremes. Valences

BOX 11.3

Expectancy Theory

E:P Expectancy	P→O Expectancy	Valence
Perceived probability of successful performance, given effort	Perceived probability of an outcome, given successful performance	Perceived value of each outcome
Effort →	**Performance →**	**→ Outcome A**
		→ Outcome B
		→ Outcome C

may take on a value from $+1.0$ to -1.0. For example, an employee who is strongly attracted to monetary rewards will assign a high positive valence to the outcome of a pay raise, while an employee who strongly values time with his or her family will assign a negative valence to the outcome of a time-demanding promotion.

Expectancy/valence theory posits that an employee's motivational force for a particular behavior is determined by multiplying the E→P expectancy times the P→O expectancy times the valence of the outcome. Hence, the theory predicts that the motivational force to behave in certain ways is greatest when the individual believes that performance at the desired level is possible (high E→P expectancy), when he or she believes that the behavior will lead to outcomes (high P→O expectancy), and when these outcomes have high attractiveness to the individual (high positive V).

The three factors contributing to the motivational force are based entirely on the subjective perceptions of the person involved. Therefore, two individuals in the same situation often choose different modes of behavior.

What are the strengths of Expectancy/valence Theory? Apply this theory to a concrete example at work.

Applications of Expectancy/Valence Theory

The expectancy/valence theory of motivation provides a valuable management tool. The model explains why certain individuals will be motivated to perform a specific behavior, while other individuals may not be so motivated. Similarly, it explains how an individual who is eager to work on some projects can be strongly reluctant to work on other projects. A manager who is familiar with the ideas of E→P expectancy, P→O expectancy, and valence will learn to understand many of the actions of employees that previously seemed unreasonable. When an employee makes a decision, it is only natural that he or she will choose the behavior that he or she feels is most likely to satisfy his or her needs. If the manager can identify which goals are most important to individuals (valence), the individuals' perceptions of the effectiveness of a successful performance (P→O expectancy), and individuals' views of their capability to perform well (E→P expectancy), then the manager can assign employees to tasks which they will find motivating. Expectancy/valence theory suggests that when managers select an employee to carry out a specific task, they should choose an employee who feels confident that he or she can perform well, and who is reasonably certain that good performance will lead to attractive consequences. If managers fail to recognize the E→P expectancy, P→O expectancy, and the valence an employee has for a particular behavior, then managers may be offering the right job to the wrong person.

Expectancy/valence theory posits that employees have assumptions about what will happen to them. Individuals faced with a motivational choice will attempt to relate the options presented by their work environment to their personal needs and values. Since each person approaches a job with a unique set of needs and experiences, people in the same organization will develop different expectancies of what kinds of behavior lead to rewards.

In addition, employees often perceive situations inaccurately. Indeed, the more the situation involves important needs (e.g., promotion and salary), the more individuals are likely to distort reality. Nadler et al., stated that people do not accurately see the world and it is because of this that they sometimes appear to behave irrationally. They believed that when people do not correctly perceive their performance outcomes, they will behave in what they believe is rational behavior. Nadler et al., (1979) said that because of these misconceptions of employees, many of the factors that managers use to motivate employees fail. Thus, while expectancy/valence theory provides a cogent model for conceptualizing motivation and behavior, managers must not disregard intervening human and environmental variables.

The expectancy/valence model is particularly valuable when used as a guide in predicting the behavior of individuals in organizations and in elucidating many of the seemingly obscure motives for this behavior. If applied prudently, expectancy/valence theory enables managers to create jobs that will engender a high degree of motivation. In addition, expectancy/valence theory helps managers to select employees who will be motivated to perform specific tasks, and to offer appropriate rewards, whether cash, stock, or increased autonomy in work. Applied correctly and carefully, these factors can all help to raise levels of employee motivation. It is this magical combination of motivating tasks, rewards, motivated workers that leads to employee satisfaction and organizational efficiency.

> Which theory of motivation makes the most sense to you? Which theory would you be most likely to apply with your employees on the job?

Summary

Employee motivation is a complex process. Although the sources of behavior seem all too obvious, they are often difficult to untangle. In this section we discussed just three of the many theories of motivation. Need hierarchy theory postulates that employees are concerned with fulfilling specific needs and that they will be motivated to perform those behaviors that they feel will lead to rewards capable of satisfying these needs. Operant conditioning theory suggests that the dispensation and withdrawal of rewards and punishments will act to reinforce or discourage certain behaviors. Managers can often control the release of rewards or punishments themselves, but it is important to realize that the work environment dispenses its own reinforcers, which are not necessarily under the manager's control. Expectancy/valence theory outlines an empirical reasoning process that guides employees in their choice of which behavior to perform, based on the employees' subjective perceptions.

Prudent managers appreciate that there are many interacting forces that shape employee motivation and subsequent behavior. It is crucial to recognize that each employee has a unique set of needs, experiences, and expectations. Sensitivity to these issues enables managers to discover the sources of behavior and lay the foundation for improved motivation, performance, and satisfaction.

Key Words

motivation *293*
operant conditioning *295*
need hierarchy theory *298*
physiological needs *299*

safety needs *299*
belongingness needs *300*
esteem needs *300*

self-actualization needs *300*
pavlovian conditioning *305*
valence *310*

Exercises

Exercise 1 "Shoot it!": Effect of Manager/Employee Relationships on Motivation

Objective: To show participants how an employee's relationship with his or her supervisor affects performance

Materials:

1. One empty wastebasket
2. Twelve tennis balls

Procedure:

1. Select six students to participate in this exercise, while the remaining participants will be observers.
2. Choose three of the participants to serve as employees and the other three participants to serve as managers.
3. Send the three employees out into the hall.
4. Explain to the three managers that they will each have an employee. Their employee will be blindfolded and will attempt to shoot 12 tennis balls, one at a time, into a wastebasket. Have a wastebasket eight feet from where the employees will be shooting. Tell everyone else to write down their observations of the following process.
5. Tell the first manager that once his employee begins to shoot, he should be aggressive and should belittle and mock his employee. If his employee misses the shot say things such as, "Can't you shoot? Can't you play ball? What a dumb shot!

A fourth-grader could throw better than you!" Tell the first manager to go into the hallway and retrieve an employee. Blindfold the employee and have the manager explain that he will be trying to get as many tennis balls into the wastebasket as possible, while blindfolded.

6. Once the first manager and employee are finished, tell the second manager that once his employee begins to shoot he should say absolutely nothing. Tell him to go into the hall, choose an employee, blindfold him, and tell him to try to get as many tennis balls into the wastebasket.
7. Finally, tell the third manager that he should be supportive when his employee is shooting. Tell him to say things such as "Throw a little more to the right! That's it, you got one in!" Tell the third manager to go into the hall, get the last employee, blindfold him, and tell him to shoot as many tennis balls into the wastebasket as possible.
8. The facilitator should record how many balls each person got into the basket. Usually, the supportive feedback-giving trainer's employee has the most balls in the wastebasket.
9. The facilitator should
   - ask each employee how he felt during the exercise;
   - ask each manager how he felt during the exercise;
   - lead a discussion on the role of feedback in motivating employees.

Exercise 2 What do People Want from Their Jobs?

Objective: To give participants an opportunity to discuss what factors motivate employees

Procedure:

1. Distribute copies of the form, "What do People Want From Their Jobs?", that is attached. Divide the participants into subgroups of three to five people each.
2. Have each individual, working alone, rank how he thinks *employees* would prioritize the list. Tell them to rank the most important factor as 1, the next most important factor 2, and so on. Have them enter their ranking in the column headed "Individual."

3. Next, have the participants convene in their groups and attempt to come to a consensus on the rankings. Have them enter their group's ranking in the column headed "Group."
4. Once all the rankings are recorded for each group, tell participants that the same scale has been given to thousands of supervisors and employees around the country.
5. Have each individual enter the employees' scores under the heading "Employees."
6. Point out to participants that the top three items marked by the employees as motivating are the last three felt to be important for them by the supervisors. It seems supervisors don't know what their employees want from the organization or their supervisors.

7. Lead the participants in a discussion:

Compare your individual and group ratings with the ratings in the "Employees" column. How do they differ? What factors might account for the differences?

Why do you suppose the supervisors' ratings are so different from those of their employees?

***

Motivating Factors within Organization	Individual	Group	Supervisors	Employees
Tactful discipline				
Interesting work				
High wages				
Feelings of being included on things				
Job security				
Promotion in the company				
Personal loyalty of supervisor				
Full appreciation of work done				
Good working conditions				
Help on personal problems				

Source: Lane, B. (1996). *Managing People: A Practical Guide*. Bookworld Services. Third Edition, 4–12, 14–15.

Exercise 3   Off-Season Layoffs

Objective: To encourage participants to explore motivation of employees within an organization

Procedure:

1. Divide participants into groups of three to five people each. Have each group select a leader.
2. Read the following scenario to all participants:

You are an executive team of managers at a renowned beach and tennis resort in Naples, Florida. It is August, which is the off-season for this resort because of the extremely hot weather. You recently announced that the workforce has to be reduced by 10 percent in the next two weeks in order to remain profitable during the off-season. Many of the employees are worried that they will be part of the 10 percent. They do not trust upper management and many employees have exhibited decreased performance and a lack motivation to continue working for fear that they will not have a job tomorrow anyway.

The executive team is told by the CEO to develop a plan to improve employee motivation and morale. The CEO is worried that many of the employees will go ahead and quit since they fear their job is on the line. While developing your plan of action, think about the key causes of the employees' lack of motivation, what you could have done differently, and how you can convince the employees to stay with the hotel (if they are not among the ones being laid off).

3. Give each team 30 minutes to devise their plan of action. Let them know that they will be presenting their plan of action to the other participants and will have to back up their opinions and decisions.

Endnotes

Alderfer, C. P. (1972). *Existence, Relatedness, and Growth*. New York: The Free Press.

Anonymous. (2005). 10 common problems managers face when motivating employees—and suggestions to solve them. *Employee Motivation and Incentive Strategies*, 6(8), 4.

Anonymous. (2005). Spotlight on: American Express incentive services. *Sales and Marketing Management*, 157(9), 56.

Anonymous. (2006). New generation organizations: Motivating employees through creative working practices. *Strategic Direction*, 22(11), 22.

Bartlett, M. (2005). Staff incentives: What credit unions have found works & doesn't work in motivating employees. *Credit Union Journal*, 9(38), 56.

Chiang, C. (2006). *An Expectancy Theory Model for Hotel Employee Motivation: The Moderating Role of Communication Satisfaction*. Manhattan, KS: Kansas State University.

Cottringer, W. (2003). Light their fires. *Supervision*, 64(6), 12.

Cross, L. (2003). Motivating a company's best assets. *Graphic Arts Monthly*, 75(11), 38.

Ducharme, M. J. & Podolsky, M. (2006). Variable pay: It's impact on motivation and organisation performance. *International Journal of Human Resources Development and Management*, 6(1), 68.

Duncan, J. (2003). Stock ownership and work motivation. *Organizational Dynamics*, 30(1), 1–11.

English, G. (2005). Understanding and motivating employees at WHSmith. *Strategic HR Review*, 5(1), 28–31.

Garg, P. & Rastogi, R. (2006). New model of job design: Motivating employees' performance. *The Journal of Management Development*, 25(6), 572.

Gordon R., K. A. (2004). Beyond Maslow's hierarchy of needs: What do people strive for? *Performance Improvement*, 43(10), 27–31.

Hackman, J. R. & Lawler E. E. (1971), Employee reactions to job characteristics, *Journal of Applied Psychology,* 55, 259–286.

Hammer, M. (1971). The application of behavioral conditioning procedures to the problems of quality control: Comment. *The Academy of Management Journal*, 14(1), 529–532.

Haubrich, J. G. (2005). Compensation and incentives. *Chief Executive*, 5.

Herzberg, F. (1959). *The Motivation to Work*. Second Edition. New York: Wiley.

Hobson, C. J., Kesic, D., Rosetti, D., Delunas, L., & Hobson, N. G. (2004). Motivating employee commitment with empathy and support during stressful life events. *International Journal of Management*, 21(3), 332–337.

Howatt, B. (2003). Getting it done: Become a motivational manager. *Credit Union Management*, 26(3), 6.

Macdonald, B. (2004). Tips for motivating employees. *The Canadian Manager*, 29(2), 12–13.

Maslow, A. H. (1943). A theory of human motivation. *Psychological Review*, 50, 370–396.

Nadler, D. A., Hackman, J. R., & Lawler, E. E. (1979). *Managing Organizational Behavior*. Boston: Little Brown Publishers.

Parr, C. A. (2005). Managers: The critical link—in a successful rewards and recognition program. *Workspan*, 48(11), 18–21.

Rottier, A. (2001). Motivate or risk losing top execs. *Workforce*, 80(11), 18.

Stajkovic, A. D. & Luthans, F. (2001). Differential effects of incentive motivators on work performance. *Academy of Management Journal*, 43(3), 580–590.

Sujansky, J. G. (2003). Lead, motivate, retain. *Incentive*, 177(7), 63.

Van Yperer, N. W. & Hagerdorn, M. (2003). Do high job demands increase intrinsic motivation or fatigue or both? The role of job control and job social support. *Academy of Management Journal*, 46(3), 339–348.

Wilson, S. (2006). Motivational metrics. *Restaurant Business*, 105(10), 14.

Wiscombe, J. (2002). Rewards get results: Put away your cash. Whether it's productivity, safety, or another business result, public praise and non-cash rewards are strong motivators. *Workforce*, 81(4), 42–46.

12

COUNSELING EMPLOYEES

He that gives good advice, builds with one hand; he that gives good counsel and example, builds with both; but he that gives good admonition and bad example, builds with one hand and pulls down with the other.

—Francis Bacon, Sr.

CHAPTER OUTLINE

Introduction

Identifying an Employee in Need
    Job-related Problems
    Family-related Problems
    Other Employee Concerns

The Core Conditions for Effective Counseling
    Empathy
        Empathy scale
    Respect
    Genuineness

The Managerial Role in the Counseling Model
    Exploratory Phase
    Employee Self-Understanding Phase
    Constructive-Action Phase

Counseling Techniques
    Develop Reflection Skills
    Use of Open and Closed Questions
    Behavioral versus Evaluative Feedback
    Accept Silence
    Use Freeing, not Binding Responses
    Create an Accepting Environment
    Learn Stress Listening

Common Counseling Behaviors
    Inappropriate Behaviors
    How *not* to Counsel an Employee
    How to Counsel an Employee

Avoidance of Counseling
    Why Employees do not Seek Counseling Help

Managing Crisis Situations
    Process for Crisis Intervention
    The Suicidal Employee
    The Cardinal Rule of Suicide Prevention: *Do Something*

Making Referrals
    Indications that a Referral Should be Made
    How to Refer an Employee for Further Help

Summary

LEARNING OBJECTIVES

After reading this chapter, you will be able to do the following:

    1. Identify three distinct types of problems and give an example of how each could have detrimental effects on the organization.

2. Explain the three necessary conditions for effective counseling.
3. Describe the components of each phase of the counseling process.
4. Give specific examples of how you could use four of the counseling techniques.
5. Explain two common, but inappropriate, counseling techniques and state why the technique is not conducive to effective counseling.
6. Define a type of crisis situation and explain the actions a manager would take to resolve it.
7. Describe a situation in which making a referral would be the appropriate way to approach an employee's problem.

Scenario: Corrected Carla

Carla, a new desk clerk in the busy Metro Hotel has come to you to discuss relations with her immediate supervisor. Erin, the front desk manager, has been employed by the hotel for over eight years.

"I'm losing patience with Erin. I feel like her sole purpose is to look at what I'm doing and find fault with it. I like to think that I learn quickly, but with so many meticulous details to remember, I'm going to forget something here and there. But that's human, right? I understand the purpose of "coaching" to correct errors, but Erin takes it to the extreme. Every time she approaches me, I try not to make eye contact, because I always feel like she's going to point out my latest "screw-up." Worst of all, she treats me like I'm one of her children. I'm 19 years old . . . not three.

Mrs. Paul, a guest, recently asked that I place all of her mail on the desk in her hotel room rather than in her box at the front desk. I noted her request and left a message on Erin's voice mail to make sure that she was also aware of the request. Later that day, Erin stopped by the front desk with her condescending attitude and said, 'I just listened to your voice mail about how to process Mrs. Paul's mail. Didn't I tell you how we handle these requests when I trained you four months ago?' I explained to her that I didn't recall her teaching me that. Determined to prove herself right, she took the training manual from the front desk drawer and searched for the proper procedure. She couldn't find it listed anywhere and walked away from the desk, pouting. I hate to admit it, but I enjoyed seeing her make a fool out of herself. It's time for her to learn that we're all fallible, herself included."

Situations such as the predicament that the desk clerk in this scenario found herself in are all too common in today's hospitality industry. In this chapter we will discuss the value that a manager can add to his or her organization by employing various counseling techniques.

INTRODUCTION

Counseling, the process of listening to someone's problem and guiding them as they solve it, is an important managerial skill. Helping a troubled employee does not require an advanced degree or a special license. An interested, sensitive manager can understand the dynamics of the employee's problem as well as an outside professional can. Managers who have learned the basic skills of counseling can help employees function productively and will be invaluable to their organization.

Why should the manager who already has a frenetic schedule and myriad responsibilities also assume the role of counselor?

1. The manager's dedication to an employee in a helping relationship leads to employee commitment to the organization. This, in turn, leads to maximization of human and financial resources.
2. Healthy employees make healthy organizations.
3. Helping someone in need is one of the most personally satisfying experiences a manager can have.
4. Helping someone else grow enables the manager to grow.

> Do you agree that managers have a responsibility to serve as counselors to their employees who face problems at work? Explain.

IDENTIFYING AN EMPLOYEE IN NEED

For the above four reasons, managers should take the time to learn how to help an employee in need. The first step toward being able to do this is to identify an employee who has a problem. Sources of problems for employees include the following:

1. Job-related problems
2. Family-related problems
3. Other problems generated from outside the organization.

Job-related Problems

Job-related problems can be generated in many ways, from poor working conditions to dissatisfaction with the job itself. The pressure and stress of working with others can create problems for employees such as reduction in group cohesiveness or increased irritation as a result of the habits and behaviors of others that the employees may find annoying. Hitting a career plateau or fearing imminent retirement can create additional job-related problems.

Compelling data indicate that the number of employees with financial problems that affect their work is increasing (Rives, 2004). It has been estimated that 25 percent of all employees in the United States are experiencing stress from significant financial pressures to the extent that their productivity is negatively affected (Armour, 2005). Garman and his colleagues also suggested that in some organizations 40 percent to 50 percent of employees may be experiencing financial stresses that negatively affect their productivity.

Others (Schaitberger and Dell, 2007) agree. A study on the impact of financial problems found that more than half of the respondents were under financial stress, a quarter reported being under "severe financial stress," and over 10 percent reported experiencing "overwhelming" financial stress. A 2006 survey (Shumway et al.,) revealed similar results, reporting that more employees indicated that they were "troubled by" financial problems than by issues of alcohol or drug-related concerns. The highest rate of the eight concerns presented (psychological, family, medical, financial, employment, legal, alcohol, and drug), however, were those related to family matters.

Family-related Problems

Family-related problems can have a profound effect on employee job performance. Family crises such as death, divorce, and major illnesses, as well as family pressures that conflict with job demands, are all situations in which employee productivity is likely to decrease. Managers need to be able to identify these problems quickly and offer appropriate counseling solutions.

Perhaps one of the fastest growing problems affecting hospitality workers is eldercare. According to one study (Grensing-Pophal, 2003), there are over $25 billion in costs associated with lost productivity due to dealing with aging parents or other relatives. Employees increasingly discover that they must take off time from work to take loved ones to doctor's appointments and deal with a wide range of financial concerns.

Managers are also finding themselves discussing old problems created by new technologies. Employees' inability to "switch off" from their work and enjoy time with their family has a number of consequences, not the least of which is "Not tonight, Darling." O'Reilly (2007) gives an example of one staff member who complained that her husband kept his BlackBerry on their pillow.

While new issues have been added to the mix of employees' family concerns, there has been little success in resolving the more traditional problems of child care, transportation, divorce, domestic violence, and legal help that have required counseling and support. In low income neighborhoods, in particular, these issues have not gone away and absenteeism and other consequences of family dilemmas continue to have a dramatic impact on the workplace. The new complexity in this mix is the fact that the US workplace is becoming increasingly diverse. By 2050, minorities may represent nearly 40 percent of the population (Owens, 2006). Counseling employees effectively will have additional challenges in that managers will be expected to acquire cultural competence as they take into account each employee's personal profile, including not only age but also such characteristics as race and sexual orientation.

> Do you know of someone who has personal problems that affect their performance on the job? What is the specific situation? Do you believe that it would be helpful for their manager to counsel them?

Other Employee Concerns

Financial, legal, and social troubles outside the organization can cause problems of which managers need to be aware. Each one of these problems can lead to substantial costs to the organization resulting from accidents, absenteeism, turnover, and lost productivity.

In addition to the stress caused by poor personal finance decisions, the following statistics indicate other pervasive problems that may affect employees in and outside of the workplace.

1. Chemical dependency cost the US economy in excess of $238 billion a year; and over 69 percent of these costs are from productivity losses due to drug-related illnesses and deaths (Drug-free workplace statistics; Hafer and Blume, 2002).
2. Alcoholics and problem drinkers are absent from work 3.8 to 8.3 times more often than other employees. In addition, illegal drug users are absent from work an average of five

days per month. In Alaska alone in 2003, productivity was reduced by \$106 million due to alcohol and over \$30 million due to drug use (Drug-free workplace statistics, 2000; Campbell, 2006).

3. Approximately one out of two marriages will end in divorce; women in their 40s and 50s now initiate over 65 percent of these divorces (Rosenblum, 2007).
4. Depression and anxiety disorders—the two most common mental illnesses—each affect 24 million adults annually (National Institute of Mental Health).
5. Employees miss 175,000 days of work per year because of domestic violence alone (Johnson and Gardner, 1999).

The costs to the organization aren't limited to accidents, absenteeism, turnover, and lost productivity; they also include low morale and poor employee and customer relations. These challenges are being met in some organizations by the development of employee assistance or counseling programs. In organizations that lack these programs, the need for supervisory employees with the skills to recognize employees with problems is even greater.

THE CORE CONDITIONS FOR EFFECTIVE COUNSELING

Research on counseling has suggested that there are certain core conditions that are essential to effective counseling. These core conditions include giving empathy, showing respect, and being genuine.

Empathy

The most critical ingredient in counseling is **empathy**—understanding the feelings and personal meanings of the employee and communicating this understanding to him. Being empathic involves paying attention to and understanding the inner world of the employee as he perceives it. With empathy, the manager or counselor can assist the employee in gaining a clearer understanding of, and thus greater control over, his world and behavior. Carl Rogers describes empathy as experiencing the individual's private world "as if it were your own, but without ever losing the 'as if' quality" (Rogers, 1961).

As employees find the manager or counselor listening acceptingly to their feelings, they become able to listen acceptingly to themselves. As the empathic manager or counselor is genuine and nonjudgmental, employees are able to drop facades and develop themselves more fully.

While most people use the word "sympathy" to denote feelings of caring, in counseling it is better to feel empathy than sympathy. By definition, the sympathetic counselor personally experiences the employee's emotions. Not only would this be difficult (if not impossible), but the counselor's emotions would get in the way of helping. The empathic counselor, on the other hand, attempts to understand the employee's emotions without experiencing them.

Learning to use empathy can help the manager to achieve the following:

- Increase communication as personal barriers are broken down
- Enhance understanding of behavior, both the manager's and the employee's
- Sharpen his or her perception in various situations by seeing things through another person's eyes
- Enhance his or her ability to help others.

A manager may also experience barriers when attempting to communicate empathy. These include the following:

- Thinking in terms of stereotypes
- Focusing on only one aspect of an individual's behavior, i.e., being narrow-minded
- Centering only on one's own needs or emotions
- Maintaining a distance between themselves and others
- Being judgmental.

Robert Carkhuff developed various scales for training individuals in effective counseling. The following adaptation of one of these scales illustrates how the manager's/helper's responses reflect different levels of empathy for the helpee's verbal and behavioral expressions (Carkhuff, 1969).

EMPATHY SCALE

Level 1: The manager's/helper's responses either do not attend to or detract significantly from the helpee's expressions in that they communicate significantly less of the helpee's feelings and experiences than the helpee himself has communicated. The manager/helper communicates no awareness of even the most obvious, expressed surface feelings of the helpee. The manager/helper may be bored or simply operating from a preconceived frame of reference which excludes that of the helpee.

Level 2: The manager's/helper's responses subtract substantial emotion from the helpee's expressions. The manager/helper may communicate some awareness of obvious, surface feelings of the helpee, but his communications drain off a level of affect and distort the level of meaning. The manager/helper may communicate his own ideas of what may be going on, but they are not congruent with the expressions of the helpee.

Level 3: The manager's/helper's responses essentially are interchangeable with the helpee's expressions in that they express the same affect and meaning. The manager/helper responds with accurate understanding of the surface feelings of the helpee.

Level 4: The manager's/helper's responses add noticeably to the helpee's expressions by expressing them at a deeper level than the helpee was able to communicate. The manager/helper communicates his understanding of the expressions of the helpee at a level deeper than they were expressed and thus enables the helpee to experience and/or express feelings he was unable to express previously.

Level 5: The manager's/helper's responses add significantly to the helpee's expressions by accurately expressing them at deeper levels than the helpee was able to communicate. The manager/helper responds with accuracy to all of the helpee's deeper as well as surface feelings.

It is essential that the manager/helper communicate at least at Level 3 on the Empathy Scale to facilitate the helping relationship. If rapport and mutual understanding have developed, the manager may attempt to practice empathy at Level 4. Level 5 is beyond what a manager who has not had extensive counseling training can or should do.

> As a manager, do you predict that it will be easy for you to empathize with members of your staff or department? What have people told you in the past about your ability to be empathic?

Respect

Respect is the counseling ingredient that requires the manager/helper (1) to regard the helpee's feelings and opinions as valid, and (2) to understand that the helpee can best solve his own problems, with some help from the manager/helper. It is not appropriate for the manager to resolve the employee's problems for him; this would diminish the employee's sense of self-worth and self-respect. Rather, the manager uses unconditional positive regard—respect—to free the employee from censoring his words and encourage open and honest communication. Respect is often communicated by actions rather than words. Examples of such respect-oriented behavior include being "for" the employee, willingness to work with the employee, regarding the employee as unique, suspending critical judgment, and expressing reasonable warmth.

Genuineness

Genuineness is the counseling ingredient whereby the manager/helper's feelings are congruent with his or her expressions to the employee. Managers must be real, honest, and up front, with no facades; they must be "who they are" and openly express their true feelings to the employee. They must also be able to say, "I don't know" when one feels he or she does not have a helpful response.

Employees who perceive the manager/helper as genuine are more likely to be genuine themselves. They will be more comfortable about expressing, rather than masking, their true feelings and more likely to trust the manager with their problem.

The following behaviors are recommended:

- Be willing to commit to others
- Strive for employee independence in relationships
- Communicate without distorting the message
- Listen to employees without distorting their message
- Be concrete in communications.

"YOU'RE RIGHT, I'M ARROGANT AND BOSSY, AND RELATE to OTHERS INAPPROPRIATELY. READ THAT BACK."

How will you make sure that your employees feel comfortable talking with you? In what ways will you communicate your respect and sincerity?

THE MANAGERIAL ROLE IN THE COUNSELING MODEL

There are three basic principles to be followed before the manager offers counseling to an employee. The manager must be certain that he or she is well centered; it is imperative that a manager not use the counseling experience to satisfy personal needs. The manager must be aware of biases on his or her part that might impede the growth of another person. The manager must believe that the personal growth of the individual he or she is helping is possible.

The goal of the manager is to help the troubled employee find his or her own solution to the problem. The responsibility remains with the employee; the manager merely facilitates the helping process. There are two reasons for this. One is that such an attitude will communicate trust, confidence, and respect to the employee. It may even be the first time that the employee has been shown such confidence. Another is that it develops a problem-solving model for the employee to use with future problems. If the manager can develop a pattern for arriving at problem resolution together with the employee, the employee is likely to become more independent and continue the process on his or her own.

The counseling process incorporates three phases:

1. Exploratory phase
2. Employee self-understanding phase
3. Constructive-action phase.

Exploratory Phase

When a problem has been detected and the manager has chosen to counsel an employee, there are several things to keep in mind. First, set up an appointment to meet one-on-one with the employee. The meeting should be conducted in a quiet place, where there will be no interruptions. It is also recommended that neither party sit behind a desk and that a box of tissues is kept handy.

When the meeting begins, state the purpose of the meeting. Beating around the bush will only increase the level of anxiety for the manager and the employee. In this phase, the manager should convey to the employee that the immediate goal of the meeting is to explore his or her concerns. In order to do this the manager must build rapport. The manager should start by giving close attention. Good eye contact and a lean-forward posture are essential. During this stage the manager must try to understand at the level of the employees affect, rather than attempting a deeper, more insightful level. Pay attention both to the words (cognitive content) and to the feelings behind the words (affective content).

Employee Self-Understanding Phase

The goal of employee self-understanding phase is for the manager to facilitate a shared understanding of the employee's feelings about his or her own problem. In this stage it is important to communicate empathy, so that the employee knows that the manager understands how he or she feels. The manager should forget how he thinks the employee should feel. By responding accurately to both the words and the feelings behind the words, the manager can tell the employee that he knows what it is like to be in his or her shoes.

Through a continuous process of reflecting and clarifying what the employee is saying, the manager assists the employee in coming closer to the core problem. It is best for the manager to paraphrase what he or she has heard to insure understanding of the problem. If the manager paraphrases a comment incorrectly, it is likely that the employee may correct the manager, thereby communicating an even better picture of the situation.

Constructive-Action Phase

Once the employee has exhausted the discussion of his or her feelings, it is time to make a transition to the problem-solving phase. During this stage, the manager will be facilitating a process that develops the employee's ability to solve his or her own problems. If the process is shared and developed into a step by step course of action, the employee will acquire a skill that will be useful for future problem solving.

By letting the employee choose the solution, the manager has placed responsibility on the employee to solve the problem. The employee understands that he or she has come up with the solution and thus may be more committed to solving the problem. The transition to this stage may take the form of such questions as the following: "What kind of solutions have you considered?" or "What do you see as alternatives?" Or it may involve a summary of the issues with which the employee has been grappling.

After developing a list of alternatives, the employee must choose among them. A useful way of choosing is first to prioritize the employee's values and then to assign points to each alternative, based on how it fits with the employee's values. If the employee does arrive at a solution, make sure the employee can live with the consequences of the decision. Also, determine how he or she will react if the solution does not work.

Finally, the manager should strive to achieve closure. The following remarks may be helpful in leading to closure:

1. "Is there anything else you want to talk about?"
2. Reflect on the solution, for example, "You are going to do X."
3. "How do you feel now?"
4. Summarize the entire session.
5. "I sense we're going around in circles—perhaps we've touched all the bases. Let's stop for today, think about it, and talk some more later."

Before the employee leaves the office, the manager should restate what has been said and what goals and objectives have been set. The manager should thank the employee for his trust in bringing the problem to the manager's attention. A follow-up meeting should be scheduled where progress or roadblocks that have arisen can be discussed. At this point, if the manager lets the employee know that he or she is open to discussing problems that have occurred during the solution phase, the employee will be more willing to voice problems, rather than covering them up with a false sense of well-being. The follow-up meeting should be followed with more meetings to make sure that the employee stays on the right track.

Imagine yourself working through each stage of the above model. What stages will you find particularly easy? Where do you anticipate you will encounter frustrations or obstacles? How might you prepare to be effective in this process?

COUNSELING TECHNIQUES

There are six valuable counseling techniques that may be used by a manager when interacting with an employee to help make their time together more productive.

Develop Reflection Skills

Reflection is an important counseling technique. It is simply a restatement by a manager/helper in a nonjudgmental manner of what the employee already has said or has indicated through tone of voice and body language.

Reflection is saying to another person the essential elements of what they have communicated to you. They may have said it, implied it, behaved it, or nonverbally communicated it. For example, "It sounds as if you are saying . . ." A rule of thumb for reflecting: When reflecting, the manager must restrict himself to what the employee has communicated. The manager may supplement verbal communication by inferring from behavioral communication. But don't play armchair theorist and make deductions that may be inaccurate.

EXAMPLE:

Inferred Reflection. "From the way you keep shredding that piece of paper I can tell you are upset."

Armchair Theorist. "Are you nervous because of some unpleasant secret you're trying to hide?"

Reflection is particularly effective in helping people clarify their feelings. It is the process whereby the manager and employee come to a concise expression of the employee's problem and ensure that it is mutually understood. It serves several purposes:

1. Reflection facilitates understanding.
2. Reflection often encourages further expression.
3. Reflection conveys to the employee that the manager is understanding or trying to understand what he is saying.
4. Reflection is a check on the accuracy of the manager's hearing, comprehension, and insight.
5. If done with genuineness and respect, reflection communicates the manager's ability to empathize, which in turn elicits trust and more sharing.

There are two levels of reflection: direct paraphrase and additive reflection. **Direct paraphrase** conveys to the employee that the manager is genuinely trying to follow and understand what the employee is saying. It also crystallizes the employee's comments in a concise way, extracting the essential content and providing a check for the manager and employee regarding communication. An example of direct paraphrase is "It sounds as though you are feeling frustrated in your daily activities."

The second level of reflection, **additive reflection,** occurs when the manager picks up on some aspect, feeling, or problem that was not stated, but was implied or suggested in some way by the employee. This reflection elicits more feelings and/or helps the employee probe his feelings in greater depth. The employee may be encouraged to explore the situation more deeply. A manager/helper should use additive reflection judiciously and sparingly. An example of additive reflection is "You say that you have trouble getting to work, which suggests there is little that motivates you to come in every day."

For a manager to reflect well, he or she should do the following:

1. Pay attention and concentrate. Focus on the whole person.
2. Develop the ability to remember.
3. Understand that feelings are not the only thing the manager might hear and wish to reflect.
4. Reflect at the same level of affective intensity that the employee communicates.

Use of Open and Closed Questions

Closed questions encourage simple yes-or-no answers, whereas open questions encourage the employee to respond at some length. In some cases, it may simply be a matter of rephrasing a question to get the employee to do the work. For example, if the employee is discussing a pervading sense of fatigue and boredom and says, "I seem to just wander through my days and don't accomplish anything," typical closed responses would be: "So you don't have much purpose right now?" or "If only you were doing something more important."

Each of these questions focuses on only one aspect of what the employee said. Furthermore, both put the manager in charge of the flow of communication. The employee will just answer "yes" or "no" and won't push further toward deeper understanding.

An open question shifts the responsibility of communication back to the employee, who then must work through the question with possibly a deeper processing of emotions. An example of an open question might be: "How does that feel? What's the feeling you have about yourself when that happens?"

This type of question is ideally suited for employee counseling in that the employee can pick up on the most important elements of his problem. Compare the following closed questions with their open counterparts:

Closed	Open
"Are you feeling discouraged?"	"What does that feel like?"
"Are you feeling angry at your boss or at yourself?"	"What's the feeling behind that comment?"
"Does that mean it's not worth trying?"	"What does that mean for you?"

Create your own examples of open and closed questions. In the past, which type of question would you have been most likely to ask?

Behavioral versus Evaluative Feedback

Behavioral feedback focuses on the observable facts about an employee and gives the employee a chance to evaluate these facts. Conversely, evaluative feedback passes judgment on the employee and puts him on the defensive.

Evaluative	Behavioral
"Mary, you're not doing a very good job."	"Mary, last week three guests complained about the way you treated them."
"Al, you're just stubborn."	"Al, you've disagreed with four of the five things I've suggested."
"Joe, you don't listen to anything I say."	"Joe, I've had to ask you that question five times now."

When one uses evaluative responses in a counseling session, the employee may feel as if he is being attacked by the manager. If this feeling pervades, the employee may resist help. Using behavioral responses presents the problem at hand and leaves room for discussion.

Accept Silence

One of the most powerful tools in any manager's repertoire of listening skills is the use of the pause or silence. The manager is likely to feel more comfortable in the counseling role than his subordinate is in the helpee role; the pressure is far greater on the employee. A pause can give the employee time to collect his or her thoughts. There is an implication in silence or a pause that suggests more is expected.

Silence can also be threatening to the employee and may hinder the counseling process. The manager must be aware of when and why he is using silence and the effect it is having on the employee. Silence should be a positive sign that the manager is giving the employee "room to think," rather than a cold shoulder.

How comfortable are you with silence? Provide an example to illustrate.

Use Freeing, not Binding Responses

There are certain responses that work to free the helpee and increase his/her autonomy, while other responses have binding effects that diminish autonomy. Here are examples of both.

Responses with freeing effects are the following:

1. *Active attentive listening*—responsive listening.
2. *Paraphrasing*—testing to ensure that the message you got was the message that was sent.
3. *Perception check*—showing your desire to relate to and understand the helpee as a person.
4. *Seeking information to help you understand the helpee*—questions directly relevant to what he or she said.

Responses with binding effects are the following:

1. *Changing the subject without explanation*—for example, to avoid the other's feelings.
2. *Interpreting the helpee's behavior*—"You do that because your mother always . . ."
3. *Advice and persuasion*—"What you should do is . . ."
4. *Denying his or her feelings*—"You don't really mean that!" or "Everyone has problems like that."

Create an Accepting Environment

Managers/helpers should create an accepting environment in which the employee is not on the defensive. The following are examples of phrases that put the employee on the defensive:

- "You should . . ."—conveys a controlling attitude to which the helpee will often respond with a conforming phrase like, "OK, I will."
- "This is the way to . . ."—tells the helpee what to do, and leads the helpee to avoid taking initiative, saying or thinking "My ideas are no good."
- "You are wrong . . ."—shames the helpee into hiding and denying problems, thinking "I won't tell . . ." out of fear of being criticized.

On the other hand, the following phrases help to create an accepting environment:

- "I hear you what you are saying . . ."—lets the helpee know that you are really listening, and creates an environment in which the helpee is willing to experiment with solutions and be creative.
- "What you say has value . . ."—conveys understanding and boosts the employee's confidence and desire to improve.
- "You can tell me and trust me . . ."—creates an atmosphere of sharing that encourages the employee to open up and let you help.

Learn Stress Listening

Many times the manager finds himself in an undesirable angry confrontation with an employee, and thus before working at discovering the core problem, he must first take steps to resolve the conflict. Even though anger is the employee's problem it is up to the manager to be responsive. By following some of the basic principles of stress listening, anger may be converted into a productive working relationship.

- Avoid sharing anger. Remain calm, matter-of-fact, and empathic. This will serve not only to calm the employee, but the manager will then control his own anger and begin to attack the problem.
- Respond constructively.
- Avoid small talk.
- Maintain comfortable eye contact.
- Prevent interruptions.
- Do not hide behind a desk.

Ask questions to try to uncover the source of the anger.

- Separate fact from opinion.
- Avoid hasty opinions.

The goal of stress listening is for you not to do or say anything to add to the employee's anger.

COMMON COUNSELING BEHAVIORS

Inappropriate Behaviors

Many managers, despite their best intentions, exhibit behaviors or make comments that are inappropriate. Whether they are new to the practice of counseling or just unaware of potential side effects, managers need to know where to draw the line. The following techniques are examples of inappropriate managerial approaches to counseling.

Getting tough. Managers may try the "shape up or ship out" approach to solving problems with employees. The manager tells the employee what is expected of him and then gives him an ultimatum. No room is left for discussion or compromise. Though this tactic may frighten some employees into action, its results are not long-lasting. Many employees will start to resent the manager for this behavior and begin to give up altogether.

Being extra nice. The manager may decide to give the employee more time, more space, and many concessions to persuade him to change his attitude. The employee will perceive that the worse he becomes, the more latitude he will be given. The manager will lose control of the situation and the employee's respect.

Making the employee miserable to the point of resignation. The manager attempts to force behavioral change by making the employee miserable through such ploys as increased workload, undesirable job assignments, or harsh criticism in front of peers. This approach usually backfires on the manager. Other employees will notice his abhorrent behavior and begin to resent and mistrust him or her.

How *not* to Counsel an Employee

In his brilliant article, "The Mrs. Lincoln Response" (derived from the sick joke "Other than that, Mrs. Lincoln, how did you like the play?"), Brooke Collison examines the different ways in which individuals respond inappropriately to people in distress (Collison, 1978). Following are the five inappropriate responses:

1. "Are you okay?" This is asked by newcomers to an accident scene where the person in question clearly isn't "okay." The accident victim frequently says, "Yes, I'm okay" and the questioner shows relief. He is off the hook and grateful that no further action is necessary, because the person is "okay."
2. "How are you?" Many times the questioner does not listen to the answer to the question, expecting an answer of "fine." Often the response is "lousy" or "not good."
3. "A friend of mine . . ." You tell someone in distress that "your friend" had a problem similar to his but it was much worse and had dire consequences, or that the "your friend's" problem turned out to be inconsequential. Thus he should be grateful that his problem is not so bad (by comparison) or that things could probably turn out as well as they did for "your friend," so don't worry. This response helps shift the focus away from the person in distress, and the speaker distances himself from the suffering person.

4. "I feel really terrible." This response to someone's pain makes the sufferer regret that he has shared his problem and caused you to suffer, too. Next time he will spare you and not share his problem.

5. "You shouldn't feel that way." This is a denial of feelings. The person who has been told his or her feelings are "wrong" becomes apologetic, guilty or silent.

> Has anyone ever made you defensive by behaving in one of the ways mentioned above? What was the situation? What was the outcome?

How to Counsel an Employee

The following are a few basic guidelines that would be beneficial for a manager to follow when counseling an employee.

- *Be specific*. Managers should give employees specific examples of the employee's performance. If a manager cannot cite specific examples of poor performance, then the employee has no basis for developing a plan for improvement. At this time, the manager should also cite positive aspects of the employee's performance.
- *Be consistent*. The manager should be consistent in identifying performance problems with all employees, not with just a select few.
- *Respond in a timely manner*. Feedback and counseling is only effective if done in a timely manner. If a manager waits too long to intervene, the employee may not realize the severity of his poor performance or behavior, and the remainder of the work group may begin to suffer as well.
- *Maintain credibility*. The manager must be perceived as a fair and accurate source of information. It would be wise for the manager to keep a file on all employees recording both inadequate and outstanding behaviors. The manager may also wish to keep notes on what was discussed during a counseling session so that in follow-up sessions the helpee knows the manager cared enough to remember.
- *Listen carefully*. The manager must listen carefully to the employee. It is necessary to understand and appreciate the employee's point of view. Only if the manager and the employee work together will the problem be resolved.

AVOIDANCE OF COUNSELING

Why Employees do not Seek Counseling Help

Sometimes, although an employee may be experiencing a severe short-term problem, he or she does not seek help. An employee in this case may feel that his or her situation is hopeless and that nothing can help it get better. Alternatively, he or she may fear change or harbor concerns about confidentiality and how reporting a problem may change how he or she is treated in the workplace.

By the same token, managers sometimes do not offer counseling when they could. Several common excuses for this behavior include lack of time, lack of skills, intimidation, friendship, pity or a lack of empathy. Unfortunately, choosing not to offer counseling assistance to an employee in need for one or more of these reasons will ultimately be more detrimental to the organization. Because of the benefits to the troubled employee, to you, and to your company, it is worthwhile to notice employees who appear to need help and to offer it.

It is important for the manager to be able to recognize the troubled employee. Even the most attuned and vigilant manager can miss important clues, such as inattention, listlessness, nervousness, chronic lateness, deteriorated appearance, unexcused absences, arguments with other employees, and self-deprecating remarks. Managers should be aware of these signs and should talk to the employee who exhibits any of them. Other problems arise as a result of the working environment. Employees may be in over their heads, or not challenged at all. Conflicts between supervisors and employees may occur, or the employee may feel that he or she has been treated unjustly. Regardless of where the problem originated, effective managers are willing to recognize these problems and take necessary steps to help the troubled employee.

Employees may approach their managers for information, but their questions may mask deeper problems. Afraid to tell what is really on their minds, they may start with a "safe" question to assess the manager's willingness to discuss deeper concerns. The following signals may indicate deeper problems:

Undue concern about a simple problem.

Denial of the importance of an unstated problem, saying, "It doesn't matter."

An inability or hesitancy to focus on the issue at hand. In this situation, the employee seems confused and unable to respond to your questions.

A lack of congruity between verbal and nonverbal expression. The employee tells you things are great but looks miserable.

Overdone, nervous, or inappropriate joking or laughter. The employee laughs or jokes about his problems and won't discuss them seriously.

Lack of eye contact, for example, the employee looks down at her shoes instead of looking at you.

A reluctance to terminate the counseling session.

Certainly this list of signals is not exhaustive. Moreover, it is important to remember that these behaviors do not always indicate a problem; the employee who looks down at her shoes may just be shy. But when the manager suspects that employees have more on their minds than they disclose, it is helpful to describe their behavior without making judgments about it. A certain amount of probing may be necessary to unearth the employee's real concerns, but effort on the manager's part to do this will have long-lasting beneficial results for all parties involved.

Fred, the restaurant manager, worried about two of his staff members. Sean, the Maitre d', had been coming in late for his dinner shift, and Fred thought he smelled alcohol on Sean's breath. In addition, Erica, a waitress, had been arriving at work with red-rimmed eyes, indicting she had been crying. Fred thought that he should approach them and ask if they would like counseling help.

When Fred came to Sean with this in mind, Sean responded, "Things are going well in the restaurant. We are busy every night. What could you possibly want to see me about?" Fred repeated that he only wanted to meet with Sean in private. Then Fred asked Erica if she could come to his office when she had a chance. She said, "Did I do something wrong?" Fred responded, "No, I just would like to speak with you."

Erica came almost immediately, and Fred said, "Erica, I've been noticing that you have been upset. Is something bothering you?"

Erica nodded and responded, "Yes. It's that Marti! The minute I walk in she is all over me. I wish she'd just leave me alone!"

"She is your shift manager . . . do you want me to speak to her?" asked Fred.

Erica half smiled. "No, you're right. She's just doing her job. I guess it's not really her that's bothering me. The truth is . . . I'm a single parent and am having problems making this job work. I have to drop my daughter off at the sitter, sometimes before dawn. It can be so cold and I have to take her from her warm little bed and drive her across town in the freezing cold. Then I leave her all day and sometimes when I pick her up she is already asleep for the night. Sometimes she calls the sitter 'Mommy' and I feel like I hardly get to see her."

Fred said gently, "So you are missing your daughter."

Erica began to cry. "I'm sorry," she said, "but I just feel so hopeless about all this."

"How do you feel about working?" Fred asked.

"I don't have a choice, do I?" Erica snapped back.

"No, think about it. This isn't going on your review. I've seen you look pretty happy here. You relate well to the customers. Your performance is very good. So, how do you feel about working?" asked Fred.

"Well, I'm not one of those people who could sit home on welfare. And you are right; as jobs go I do like this one. I like being able to provide for little Rosie and me."

"So the job's not the problem?"

"Rosie's not the problem either. She is an angel. And the sitter's not the problem. She's like a sweet old grandmother. The problem is that I don't get enough time with Rosie."

Fred asked, "What could you do about that?"

Erica thought a little while and then said. "Well, I could ask Mrs. Jenkins to make sure she has a good nap every day so she's awake when I get there. I could try trading shifts with someone on the 3 to 11 and see if that would work better; then she would be asleep for most of my shift and I could take her to the sitter in broad daylight. If it seemed better, could I ask for a change the next time one of those shifts comes available?"

"I'd be open to that," replied Fred, "but you still have a tough road ahead of you. I know the employee assistance program has excellent counselors, and they will find someone who will help you. Let's call them and see what they have to offer. You're doing great on your own, but wouldn't it be nice to have some help when you hit these rough spots?"

Erica answered, "I'm not willing to take much more time away from Rosie. May I leave work to go to my appointments with the counselor?"

Fred responded, "Yes, I will let you off from work to go to your sessions. We just have to find someone to cover for you. Other employees have been very happy with the help they have received. Here's the number. Why don't you make the call? I need to go check on the kitchen before lunch." Erica agreed to do this, and decided that this might be a good solution to her problems.

Sean never came in, so toward the end of the evening dinner hours, Fred went to Sean and asked him to come to his office. Fred said to Sean, "I noticed that you've been coming in late, and I've smelled liquor on your breath."

Sean responded, "No way, man!"

Fred said, "Would you care to see a counselor in the employee assistance program?"

Sean answered, "No, I don't have any problems!"

Fred calmly responded, "You may not recognize you have a problem, but I do. Both your appearance and your attitude are far less appropriate than when you were hired. I believe it won't be long before the guests are able to see your problem, and when that happens, my responsibility will be clear."

"Are you threatening me?" Sean exclaimed.

"No," replied Fred, "your drinking is threatening you in ways I never could. If you were honest, you would admit that this is more than a work issue. But while I respect you, and I would like to see you get the help you need to pull yourself together, my ultimate responsibility is to this business. You are an important part of our team here and we rise or fall together. I can't have you continue in the direction you are going. Call AA. Check in with the employee assistance program and work with someone there. I've met many of the counselors, and they do good work. You may choose whether you would like a man or a woman."

Sean retorted, "I don't want to go!"

"Well," Fred said, "you can choose to try to do this on your own. I hope you can do it. We will meet again at the end of the week and see where we are."

MANAGING CRISIS SITUATIONS

Managers may also be called upon to help an employee in a severe crisis situation. The goal in these situations is to make a referral to a professional counselor as soon as possible. However, sometimes it is not feasible to make a referral right away. The manager may feel that a need to hang in with the employee until the appropriate time to make a referral. This section will prepare managers to handle a crisis situation.

Crisis may be defined as the inner state of a person reacting to stress when normal coping methods have broken down. **Stress** occurs when the demands placed on a person by his or her environment exceed the person's coping skills. **Coping methods** are the usual way the employee handles stress, which may be **adaptive** or **maladaptive.**

A crisis is intensive and time-limited, generally within a six-week period, and pushes toward some kind of resolution. During crises, the employee's habits and coping mechanisms are suspended and he or she is especially open to new methods of coping. There is a rise of energy during crises, signified by emotional turmoil, which can be focused and directed toward crisis resolution.

What are some of the specific crisis situations that you might anticipate as a hospitality manager?

Process for Crisis Intervention

Crisis counselors suggest the following steps for intervening in crisis situations:

1. Make contact with the employee at a feeling level rather than the factual level. Identify the employee's feelings and accept his right to feel that way. Then reflect your response to his feelings.
2. Explore the current dimensions of the problem, focusing on the previous six to eight weeks. Identify the event that precipitated the immediate crisis. Ask open-ended questions so the employee does most of the talking. Ask the employee to be concrete and specific.

3. Summarize the problem with the employee so that you agree on the main elements.
4. Focus with the employee on specific areas of the problem to be considered. Two criteria are important:

   • Area selected should be the one causing the employee great pain.
   • Area selected should be susceptible to some immediate action with likelihood of results.

5. Explore different modes of action. Ask the employee what he would like to do, what he fears doing, and what he has done in similar situations. If the employee cannot come up with possible modes of action, ask how he feels about some you suggest.
6. Specify a plan of action that defines what the employee will do. Arrange in advance for the employee to return if the action plan fails.

The Suicidal Employee

A suicidal employee is the most critical crisis a manager may face. In this section, we provide information about suicide and make suggestions for managing the situation. Depression, which affects over 30 million people in the United States, may predispose people toward ending their lives, although the suicide itself may be triggered by another event. Loss, loneliness, and hopelessness are the factors that lead to suicide. Approximately 35,000 Americans commit suicide each year; however, as many suicides are not reported as such, the accurate figure may approach 100,000 each year. The American Society of Suicidology (2006) figures for 2004 indicated that there were well over 800,000 suicide attempts.

Four out of five people who commit suicide have previously given clues of their intention to do so. The danger signs of suicide include previous attempts or threats to commit suicide, a tendency toward isolation, especially in conjunction with other personality changes or odd behavior, and an obsession with putting all personal affairs in order.

The Cardinal Rule of Suicide Prevention: *Do Something*

If someone you know threatens to end his life *or*

If someone you know has undergone drastic changes and begins giving away personal possessions or preparing a will, *get help.*

If you detect signs that someone is considering suicide, don't be afraid to ask, "Has suicide been on your mind?" If they are not thinking about suicide, your mentioning it will not increase the probability. If they are thinking about it, your interest in them will probably come as a relief. Don't act shocked or make moral judgments. It is okay to ask specific questions about how he feels and why he wishes to end his life. The manager should offer suggestions about alternative ways of coping with his problems.

Assess the lethality of his situation by determining if he has a specific plan such as accumulating drugs or buying a gun. Remember, the more specific the plan, the greater the risk of suicide. Managers must reassure the employee that something can be done for him and encourage him to accept professional help.

Have you ever known someone who was suicidal? Was appropriate help readily available to this person? Would you have been prepared to refer this person to an appropriate resource?

MAKING REFERRALS

Indications that a Referral Should be Made

As a manager/helper it will become clear that certain problems should be referred to professionals rather than tackled alone. Simply by approaching the troubled employee and addressing the situation, a manager may perform an important function: motivating the employee to seek professional assistance. When an employee asks for help, the following situations may indicate that a referral is in order:

- Undue concern about a simple problem.
- Tendency to accept suggestions offered without reasonable consideration.
- Inability to focus on the issue at hand.
- Lack of congruence between verbal and nonverbal communication.
- Overdone or inappropriate joking or laughter.
- Lack of eye contact.
- Reluctance to terminate the session.

It is not appropriate for a manager to do long-term counseling of an employee with personal, emotional, or mental problems. However, recognizing troubled employees, helping when possible, and referring the employee for professional help when necessary is well worth the effort.

How to Refer an Employee for Further Help

Knowing how to make referrals is as important as knowing to whom to make the referrals. It is important to try to go beyond matching a problem with the correct phone number or office. Taking time to establish rapport with employees will give them the impression that someone really cares about them. There are several techniques that managers can use to make referrals more personal. Refer the employee to a specific person(s) rather than to an agency or organization. Offer several alternatives if the employee's needs are not clear, if the employee seems reluctant to go to a particular agency, or if several services seem appropriate. The manager should delay making a referral if he is not familiar with the appropriate organization or does not know which service or which person would handle the problem best. Have the employee wait while you make a phone call or two. Communicate the desire to learn what happens after the employee leaves your office.

Referrals to informational resources are not likely to have an emotional effect on employees. On the other hand, referrals for counseling or therapy may generate the stigma attached to "going for help." The sensitivity you demonstrate in making referrals may determine employees' willingness to accept suggestions.

It is rarely fruitful to insist that employees accept referrals. If an employee does not want the help offered, it is unlikely that he or she will benefit from it. On the other hand, it is possible to make difficult referrals acceptable to employees. If the situation is potentially lethal, the manager should not leave until the employee has accepted a referral. The manager should leave work and go with the person to the nearest source of appropriate professional help.

Occasionally, it will be necessary to refer an employee to a therapist. The people most likely to benefit from therapy are those strong enough to confront themselves and acknowledge the need for personal development. The point to communicate is that referral for therapy or counseling is in fact an expression of the manager's confidence in their capacity for improvement.

For a great number of people, the mere mention of therapy brings to mind "craziness" or "sickness," thoughts damaging to self-esteem and barriers to acceptance of referral for therapy. Here the point to get across is that the difference between advising and therapy and is one of degree rather than kind: therapy is a more intensive and wide-ranging form of problem exploration than advising.

Employees may ask manager's to arrange referrals. If an employee makes such a request, it is useful to discuss with him or her exactly what information should be relayed to the referral resource, because the employee may wish to relate his or her own story when the time comes. It is best to make referral calls in the employee's presence so he or she will know exactly what you said.

What can you do now to prepare yourself for this important management role?

Summary

In this chapter we have explored the various ways in which an employee's problems—ranging from alcoholism to family-related problems—can affect the employee's ability to do his or her job. Outlining the many different categories of problems employees may encounter in and outside of the workplace, we offer some basic strategies and rationale for providing counseling to employees who may need help.

We offer six practical techniques that enhance the counseling process and outline the three stages of the counseling process—the exploratory phase, employee self-understanding phase, and constructive-action phase. We suggest strategies for closing a counseling session to encourage further manager–employee interactions on matters in which the employee may seek help. Finally, we emphasize the importance of identifying crisis situations and making referrals for employees if they are needed. Opening up communication with employees will be an invaluable skill for all managers who take the time to master it.

Key Words

counseling *319*	reflection *327*	stress *335*
empathy *322*	direct paraphrase *327*	coping methods *335*
respect *324*	additive reflection *327*	adaptive stress *335*
genuineness *324*	crisis *335*	maladaptive stress *335*

Exercises

Exercise 1   The Empathic Manager

Category: Counseling/Coaching/Feedback

Objective: To help participants understand and practice empathy in counseling employees

Group Size: Groups of 3–5

Time Frame: 60–90 minutes

Materials: Handout 1 and Handout 2 for each participant.

Procedure:

1. Explain the effectiveness and use of empathy using Handout 1.

2. Divide participants into groups of 3–5.

3. Distribute Handout 2 and ask participants to work in their groups to uncover the emotions and feelings underlying the statements. When emotions are identified, ask them to write down empathic responses that reflect these emotions. Allow them enough time to examine carefully.

4. As a class, discuss each statement and come up with a list of effective responses as a manager who is counseling a subordinate.

***

EMPATHETIC MANAGER

Handout 1: Empathy

One of the effective communication skills used in counseling is empathy. Empathy is a way of communication where you identify, understand, and reflect the other person's feelings and behaviors from his or her point of view. Empathy in counseling is effective because it allows the individuals to open their feelings to the counselor. As a manager, using empathy in counseling your subordinates and colleagues will help you build effective working relationships.

Steps for exercising empathy in counseling

The first step in practicing empathy is to reflect the individual's emotions in your response to the statement or the behavior that is presented by him or her.

1. Listen carefully to the statement.
2. Listen carefully for the message that the individual is trying to communicate to you.
3. Look for the feelings and emotions that form the basis of what he or she is saying and/or doing. Study
   - choice of words
   - facial expressions
   - tone and pitch of voice
   - body language
   - eye contact.
4. Understand his or her feelings and emotions.
5. Communicate your understanding by reflecting his or her feelings and emotions identified.
   - Reflect emotions that are presented. For example, you can say,
     a. You are upset.
     b. You are happy.
     c. You feel a lot of stress.
     d. You think it will not work out.
   - Reflect emotions that are implied in behavioral statements. For example, you can say,
     a. You feel like punching him: implied emotion is anger.
     b. You feel like running away: implied emotion is anxiety.

(continued)

(continued)

    c. You feel like crying: implied emotion is sorrow or joy.

    d. You feel like hiding under the desk: implied emotion is embarrassment.

- Reflect emotions that are implied in experiences that are expressed by the individual. For example, you can say,

    a. You feel like you are being ignored: implied emotion is resentment.

    b. You feel like you are never going to get the job done: implied emotion is anxiety.

    c. You feel like all customers love you: implied emotion is joy.

    d. You feel like you may be transferred to another department: implied emotion is anxiety or excitement.

***

EMPATHETIC MANAGER

Handout 2: Scenarios

Scenario 1: Housekeeping Supervisor, male, 28 years old

I enjoy working at this hotel. The job is right for me and I feel like I do a good job. But when I look at myself in the future, I don't see myself getting anywhere. The best I can do is to become Assistant Housekeeping Manager at this hotel. And then what? I don't know much about Front Office, but one thing I know for sure is that I don't enjoy guest contact positions. I like being behind the scene, but this does not help me get anywhere. Should I start looking for something outside the Industry?

You are his boss.
What are the feelings and emotions that form the basis of his statement?

What can you say to him?

***

Scenario 2: Restaurant Manager, female, 35 years old

Recently, I am having problems with my subordinates. It seems to me that the morale in the restaurant has gone down the drain after I hired John, Assistant Manager. He is very aggressive and gets done what he needs to get done . . . sometimes upsetting other people. We are opening another restaurant in town and I am grateful for his help, and I really like his work. But others don't seem to feel that way. I am torn. I need his help to free myself up to do some work on the new restaurant, but employees are unhappy.

You are her colleague.
What are the feelings and emotions that form the basis of her statement?

What can you say to her?

***

Scenario 3: Sales Manager, male, 26 years old

"I am really in trouble. I am losing a lot of accounts recently. When I compare myself to Sherry—she joined the Sales department at the same time that I did—she does so much better. My boss threatens me that there will be no bonus for me this summer if my results don't improve. We just bought a house and we need money. I feel tired and overworked, and it shows. On the other hand, Sherry looks so confident and is having a great time both professionally and personally. It seems to me that she is favored by our boss for some reason or another. . . . it is very unfair."

You are his colleague.
What are the feelings and emotions that form the basis of his statement?

What can you say to him?

***

Scenario 4: Sous Chef, female, 35 years old

I am recently having problems sleeping. I have seen the doctor who gave me some pills, but still I am not sleeping very well. It affects my job, it affects my attitude at work. I feel grumpy and irritated all day. My colleagues don't seem to care how I feel. All they do is talk behind my back that I am being lazy. I don't have friends here anymore, but I don't care. But I can't quit, because I've got mouths to feed at home.

You are her boss.
What are the feelings and emotions that form the basis of her statement?

What can you say to her?

***

Source: Adapted from "Getting to the Heart of the Matter:" Baily, Roy, (1991). 50 *Activities for Developing Counseling Skills In Managers,* Amherst, MA: Human Resources Development Press.

Exercise 2   Zach & Zoë's Ice Cream Shoppe

Category: Providing Feedback

Objective: To learn how to have more effective managerial communications and how to provide constructive feedback

Number of Participants: 20

Time Frame: 50 minutes

Materials: One copy of the Zach & Zoë's case and one feedback form per participant

Procedure:

1. Distribute the Zach & Zoë's case and ask each participant to read it.

2. Ask two volunteers to role-play the two characters and to perform the ensuing scene.

3. Debrief and discuss the importance of providing constructive feedback to employees.

Discussion Questions:

- How could Lily Amber have better managed her employees?
- How could Lily have avoided this scenario with Cassie?
- How could Lily have improved her communication skills?

***

OBSERVER'S FEEDBACK FORM

A. Watch the role play carefully and make notes in the space provided below prior to the general review and discussion.

Lily Amber's Behavior & Comments	Cassie Mae's Behavior & Comments

(continued)

(continued)

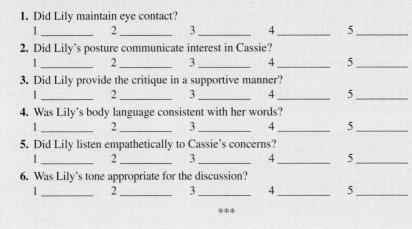

  B. Please indicate the appropriate rating, with "1" representing excellent and '5' poor.

    1. Did Lily maintain eye contact?

    1 _____   2 _____   3 _____   4 _____   5 _____

    2. Did Lily's posture communicate interest in Cassie?

    1 _____   2 _____   3 _____   4 _____   5 _____

    3. Did Lily provide the critique in a supportive manner?

    1 _____   2 _____   3 _____   4 _____   5 _____

    4. Was Lily's body language consistent with her words?

    1 _____   2 _____   3 _____   4 _____   5 _____

    5. Did Lily listen empathetically to Cassie's concerns?

    1 _____   2 _____   3 _____   4 _____   5 _____

    6. Was Lily's tone appropriate for the discussion?

    1 _____   2 _____   3 _____   4 _____   5 _____

***

ZACH & ZOË'S CASE

Actors: Lily Amber, Manager, Zach & Zoë's Ice Cream Shoppe

        Cassie Mae, Teenage Scooper, Zach & Zoë's Ice Cream Shoppe

Situation: Lily Amber is the Manager of two Zach & Zoë's Ice Cream Shoppes. Lily has been in this position for two years and supervises a total of 20 people (10 in each store), for day and night shifts. The scooper's responsibilities range from scooping ice cream, making the ice cream specialties, such as sundaes, shakes and cakes, and cleaning up. One of these scoopers is Cassie Mae.

    Cassie is an 18-year-old recent high school graduate. Cassie's prior work experience includes being a busgirl at a local family restaurant and selling jewelry in a small department store. Lily hired Cassie three months ago from among half a dozen job applicants. What impressed Lily about Cassie were (1) her plans to enroll in the local university; (2) her prior work experience; (3) references that reported Cassie as reliable, friendly, honest, and bright.

    Zach & Zoë's employees are on probation for their first three months, after which they are considered permanent. Cassie has completed the three-month probationary period and Lily is now required to give a performance review. It's 10:00 a.m., the Zach & Zoë's store is quiet, and Lily has asked Cassie to sit down at a table and talk.

Lily Amber's Role: Your job is hectic. Supervising two stores with a total of 20 employees allows little time for planning. You often feel that all you do each day is run around "putting out fires." Because of your hectic pace, you haven't had time to point out a few of Cassie's problems. As with other employees, you plan to use the three-month review as an opportunity to tell Cassie that her job performance has been satisfactory on the whole, but two things concern you. First, Cassie has long hair and is required by health regulations to wear it pulled back with a Zach & Zoë's baseball cap at all times. You've had to remind her four or five times to pull it back and put on the baseball cap. Second, you're aware that Cassie has been dating Justin—another employee at Zach & Zoe's. You don't consider the fact that they're dating to be your business, but what does concern you is that the two show demonstrative affection, such as kissing and caressing, toward each other while working behind the counter. You've decided to extend Cassie's probation for one more month. Based on Cassie's performance during the additional month probation, you will either give her the standard three-month raise of 50 cents an hour or terminate her employment.

Cassie Mae's Role: You've been on your job three months. You find it strange that your boss, Lily Amber, hasn't said one word to you about how well you've been performing. This lack of communication has been bothering you for a number of weeks, but you haven't brought it up because you think it's Lily's job to initiate such discussion. This lack of communication got so bad last week that you actually thought about quitting.

The only reason you didn't is that Justin—a coworker you've been dating—convinced you not to. Justin agreed with you that Lily is curt, thoughtless, and a poor communicator. But you think you've been doing a good job, especially since you mastered the cake-making technique, you like your coworkers, and the promotion opportunities at Zach & Zoë's are good. As you sit down to talk with Lily, you expect her to tell you that you're one of the best employees and that you can expect a pay raise of 50 cents (you are currently making minimum wage). After all, you are conscientious, energetic, and have memorized all the flavors and recipes for Zach & Zoë's signature ice cream specialties. The only comments Lily has ever made to you that could even be perceived as negative were on the few occasions that you forgot to wear your baseball hat to control your hair. Also, before you started dating Justin, you asked him to make sure that dating a coworker was not in violation of the Zach & Zoë's policies. He told you that it was not against the procedures and that many couples had in fact met at Zach & Zoë's.

Exercise 3   Counseling Role Playing

Objective: To have participants practice counseling in situations that will most likely occur during their management career

Procedure:

1. Hand out worksheet with each scenario and have participants sit in a circle.
2. Give the participants time to read and think about how they would play each role. Ask for seven volunteers to act out each scenario (two for the Greg and Jerry case, three for the Fred and Sam case, and two for the Ben and Lynn case).
3. Have the first set of role players stand within the circle.
4. Distribute the Feedback Handout and have the rest of the participants write down feedback for the managers in the scenarios that they will share after all of the scenarios have been acted out.

***

SCENARIO 1: GREG AND JERRY

Greg's Case

As he made his way to the kitchen, Greg pondered his impending talk with Jerry. It was so difficult to address the subject of personal hygiene in the workplace. His coworkers had approached Greg yesterday about Jerry's body odor. They were ill-at-ease complaining about it but said the problem was unbearable in the kitchen. Greg had often noticed a pungent odor in the kitchen. He had not realized that one individual was responsible for the problem and making the others unhappy. Greg now learned that productivity in the kitchen was suffering because coworkers refused to get close to Jerry. They feared that confronting Jerry about it might create hostility and resentment. Greg knew the responsibility was his, yet in his 14 years at the restaurant he had never had to deal with a situation like this one. He hoped his management expertise wouldn't fail him now.

Jerry's Case

Jerry knew that something was up. Greg, his supervisor in the kitchen at the restaurant, was on his way down to meet him. He had made it sound like it was no big deal—that meant it probably *was* a big deal. Jerry had no clue what it was about. He asked a few coworkers whether they had any idea, but they said they didn't. They acted a bit sheepish, though, and Jerry noticed they were in a hurry to end the conversation and get back to work. Come to think of it, that happened a lot. Jerry was still pondering his fate when Greg arrived in the kitchen. They went into the chef's office and Greg closed the door. Jerry wondered if his breath smelled okay.

***

SCENARIO 2: FRED AND SAM

Fred's Case

Your new MP3 player was in your locker at the start of your shift. You clearly remember locking it safely inside when you first arrived at work. At 4:30 p.m., you opened your locker to find that the player was missing. It had to be Sam who took the player. After all, this morning he was admiring it, saying how much he'd like to have one, but couldn't afford it. You demanded that Sam return the item to you, and he denies stealing it. Now, you're going straight to see the Dining Room Manager . . . and Sam's right behind you.

Sam's Case

Fred, your coworker in the main dining room, is accusing you (in a less-than-subtle tone) of stealing his MP3 player. This morning, in the locker room before work, you did tell Fred how much you want one (and that you cannot afford one right now). But you certainly didn't steal it. Perhaps he left it lying out instead of locking it away as he so "clearly" remembers. You wish you could help him locate it, but the truth is that you had nothing to do with the situation. If he can't keep track of his belongings, he shouldn't bring them to work! Fred demanded that you return the item, but you didn't take it! Now, he's going to the Dining Room Manager's office . . . and you're right behind him.

***

SCENARIO 3: BEN AND LYNN

Ben's Case

Ben knew how to take a hint. He also knew how to give one, and when he began hinting to Lynn that it was time for her to retire, he wasn't satisfied that the message had gotten through. That was six months ago, and now it was time for another performance review. Ben's strategy had been to urge Lynn gently but firmly to relinquish some responsibility, work fewer hours, and shorten her work week by a day or two. The idea was to ease her gradually out of the restaurant. Lynn had joined the Pelson Restaurant 40 years ago and had been highly esteemed by its founder. But her star had been fading for several years. Her drive to excel was diminishing, her memory was failing, and her attitude was increasingly apathetic. What's more her technical expertise was more or less obsolete. Still she resisted Ben's attempts to phase her out diplomatically. Ben was not willing to allow Lynn to stay on indefinitely. A dynamic employee was waiting in the wings to assume Lynn's position. If it were not made available soon, the employee planned to seek career opportunities elsewhere. Ben knows that Lynn has considerable pension funds, so money is not the issue. He decides to adopt a stern tone with Lynn at her performance review.

Lynn's Case

Lynn dreaded her upcoming performance review with Ben. At her last review six months ago, they had tried to set her on the road to retirement. It's a safe bet they would try again today and even more forcefully. Lynn was aware that some of her spark had gone out in the last few years. She could never match the productivity she had achieved in those first pioneering years at the Pelson Restaurant. But she felt she knew the restaurant and the industry better than anyone else on the payroll. If the founder were still alive he'd back her up on that 100 percent. Instead, these young Turks on the executive staff thought they had all the answers. Lynn could teach them a thing or two about management! Lynn realized she was the last of the old guard at the Pelson. Ben was a decent supervisor and Lynn didn't want to create a scene at the performance review. Nevertheless,

(continued)

(continued)

she was unwilling to be put out to pasture. She felt she deserved more courtesy and respect than that. Besides, what was waiting for her in retirement? Quilting bees? Mahjongg? Taking in stray cats?

***

Feedback Handout

1. At the beginning, how did the manager make the employee comfortable?

2. How did the manager show empathy in his or her counseling?

3. What were the indications that the manager was listening to the employee?

4. Would you change any of the vocabulary the manager used during the counseling session?

5. Did the manager schedule a follow-up meeting?

***

Exercise 4   Jade Hotels Case

Category: Coaching/Counseling

Objective: To develop counseling skills and to provide constructive feedback

Number of Participants: 20 participants

Time Frame: 50 minutes

Materials: One copy of the Jade Hotels case and one feedback form per participant.

Procedure:

1. Distribute the Jade Hotels case and ask each participant to read it.

2. Ask two volunteers to role-play the two characters and to act the ensuing scene.

3. Debrief and discuss the importance of providing constructive feedback to employees.

Discussion Questions:

- How could Morgan Kase have been a more encouraging manager?
- How could management provide continual improvement initiatives for employees?
- Why is active listening an important attribute for a manager?

***

OBSERVER'S FEEDBACK FORM

A. Watch the role play carefully and make notes in the space provided below prior to the general review and discussion.

Morgan Kase's Behavior & Comments	Alex Wicker's Behavior & Comments

B. Please indicate the appropriate rating scale, such that '1' represents excellent and '5' poor.

1. Did Morgan approach Alex in a supportive manner? Did he put her at ease?

1 _____ 2 _____ 3 _____ 4 _____ 5 _____

2. Was the problem stated directly and objectively?

1 _____ 2 _____ 3 _____ 4 _____ 5 _____

3. Did Morgan highlight Alex's strengths along with stating the problem?

1 _____ 2 _____ 3 _____ 4 _____ 5 _____

4. Did Morgan encourage Alex to communicate and explain her behavior?

1 _____ 2 _____ 3 _____ 4 _____ 5 _____

5. Was Morgan open with suggestions to improve the situation?

1 _____ 2 _____ 3 _____ 4 _____ 5 _____

6. Did Morgan set a follow-up time and date for a progress meeting?

1 _____ 2 _____ 3 _____ 4 _____ 5 _____

***

JADE HOTELS CASE

Actors: Morgan Kase, Regional Corporate Sales Manager, Jade Hotels

Alex Wicker, Corporate Sales Manager, Jade Hotels, SF

Situation: Morgan Kase is the Regional Corporate Sales Manager of the northwestern territory for Jade Hotels, which totals five hotels in California and Oregon. Based in LA, Morgan oversees 10 corporate sales managers and 15 corporate sales assistant managers. Since Jade Hotels occupies an exclusive, small, upscale business travelers' niche, the sales managers and assistant managers must work closely to secure a high level of customer satisfaction.

Alex Wicker is one of these assistant sales managers and has been in the San Francisco property for two years. Before that she worked as a sales manager for a large franchise hotel company. Morgan Kase has been the Regional Corporate Sales Manager for 12 months. Prior to this, Morgan was the top-producing corporate sales manager for the San Francisco property.

Morgan Kase's Role: You have not been pleased with Alex's job performance, so you decided to review her performance file. Alex's first six-month review stated: "Enthusiastic. A bit unorganized but willing to learn. She is bright and seems to have a lot of potential." A year after, her supervisor had written, "Alex seems to be losing interest and seems very unorganized. Often short with clients. Did not mention these problems to her previously. Hope that Alex will improve because long-term commitment and potential in question."

You have not spent much time with Alex. With headquarters in Los Angeles and Alex at the San Francisco property, your offices are far apart and you have little interaction. The real reason for your weak rapport, however, is probably that Alex is not the easiest person to talk to and you have little in common. When you accepted the Regional Sales position, you decided to wait some time before moving to Los Angeles to make sure everyone at the San Francisco office had a good grasp of the accounts and knowledge of the client base.

But Alex's problems have gotten too visible to ignore. She is consistently missing quarterly sales projections. Based on total sales, Alex is your lowest performer and her month-end reports are constantly late. After reviewing last month's performance reports, you made an appointment to meet her today at 9:00 a.m. at her office. Unfortunately, Alex was not in her office when you arrived for the appointment. You waited 15 minutes and then gave up. Alex's administrative assistant tells you that she regularly comes in late for work in the morning and takes very long coffee breaks in the afternoon.

Last week, Bettine Herman, Alex's fellow assistant sales manager, complained that Alex's behavior was demoralizing to her and to some of the other sales managers.

You don't want to fire Alex. Finding a replacement in the current tight labor market would be very difficult. Moreover, Alex's strong personal contacts with the hi-tech industry have resulted in strong accounts for Jade Hotels. The accounts Alex has opened have generated about 60 percent of the SF property's overall business. If Alex were to leave Jade Hotels and go to a competitor, she would probably convince the accounts to follow her to her new place of employment.

Alex Wicker's Role: Corporate hotel sales have been pretty profitable for you. From your previous job at the franchise hotel, you developed many contacts with hi-tech firms. You cultivated these relationships and brought these accounts to Jade Hotels. In fact, probably 60 percent of the major accounts have been

from these accounts and others with whom you have personal ties.

Although your hi-tech clients and friends provide you with a lot of business, you realized early in your first year at Jade Hotels that Corporate Hotel Sales required more sophisticated communication, financial, and computer skills. You never acquired these skills, because immediately after high school you became a wife and mother. Most of the other sales managers are college-educated and some even have MBA's. You have been too embarrassed to ask for help because you are older than most of the other sales managers. Consequently, it takes you a bit longer than the other managers to write memos and letters to clients, and to complete the month-end reports, whose format requires the integration of Word and Excel.

To try to get up to speed, you have enrolled in an 8:00 a.m. extension course in Microsoft Office Suite at the local community college. While this course makes you about a half hour late for work three times a week, you believe that in the long run it will be worth it. You are hoping that the business communications course you signed up for will have equal payoff.

You are working on it in the evenings and during your breaks at work.

At the moment, all of this is a bit overwhelming and you have fallen a little behind in your work. You overheard some of the other sales managers discussing your lack of teamwork a couple of weeks ago, but you're too busy with coursework to worry about that. Besides, once you finish the courses, you know you'll be right up there with the best of them. For now, you are still pulling your weight with the hi-tech accounts. In fact, you are taking an accelerated sales course during the weekends to increase your skills and position yourself to become a Corporate Sales Manager within the next six months.

Bettine Herman, the sales manager whose office is adjacent to yours, mentioned that your supervisor, Morgan Kase, was at your office today for a 9:00 a.m. appointment that Morgan had scheduled yesterday. You went to your class as usual and completely forgot about the meeting. Fortunately, Morgan is up from Los Angeles all day and you reschedule another appointment in 30 minutes to see what she wanted to discuss with you.

Endnotes

Anonymous. (December 2006). Employee financial concerns can affect employers' bottom line. *Tri-State Defender*, 55(52), 13–15.

Armour, S. (October 5, 2005). Money worries hinder job performance. *USA Today*. Money 1B.

Beckwith, R. (January 2, 2007). A new lifeline helps the poor stay on the job: Child care, transportation, legal help to be coordinated. *Knight Ridder Tribune Business News*, 1–2.

Bushweller, K. (2005). Counselors want aid to help gay students. *Education Week*, 24(20), 12–14.

Campbell, M. (April 2, 2006). Substance abuse costly to employers. *Knight Ridder Tribune Business News*, 1–2.

Carkhuff, R. R. (1969). *Helping and Human Relations*. Vol. 1. New York: Holt, Rinehart & Winston.

Collison, Brooke B. (1978). The Mrs. Lincoln response. *Personnel and Guidance Journal*, 180–182.

Devaragan, R. (2004). Counseling in the corporate context. *Business Line*, 1.

Elliott, K. & Shelley, K. (2005). Impact of employee assistance programs on substance abusers and workplace safety. *Journal of Employment Counseling*, 42(3), 125–133.

Grensing-Pophal, L. (2003). Aging America. *Credit Union Management*, 26(1), 40–44.

Hafer, F. & Blume, E. R. (2002). The growing cost of doing nothing. *Electric Perspectives*, 25(1), 36–44.

Johnson, Pamela R. & Gardner, S. (1999). Domestic violence and the workplace: developing a company response. *The Journal of Management Development*, 18(7), 590.

Joo, S. & Grable, J. E. (2000). Improving employee productivity: The role of financial counseling and education. *Journal of Employment Counseling*, 37(1), 2–16.

McIntosh, J. (2006). US suicide data for 2004. *American Association of Suicidology Final Annual Report*.

National Drug-Free Work Place Alliance. Drug Use Facts. Retrieved January 29, 2008 from the World Wide Web: http://www.ndfwa.org/

NIMH. (1999). MHIC: Mental illness and the family: Mental health statistics. *National Mental Health Association*. Available at: <http://www.nmha.org/infoctr/factsheets/15.cfm>

(December 6, 2003). Wellness programs: Online poll shows only 9 percent of employees enroll in corporate wellness programs. *Obesity, Fitness and Wellness Week*, 36–37.

O'Reilly, S. (2007). Not tonight, darling. *Personnel Today*, 12.

Owens, D. (2006). EAPs for a diverse world. *HR Magazine*, 51(10), 91–95.

Rives, K. (September 24, 2004). Firms' employee assistance programs branch into providing financial advice. *Knight Ridder Tribune Business News*, 3.

Rogers, C. (1961). *On Becoming a Person: A Therapist's View of Psychotherapy*. London: Constable.

Rosenblum, G. (April 2, 2007). Divorce: Women who walk. *Knight Ridder Tribune Business News*, 1.

Schaitberger, B. & Dell, P. (2007). Financial, EAP counseling can improve fiscal, physical health. *Employee Benefit News*, 1.

Shepherd, L. (2006). Mental illness exacts a high financial, human toll. *Employee Benefit News*, 3.

Shumway, S., Bell, M., & Arredondo, R. (2006). Financial planners and employee assistance programs: An opportunity for practice building. *Journal of Personal Finance*, 5(1), 26–37.

Strazewski, L. (2005). Investing in EAPs—Employee assistance programs. *Rough Notes*, 148(7), 52–55.

Wasmer A. L. (2005). Coping with divorce. *HR Magazine*, 50(5), 58–64.

13

POWER AND POLITICS IN HOSPITALITY ORGANIZATIONS

Power is America's last dirty word. It is easier to talk about money—and much easier to talk about sex—than it is to talk about power. People who have it deny it; people who want it do not want to appear hungry for it; and people who engage in its machinations do so secretly.

—Rosabeth Moss Kanter

CHAPTER OUTLINE

Introduction

Power and its Attributes
    Definitions of Power
    Influence versus Power
    Attaining Power
    The Nature of Power

Approaches to Power
    Rational Approach
    Critical Contingencies Approach
    Strategic Contingencies Approach
    Organizational Culture Approach

Going from Powerful to Powerless
    Overemphasizing Credentials
    Unclear Wants
    Confluence

Going from Powerless to Powerful
    Personal Power Characteristics
    Positional Power Characteristics

Types of Power (Power Bases)
    Legitimate Power (Authority)
    Reward Power
    Coercive Power
    Expert Power
    Referent Power

Outcomes of Using Different Power Bases
    Outcomes of Power
        Commitment
        Compliance
        Resistance
    Understand Power Bases

Organizational Politics
    Political Tactics
        Control information and resources
        Cultivate favorable impressions
        Gain support of others
        Align oneself with others more powerful
    Benefits and Disadvantages of Organizational Power
        Negative outcomes of power
        Positive outcomes of power

Empowering Others
  The benefits of sharing power
  Ways power can be shared
  Examples of organizations that empower

Summary

LEARNING OBJECTIVES

After reading this chapter, you will be able to do the following:

1. Compare and contrast the four approaches to power: rational, critical contingencies, strategic contingencies, and cultural.
2. Describe three ways a manager can go from being powerful to powerless.
3. Name four personal characteristics that foster power.
4. List the five characteristics of one's position within an organization that may impact the attainment of power.
5. Identify and explain each of the five power bases.
6. Explain which motivational outcomes will likely result from the use of each of the five power bases.
7. Discuss five ways a manager or supervisor can empower others within the organization.

Scenario: Climbing the Ladder

Nadia had worked hard as a new Assistant Front Desk Manager at The Wave, an upscale resort hotel on the coast. She realized that very few senior managers were women, and was determined to climb the ladder of success in this 800-room property. Her ultimate goal was to be corporate VP of Human Resources, although she realized that there would be a lot of hard work between her current job and her dream.

When Nadia first arrived, it was obvious to her that she would need to make friends with some of the other managers who might be in positions to help her career path. She wasted no time in finding out when the Front Desk Manager went to lunch and made sure that their paths crossed. She got to know those in other departments as well so that when it came time to select employees for special recognition she was confident everyone would know who she was. She was always conscious of the image she presented, and carefully managed impressions through her clothes and internal communications.

Soon Nadia's deliberate efforts paid off, and when, within six months of her employment, the Front Desk Manager was made Rooms Division Manager, she was promoted to his position. The next year she was made Rooms Division Manager, working with a team of many direct reports. Everyone at The Wave knew of Nadia—if not personally, then they had heard stories about what she had accomplished. As Rooms Division Manager, she consistently secured resources for her department by aligning herself with other managers who had promised to support her proposals. She was influential in almost all major decisions, from the renovation of the south wing of the property to providing suggestions for marketing campaigns.

(continued)

(continued)

Once Nadia's influence was secure, she began to do favors for her "friends" and others who had helped her meet her goals. She was able to sway the Executive Committee by reaching out to several of its members in advance of important decision-making meetings. Soon, it was a known fact that in order to have any proposal succeed you would need to make sure you had Nadia's approval. When anyone challenged her authority, there were consequences. The inability to criticize or disagree with any idea Nadia supported soon resulted in less active participation by other members of the Executive Committee. Resentment built, but everyone was afraid to speak up.

Nadia recognized her power and enjoyed it. She was a high risk taker and worked hard to make The Wave one of the best resort hotels in the area. Soon her accomplishments were recognized by the corporate office, and the Regional Manager made frequent visits to get her opinion on plans that would affect the entire chain. The writing was on the wall—it was only a matter of time before she would realize her dream of getting into the corporate suite.

After reading this chapter, you will be able to answer these questions about the opening scenario:

1. Give examples of how Nadia went about increasing her power.
2. Do you think she was ethical in her approach to getting ahead?
3. If you were a new front desk employee at The Wave when she was Reservations Manager, how do you expect you would feel about Nadia?
4. Do you feel that it is generally helpful or harmful for someone to have such a significant amount of power in an organization?
5. Do you imagine that the organization benefited or was harmed by Nadia's influence? Give examples of how she might affect both the hotel's reputation as well as its culture and human resource function.

INTRODUCTION

Power. The word conjures up different images for different people: influence, fear, natural power like the thundering waterfall, the roaring hurricane, the cataclysmic earthquake. As the opening quote suggests, "power" may indeed be America's last dirty word. But where did this negative image come from? Some theorists suggest that it arises from our experiences of being hurt by a boss, parent, or lover who has wielded power over us. In fact, the United States was born out of a rebellion against power.

But people also recognize that power is an essential ingredient in our society. They realize that leaders in all facets of society, whether the president of a university or of a country, must have power in order to lead. This amalgam of positive and negative connotations has resulted in ambivalent attitudes toward power.

Steven Spielberg's *Schindler's List,* one of the most moving films ever made about the Holocaust in Nazi Germany, demonstrates the ambivalent nature of power in its application. *Schindler's List* is based on the true story of Oskar Schindler, who was born in the Austrian

Empire and became a member of the Nazi party. Schindler took full advantage of his power and influence to save the lives of more than 1,000 Jews who would otherwise have been sent to death camps. Oskar Schindler attempts to wield his influence over Amon Goeth, an especially brutal Nazi commander who held authority in several death camps throughout World War II, by explaining the noble use of power. Schindler says to Goeth:

> Power is when we have every justification to kill—and we don't. That's power. That's what the emperors had. A man stole something, he's brought in before the emperor, he throws himself down on the floor, he begs for mercy, he knows he's going to die . . . and the emperor pardons him. This worthless man. He lets him go. That's power. That's power.

In the film, Goeth considers this proposition about the nature of power, but cannot find it convincing enough to stop him from exercising his power through killing. After the war, the real Goeth was tried and executed for crimes against humanity. Schindler, on the other hand, was honored with a tree planted in his name on the Avenue of the Righteous in Jerusalem (*Schindler's List*). These kinds of stories demonstrate the vast potential that power has to bring about change, but also show that power can take vastly different directions. In *Power and the Corporate Mind,* Zaleznik and Kets de Vries (1975) express society's ambivalence toward power:

> Power is an ugly word. It connotes dominance and submission, control and acquiescence, one man's will at the expense of another man's self-esteem. . . . Yet it is power, the ability to control and influence others that provides the basis for the direction of organizations and for the attainment of social goals. Leadership is the exercise of power.

This suggests that the key to understanding power is to realize that power is a dimension of leadership. Pfeffer (1992) has argued that many organizations suffer because they have accepted the negative connotations of power and have slipped into passivity. Pfeffer contends that because power contains the potential to be a destructive or productive force, people must learn to understand it and manage it. The proper use of power requires the embrace of a moral universe that controls the destructive potential, but takes advantage of power's potential to create positive results.

In this chapter we examine several different aspects of power. We will first establish a definition of power, and later examine some attributes of power. We will then focus on four general approaches to departmental power. We will take a look at powerlessness and how to avoid it. We will also examine the five main types of power and the responses they typically elicit, and follow with a discussion of the three organizational sources of power. Next, we will discuss the need to share power within organizations to maintain relationships that can increase leaders' power and influence throughout the organization. We will conclude by providing today's managers with some tips on using power to get things done, while avoiding the traps associated with the exercise of power.

What images come to your mind when you think of "power?" What have been the experiences that led you to that response?

POWER AND ITS ATTRIBUTES

Definitions of Power

Let's first establish a workable definition of power. It is important to realize that there are as many definitions of power as there are instances when it is used. We will use a definition established by R. A. Dahl, a pioneer in the field of power. Dahl (1957) defined **power** using this scenario: "A has power over B to the extent that he can get B to do something B would not otherwise do."

Influence versus Power

Kyle was having a difficult time getting things done. He reasoned that his employees were the problem. For the most part, they had a careless attitude toward their work. They did what they could get away with. When he arranged trainings for them, they did not seem to implement the strategies and certainly not the attitudes that Kyle wanted. Kyle complained, "I've worked hard to get to my position. I went to an excellent college. I have a terrific resume. I used networking to achieve this position. I am in charge of all of food and beverage for this hotel. I have power and authority, but these people make me look like a complete failure!"

Martha, one of the food prep workers, had a different point of view. "Oh, King Kyle. He certainly seems to enjoy acting like he's in charge, but who does all the work around here? Did he ever work in a kitchen? I doubt it. He is full of innovative ideas that take up too much time or just plain don't work. I have children older than he is. Just because he got the job doesn't mean he knows what he's doing. Estelle, the cook, runs things in the kitchen. She's been here for 18 years and she really knows what's going on. When Kyle tells us to do something we act like we agree, and then we go see how Estelle wants it done. Kyle went to a seminar for a week and, actually, it was an improvement. But if Estelle is out sick for even a day, the whole place falls apart.

It is also useful to differentiate between influence and power. In the case above, Kyle had power, but the cook Estelle seemed to have all the influence. **Influence,** then, is using power bring about desired results. Access to decision-making processes causes individuals, or groups, to have varying degrees of impact. When the impact leads to the acceptance of the final decision, it has become power.

Let's think about how power, **authority,** and influence might work in a hotel. The general manager of a hotel gives input to the food and beverage director on how to handle a catered event. If the F&B director considers the general manager's advice in his decision-making process, it is assumed that the general manager has a degree of influence with him, which stems at least partly from her formal authority over the F&B manager's actions. When the general manager's advice becomes his final decision on a regular basis, then the general manager has established power over her subordinate. Keep in mind that power is neither good nor bad; power simply *is*. It is, rather, how the power is used that is perceived as being either good or bad. Manipulation is bad, but we need not feel that power is corruptive.

Would you rather have influence, or power? Explain.

Attaining Power

Although some people complain that thin, beautiful people get more respect and more power over others, research shows that there is much more involved in attaining power. For example, leaders learn to capitalize on others' natural tendency to defer to experts or authorities, using their leadership skills to gain power (Cialdini and Goldstein, 2002). As Pfeffer (1992) reminds us, because power can be used for any variety of purposes, responsible leaders should know both how to use power well and how to recognize and counter the irresponsible exercise of power. We suggest that you learn about power management so you can use power to your advantage and defend yourself and your organization against the misuse of power.

The Nature of Power

Is the amount of power in the world limited? The historical viewpoint of power is that it is fixed in nature. This theory, also referred to as the zero-sum quantity, implies that if one individual gains power, then another must lose the same amount. However, theorists have developed a different concept, claiming that power is elastic or infinite in nature (Parsons, 1963). This theory allows individuals to accumulate power, but not at the expense of others.

Does power have to be exercised to exist? Dahl (1957) says the presence of potential power assumes that power does not have to be exercised to exist. Other theories revolve around a behavioral perspective that states that the existence of power depends strictly on observable behaviors, or actual power. Wrong (1995) combines potential and actual power into a concept he refers to as capacity, whereby an individual (or group) can possess power without exercising it, as long as it is believed that they will exercise it. Consequently, capacity is dependent on previous actions of power.

APPROACHES TO POWER

Rational Approach

There are four general approaches to power. The rational approach as established by Weber (1949) is based on hierarchical authority. Authority and the distribution of power in this approach are based upon the organizational chart. Hence, the general manager has power over (or more power than) the front desk manager; and the front desk manager has power over the front desk assistant. While it is true that authority is always distributed according to the organizational chart, is actual power distributed the same way? We must differentiate between authority and power. While authority can be defined as the *right* to control the actions of others, power is the *ability* to control the actions of others (DuBrin, 1981). An individual's position within the organizational hierarchy or his or her expertise in a particular area creates authority, but it may or may not create power. That is, a person who holds an authoritative position can be powerful or powerless, depending upon how he or she engages personality factors and other power bases.

Conversely, powerful people within organizations do not always hold positions of authority. Although the secretary of a department may hold one of the lowest positions of authority, if that secretary falls ill or refuses to cooperate with you, you may well find that accomplishing any simple task becomes nearly impossible. In dealing with a potential employer, insulting the secretary is one of the surest ways to guarantee that you won't get an interview. The word of caution here is to remember that the people in authority are not necessarily the people who hold the most power in an organization.

"But how do you know for sure you've got power unless you abuse it?"

Think of someone you have known, or know of, who does not have authority but does have power. How is that possible?

Critical Contingencies Approach

These sorts of conflicts inspired Pfeffer and Salancik to devise a theory that is more political in nature. Their critical contingencies approach uses a situational model to explain power. They state that the person or department that acquires power is the one that is most able to cope with the critical problems and uncertainties that face, for example, a legal firm (Salancik and Pfeffer, 1977). In the event of a big lawsuit, the legal department would gain power over organizational decisions, since they are most apt to deal with this critical problem. Their power may begin to supersede their previous boundaries and enter into other organizational areas such as product development and operations. Through time, the head of the legal department may become the head of the organization, just as the vice president of marketing becomes president when market share is a problem, or the vice president of finance becomes president when there is a recession.

Strategic Contingencies Approach

Hickson et al. (1981) have advanced a model of strategic contingencies, in which people gain power because they:

1. help reduce the level of others' uncertainty;
2. have a high degree of centrality in the organization; and
3. perform duties that are indispensable to the organization to gain power.

The strategic position of those critical employees increases their visibility in dealing with urgent and pressing organizational problems. This visibility increases their potential power, but may or may not help them attain unlimited advancement. For more information on the uncertainties in this equation, see our section on the potential pitfalls of expert power.

Organizational Culture Approach

Whereas the critical contingencies and strategic contingencies models rely on the theory that the external environment determines who has power, the cultural model depends on an internal source. The cultural model states that the department that has values that are congruent with those of top management will be the department with the most power. If your hotel's top management is all about the bottom line, then the marketing department may have the most power.

In hospitality organizations, which department would you suspect has values that are most congruent with those of top management?

GOING FROM POWERFUL TO POWERLESS

How do you learn to become powerful? Power is a natural state; no one has to be taught to be powerful. Look, for instance, at children under the age of six.

Children are clear about what they want. Even before they learn to speak, they cry, point gesture, and fuss until they have obtained what they want. Even older children do not cooperate with adults that offer no reward. Children are not coy about their motivations: they gloat when they get what they want and pout when they do not receive it. They can be tenacious strategists when confronted with an obstacle that prevents them from getting what they want. They will begin by asking, maybe pestering, then move on to crying, pouting, tantrums, or even trickery. If something is wanted badly enough, a child will not stop pursuing it until the objective is either obtained or irrevocably blocked.

If power is a natural state, then why do so many people see themselves and others as powerless? As children are raised into adults, we teach them manners, cooperation, and submissiveness to authority. Part of moving from childhood to adulthood is a resumption of responsibility and power. So as children and young adults, we all learn to surrender power to varying degrees. In the following section, we discuss three ways people in management continue to disempower themselves.

Overemphasizing Credentials

Overemphasizing credentials refers to responding inappropriately to other people's credentials. Credentials can take many forms, such as organizational rank, academic degrees, real or implied experience, and status. And the moment you allow the so-called expert to make decisions for you, you have thoroughly disempowered yourself. One should seek the advice of credentialed consultants, but retain the decision-making responsibility and power. When seeking an opinion from an individual with credentials, listen to what the individual has to say but choose to agree, disagree, or modify the opinion. The individual who takes credit for the final decision retains the power, regardless of the decision and who initially suggested it. In this context the popular aphorism, "Knowledge is power," can be translated to Decision is power.

Give an example of where you have listened to an expert for his or her opinion, but have kept the option of making the final choice yourself. In that situation, did you have "power"?

Unclear Wants

Many people are powerless to get what they want because they do not know what they want. They do not take the time to think about their needs and goals; they often act spontaneously. In the hospitality industry, for example, the food and beverage director may originally say that he wants more employees in order to provide better customer service. However, once he hires the additional employees, he may realize that in spite of an abundance of employees in the dining room, the customers are still receiving poor service. The manager did not *want* more employees; he wanted better customer service, which could have been accomplished through additional training. The food and beverage director may have lost the power to get additional training after he mistakenly hired more employees. Managers should take time to figure out exactly what it is they want or risk losing power within the organization.

Confluence

Confluence typically refers to an area where two separate bodies of water join to make a third body. **Confluence** basically means coming together. Upstream you can identify two distinct bodies of water, but once you get to the area of confluence, you can't tell from which upstream body a water molecule came. This principle applies to people within an organization. Individual employees tend to support group effectiveness by showing individual strength in energy, creativity, and risk-taking. Confluence occurs whenever the benefits of confluence—feelings of security, belonging, and calm—trump the importance of individual self-awareness. There is a temptation especially among those new to management to fall into the trap of confluence. A new manager might try to befriend his employees and in the process transfer power away from himself, a process that benefits neither the manager nor the employees.

GOING FROM POWERLESS TO POWERFUL

The hospitality industry is unique in that we put the customer at the top. "The customer is always right." A hospitality manager must perform an unusual balancing act by accommodating the customer and maintaining authority over the staff. Whetten and Cameron (2002) have discussed a number of characteristics that guide the level of power an individual can attain. These attributes fall into two broad categories: personal and positional.

Personal Power Characteristics

Personal power characteristics are particularly important to the hospitality industry, where so much of what we provide is personal in nature. According to Whetten and Cameron, four main personal characteristics (PEEL) foster power:

- *Personal Attraction*—The affective appeal exuded by that person, which may involve charisma.
- *Expertise*—The cognitive abilities and specific knowledge the individual possesses.
- *Effort*—The demonstration that the individual is committed to a particular course of action.
- *Legitimacy*— The credibility of the individual attempting to gain power.

Positional Power Characteristics

In conjunction with these personal characteristics, factors relating to one's position can also play a significant role in an individual's ability to achieve power. The characteristics of one's position that may impact the attainment of power are as follows:

- *Centrality*—The individual's level of access to information within the network.
- *Criticality*—The impact of the tasks performed within the organization's larger goals.
- *Flexibility*—The amount of discretion and independent decision making given to individuals holding the position.
- *Visibility*—The extent to which influential people see the task, its results, and the person responsible for its accomplishment as linked.
- *Relevance*—The fit between the task and the priorities of the organization (Whetten and Cameron, 2002).

By honing your personal leadership skills, as well as paying attention to how you can make the most of your position within the organization, you can increase your power potential. Review the opening scenario. Compare Nadia's tactics with the concepts described in these last two sections. See if you can identify her strategies. We now turn to an examination of the various bases by means of which power can be exercised.

> Look at the positional power characteristics again. Which do you anticipate will be easy for you to master? Which will be more difficult?

TYPES OF POWER (POWER BASES)

How do people exercise power? French and Raven (1959) have identified five distinct types of power, or power bases.

Legitimate Power (Authority)

Legitimate power (authority) is the legitimate right of the leader to make certain types of requests due to their structural position in the organization. For example, the general manager tells the front desk manager to improve his attitude. The general manager gives the order comfortably knowing that her organizational position allows her that power (even though it may not be an effective way to handle the situation).

Reward Power

Reward power refers to the leader's control of rewards that are valued by the subordinates. Reward power is often used as a device of motivation for salesmen, who get a certain percentage commission on what they sell. The reward does not always have to be money. One way a hotel manager can use reward power is by keeping track of how many days each employee arrives late to work, and if an employee is on time every day for the year the manager can give him an extra week off. When a general manager was asked how he justified this reward, he explained that he had once worked for a hotel that did not monitor the arrival of its employees, resulting in an informal five- to ten-minute grace period and poor guest service. He calculated that by coming to work five minutes late each day, an employee misses more than five days by the end of the year. He said, "I'll give them the five days off if I can count on them to be on time to serve the guests." In order to make use of reward power, managers must have authority over sufficient resources to direct the distribution of rewards.

Coercive Power

Coercive power is the leader's control over punishments. Although exercising coercive power rarely results in increased employee performance, there are times when it may be acceptable. One hospital has a policy that states, "If you are going to be late, don't bother coming back—ever." This strategy differs greatly from the reward power situation above, but so does the situation. Coercive power includes the use of force, which depending upon the leader's position could mean anything from a bad report noted on an employee's record to the invasion of a country that refuses to comply with another country's wishes. Certain types of bullying, harassment, and victimization involve the use of coercive power as a display of physical power. When people think of the negative aspects of power, coercive power, which tends to be unpopular, comes to the fore.

Expert Power

Expert power is the leader's task-relevant knowledge and competence as perceived by the employees. The recognition that an individual commands a specialized area of knowledge leads others to seek his or her advice in that particular area. Individuals can rise quickly in an organization by having expertise in a particular area of the company's need. However, this power may be limited by changes in the company's needs and by the danger that the individual may become "stuck" at a particular level because of his or her expertise. This is similar to the experience of actors and actresses who excel in one sort of role or character and subsequently experience difficulty in securing different types of roles. Use expert power in conjunction with other power bases in order to minimize this effect; remind others that you are not a "one-trick pony."

Referent Power

Referent power is the subordinate's loyalty to the leader and the desire to please that leader. A supervisor reported that he worked one summer in a restaurant for a general manager who was excellent at using referent power. The employees would do anything for the general manager, who had an uncanny knack for making people feel good about themselves. When they did a job well, he would let them know about it, and also let everyone else know. His employees always did their best to please him, no matter how trivial the task (French and Raven, 1959). Referent power also includes the employee's recognition that the leader can either help or hurt his or her future prospects by making recommendations to others within the organization, or to other potential employers.

Which type of power do you find most interesting? Give an example of two of the different types described.

OUTCOMES OF USING DIFFERENT POWER BASES

Research by Yukl and Taber (1983) revealed that the majority of effective leaders rely mostly upon expert and referent power to influence subordinates. Effectiveness of leadership can be seen through employee satisfaction and work performance.

Outcomes of Power

After the leader has used one of the five power bases, the motivational outcome can be classified according to whether it results in commitment, compliance, or resistance in the subordinate. Yukl and Taber also define each of the classifications as follows:

COMMITMENT   Commitment is the ideal result of a leader's power. When employees are committed, they are enthusiastic about carrying out the leader's requests and make a maximum effort to do so. Committed employees see their goals in alignment with the leader's requests and feel confident about the leader's ability to make decisions and recommendations for action.

COMPLIANCE   When an employee complies, it is only a partly successful outcome of the leader's power. Subordinates go along with the leader's requests without necessarily accepting the leader's goals. They are not very enthusiastic and make only the minimal effort required. They lack confidence in the leader's vision and in the potential outcome of his effort. Nevertheless, they do not actively oppose the leader's requests.

RESISTANCE   Resistance, as most managers can attest, is a clearly unsuccessful outcome. Subordinates reject the leader's goals and may pretend to comply, but actually attempt to delay or sabotage the task.

As figure 13.1 clearly illustrates, expert and referent power tend to result in employee commitment, legitimate and reward power tend to result in employee compliance, and coercive power tends to result in employee resistance. Yukl and Taber, however, are quick to point out the limitation of their study: it overlooks the leader's skill in exercising the power. They assert that the result or outcome will depend as much on the leader's skill in applying the different power bases as on the actual type of power used. They say it is quite possible that expert and referent power could result merely in compliance or even resistance if not used skillfully. By the same token, authority and reward power could result in subordinate commitment when used in an appropriate situation by a leader with the charisma and skill to make the best use of these bases of power. Other researchers have also agreed that the exercise of power can lead to conflict with employees.

> Which type of power listed in Figure 13.1 seems most effective? Do you agree with the conclusions of the grid regarding the degree to which each fosters commitment, compliance, and resistance? If you had to choose, would you rather have commitment or compliance from your employees?

Power Source	Commitment	Compliance	Resistance
Legitimate Power	Possible	LIKELY	Possible
Reward Power	Possible	LIKELY	Possible
Coercive Power	Unlikely	Possible	LIKELY
Expert Power	LIKELY	Possible	Possible
Referent Power	LIKELY	Possible	Possible

FIGURE 13.1   Outcomes that result from different types of power (Yukl and Taber, 1983)

Understand Power Bases

Rahim et al. (2001) argue that the power bases are interrelated, and that the types of situations in which these types of power are exercised may influence their effectiveness and potential to create conflict. Yukl and Taber also emphasize the importance of situation in the utilization of different types of power. It is misleading to draw the conclusion that expert and referent power are always the best options.

Reward power has been proven to be very effective in improving employee performance and motivation in some situations, and punishment has been proven, at times, to be effective in getting employees to abide by rules and regulations. Coercion, however, should be reserved for rare instances. David McClelland states that, "Slaves are the most inefficient form of labor ever devised by man. If a leader wants to have far-reaching influence, he must make his followers feel powerful and able to accomplish things on their own." Clearly the use of coercive power will tend to result in resistance in the majority of situations.

A study conducted in the Netherlands has also indicated that leaders draw on different power bases depending upon the specific type of situation they must resolve. The authors differentiate between crisis and noncrisis situations. When a crisis is not imminent, leaders tend to prefer to consult openly with their subordinates. However, in the midst of a crisis, they often rely on their referent and expert power to direct the course of action required in order to solve the problem at hand (Mulder et al., 1986). In crisis, leaders become more like sports coaches who must make full use of their power as experts to direct a game, rather than wasting precious time in consultation with others.

Yukl and Taber maintain that, "A leader's effectiveness stems from knowing the appropriate type of power to use in each situation and how to exercise this power skillfully to maximize subordinate commitment." In some cases, this may also involve the exercise of leadership skills—knowing when to delegate power to talented subordinates, and when to give employees the opportunity to give their own input. Studies show that this type of power sharing, when deployed appropriately, can lead to increased productivity, job satisfaction, and morale. It can give employees both a stronger sense of job-related meaning and self-determination, and bring innovative ideas to the organization (Silver, 2001; Hansen, 2003).

ORGANIZATIONAL POLITICS

Throughout this chapter, we have discussed power and how it can be used to successfully influence the actions of others. Individuals within an organization often use their power to influence others to accomplish personal goals, which are not always aligned with organizational goals. When these individuals use their power to take action, they are engaging in **organizational politics.** Anyone within an organization can use politics; it is not restricted to management. Often, an individual participating in organizational politics is placing self-interests above organizational interests (Greenberg and Baron, 2000). There are often situations within an organization that increase the probability of individuals participating in political behavior. Some of these situations include the following (Hellriegel, 1995):

- Unclear organizational goals
- Competition among individuals and groups for scarce resources
- Rewards for political behavior within the organization
- Individuals have different information about the situation
- Decision-making procedures and performance measures are unclear.

What comes to mind when you hear the term "organizational politics?" Do you think of it as a generally positive or negative behavior? Why is that the case?

Political Tactics

When an individual does decide to "play the game" of organizational politics, there are several tactics that he or she may decide to use to reach his or her desired goal (Greenberg and Baron, 2000).

CONTROL INFORMATION AND RESOURCES Withholding information or keeping important news to oneself has several negative consequences. Perhaps of most concern is the fact that others must rely on the person with information to make important decisions since no one else has access to key facts.

CULTIVATE FAVORABLE IMPRESSIONS Impression management is a fact of organizational life. Employees are always working to make the best possible impression on their supervisors because they realize that they need this individual's good will and support. When someone goes out of his or her way to cultivate a favorable impression at the expense of doing their best job, however, this activity becomes an obstacle to productivity. Misleading impressions are a source of conflict among colleagues as well.

GAIN SUPPORT OF OTHERS In order to ensure that your ideas are accepted and proposals passed, you need the support of others. When employees obtain this support through a deliberate strategy, their behavior falls into the category of "political."

ALIGN ONESELF WITH OTHERS MORE POWERFUL Organizational life provides opportunities to interact with all types of people. When an individual makes friends or does favors for someone primarily because he or she believes the person may be in a position to help them out in the future, their actions are political. Often employees side with senior managers and try to make sure that those in power see them in a favorable light, hoping for reciprocation at a later point in time.

How do you, personally, go about cultivating positive impressions in the workplace? At school?

Benefits and Disadvantages of Organizational Power

As emphasized earlier, organizational power can be used to make the organization healthy and productive, or it can bring harm. Let's look at some specific outcomes that result from the use of power.

NEGATIVE OUTCOMES OF POWER Whenever individuals pursue their own goals at the expense of others, there is a chance that they will bring harm to the organization or to other employees. It is obvious that use of oppressive power tactics reduce job satisfaction and harm morale. While high satisfaction encourages productivity, dissatisfaction is likely to lower employee performance.

The inappropriate use of power can also prevent organizational goals from being reached. When individuals pursue their own agendas, the welfare of the company is easily overlooked. There is often a waste of energy and other resources.

Perhaps one of the most harmful negative outcomes of power is when incompetent individuals are promoted or are given responsibilities for which they are not qualified. These people often command a high salary which creates even more resentment and the perception of injustice among coworkers. Over time, damage is likely to be done to the organization's reputation and image which may have a long-term negative effect.

POSITIVE OUTCOMES OF POWER

While it is easy to see how those with power might harm organizations, scholars have also studied the negative effects of powerlessness. In fact, researchers have come to believe that managers who have power are able to accomplish goals and facilitate positive change. It is when individuals feel powerless that they become demoralized and ineffective—and when they are most likely to resort to political tactics. One stream of research indicates that the most effective leaders seek and need power, and use it productively. Individuals who are able to accomplish important tasks almost always enjoy the process of influencing others. Even the employees themselves prefer to be supervised by someone perceived to have power, as it is easier for them to network with others who can help them solve job-related problems or acquire necessary information.

A range of positive outcomes are associated with the manager who has power, including accomplishment of personal goals, getting the task accomplished efficiently, increased visibility and recognition, career advancement, and higher levels of confidence. Other outcomes are listed in Box 13.1. Those who have power are particularly effective during times of turbulence and change, as they are able to bring employees together around common goals and reduce tension and fears associated with the change process.

BOX 13.1

Positive Outcomes of Organizational Power

Easier to interact with senior decision makers
Among first to know about changes in policy or staffing
Empowered to set agendas and put priorities on the table
More successful in getting budgets and expenditures approved
Able to actively support junior members of the organization
Influential when speaking on behalf of someone in trouble with the organization

Source: Adapted from Whetten and Cameron, 2002.

Do you think that someone can be effective in an organization—at any level—without some sort of power? Explain.

Empowering Others

In our analysis of the dynamics of power, we have indicated that authority and power flow from the top to the bottom of organizations. However, authority and decision-making power can be distributed in a number of different ways. For example, in a highly centralized organization, the bulk of both authority and power tend to be centralized at the top of the organization. This would be the case in a small society ruled by a chief, in which the chief personally looks after daily operations and personally settles disputes. However, as the size of a society—or any other kind of organization—increases, this type of centralization becomes impossible.

Different forms of leadership and different ways of distributing power become essential to the smooth conduct of business. Look around the world. National governments distribute power in very divergent ways, ranging from the absolute power of a dictator to highly dispersed distribution of power from the national and state to the local level. In this section, we will discuss a number of theories about why power should be shared within organizations and methods for doing so.

THE BENEFITS OF SHARING POWER   Leaders are necessarily dependent upon others for their power. Think about it. If you were alone on a desert island, how could you be powerful? There would not be anyone upon whom to exercise power—except for monkeys and other animals—nor anyone to appreciate your level of influence. Leaders are involved in dependency relationships with their followers, and must be careful not to alienate their subordinates (Winfield et al., 2000). One way to maintain positive relations with employees and improve customer service is to **empower** employees and middle managers by giving them authority and power to make certain key decisions about their operations. In recent years, researchers have begun to advocate the formal sharing of power within organizations.

WAYS POWER CAN BE SHARED   Whetten and Cameron (1991) offer several suggestions for empowering others in the organization. These suggestions involve increasing the positive energy and level of cooperation within the workplace.

- Include subordinates in the assignment of tasks.
- Encourage collaboration in work projects.
- Reward accomplishments publicly and personally.
- Express confidence in subordinates.
- Foster initiative.

These are undoubtedly noble goals, but they are not easy directives to implement. Which responsibilities should be delegated to people will depend upon the nature of the organization and the position of the subordinates. In a hotel restaurant, for example, the headwaiter or waitress can be responsible for choosing the next day's color scheme of tablecloths and napkins, rather than relying on dictates from the dining room manager. This small delegation both relieves the dining room manager of a small responsibility and increases the head server's sense of responsibility and accountability for the restaurant's operation. Greenberg and Baron also argue that the level of centralization or decentralization can have an impact on individuals' level of job satisfaction. Specifically, the more workers feel empowered to take action in matters that impinge upon their daily tasks—instead of always having to consult upper management before making a decision—the more satisfied they will be with their work (Greenberg and Baron, 2000).

What are the dangers of empowerment? What variables are most important when selecting employees to empower in a particular high-level position?

EXAMPLES OF ORGANIZATIONS THAT EMPOWER   Cruise lines provide a vivid example of organizations that depend on empowered employees. As cruise passengers become more sophisticated, they also have become more demanding and more diverse. Consequently, employees require a range of responses in meeting guests' expectations. Service is not only a competitive advantage, but employees depend directly on passenger feedback and ratings for their job success. Given the variety of demands and the importance of service quality, passengers often influence the nature of service delivery more than managers. Employees respond to passengers according to their perceptions of the individual's needs and preferences, which requires an empowered work environment.

Axelrod (2000) argues that in order to create an empowered organization, in which more employees feel a sense of ownership of their work and responsibility for the success of the larger organization, there must be a free flow of information within the organization. Withholding information leads to excessive dependency, whereas sharing information allows a wider circle of people to gain initiative to have a positive impact on the operation of the organization. Sharing information increases the level of trust among members of the organization, and enables more people to connect with ideas and with colleagues.

From your personal experience, what hospitality organization would you give an A+ to with regard to employee empowerment? Explain the reason for your choice.

Summary

In this chapter we have discussed the ambivalence many people often feel toward the use of power. An individual has power when he or she can get other individuals to do something they would not otherwise do. We discuss four approaches one can take when thinking about power: rational approach, strategic contingencies approach, critical contingencies approach, and cultural approach.

There are five types, or bases, of power that we describe: legitimate power, reward power,

coercive power, expert power, and referent power. A manager will elicit various responses from subordinates under each form of power. As we discuss, coercive power should be used as little as possible because it often causes resistance among subordinates. We explore ways of increasing power potential, and the negative and positive outcomes of power. We then offer ways of helping maintain necessary business relationships by empowering subordinates.

Key Words

power *355*
influence *355*
authority *355*
confluence *359*

legitimate power *360*
reward power *360*
coercive power *361*
expert power *361*

referent power *361*
organizational politics 363
empower *366*

Exercises

Exercise 1   A Resource Control Exercise

Category: Power

Introduction:
This is a bargaining and resource control exercise that involves participants in a complex set of group relations. For the exercise, each of the four groups will view a central model of a structure to be built with a set of tinkertoys, Lincoln logs, Legos, or any other construction items. One completed structure is presented to the teams.

Each group is awarded points for completing their duplicate structure. They may also accumulate points by having excess building materials. Excess resources only provide a team with points *after* their structure is completed. If their structure is not complete, no points are assigned.

The objective of getting the most points may be explicitly stated and rewarded or not, depending on the wishes of the instructor. If the objective is not specified, the instructor can later discuss the implicit assumptions and social definitions to team members attached to the "game."

This exercise utilizes sets of a child's building materials to illustrate complex management issues. Participants explore issues of resource dependence, power, and ethics.

Group Size: Four groups of 9–11 members each.

Time Frame: Approximately one hour

Materials: Four "basic" sets of building materials.

Resource Acquisition: Groups will receive two points for every piece of building material they have left after the structure is complete.

RESOURCE-BASED GROUP COMPOSITION

Group 1: Provide this group with nearly all of the pieces they need to complete the structure and thus are in control of most of their needed resources. This group also possesses many of the pieces needed by other groups to complete their structures. This is the powerful "resource-rich" group.

Group 2: Provide this group with a lot of "raw materials," but include few of the pieces that they or the others need to successfully build the structure. Though at first it may appear to be resource-rich, this group is actually resource-poor and powerless.

Groups 3 and 4: These groups are provided with a moderate amount of the pieces that they need to build their structures. Each of these groups must rely to some extent on other groups for critical resources but are not as resource-poor as Group 2.

Instructions to Participants

Show the groups the model structure and remind them that they will receive two points for each piece of building material or "excess resources." Additional instructions to participants may be given by the instructor at the instructor's discretion. Such added instructions may include the following:

1. You may negotiate or bargain across groups for resources;
2. You are competing for the most points;
3. You have 20 minutes before point totals are counted;
4. There are no rules other than those explicitly stated; and/or
5. The first five minutes of the exercise may only be used to plan your strategy. You may not bargain or put pieces together until after this initial five-minute planning period is over.

Factors to Consider when Running the Exercise

Participants often take pieces off the model structure to use in their own structure. This can be used as a basis for discussion of common resources and ethics. For example, the instructor could ask, "Is taking pieces off the model an ethical thing to do?"

Exercise 2   Using Influence Strategies

Category: Power

Instructions: Circle the appropriate number below to indicate how often you use each of the following strategies for getting others to comply with your wishes. After you have completed the survey, use the Scoring Key to tabulate your results.

***

ACTIONS

RARELY   ALWAYS

1. "If you don't comply, I'll make you regret it."
   1   2   3   4   5
2. "If you comply, I will reward you."
   1   2   3   4   5
3. "These facts demonstrate the merit of my position."
   1   2   3   4   5
4. "Others in the group have agreed; what is your decision?"
   1   2   3   4   5
5. "People you value will think better (worse) of you if you do (do not) comply."
   1   2   3   4   5
6. "The group needs your help, so do it for the good of us all."
   1   2   3   4   5
7. "I will stop nagging you if you comply."
   1   2   3   4   5
8. "You own me compliance because of past favors."
   1   2   3   4   5
9. "This is what I need; will you help out?"
   1   2   3   4   5
10. "If you don't act now, you'll lose this opportunity."
    1   2   3   4   5
11. "I have moderated my initial position; now I expect you to be equally reasonable."
    1   2   3   4   5
12. "This request is consistent with other decisions you've made."
    1   2   3   4   5
13. "If you don't agree to help out, the consequences will be harmful to others."
    1   2   3   4   5
14. "I'm only requesting a small commitment (now)."
    1   2   3   4   5
15. "Compliance will enable you to reach a personally important objective."
    1   2   3   4   5

SCORING KEY—USING INFLUENCE STRATEGIES

Retribution	*Reciprocity*	*Reason*
Item Score	**Item Score**	**Item Score**
1 ____	2 ____	3 ____
4 ____	5 ____	6 ____
7 ____	8 ____	9 ____
10 ____	11 ____	12 ____
13 ____	14 ____	15 ____
Total ____	**Total** ____	**Total** ____

Primary influence strategy: _____ (highest score)

Secondary influence strategy: _____ (second highest score)

Exercise 3   Unequal Resources

Category: Power

Objectives:

- To provide an opportunity for observing group use of resources which have been distributed unequally
- To observe bargaining processes

Group Size: This task may be done with clusters of "groups" of from one to four members each. If more than one cluster of four groups is used, the facilitator may add the dimension of competition between and within clusters. The facilitator may ask that several participants volunteer to be process observers.

Time Frame: Approximately one hour, depending upon the number and complexity of the tasks assigned

Materials:

1. Scissors, ruler, paper clips, glue, black felt-tipped markers and construction paper in six colors.
2. Unequal Resources Task Sheet for each group.
3. Large envelopes to hold each group's resources. In the example below, the envelopes will contain the following resources as designated by group:

Group 1: scissors, ruler, paper clips, pencils, and $8\frac{1}{2}'' \times 11''$ sheets of paper (two red and two white).

Group 2: scissors, glue and $8\frac{1}{2}'' \times 11''$ sheets of paper (two blue, two white, and two gold).

Group 3: felt-tipped markers and $8\frac{1}{2}'' \times 11''$ sheets of paper (two green, two white, and two gold).

Group 4: $8\frac{1}{2}'' \times 11''$ sheets of paper (one green, one gold, one brown, one orange, and one purple).

Physical Setting: Table and chairs for each group. These should be placed far enough away from each other so that each group's bargaining position is not betrayed by casual observation.

Procedure:

1. The facilitator asks groups to be seated at their individual tables and distributes an envelope of materials and a Task Sheet to each group.
2. The facilitator asks the group not to open their materials until he tells them to begin the process. He then explains that each group has different materials but that each group must complete the same tasks. He explains that they may bargain for the use of materials and tools in any way that is mutually agreeable. He emphasizes that the first group to complete all tasks is the winner. (If clusters are competing, there will be both a group winner and a clusterwinner.)
3. The facilitator gives the signal to begin and attempts to observe as much group and bargaining behavior as he can, so that he can supply some of the feedback during the final phase.
4. The facilitator may alter the complexity of tasks and distribution of resources to fit many different kinds of groups and age levels. When it is being used as a teaching tool, analogies may be drawn between this experience and how minority groups or underdeveloped nations relate to those with more power.

UNEQUAL RESOURCES TASK SHEET

Each group is to complete the following tasks:

1. Make a $3 \times 3''$ square of white paper.
2. Make a $4'' \times 2''$ rectangle of gold paper.
3. Make a five-link paper chain, each link in a different color.
4. Make a T-shaped piece $3'' \times 5''$ in green and white paper.
5. Make a $4'' \times 4''$ flag, in any three colors.
6. Complete the list with different attributes.

The first group to complete all tasks is the winner. Groups may bargain with other groups for the use of materials and tools to complete the tasks on any mutually agreeable basis.

Exercise 4   Domination

Category: Power

Summary: Participants form a line according to how dominant they feel they are.

Objectives:

- Assertiveness
- Self-perception
- Motivation

Time Frame: 15 minutes

Materials: None

Procedure:

1. Designate one end of the room for *most* and one for *least.*
2. Ask for three volunteers, put one at each end of the room and one in the middle. Ask the others to line up in equal-sized groups behind them.
3. Explain that they are categorized according to *dominance* and ask them to get themselves into the position they are happy with, by "force" if necessary.
4. Participants should then discuss their reactions. Bring out the fact that some people fought (i.e., were dominant) to secure a *less* dominant position.

Commentary: Some people will use another as a benchmark, some will have other ways of deciding where to put themselves, and these can be explored.

Variation: A twist can be added with a decision-making task for the group (e.g., electing a group leader, choosing a name for the group, deciding on a start time for the next day) in which *votes* are distributed so that those who are least dominant are allocated the most votes (least dominant getting a number of votes equal to the number of group members, most dominant getting one vote, etc.). The group can then discuss the nature of leadership and qualities that make a good leader.

Endnotes

Axelrod, R. H. (2000). *Terms of Engagement: Changing the Way We Change Organizations.* San Francisco, CA: Berrett-Koehler Publications. pp. 150–151.

Cialdini, R. B. & Goldstein, N. (2002). The science and practice of persuasion: From business owners to busboys, the ability to harness the power of persuasion is often an essential component of success in the hospitality industry. *Cornell Hotel and Restaurant Administration Quarterly, 43,* 40–52.

Dahl, R. A. (1957). The concept of power. *Behavioral Science, 2,* 201–215.

DuBrin, A. J. (1981). *Human Relations: A Job-Oriented Approach.* Reston, VA: Reston Publishing Co.

French, J. R. P., Jr. & Raven, B. H. (1959). The bases of social power. In D. Cartwright (Ed.), *Studies in Social Power.* Ann Arbor, MI: Institute for Social Research. pp. 150–167.

Greenberg, J. & Baron, R. A. (2000). *Behavior in Organizations: Understanding and Managing the Human Side of Work.* Seventh Edition. Boston: Allyn and Bacon. p. 169.

Hansen, F. (2003). Power to the line people: There's a revolution in compensation, led by companies like Marriott and Dow. They establish market prices for pay, and let line managers make the salary calls. The results are impressive. *Workforce, 82*(6), 71–75.

Heller, F. A. (1976). *Decision Processes: An Analysis of Power Sharing at Senior Organizational Levels.* Handbook of Work, Organization, and Society. p. 687.

Hellriegel, D., Slocum, J., Jr., and Woodman, R. (1995) *Organizational Behavior.* Seventh Edition.

Minneapolis, MN: West Publishing Company. pp. 355–358.

Hickson, D. J., Astley, W. G., Butler, R. J., & Wilson, D. C. (1981). Organization as power. In L. L. Cummings & B. M. Staw (Eds.), *Research in Organizational Behavior, 4.* Greenwich, CT: JAI Press. pp. 151–196.

Kanter, R. M. (1979). *Life in Organizations: Workplaces as People Experience Them.* New York: Basic Books.

Karp, H. B. (1985). *Personal Power: An Unorthodox Guide to Success.* New York: American Management Association. p. 24.

Kotter, J. (1979). *Power in Management.* New York: AMACOM.

May, R. (1972). *Power and Iinnocence.* New York: Norton.

Mulder, M., de Jong, R. D., Koppelar, L., & Verhage, J. (1986). Power, situation, and leaders' effectiveness: An organizational field study. *Journal of Applied Psychology, 71,* 566–570.

Pfeffer, J. (1992). Understanding power in organizations. *California Management Review, 34*(2), 29.

Rahim, A. M., Antonioni, D., & Psenicka, C. (2001). A structural equations model of leader power, subordinates' styles of handling conflict, and job performance. *International Journal of Conflict Management.* Bowling Green (OH): *12*(3), 191–211.

Raven, B. H. (1992). A power/interaction model of interpersonal influence: French and raven thirty years later. *Journal of Social Behavior and Personality, 7,* 217–244.

Salancik, G. & Pfeffer, J. (1977). Who gets power and how they hold on to it. *Organizational Dynamics*, 3–21.

Schindler's List. Director, Steven Spielberg. Screenplay, Steven Zaillian. Based on the book by Thomas Keneally. Film information from http://www.schindlerslist.com.

Silver, S. (2001). Power to the people. *Training*, *38*(10), 88.

Weber, M. (1949). The Methodology of the Social Sciences (eds. E. A. Shils and H. A. Finch), The Free Press, New York (translated from the Gernan original.

Whetten, D. A. & Cameron, K. S. (2002). *Developing Management Skills*. Fifth Edition. New York: Harper Collins, 282–290.

Winfield, P. W., Bishop, R., & Porter, K. (2000). *Core Management for Human Resources Students and Practioners*. Boston: Butterworth/Heinemann. pp. 80–81, 313.

Wrong, D. (1995). *Power: Its Forms, Bases and Uses*. New Brunswick, NJ: Transaction Publishers.

Yukl, G. & Taber, T. (1983). The effective use of managerial power. *Personnel*, 60.

Zaleznik, A. & Kets de Vries, M. (1975). *Power and Corporate Mind*. Boston: Houghton Mifflin.

14

LEADING HOSPITALITY ORGANIZATIONS

I am certainly not one of those who need to be prodded. In fact, if anything, I am the prod.
—Sir Winston Churchill

We have to undo a 100-year-old concept and convince our managers that their role is not to control people and stay 'on top' of things, but rather to guide, energize, and excite.
—Jack Welch, Former CEO of General Electric

CHAPTER OUTLINE

Introduction

History of Leadership Research
    Traits: Leaders Born or Made
    Leadership Behaviors
    Contingency Theory
    Leading versus Managing

Types of Leadership
    Transactional Leadership
    Transformational Leadership
    Servant Leadership

Charismatic Leaders
    The Power of Speech
    The Power of a Promise
    The Power of Persistence

The Leadership Spectrum
    The Authoritarian Approach
    The Laissez-Faire Approach
    The Participatory Approach
    The Collective Approach

The Dilemmas of Leadership
    The Pygmalion Effect
    The Accessibility Dilemma
        Interrupters
        Smothering leaders

Checks and Balances of Leadership
    Checks on Leader Power
    Leadership Assessment
    Assessment instruments
    Assessment center

Summary

LEARNING OBJECTIVES

After reading this chapter, you will be able to do the following:

1. Explain the difference between a leader and a manager.
2. List three differences between transactional and transformational leadership.
3. Define "charisma" and list three characteristics of a charismatic leader.
4. Identify the four approaches that managers can use when leading others.
5. Explain the benefits of using the participative approach when leading.
6. Discuss how a manager can take advantage of the Pygmalion effect.
7. Describe three checks and balances to a leader's power within an organization.

Scenario: Michael's Mandate

Michael Craven is a manager with Mylo's Restaurant Company. The restaurant was closed in September after a news release issued by the County Health and Human Services Agency claimed that at least ten people had become ill with apparent Shigella infections after eating at Mylo's Restaurant in late August, three of whom were hospitalized. Although restaurant health inspection failed to prove that the restaurant was culpable, the negative press exacerbated low attendance problems.

Downturns in the business have made it necessary to prepare for a reduction in the workforce. The terminations will be permanent and there are no termination benefits. The executive committee has identified five employees as the first ones to be considered for termination. All of the five employees are at the same organizational level, but are from different areas of the restaurant. Shaquille Singletary is a server; Jessica Lopez is a bartender; Matthew David is a cook; Martha Roger is an expediter; and Roger Clement is a baker. One must be terminated, and the rest ranked for future termination. Michael has a cordial working relationship with all of these employees and regrets having to let any one of them go. He must determine who will be the first to go, the next to go, and so on.

In spite of the executive committee's mandates, Michael hopes to use his leadership skills to rejuvenate the restaurant and increase business. He has always been one to persevere in the face of adversity. His employees are loyal to him because of his skill in running the restaurant and his charisma and consideration in his relationships with them. He will rely on their support in his attempts to save Mylo's Restaurant. Michael's situation requires him to do far more than merely manage. The time has come for him to lead.

INTRODUCTION

Who comes to mind when you hear the phrase the "perfect leader?" Perhaps it's a national leader. Or was it the coach of the soccer team you played for as a child? Or was it your high school science teacher?

What do leaders look like? How do you identify a successful hospitality leader?

You have become familiar with a range of skills and principles applied by men and women who are interested in making a positive impact—either in their work relationships, their teams, their departments, or the larger organization.

The leaders you encounter come in a variety of shapes and sizes, depending upon their mission and goals, the specific context, and the nature of the workforce involved. You have seen that effective leaders are always grounded in solid values that enrich the workplace and respect the backgrounds of employees. True leaders, however, also have concern for the communities in which they work. Fairmont Hotels & Resorts, for example, initiated a brand-wide commitment to focus on what the company can do for the earth by committing to use sustainable, locally sourced products in their food service operations.

Serge Simard, the director of Food and Beverage at the Fairmont Royal York in Toronto, said when he was Vice President of Food and Beverage at the Fairmont San Francisco, "Our Guests are . . . experienced diners, and they are becoming more conscious of how consumer choices affect the planet." Social responsibility is becoming a leadership requirement, and Fairmont is leading the way.

Other leaders also have applied the principles in this text to achieve their high priority goals. Howard Shultz who, with his partner David Olsen, purchased Starbucks in 1987, clearly established a corporate philosophy, saying, "Treat people as family and they will be loyal." Pedro Man, President of Starbucks Coffee Asia Pacific, echoes this view, saying, ". . . our people are highly valued partners in creating the unique Starbucks Experience. It is their passion, knowledge, and unsurpassed expertise and enthusiasm which help to create a truly outstanding coffee experience." The success of the company's introduction in Asia has been attributed largely to its focus on the total guest experience and the people employed to create that experience. Strong leadership with a clear vision has distinguished the Starbuck brand.

Leaders who are honest, compassionate individuals have achieved impressive results in all areas of hospitality. The family-based, employee-centered approach contributed to the success of Marshall Management, a Maryland-based operating company. Its president, Mike Marshall, was quoted as saying, "We're a family company and we operate every hotel as though we own it. The company also continuously improves, adopting the best practices and tailoring them to their specific operation to keep all stakeholders satisfied."

Effective leaders, as you have seen, also foster creativity. Monty Schiro, President and the creative force behind Food Fight, shares his views. Food Fight retains a portfolio of retro-trendy diners, an upscale Italian bistro, as well as Asian and southwestern concepts. Schiro prides himself on doing things that are "unique." That means constant change and, Schiro adds, "surrounding myself with the people who know the things I don't know."

The importance of clear goals and a cohesive team was reinforced by the experiences of Mark Cox, chef and owner of Mark's American Cuisine in Houston, Texas. Quoted as saying, "It's important that everyone has a common understanding of why we are here and what we are working on achieving," Chef Cox has been credited with establishing an esprit de corps in his kitchen that sets his restaurant apart.

As you think about hospitality leaders, you will find that each one brings slightly different skills and perspectives to this important role. Are leaders born or made? Are they take-charge authoritarians or facilitative partners? If you think about your own strengths, carefully consider the principles you have learned, and then apply the ideas in this text, you may just find that the effective leader your colleagues or classmates talk about is you!

Serving as a leader carries different responsibilities in different environments. However, one common thread exists among all leaders; they are charged with the task of guiding others toward a shared goal or interest. It's often impossible to fully satisfy everyone's interests. Furthermore, each of us responds differently to varying styles of leadership. This represents one of the challenges of leading people. Some people perform better working under close supervision with a strict set of guidelines. Others prefer a more liberal work environment where they can work at their own pace, still getting the job done, but without constant input from a superior. Thus, ideal leaders do not subscribe to a single management theory. Instead, they know how and when to adapt to effectively meet the needs of different staff.

Every manager wants tips on enhancing leadership skills. In this section, we discuss what management researchers have learned through their myriad studies of leadership. We will discuss dimensions of leadership that have been studied and assess them for today's managers.

HISTORY OF LEADERSHIP RESEARCH

Leaders have emerged throughout history, yet neither researchers nor practitioners have come to an agreement regarding how leadership should be defined. In fact, the term "leadership" has only been in use for approximately 200 years (Yukl, 1994). While most would agree that leadership involves the process of influencing followers in some manner, many other dimensions continue to be debated. The following sections review the development of approaches to leadership research.

Traits: Leaders Born or Made

Perhaps one of the most active arguments centers on the extent to which leadership can be "learned." Early researchers concluded that leadership required a combination of personal traits that could not be taught (Klop and Rea, 2006). Many studies focused on the differences in personality between leaders and followers. Although this research stream is still active, scholars have reached no definitive conclusions or agreement regarding exactly what traits distinguish highly effective leaders.

For instance, although there is evidence to support the idea that many leaders are endowed with strong, attractive physical features, good looks are certainly not an essential ingredient in the leadership recipe. Nor, in fact, is intelligence. Although intelligence is certainly an asset to a leader, research has shown that exceptional intelligence is not a necessity for individuals to be effective.

Some researchers believe all that is needed is for the leader to be intelligent *in comparison* to the people he or she is leading. This is a debatable issue and certainly depends upon one's definition of intelligence. There are many examples of groups in which employees have higher IQ's, or better college transcripts, than their leaders. Perhaps conventional measures of intelligence are not what are important here. Other forms of intelligence, such as common sense, an understanding of human nature, and the ability to visualize long-range goals are probably much more valuable to a leader than "book smarts" (Bass, 1990).

How does one acquire those elusive elements of the leadership equation? Although many people believe that there is no precise formula for effective leadership, it is helpful to have an idea of some characteristics, which, if not universal, are at least observed frequently among successful leaders. Researchers have compiled hundreds of lists of traits, which researchers tout as the keys to effective leadership. Box 14.1 presents a list of desirable leadership traits that have appeared repeatedly in research studies (Bass, 1990).

What leadership traits do you feel you have that will help you be a hospitality leader? What traits do you feel will need to be further developed?

Leadership Behaviors

During the mid-twentieth century, researchers turned their attention to the study of leadership behavior. This appeared to be a productive stream because behaviors were more observable than personality traits and most scholars agreed that behavior was something that could

BOX 14.1   Leadership Traits

Self-starting	Stands by team	Tolerant of frustration
Well-informed	Alert	Assertive
Ambitious	Clear thinking	Competitive
Concrete	Decisive	Dynamic
Cultivates relationships	Emotionally stable	Energetic
Extraverted	Group-oriented	Honest
Intelligent	Mentally healthy	Reality-oriented
Optimistic and confident	Pragmatic	Productive

be taught and developed. If leaders simply demonstrated certain behaviors, then perhaps anyone who was capable and motivated could be successful in leadership positions.

While progress was made by those who studied leadership behaviors, the approach had obvious limitations. For one, it relied on an oversimplified view of the leadership role. Most importantly, it did not address issues of interpersonal dynamics, organizational culture, changing leadership contexts, and other key variables.

Contingency Theory

It has only been during the past 50 years that leadership contexts have been viewed as an important dimension of leadership behavior. Contingency theory considers how the leader's personal style, behavior, and other variables are impacted by the given situation.

In this regard, researchers would explore issues related to industry segment. That is, do leaders on cruise ships or in the airline industry have different competencies than those in hotels? Is the hospitality industry a unique service environment such that industry leaders depend on a set of distinctive people-centered skills for their success?

Contingency theory also explores the needs of a particular period in time. Are some individuals better leaders in crises situations, while others might distinguish themselves when the focus is on building trust or negotiating with foreign partners.

Give an example of a leader who was "the right person at the right time;" that is, whose effectiveness was linked to the historical period or to the specific events going on at the time.

Leading versus Managing

The terms "leader" and "manager" are often used interchangeably in everyday speech. However, there is a difference between leaders and managers and it is important to distinguish the two. Leaders go beyond just managing, beyond just organizing, controlling, coordinating, and planning. A **manager** has a short-term view of the organization, supervising daily, weekly, and monthly operations. A **leader** provides long-term guidance, developing a clear vision and strategic plan. A manager's primary function is to implement the leader's vision and strategic plan throughout the organization. Leaders create an effective synergy among employees, organizational tasks, and themselves.

Leaders must help to refine natural talent, teach employees new skills, and guide employees' work efforts in the direction most beneficial to both the individual and the organization. They must aid in the coordination of group performance and in the establishment of communication with the environment external to the organization. Through all of these processes, leaders learn how to transform mundane tasks into extraordinary opportunities for service and growth (Alvesson and Sveningsson, 2003).

In addition, the leader serves as a symbol of the goals and ideals of the organization and, through sensitive guidance, provides the inspiration for achievement of these goals and ideals. With this in mind, we find that there remain numerous types of leadership and a variety of approaches that can be taken to accomplish leadership goals.

If we agree that management and leadership functions are different, what would you say is the most important distinction between a leader and a manager?

TYPES OF LEADERSHIP

Researchers have differentiated between different leadership approaches. The three most common are transactional, transformational, and servant leadership. We find that most interactions between leaders and followers are of the *transactional* type, which means that they are based on an exchange. *Transformational* relationships, which involve shared values and common goals, are much more rewarding and powerful (Tracey and Hinkin, 1994). With the development of many information workers who are empowered to work independently, servant leadership has also become an important concept. Next, each of these three types are discussed.

Transactional Leadership

Transactional leadership is based on a series of exchanges—"You can expect a raise if you manage to improve the efficiency of the housekeeping staff;" or, "Fill the hotel every night for six weeks and I'll make sure to recommend you for a promotion." Such bargaining is rational and calculated, and although it often provides a temporary increase in motivation and performance, its potency is not enduring. For one thing, by offering compensation, a leader may make the employee wonder if the job is perhaps more distasteful than he or she realized. People who are satisfied with their jobs perform tasks with enthusiasm and enjoyment. If they see that their leader is trying to charm them with offers of a "trade," they may become unnecessarily suspicious of and displeased with their work situation. Individuals involved in a transactional relationship share no common bonds beyond the immediate purpose of their transaction. No all-pervasive vision unites them in pursuit of a sublime goal.

Give an example of a transactional leader you encountered in your past and the exchange you had with them. Were you highly motivated—and was that motivation sustained? Explain.

Transformational Leadership

Transformational leadership is based on the idea that, by bonding together, leaders and followers can accomplish more and be more mutually satisfied than they would if they each worked separately. In a transformational relationship, there is no forced bargain—any member has the freedom to back out of the deal at any time if he or she is not satisfied. Hence, there is no sense of being forced into an unwanted obligation. Furthermore, since there is no mention of a "reward for service," individuals feel that they are working for their own personal satisfaction, not just to "pay back" the boss. Transformational leaders unite followers with a common goal and ignite them with the desire to reach that goal. Those who enter into a transformational relationship are inspired to work together because they believe that they will flourish both individually and within the context of their leader–follower relationship.

When we think of the great leaders who have affected the course of history, those who come to mind are paragons of transformational leadership. Abraham Lincoln, Martin Luther King Jr., and Mohandas "Mahatma" Gandhi—each of these leaders had a powerful vision with which they influenced the world, and an equally strong commitment toward fulfillment, which they managed to infuse into their followers (Yammarino, Dansereau, and Kennedy, 2001). Lincoln spoke of a government "of the people, by the people, and for the people." This vision epitomizes the ideals of transformational leadership. Similarly, King's famous "Dream," did not remain merely *his* dream; through his leadership, he made it the dream of an entire generation. In his turn, King drew the inspiration for his techniques from Gandhi's philosophy of nonviolent resistance, which Gandhi used to unite Indians to drive the British colonial government out of their country. All three were deeply committed to backing up their messages with ethical behavior that reflected their ideals, another critical aspect of good leadership (Lussier and Achua, 2001).

The above examples should not be dismissed as historic melodrama. These messages, filtered down to scale, can form the basis for successful leadership in a variety of industries. The promise of leadership of, by, and for employees can go a long way toward stimulating involvement, dedication, and loyalty. Sharing the goals of the organization with employees will give them a common dream for which to strive. By blending the needs of employees with the goals of the organization, a leader can create a unity of purpose throughout the organization. Employees who believe that their goals and the company's goals are one and the same will trust and love their corporate family, and will find themselves asking what they can do for their organization.

Servant Leadership

The term "servant leadership" suggests the philosophy of this approach. The leader views everyone in the organization as empowered employees who have a good idea of their personal needs and abilities. Consequently, the leader takes his or her cues from the employees in helping them achieve goals that they have set for themselves.

Naturally, employee goals must be aligned with the larger organization's mission and vision. The leader's role, however, is to assist all employees in becoming more knowledgeable, healthier, and more independent. As a result, employees are more motivated, satisfied, and organizational effectiveness is increased.

As you might imagine, not every leader is well suited to be a servant leader. Researchers have discovered that servant leaders must be able to inspire employees and gain their trust.

Teamwork is often an important part of the organizational culture, and emphasis is placed on clarifying and expressing organizational values.

Do you think servant leadership generally works well in hospitality organizations? In some departments better than others? Explain.

CHARISMATIC LEADERS

When a leader's appeal is so universal that it seems almost magical, it is usually attributed to "charisma." **Charisma** is the catchword that we use to describe those unique individuals who engender instantaneous trust, respect, and cooperation. Charisma is the stuff of which legends are made; yet it is tangible, tractable, and broadly applicable. The hospitality executive who is familiar with the ingredients of this dazzling quality commands a valuable and versatile leadership tool.

The *American Heritage Dictionary* defines charisma as "a rare quality or power attributed to those persons who have demonstrated an exceptional ability for leadership and for securing the devotion of large numbers of people." The word is derived from the Greek word *kharisma*, which means "favor, divine gift." Indeed, theology has incorporated the word charisma to designate "a divinely inspired gift or power, such as the ability to perform miracles." Although today's organizational leaders cannot claim to walk on water, the mystique surrounding exceptional leaders often carries them to heroic proportions in the eyes of their followers.

Historically, charismatic leaders have arisen in times of spiritual or political upheaval. They appeal to distressed people because they provide a feeling of safety, a solid identity, and a unifying purpose (Yukl, 1994). Charismatic leaders are capable of mobilizing the emotional forces of large groups of people. Mahatma Gandhi and Martin Luther King, Jr., exemplify the qualities of charismatic leadership because they appealed to the masses in their time of need. They offered a solution to widespread problems. They impressed people with their steadfast vision and their courage to challenge authority.

The Power of Speech

Charismatic leaders carry their source of power in their personal presence. They know how to use their expert communication skills and rhetorical ability to capture the emotions of their followers. Forceful, persuasive speech is a trademark of the charismatic individual; rhythm and repetition are common features in charismatic oratory. Mahatma Gandhi and Martin Luther King, Jr., mesmerized their followers with repetitive chants and dramatic crescendos. Their speeches resembled the prayer of devoted worshipers. Indeed, these leaders attracted and transfixed throngs of their own devoted worshipers, engaging them in fervent rhetorical exchange. The orations of charismatic leaders are structured on a pattern of call-and-response and are punctuated with rhythmic pauses intended to generate an echo from the crowd.

Of course, a hotel or restaurant manager cannot indulge in high-level oratory in order to demonstrate charisma. However, managers can distill the above concepts into a practical set of communication guidelines. Primarily, it is important to be articulate. Managers who communicate ideas clearly and confidently will be more effective leaders than managers who remain muddled and wishy-washy. How can managers hope to inspire confidence and loyalty when they appear unsure of their own beliefs? Followers search for a leader who serves as a steadfast symbol of organizational goals and values. If the leader is hesitant and indecisive, then the followers will be even more so.

Second, hospitality managers can draw on the aforementioned speech patterns in order to lend charisma to everyday interactions. Leaders can utilize the theme of call-and-response by encouraging employee participation in conversations. Repetition is a wonderful method of instilling organizational values. After leaders have presented their perspective, they should allow employees to express these ideas in ways that make sense to them personally. Employees will remember conversations more readily if they can stamp the interaction with their own input. The employee who puts his or her personal mark on a project will be inspired to strive for excellence.

Identify someone you believe is a charismatic leader due in large part to his or her use of language and speech (this can be from politics as well as from the business world). Describe the person you selected and explain why you believe he or she is charismatic.

The Power of a Promise

A second feature associated with charismatic leaders is the offer of a promise. Any manager can order employees to perform tasks, but it takes charisma to channel these tasks toward a grand purpose. Any leader has the power to control the happiness of his or her followers, but only charismatic leaders understand how to use this power in order to unite themselves with employees in pursuit of common goals. Charismatic leaders promise each employee the opportunity to achieve a goal that holds personal significance for that individual. This promise provides a chance for the follower to endow his or her work with meaning.

Charismatic leaders offer a transformational relationship rather than a transactional one. Charismatic leaders have a dream and a message that they share with their followers. Instead of saying "Do this for me," the charismatic leader suggests, "Let's join together in our efforts and benefit together through our success." Theoretical charismatic leaders offer a promise of ultimate salvation. Real-life business leaders give employees something special to strive for, leading them to have confidence in their abilities and trust in the power of cooperation. The "salvation" which industry leaders can offer is the promise of personal fulfillment within the context of a supportive organizational environment.

Give an example of a "promise" that has been made by a hospitality leader.

The Power of Persistence

The third, and most important quality of charismatic leaders, is the ability to convey a sense of utter conviction in their beliefs. The charismatic leader must be brave enough to challenge authority, even at a risk to his or her well-being. Charismatic leaders gain the trust of their followers by demonstrating that they are willing to devote everything toward the pursuit of a cause. It is this dedication, this unyielding belief in the righteousness of one's actions that draws others into the quest and instills the values of their leader in them.

While managers are not expected to go to extremes for the sake of a menu revision or a new store promotion, they should be willing to pursue goals with unfailing determination. Leaders set the example for dedication among their employees. If leaders do not convey absolute certainty that what they are doing is right, employees will be skeptical. If the leader is not willing to pull out all the stops for a project, how important could it be? Employees look to their leader for guidance.

A *manager* provides a list of tasks and duties, but a *leader* knows how to give meaning to these mundane activities. *Charismatic leaders* capture the trust of their followers and lead them to cherish their ideals with a passion equal to their own. Authentic leaders pay careful attention to their behavioral integrity, which Tony Simons has shown to be an integral part of building and retaining employee commitment. When leaders keep their words and actions aligned with each other, the bottom line proves that integrity is well worth the effort. Consistently demonstrating words through action has been shown to decrease employee turnover, and to increase employee performance (Simons, 2002a, b, January).

Recent corporate scandals have demonstrated the critical importance of developing authentic leadership skills, through enhancing the moral capacity, courage, and resiliency of leaders. Lack of authenticity can eat away the fiber of the company and break down employees' trust. Leaders must recognize the moral dilemmas involved in their decisions, consider alternatives, and make resolutions that take the needs of many stakeholders into account (May et al., 2003). Getting employees' attention and maintaining their trust is essential, but it is not easy. We will now address various theories of effective leadership.

THE LEADERSHIP SPECTRUM

All of us have at some time in our life encountered an authority figure that can be described by no kinder adjective than "smothering." We all know how frustrating it can be to work with such a manager. Although this type of leader leaves no room for mistakes, he or she also eliminates the space for creativity. Equally frustrating, however, can be the leader who gives too little guidance. Although such a manager certainly cannot be accused of coming on too strong, his or her employees often feel left in the dark about what they should be trying to accomplish.

The extent to which a manager should assume the role of dictator is dependent upon the individuals involved and the type of task desired. The accounting department probably requires and appreciates a manager who pays attention to detail, stresses accuracy, and establishes a predictable routine. The marketing department, however, is more likely to thrive under a supervisor who encourages flexibility, spontaneity, and departure from conventional thought patterns.

The leadership process is filled with variations. In an attempt to make some sense out of the leadership cornucopia, researchers have defined a model based on three basic types of leaders—the authoritarian, the laissez-faire, and the participatory. We also discuss a fourth model of leadership—collective.

The Authoritarian Approach

Authoritarian leaders make all decisions themselves, without consulting subordinates. This type of leader gives orders and expects them to be followed without complaints or considerations. In some situations this leadership style is highly effective.

A basketball team, for example, would not function if the coach stopped to discuss each decision with every player. During a game, there is not enough time to allow every team member to shape each play to his or her personal satisfaction. If each basketball player were given the chance to restructure every strategic move, the team would not have a very successful season! Fortunately for the coach, the players, and the fans, a basketball team is structured in such a way that it flourishes under authoritarian leadership. Since the team members have no time of their own to plan and negotiate, they learn that it is wise to heed the coach's advice, even though in their minds it may be incorrect at times.

The Laissez-Faire Approach

A second type of leadership style is called laissez-faire, which is translated from the French to mean "leave it be." This is leadership at its most "mellow," a "live and let live" approach. A typical **laissez-faire leader** will delineate the goals of the organization, but will allow employees to go about attaining these goals in whatever way they wish. This type of leadership grants a high degree of autonomy to subordinates, and although certain individuals may be responsive to such a method, many feel frustrated and confused. Managers should not forget that many people want to have a leader to provide guidance. The existence of such a person gives them a sense of security as well as someone to please. Many employees do not function efficiently without some semblance of a track, a plan, or a flowchart to guide them. However, the laissez-faire style works well with highly skilled, highly motivated experts, whose jobs encourage creativity and divergent thinking.

The Participatory Approach

Of course, not all organizations function like a basketball team or a highly skilled professional. There are many institutions that require a more democratic interplay between leaders and followers in order to inspire productivity and maintain employee satisfaction. These organizations will thrive under a participatory leadership style. **Participatory leaders** routinely involve their subordinates in the decision-making process. This theory of leadership is based on the idea that the key to good leadership is good "follower-ship." Participatory leaders understand that power derived from the group is infinitely more valuable than an empty label or authority associated with status or position.

Within the participatory leadership style there is a wide spectrum of interpretation. Some participatory leaders prefer to retain complete control over final decisions, while others relinquish this ultimate authority to their group of followers. Participatory leaders can be *consultative* or *democratic*. **Democratic leaders** allow the group to have the last word on all decisions; they never veto the plans of their followers, even though they hold the power to do so. **Consultative leaders,** however, exercise their right to have the final say; although consultative leaders encourage participation throughout the decision-making process, in the end they retain the ultimate authority.

The benefits associated with participatory leadership are manifold. By allowing employees to contribute their firsthand knowledge of the situation, the leader conveniently increases the pool of information upon which to base decisions. Also, employees who actively participate in organizational decision making are usually more enthusiastic about carrying their plans to completion than employees who have had their orders dictated to them by an authoritative leader.

A further benefit derived from the participatory leadership approach is that employees who feel that their opinions are appreciated will feel a greater degree of job satisfaction. They will be motivated to increase their knowledge about their own work, as well as about the functioning of the entire organization, so that they can be even more valuable in future situations. In many cases, the critical factor is not that leaders know the answers to every question that could arise in their organizations, but that they know the right questions to ask, and whose advice they should seek in particular situations (O'Toole, 1999).

*"I still don't have all the answers, but I'm
beginning to ask the right questions."*

The Collective Approach

The Japanese style of management, collective management, is another model of leadership. There are many qualities in this model that are worth considering. **Collective decision-making** is a powerful method of assuring universal commitment. Non-specialized careers provide employees with a unique view of the organization as a whole, enabling them to better appreciate the central themes and goals upheld by management. Infrequent promotions deemphasize employees' concerns with money and status and strengthen group loyalty and sustained commitment. Lifetime commitment gives each employee the chance to witness the long-term effects of his or her decisions and gives a leader the chance to cultivate talent and build lasting relationships.

> Select one of the four leadership styles described above and give an example of a leadership situation where the style was highly appropriate and effective. Then, considering the same style, identify an example of another situation where it was inappropriate and less effective. What accounts for this difference?

THE DILEMMAS OF LEADERSHIP

The Pygmalion Effect

In Greek mythology, Pygmalion was a sculptor who fell in love with one of his statues. He was so enthralled with the statue that he could not eat or sleep. In the statue he saw his ideal of the perfect woman and he spent every moment staring at the marble, wishing it would come to life. In the end, the goddess Aphrodite granted Pygmalion's wish and brought the statue to life. The myth of Pygmalion has remained alive through the centuries and was the inspiration for the musical comedy "My Fair Lady." The moral of the story, the **Pygmalion effect,** is that high expectations will bring the highest results. This is the idea of the "self-fulfilling prophecy." If a leader views his or her employees as "diamonds in the rough" and communicates this faith in their potential, then hard work and patience on both sides will unearth these glistening gems.

The dark side of the story, however, is that negative expectations can bring about equally strong negative results. A leader who fails to appreciate the hidden talents of employees has little chance of uncovering them. In fact, a negative attitude will only drive positive qualities even deeper beneath the surface of the employee's personality.

Leaders of all styles have the potential to initiate a cycle of Pygmalion effects. In some cases the results can be rewarding, but in other situations they may be disastrous. For example, a negatively oriented leader cannot hide his or her negative attitude. Employees detect it, and their reaction will only corroborate the leader's initial assumptions. Employees who feel that they are not trusted often become resentful and cease to act responsibly. In extreme cases, this resentment can develop into sabotage.

Employees who are monitored at every step will lose the confidence to try anything on their own. They will learn to view themselves as helpless, stupid, unimaginative drones who are completely dependent upon the orders of their leader. This sad example demonstrates how inappropriate leadership behavior can destroy the initiative and confidence of a talented group of individuals. The reaction of employees to a negatively oriented leader will only serve to reinforce the leader's original prejudice. This evokes even more negative qualities from employees creating a vicious cycle.

This vicious cycle is the self-fulfilling prophecy transformed into an organizational nightmare and is one of the most ruthless pitfalls a leader can encounter. However, the potency of this cycle can also be harnessed in a positive direction. Participatory, or relationship-oriented, leaders appreciate the knowledge, experience, and personal qualities of employees. By encouraging employees to contribute to decision making, leaders initiate a positive Pygmalion reaction. By affirming that they value the input the employee has to offer, leaders help employees believe that they are valuable members of the organization. Confidence breeds confidence; leaders should remember that employees will be motivated to perform when they know that the boss believes in them.

> Think of a time in your life when you were victim of a self-fulfilling prophecy. What was it? How did it affect your self-confidence? Explain.

The Accessibility Dilemma

Should leaders spend their precious time "out in the field?" Leaders possess the highest level of knowledge—maybe they shouldn't waste it on low-level problems. Perhaps it is wise to maintain a mystique, keep a distance and filter the delegation of tasks through a hierarchy so as not to be bothered with any but the most esoteric issues.

When leaders insulate themselves, it leaves them with more time to get "thought-work" done, but engaging employees on the floor gives them a feeling of importance. If leaders are too insulated, they fall prey to a narrow vision and a lack of information that results in poor decisions. Hence, many people believe that the perfect leader is always available, maintaining high visibility with respect to both employees and guests. The perfect leader should be out in the lobby, down in the kitchen, cruising the grounds—omniscient yet down to earth, and ready to wash dishes or take out the garbage if need be.

There are many forces that beckon the leader to leave his or her pedestal and jump into the thick of things. Routine activities are appealing—they promise instant success. Concrete tasks are easier to manage than the complex problems that traditionally constitute the bulk of a leader's responsibility. Leaders gain respect by accomplishing the miraculous. Hence, they are easily seduced by the promise of instantaneous solutions.

Leaders who immerse themselves in the lower levels of the organization will discover a plethora of useful information. Yet is this reward worth the price they pay for diverting their efforts from long-range planning and decision making?

> Is "walk around" management always in the best interest of the organization? How do you find a balance between having time to plan and strategize and to connect in meaningful ways with first-line employees?

INTERRUPTERS   Any top-level executive is all too familiar with the numerous phone calls, visitors, unscheduled meetings, and other interruptions that creep insidiously into every waking (and sleeping!) moment. Even the purposely aloof leader cannot escape the infinite pestering disturbances that threaten to destroy any sense of privacy he or she may have envisioned. Researchers who examined a typical restaurant manager's day found that it was consumed with unplanned meetings, tours, and telephone calls. In fact, only 29 percent of the leader's day was devoted to scheduled meetings and a mere 17 percent was spent at his or her desk. Scheduled meetings and desk sessions represent the only times during which the leader can concentrate on those activities which require his or her special skills, but even these sessions are plagued by numerous interruptions. The restaurateurs studied received an average of 86 interruptions per day (approximately 10 or 11 disturbances every hour). Each contact lasted an average of 4.2 minutes. Hence, approximately 45 minutes of each hour were "wasted" on activities that distract leaders from top-level issues that they alone are equipped to handle.

If a leader who tries to be inaccessible is left with only 15 minutes an hour to devote to strategic pursuits, what happens to the leader who does not even attempt to guard his or her time? A leader's power is derived from his or her ability to do the extraordinary; yet all too often leaders become bogged down in the mundane. How do leaders find the time and space to lead?

SMOTHERING LEADERS   Some of the most successful leaders in the service industry attribute their results to sheer persistence, constant interference, and brute force. These leaders stretch "accessibility" to its most extreme interpretation—making frequent excursions out of the office and onto the floor, exerting their influence where it counts. Experienced leaders realize that it takes years, even decades, for new ideas to be assimilated and for new ways of thinking to be accepted.

Peters studied the leadership styles of highly successful business leaders and discovered that the leaders who were most successful at infusing their ideals into the corporate structure were those who ran a continuous campaign which touched not only the cities (central executive offices), but reached far into the backwoods of the organization (Waterman and Peters, 1988).

These leaders promoted their platform at every possible moment, bombarding employees with beliefs, ideas, and values in an attempt to alter the mind-set of the entire corporation.

Peters noticed several characteristics prevalent among leadership champions. Most importantly, successful leaders are *consistent*. They choose their "pet" issue and focus their efforts on this one theme until it is thoroughly ensconced in the subconscious and conscious efforts of employees at all levels in the organization. Successful companies never outgrow their obsessions with the value that built their reputation. As Peters notes, J. Willard Marriott, Sr., in his mid-eighties, still regularly visited hotel sites to instill in person his dogmatic approach to quality, returning home with long follow-up lists.

Leaders whose style is based upon constant accessibility rely upon jaw power to push their own beliefs, but the most successful leaders are also receptive to the input of others. A knowledgeable, well-intentioned leader is faced with a difficult choice when it comes to the accessibility dilemma. Of course a leader needs time alone to concentrate on top-level issues. But how can a leader make informed decisions if he or she has no communication with employees out on the job? Leaders must maintain contact with subordinates, superiors, and customers, yet they also desperately need time alone. Ideally, a leader should be able to view the organization from the outside looking in, from the inside looking out, from the top looking down, and from the bottom looking up. In reality, since it is impossible to be everywhere at once, the leader must strike a balance that suits the needs of his or her particular group at the particular time.

One of the most obvious and frustrating accessibility paradoxes is the fact that good leaders, especially those who have risen through the ranks of the organization, know much more about the company than do their employees. It is often difficult to stand back and watch employees do work which you know you could do more efficiently. Yet, even though the leader may be able to perform each job perfectly, leaders cannot functionally do every job and look after the issues that can only be solved through their own attention. For all of the necessary organizational work to be done well, leaders must learn how, when, and to whom tasks must be delegated.

Imagine a leader as a symphony conductor—instructing the instrumentalists, cueing them when necessary, drilling them when necessary, but directing the full performance. The conductor must depend on the abilities of the instrumentalists because he or she could never play all of the instruments simultaneously (Gregor and Peterson, 2000). Without teamwork, the event cannot happen successfully. Where should leaders draw the line between offering unlimited assistance and standing back in order to concentrate on issues that only they, not employees, can handle?

This dilemma is especially conspicuous when it comes to management transition. The entrepreneur, or any other leader upon whom the organization is entirely or largely dependent, will eventually be faced with the difficult task of choosing his or her successor. As leaders attempt to cultivate the next generation of executives, the interference paradox becomes a web of conflicting emotions. A leader on the verge of retirement or promotion is understandably tempted to bombard the group with his or her valuable knowledge and expert advice. To such a leader it seems urgent to teach the group everything it could possibly need to know. Leaders who visualize their impending withdrawal from the organization will be in a frantic rush to impart all of their wisdom to employees before fading into obscurity, losing the ability to correct employees' mistakes, and make crucial decisions.

Yet leaders must also realize the value of remaining inconspicuous during periods of organizational transition. Perhaps it is not a good idea to intervene in the group that you soon intend to abandon. A leader who comes on strong and then disappears will leave behind a leadership void which will be impossible to fill unless the leader has taken care to develop independence in his or her employees. Leaders should not be overly accessible to the needs of employees to the point that they become so reliant upon the leader that they are unable to think or act on their own.

When it comes to organizational transition and the replacement of managers, participatory leaders have a distinct advantage. Participatory leaders blend the two extremes of the accessibility spectrum—offering valuable advice while developing responsible, independent employees. Authoritarian leaders will find it next to impossible to choose a suitable successor because their employees have never been given the chance to cultivate their leadership skills. Organizations that are entirely dependent upon the guidance of a single individual often fail to outlive the reign of that leader.

Participatory leaders will not experience this problem. By encouraging the involvement of subordinates in decision making and by providing challenges and responsibilities which refine the leadership skills of employees at all levels in the organizational hierarchy, the participatory leader generates a leadership posterity which assures the success of the organization for many generations to come.

> What are the most important ideas you gained from this section? How will you apply them in the workplace?

CHECKS AND BALANCES OF LEADERSHIP

While participatory leaders may have patented the formula for breeding talented successors, they will run into another paradoxical dilemma—"How can I encourage participation without stifling individuality?" The corporate world has a deeply ingrained heritage of free-spirited individualism. The daring, unconventional entrepreneur is the linchpin of the free trade culture. Are leaders who stress long-term commitment, group loyalty, and adherence to organizational values asking their employees to sacrifice their individuality? Not necessarily.

Checks on Leader Power

Absolute power does not reign absolutely in the business world. In fact, it does not even exist. No matter how forceful and tyrannical a leader may be, he or she is ultimately confronted with checks and balances that threaten to limit his or her power. Good leadership draws its strength from good followership; therefore, a leader must learn to function within the constraints of an interactive relationship.

The most blatant check to leadership power is the fact that followers always retain the freedom to disobey. Since a leader is limited by the behavior of his or her subordinates, the leader's primary task is to convince followers that they will benefit more from cooperation than from rebellion. The simplest way for a leader to gain the trust of his or her group is to practice what he or she preaches. Leaders must recognize that they are symbols of organizational values and must consistently demonstrate their devotion to the company in order to elicit similar behavior from subordinates. The "do as I say, not as I do" approach does not go very far toward convincing employees that obedience and commitment are worth their while.

Another constraint that diminishes a leader's power is the need to relate each request to a common goal. A leader cannot get away with issuing commands that appear to be directed solely toward the satisfaction of personal whims. In order to gain the cooperation of followers, a leader must unite every demand with a purpose that is justifiable on collective grounds.

A third check to a leader's power is the fact that he or she must be prepared to back up rewards. The more resources over which a leader has control, the more power he or she has to offer rewards. Dangling promotions and raises in front of employees' eyes only goes so far. If leaders cannot follow through on their promises, they will lose the trust of their subordinates. Of course, rewards do not have to be monetary. A leader's resources are limited only by his or her creativity. Special recognition, added responsibility, new challenges—all of these can act as potent motivating agents and all are easily found within the boundaries of the organization.

A fourth constraint on the power of a leader is that it is impossible for a leader to monitor the actions of all employees at all times. The higher a leader rises, the more he or she must sacrifice control over those below. However, the key to perfecting the leader–follower relationship involves turning the situation inside-out. By relinquishing his or her grasp the leader leaves subordinates with several crucial degrees of freedom. Followers have the choice to obey or disobey, the choice to trust or not to trust, the choice to be committed or apathetic.

The guidelines presented in this chapter suggest how the leader may influence subordinates' choice of behavior. Not being able to be everywhere at once can be a blessing in disguise. Once leaders have instilled organizational values in employees' hearts and have boosted confidence in their minds, there is no need for them to be omnipresent. Distance provides room for employees to experiment, to stretch the limits of their creativity, and to realize the rewards of cooperation.

Leadership is a subtle process. An effective leader's magic works deep beneath the surface—energizing untapped resources and strengthening synergistic functions. The leader must be acutely aware of isolated trouble spots and must know how to apply pressure as needed, yet he or she can never lose contact with the entity as a whole.

> Describe one of the most powerful leaders you have encountered. Why did people choose to follow him or her?

Leadership Assessment

Leadership potential—and leadership effectiveness—have been assessed in a variety of ways. While no instrument or activity can predict with one hundred percent certainty how a particular individual will perform in the future or whether accomplishments can be attributed directly to a particular leader's decisions and actions, a variety of instruments and approaches exist for gathering useful information.

ASSESSMENT INSTRUMENTS   Most of the hundreds of leadership assessments now available are designed to be self-administered and self-scored. Such assessments can often be taken online, where individual responses automatically go into a database that is then used for comparison purposes. The ability to measure your performance against the established norms of a comparison set of previous test takers provides rich and useful information.

Exactly what is assessed? A variety of assessments are available that provide insight into a wide range of attributes. Perhaps the most well known and reliable assessments provide information on an individual's personal style. This information can be used to better understand his or her leadership challenges. The Myers-Briggs Type Indicator and FIRO-B have been used for both individual and team development.

Other instruments provide information on values, emotional intelligence, or cultural intelligence. Often, assessments are completed not only by the leader but also by his staff, assistants, and supervisor. This approach is called 360 degree feedback. In this process, the individual's responses can be compared to the responses of colleagues and coworkers, providing information that enables the leader to better align self-perceptions with the perceptions of others.

While some scholars have criticized assessment instruments and questioned their usefulness, the results of these surveys provide a catalyst for thinking about important dimensions of leader style, behavior, and competencies. The knowledge leaders gain from this type of assessment helps them to set personal goals and continually improve their leadership performance.

> What do you see as the strengths and disadvantages of assessment instruments when it comes to evaluating leadership effectiveness?

ASSESSMENT CENTER   Assessment centers are one of the most reliable methods of determining whether an individual is ready to increase his or her job responsibilities. The assessment center experience involves a small group of individuals, or "assessees" who are asked to move through a series of carefully designed activities. They might be asked to make an oral presentation, lead a problem-solving discussion, complete an in-basket activity, or demonstrate their creativity in a specific context. During these sessions, a team of senior managers or executives closely observe their behavior and then provide them feedback on the pre-determined dimensions.

A useful component of the assessment center is the ability of the assessors to identify "gaps" between the individual's performance during assessment activities and the expectations of the new position. While time intensive (centers often run for two or three full days), this method has proven to be one of the most reliable and constructive methods for identifying leadership potential or promoting leadership development.

> Would you like to participate in an assessment center? Explain the reasons for your answer.

Summary

Leaders are the messiahs of the managerial world. They reach beyond the mere delegation and supervision of tasks, weaving the personal needs of each follower into a universal cloak of shared values. By keeping the concepts that we discussed throughout this chapter in mind, a manager can enhance his or her leadership effectiveness.

We discuss the importance of transformational leadership, which is far more powerful than a transactional relationship. A leader is in touch with the organization as a whole. From his or her vantage point, one can appreciate the long-term implication of values and the broad-range effects of company goals. It is up to the leader to communicate this vision to his or her followers. To elicit the cooperative support and communal enthusiasm of subordinates at all levels he or she must help them comprehend the passion of those at the top of the organization.

Charisma is not as elusive as one may think. Many of the characteristics of charismatic leaders can be incorporated into a manager's leadership style. The power of speech as a leadership tool should not be underestimated. Presenting ideas clearly and confidently, using repetition as a method of subtle inculcation and engaging followers in participative call-and-response patterns are tricks of the leadership trade which can easily be incorporated into one's repertoire.

The power of a promise and the power of persistence are other tools that lend an aura of charisma to any leader. Charismatic leaders fuse organizational values with the individual needs of their followers, thereby offering each employee a promise of personal fulfillment within the organizational environment. Most important, a charismatic leader conveys a sense of conviction to her beliefs. It is important to remember that confidence breeds confidence, commitment breeds commitment, and trust breeds trust. This snowball effect is a major theme of leadership, and a crucial fact to keep in mind.

It is up to the leader to decide how tight to pull the reins. He or she should be sensitive to the needs of the group, be aware of the talents and weaknesses of each subordinate, and distinguish among those areas in which followers need guidance and those in which they are capable of standing on their own.

A leader should be aware of any negatively oriented managerial attitudes that threaten to sour his or her leadership style. He or she should aim to develop a participative-oriented behavior instead. Everybody has something worthwhile to offer; it is up to the leader to discover the hidden talents of each employee and bring each person up to his or her potential. Employees have an inner drive to be the best that they can be, a need to be challenged, and a desire to see their environment improve as a result of their efforts. A leader should give followers the benefit of the doubt. Like all people, employees will be committed to an organization that demonstrates its commitment to them.

Leadership is not a static activity. If a manager wishes to be an effective leader, he or she should pay attention to his or her followers and their environment. One shouldn't get stuck in a mind-set. One should make sure that he or she reviews each situation as it comes and decide which leadership style is most appropriate. Good leadership requires adaptability, flexibility, and dynamic enthusiasm. Managers should beware of the potential perils of *Pygmalion!* Vicious cycles are the leader's nemesis and are tough to break once they get started. Why not initiate positive cycles instead? They, too, are infectious. Self-fulfilling prophecies are valuable phenomena, provided the leader can channel them in the proper direction.

A leader should find a balance between accessibility and isolation. There are convincing arguments for both sides. It is best for the leader to size up each situation and determine how vital his or her presence is. A leader owes his or her followers the chance to try things on their own. Allowing employees to learn from their mistakes is an invaluable training method, even though it is often painful and frustrating on both sides. Determining the proper dose of intervention is a complex decision. Being in touch with the needs of followers, the capabilities of the group, and the goals of the organization will help the leader make a wise choice.

Key Words

manager *378*	charisma *381*	democratic leaders *384*
leader *379*	authoritarian leaders *383*	consultative leaders *384*
transactional leadership *379*	laissez-faire leaders *384*	collective decision-making *385*
transformational leadership *380*	participative leaders *384*	Pygmalion effect *386*

Exercises

Exercise 1 Michael's Mandate

Review the scenario at the beginning of this chapter. In this exercise we will focus on the termination mandates Michael has been given. Pretend that you are in Michael's shoes and must prioritize these terminations.

For purposes of this exercise, assume that there are no union contracts, company policies, legal requirements, or traditional business practices that constrain your decision making. Base your decision about an employee's position on the termination list purely on your own judgment of fairness to the employees and benefit for the company. The latest performance evaluations of the employees on the termination list are provided to assist you in your decisions. Please take eight minutes to make your choices individually and then attempt to reach group consensus. Once a group decision has been made, two participants will role-play the employee termination session. The remaining participants will observe the interaction and provide feedback.

***

Performance Evaluation: Shaquille Singletary

Name: _Shaquille Singletary_

Position: _Server_

Seniority: _Two years_

Biographical Information (for statistical purposes only):

Age:	_27_	Veteran:	_Yes_
Sex:	_M_	Marital Status:	_Single_
Ethnicity:	_Black_	Children:	_None_

	Low					High
Ability to work independently	1	2	3	4	5	(6)
Attendance	1	2	3	4	(5)	6
Attitude toward supervisors	1	2	3	(4)	5	6
Cooperation with coworkers	1	2	3	4	(5)	6
Decision making	1	2	3	(4)	5	6
Job-specific tasks	1	2	3	4	5	(6)
Productivity	1	2	3	4	(5)	6
Overall performance	1	2	3	4	(5)	6

Supervisor's comments (confidential): Shaquille attends night school, has completed one year of college, and is interested in supervisory work. He has received satisfactory work evaluations in the past, and his attendance is good. Recently, Shaquille received his first warning slip for taking two days off to attend a political rally after his request for leave without pay was denied. Despite his having received three innovation awards for his superior performance, I think Shaquille has too many "big ideas" for the level of job he holds. As a result, Shaquille seems to be causing some unrest among fellow employees by criticizing the restaurant's methods and practices.

***

Performance Evaluation: Jessica Lopez

Name: _Jessica Lopez_

Position: _Bartender_

Seniority: _One year_

Biographical Information (for statistical purposes only):

Age:	_35_	Veteran:	_No_
Sex:	_F_	Marital Status:	_Widow_
Ethnicity:	_Hispanic_	Children:	_One_
			Maribel, age 7

	Low				High	
Ability to work independently	1	2	3	4	(5)	6
Attendance	1	2	3	4	(5)	6
Attitude toward supervisors	1	2	3	4	(5)	6
Cooperation with coworkers	1	2	3	4	(5)	6
Decision making	1	2	3	(4)	5	6
Job-specific tasks	1	2	3	4	(5)	6
Productivity	1	2	3	4	(5)	6
Overall performance	1	2	3	4	(5)	6

Supervisor's comments (confidential): Jessica has received satisfactory work evaluations in the past, and her attendance is good. She has requested a transfer to the back-of-the-house operations should an opening occur; her high test scores make her an excellent candidate. However, Jessica is presently dating the company's executive chef. I assume that they will be married within the year.

***

Performance Evaluation: Matthew David

Name: _Matthew David_

Position: _Cook_

Seniority: _Twelve years_

Biographical Information (for statistical purposes only):

Age:	_47_	Veteran:	_No_
Sex:	_M_	Marital Status:	_Married_
Ethnicity:	_Caucasian_	Children:	_One_
			Joseph, age 25

(continued)

(continued)

	Low					High
Ability to work independently	1	2	3	(4)	5	6
Attendance	1	2	3	(4)	5	(6)
Attitude toward supervisors	1	2	3	(4)	5	6
Cooperation with coworkers	1	2	3	(4)	5	6
Decision making	1	2	3	(4)	5	6
Job-specific tasks	1	2	(3)	4	5	6
Productivity	1	2	3	(4)	5	6
Overall performance	1	2	3	4	5	6

Supervisor's comments (confidential): Although Matthew's work performance has been declining for the past few years, it is still above minimum standards. Records of prior supervisory counseling indicate his desire to stay on his present job and his assurances that he will increase his speed and performance. In the past, Matthew has shown some improvement after discussions with me but has slipped back to his former level of performance within a few days. I suspect that part of the problem is the fact that his wife has a terminal illness and is expected to live only another year and a half or two years. Matthew also serves as part-time minister for a small local congregation. His attendance, however, is excellent.

***

Performance Evaluation: Martha Steward

Name:	*Martha Steward*
Position:	*Expeditor*
Seniority:	*One and one-half years*

Biographical Information (for statistical purposes only):

Age:	*20*	Veteran:	*No*
Sex:	*F*	Marital Status:	*Divorced*
Ethnicity:	*Caucasian*	Children:	*Two*
			Caroline, age 3;
			Jonathan, age 2

	Low					High
Ability to work independently	1	2	3	(4)	5	6
Attendance	1	2	(3)	4	5	6
Attitude toward supervisors	1	2	3	4	(5)	6

(continued)

(continued)

	Low					High
Cooperation with coworkers	1	2	3	4	5	(6)
Decision making	1	2	3	(4)	5	6
Job-specific tasks	1	2	3	(4)	5	6
Productivity	1	2	3	(4)	5	6
Overall performance	1	2	3	(4)	5	6

Supervisor's comments (confidential): Martha has received satisfactory work evaluations. However, her attendance has only been fair because of work missed when her children were sick. Nine months ago Martha received a warning slip for poor attendance. Since then her record shows only two absences, one for personal illness and one for car trouble. She also was sent home one day with a fever. Recently, she indicated that her mother will soon be moving in with her to care for the children. Martha completed 11 years of school and has a weakness in basic math. Martha is a favorite with her work peers, and she makes a significant contribution to the general morale.

***

Performance Evaluation: Roger Clement

Name: *Roger Clement*

Position: *Baker*

Seniority: *Two years*

Biographical Information (for statistical purposes only):

Age:	25	Veteran:	*No*
Sex:	*M*	Marital Status:	*Married*
Ethnicity:	*Caucasian*	Children:	*Three*
			Roger, Jr., age 3;
			Ruthann, age 2;
			Ryan, age 1

	Low					High
Ability to work independently	1	2	(3)	4	5	6
Attendance	1	2	3	4	5	(6)
Attitude toward supervisors	1	2	3	4	(5)	6
Cooperation with coworkers	1	2	3	(4)	5	6
Decision making	1	2	(3)	4	5	6
Job-specific tasks	1	2	(3)	4	5	6
Productivity	1	2	(3)	4	5	6
Overall performance	1	3	4	(4)	6	6

(continued)

(continued)

Supervisor's comments (confidential): Roger is a vocational school graduate. His attendance has been perfect, but he has received marginal work-performance evaluations since he was hired. It seems that Roger is not as intelligent as other employees. When he is given assignments requiring no independent thinking, Roger does an excellent job and requires little supervision. He is unusually strong and shows an intense sense of devotion to the company and to me. In fact, one warning slip was received after he threatened an employee in the locker room who was complaining about management. Roger's wife is pregnant, and he works part-time as a gardener for the Assistant Restaurant Manager to earn extra money.

***

Termination Scoring Grid

Order of Termination

Names of Group Members	Your Score	Individuals in Your Assessment Group								Group Consensus
Shaquille										
Jessica										
Matthew										
Martha										
Roger										

***

Exercise 2 Running a Meeting Group

Category: Leadership

Introduction: Long-range planning and decision making are important tasks that leaders have to deal with on a daily basis.

- "Running a Meeting Group Exercise" brings the participants back to their workplace and enables them to role-play as a general manager. As general

manager, participants are asked to make a decision on resources allocation. This is a good exercise to put theories into practice.

Objective: Role-playing to encourage leadership in a meeting context

Number of participants: Groups of six

Time Frame: Ten minutes to review roles, 45 minutes for the meeting itself—30 minutes debriefing

Materials: Copies of role assignments

Procedure: Assign roles to each of the participants. Do not allow participants to see any other role description than their own. Allow about 5–10 minutes for players to familiarize themselves with their roles, at which point all six players convene at the "meeting." The meeting will be led by "Jan Cooper," the GM, and the ultimate goal is to determine how to allocate the $3 million among the different project options. Discussion of the process after the meeting should focus on persuasion, leadership styles, and group dynamics.

*** *

Roles:

Evan Edwards, General Manager—the five departmental directors that report to him are listed below

Britney Shears, Director of Operations—21 years with the company

Mary Tank-Mitchel, Director of Human Resources—16 years with the company

Washington Ervin, Director of Marketing—15 years with the company

Anthony Marc, Director of Food and Beverage—8 years with the company

Yu Tu, Controller—3 years with the company

Situation: The General Manager of the Pineapple Hotel, a mid-scale, full-service property in Anytown, USA, has been working with the executive committee of the hotel to prepare the budget for the next fiscal year. At the last meeting, revenue projections were established, so the next step is to estimate the capital expenditures for the next year. Each of the directors has a project they feel is crucial in the next year that will require significant capital investment. The General Manager has called the meeting to evaluate each of the projects and prioritize them in order, as to allot money to them. The Directors are expected to have prepared their "cases" for why their project is a top priority for the next year.

For the last several years the property has been experiencing financial difficulties. While these have not resulted in layoffs, there has been a severe restriction on wage increases and an absolute freeze on building alterations, travel to professional meetings, magazine subscriptions, and similar expenditures. Recently, you have heard that the company has begun to see a modest economic upturn.

Mary Tank-Mitchel's Role: As the Human Resources Director, you have been experiencing significant changes in your role in the hotel. As HR becomes more complex, more emphasis has been placed on quantifying all of your decisions in order to gain the GM's buy-in. While your financial skills are relatively advanced, you feel as though the department needs a technological facelift. This would include new computers with several very expensive software programs to serve the department's various functions, as well as significant amounts of new training to bring the department up to speed on the new technology and their changing role in the hotel. It would also include the development of a property-level Intranet to facilitate communications between employees and the management. Employees will be able to log into the Intranet on their breaks or before or after work to look at the status of their timecards for the period, change allocations to their profit-sharing plans, buy merchandise from a virtual "company store," and request time off or vacation hours. This is the newest trend in effectively managing human resources, and the increased technology will help you and your staff to have more time to concentrate on more strategic functions, rather than the previous emphasis on administration. *Project cost:* $650,000.

Anthony Marc's Role: As the Director of Food and Beverage, you have a large role in generating profits for the Pineapple Hotel. Between the kitchen, the banquet facilities, and the three other food and beverage outlets in the property, it takes experience and finesse to ensure smooth operations. As much as you believe the restaurant needs a facelift, there are bigger problems right now. During your last health inspection visit, it was discovered that several of the larger pieces of equipment in the kitchen did not pass code, and must be replaced in the next six months. Because of the urgency of the replacements, your budget for the current fiscal year will be significantly off, but you don't want this to affect your

(continued)

(continued)

ability to renovate the very-outdated dining room next year. You get the feeling, however, that the renovations will need to be put on hold because of the dent in your budget this year, despite how important
you believe the renovations will be to generating additional business. Revenues in this outlet used to be
the highest of all the food and beverage outlets, but have consistently declined over the last five years,
and you believe the condition of the facilities is to blame. *Project cost:* $1.2 million.

Washington Ervin's Role: You have been the Director of Marketing for the Pineapple Hotel for fifteen years.
In recent years, your budget has been adversely affected because the "urgency" for investment in your
projects was not viewed as highly as other departments. As a result, you're a little bitter this year, and plan
on not taking no for an answer. You want to put a great deal of money into a new advertising campaign to
boost sales for the meetings/conventions and rooms sales markets. In recent years the efforts have been
good, since you have such a great team working for you, but they have had to work with a very limited
budget, and feel this to be the cause of their not meeting sales quotas and revenue goals this year. You feel it
is unfair to demand such lofty goals of your sales managers and associates if you can't give them the
resources to do their job at such a high level. Because the revenues driven by your department are key to
the hotel's profitability, you feel that this investment is essential to the hotel's success and ability to return
profits to shareholders. You think that maybe a celebrity spotlight might be the key to the new ad campaign's
success, after all the market is competitive right now, and your property could use the added benefit of a
famous advocate. *Project cost:* $1.5 million (with the celebrity), $900,000 (without the celebrity).

Evan Edwards' Role: You are the General Manager of the Pineapple Hotel. You have good relationships with all of the executive team members, but notice every year that relations are strained around
budget allocation time. You have a pretty good idea of the projects that will be proposed at today's
meeting, but no idea of the cost of each. Things could get heated, as you realize how each director
views their project as most important. You have a *$3 million capital budget to work with* for the next
fiscal year. Which projects will you accept, which will you decline, and which will you request modification to a less costly estimate in order to accept? You sit and mull over the possibilities, stirring
your coffee, as you anxiously await the arrival of your executive committee to the meeting. They do
not know the hotel's budgetary constraint. You're not sure if you should wait to tell them until after
their proposals, or if you should lay it on the line from the onset so that those with excessive budgetary requests can trim down the cost before expecting their proposal to be approved.

Britney Shears' Role: You have been at the Pineapple Hotel since it's opening 21 years ago. You worked
up the ranks to the position you now hold, the Director of Operations. Because of your seniority, you
feel the GM should put extra thought into considering your proposal, but you also feel that the
operations departments are what make the hotel functional, so you see added incentive to put a lot of
investment in the operations. While none of your projects is particularly urgent, you would like to get
them going in the next fiscal year, because for the first time in ages you have the staff on hand to
complete them, without sacrificing operations in any other area. The low unemployment rate has really
hit the operations departments hard because of the high turnover. You've had to pay people a lot more to
get them in, and even then the retention rate in your departments (housekeeping, engineering, front
desk) is lower than the industry average. However in the last six months, through aggressive hiring
efforts, you've been able to build up your staff to the point where you can afford to put some of your
people on these key projects, but you need the money to do it. You believe that the extra challenge and
opportunity to develop people by putting them on these projects will improve your employee satisfaction ratings as well as your retention rate. The projects and estimates you have planned are as follows:

• Task and work area analysis and renovation for the housekeeping department (goal of which is to
  improve conditions for them, and hopefully their satisfaction and retention), estimate: **$500,000.**

(continued)

(continued)

- New information system for the front desk that would link all other departments to them for seamless service delivery, **$1.7 million.**
- Construction of a new workshop for the engineering department that would be built unattached to the hotel but close-by. This would also include some new equipment to replace the outdated and unsafe equipment currently being used. The purpose of the new workshop is to limit the noise, dust, and chemical "pollution" issues within the hotel, and to give them more space in which to work. The old engineering workshop is across from the kitchen, and is so cramped it is often hard to find room for materials and machinery, **$750,000.**

Yu Tu's Role: Since you became the Controller at the Pineapple Hotel three years ago, you've noticed that the hotel tends to utilize a top-down budgeting technique. This approach entails the setting of the total budget amount for large expenditures, then deciding which combination of projects will be best for the hotel while fitting within that budget. Some projects in the past have been put off indefinitely, even though you believe they are necessary, because they don't fit in the cost structure of the budget. You believe this approach is somewhat counterintuitive, as you think the better approach would be for managers to show the future value of the projects to the GM via cost/benefit and breakeven analysis. Using this approach, the project will be accepted if it offers potential returns above the breakeven, and can be shown as a necessity either to the guests or employees. You believe in the adage "you need to give a little to get a little." Your project proposition for this meeting is minimal compared to the others. You want to invest in a software program that will give managers the tools to perform such project value analysis easily with a step-by-step question-and-answer format. In addition you want to propose that next year the budget be determined more on long-term value and necessity, rather than merely budgetary fit. **Cost of program: $1,000.**

***

Exercise 3   Wheel of Experience

Category: Team Building

Objectives:

- To learn to use a team to help solve a problem
- To realize that members of a team all have individual skills and expertise that could be used to your advantage when solving a problem

Number of Participants: Between 4 and 16

Time Frame: 45 minutes to one hour, depending on the number of participants

Materials: Paper and pens

Procedure:

- Separate all participants into two groups. One group is composed of Hotel General Managers (GM), and other group consists of Front Desk Managers of a large hotel with more than 20 front desk agents.
- Have the two groups sit together in two lines facing each other, so that a front desk manager and hotel GM are facing each other.
- Explain to the whole group that the following exercise will be an experience exchange. An

experience exchange involves one person sharing their experiences about a particular problem or situation they have faced some time in the past. In this exercise, the front desk managers will be bringing real-life situations that they are facing back in their hotel to the general managers for their help, opinions, and experiences.

- The front desk manager group should now take one minute to write down a particular challenge that they are facing. The challenge should be phrased as, "The challenge at my front desk area is . . ."
- The front desk managers should now turn to the general managers facing them, and take one minute to explain the challenge. If it takes less than one minute, the GMs are free to ask any questions or clarifications, so that they are fully aware of the challenge being faced.
- The GMs should now take two minutes to respond to the challenge. They should phrase their response as, "In my experience . . ." If the GM does not have a particular experience that applies to the challenge, they should make this clear to the front desk manager.
- At the end of two minutes, the front desk managers should move to the seat next to them and present

the challenge to a different GM. This should take place until all of the GMs have seen all of the front desk managers.

- The front desk managers should write down the experiences shared with them by the GMs.
- Convene a 10-minute discussion where all participants are made aware that each of the GMs had different and helpful experiences to share, and that each was useful in some way to providing the best possible solution to the challenge.

Variations: This procedure is based on hospitality managers who work in hotel operations, using hotel front desk managers and general managers. The exercise can be easily adapted for use by any manager in the hospitality industry, for example,

- Restaurant Managers and Kitchen Managers
- Cruise Ship Hotel Directors and Cruise Directors
- Theme Park Director and Attractions Supervisors.

Exercise 4   Mini Cases

The following are situations that you are likely to encounter in your career. Read each situation carefully and state what you would do if you were the hotel manager. Consider the effective and the ineffective aspects of the possible courses of action that are open to you.

1. A group of your employees is standing around talking just before a staff meeting. One employee, who has his back to you and is unaware of your approach, refers to you using an uncomplimentary term. You overhear it, and as soon as he has said it the employee realizes you have heard it. What should you do?

2. You are new to the organization. You immediately perceive a lack of courtesy and respect among all employees. Is it wise to correct this situation? How would you go about correcting it?

3. One of your managers likes to be considered a popular person. As a consequence he rates all of his employees as "outstanding" on the performance evaluation form. You suspect that some of his employees do not deserve this high a rating. What do you do?

4. An employee has been promoted recently to a new position. It is now evident that he is not doing a good job, and the reason is just plain lack of capacity. Would you fire him, transfer him, demote him, or keep him on in the same position? Why?

5. As you are walking by, you overhear one of your managers giving wrong instructions to one of his employees. What do you do?

6. One of your managers resigns, feeling he can do better elsewhere. You do not really mind as you felt he was performing marginally at best. He asks you if he can give your name as a personal reference when obtaining another job. What do you do?

Endnotes

Alvesson, M. & Sveningsson, S. (2003). Managers doing leadership: The extra-ordinization of the mundane. *Human Relations, 56*(12), 1435–1460.

Badaracco, J. L., Jr. (1998). The discipline of building character. *Harvard Business Review, 76*(2), 115–125.

Bass, B. (1990). *Bass and Stodgill's Handbook of Leadership: Theory, Research and Managerial Applications.* Third Edition. New York: The Free Press.

Boyatzis, R. & Van Oosten, E. (2003). A leadership imperative: Building the emotionally intelligent organization. *Ivey Business Journal, 67*(2), 43–61.

Conger, J. & Ready, D. A. (2004). Rethinking leadership competencies. *Leader to Leader, 32*, 41–47.

Dessler, G. (1999). How to earn your employees' commitment. *Academy of Management Executive, 13*(2), 58–67.

Fairmont, (August 27, 2007). eConnect: Research & Resources from HSMAI Foundation.

Ferguson, D. & Berger, F. (1984). Restaurant managers: What do they really do? *Cornell Hotel and Restaurant Quarterly, 25*(1), 27–38.

Fulmer, R. (1997). The evolving paradigm of leadership development. *Organizational Dynamics, 25*(2), 59–72.

Gregor, K. & Peterson, J. S. (2000). Leadership profiles for the new millenium. *Cornell Hotel and Restaurant Administration Quarterly, 41*, 16.

Harrison, J., Chang, E., Gauthier, C., & Joerchel, T. (2005). Exporting a North American concept to Asia: Starbucks in China. *Cornell Hotel and Restaurant Administration Quarterlym, 46*(2), 275–284.

Hochwarth, P. (February 2007). In this corner: Food fight. *Restaurant Hospitality, 91*(2), 54.

Howell, J. & Avolio, B. (1992). The ethics of charismatic leadership: Submission or liberation? *The Academy of Management Executive*, *6*(2), 43–54.

Kets de Vries, M. (1994). The leadership mystique. *The Academy of Management Executive*, *8*(3), 73–92.

Kolp, A. & Rea, P. (2006). *Leading with Integrity: Character-Based Leadership*. Cincinnati, OH: Atomicdog Publishing.

Lussier, R., & Achua, C. (2001). *Leadership: Theory, Application, Skill Development*. Cincinnati, OH: Southwestern College Publications.

May, D., Chan, A., Hodges, T., & Avolio, B. (2003). Developing the moral component of authentic leadership. *Organizational Dynamics, 32*(3), 247–260.

O'Toole, J. (1999). *Leadership A to Z: A Guide for the Appropriately Ambitious*. San Francisco: Jossey-Bass.

Ruggless, R. (May 22, 2006). Mark's American cuisine. *Nation's Restaurant News*, *40*(21), 150.

Sankar, Y. (2003). Character not charisma is the critical measures of leadership excellence. *Journal of Leadership & Organizational Studies*, *9*(4), 45.

Schultz, H. & Yang, D. (1997) *Pour Your Heart into it: How Starbucks Built a Company One Cup at a Time*. New York: Hyperion. p. 127.

Simons, T. (2002a). Behavioral integrity: The perceived alignment between managers' words and deeds as a research focus. *Organizational Science*, *13*(1), 18–35.

Simons, T. (2002b). The high cost of lost trust. *Harvard Business Review*, *80*(9), 18–19.

Storr, L. (2004). Leading with integrity: A qualitative research study. *Journal of Health Organization and Management*, *18*(6), 415–417.

Tracey, J. B. & Hinkin, T. (1994). Transformational leaders in the hospitality industry. *Cornell Hotel and Restaurant Administration Quarterly*, *35*(2), 18.

Waterman, R. H. & Peters, T. J. (1988). *In Search of Excellence*. New York: Warner Books.

Watkins, E. (March 15, 2007). The Marshall Plan. *Lodging Hospitality*, *63*(4), 50.

Yammarino, F., Dansereau, F., & Kennedy, C. (2001). Viewing leadership through an elephant's eye: A multidimensional approach to leadership. *Organizational Dynamics*, 149–163.

Yukl, G. A. (1994). *Leadership in Organizations*. Third Edition. Englewood Cliffs, NJ: Prentice Hall.

15

ICEBREAKERS AND CLOSERS

Icebreakers and closers help to initiate and conclude group sessions. These exercises can help you frame group interaction in a positive way that promotes interaction among the members of the group and helps them feel comfortable with one another.

ICEBREAKERS

Icebreakers are an excellent way to bring a group of strangers together quickly through group interaction and bonding. They build trust and confidence among group members in a jovial way.

Exercises

Exercise 1   Namesake

Category: Icebreaker

Objectives:

- To help members of a newly formed group to learn others' names
- To give participants the chance to consider the meaning of their own names

Number of Participants: Up to 20

Time Frame: One minute per person

Materials: None

Procedure:

1. Begin by explaining that everyone has a way of describing their name. The clarification is often helpful to others as they try to recall your name.
2. The facilitator randomly chooses a person in the group to start.
3. Have members explain how they were given their names and then state the name they wish they had been given and why.

Exercise 2   Grandmother's Trunk

Category: Icebreaker

Objective: To help group members learn the names of other members in their group

Number of Participants: Up to 40

Time Frame: Up to 1 minute per participant

Materials: None

Procedure:

1. Read participants the following scenario: I packed my grandmother's trunk and in it I put three items:

- The first item must be a food that starts with the first letter of their name.
- The second item must be an article of clothing that starts with the first letter of their name.
- The third item must be an animal whose name starts with the first letter of their name.

2. Have each participant say what they decided to put in their grandmother's trunk.

Exercise 3   A Band of Singers

Category: Icebreaker

Objective: To encourage participants to get acquainted using familiar songs

Number of Participants: Up to 32

Time Frame: 15–20 minutes

Materials: Index cards

Procedure:

1. As the participants arrive, give them an index card with one of four songs written on it. (The facilitator should choose four nursery rhymes or other well-known songs.)
2. Have the participants begin singing the song that they were given.
3. Tell each participant to find the other participants in the group that are singing the same song.
4. Have participants introduce themselves to the other people who were singing the same song they were.
5. When everyone has arrived, have each same-song group get up in front of the class, sing their song, and introduce themselves to the everyone.

Exercise 4   Signature Hunt

Category: Icebreaker

Objective: To encourage participants to get acquainted by having to talk to all other members of the group to complete a common task

Number of Participants: Up to 40

Time Frame: 15 minutes

Materials: Xeroxed handout with signature lines and 20 random facts (see suggestions below)

Procedure:

1. At the beginning of each session it is good to start with an exercise that introduces everyone and helps participants learn the names of the people in their group. Signature hunt is an excellent icebreaker for this purpose.

2. Hand out signature sheets to each participant of the group.
3. Have participants circulate around the room and search for other group members who can sign a line that pertains to them. One person may sign up to two lines.
4. The first participant to have all signatures completed is the winner.
5. Possible items that can be included in the signature hunt are as follows:

_____ Has seen the Great Wall of China

_____ Loves to ski

_____ Plays the guitar

_____ Is an excellent cook

_____ Loves Bruce Springsteen and the E Street Band

_____ Drives a BMW or Lexus or Mercedes-Benz

_____ Is a good dancer

_____ Has been mountain biking

_____ Likes to go fishing

_____ Is an avid reader of the *Wall Street Journal*

_____ Has been to Disney world . . . and enjoyed it!

_____ Has completed a marathon

_____ Has been on the Atkins diet

_____ Prefers Coke to Pepsi

_____ Has actually picked their own strawberries . . . not at the grocery store.

_____ Has stayed at a Four Seasons hotel

_____ Has two or more siblings

_____ Ate pizza for lunch or dinner yesterday

_____ Had a pet cat as a child

_____ Loves country music

Exercise 5   I Can Help You

Category: Icebreaker

Objectives:

• To get participants acquainted with one another
• To help participants realize that using other people as a resource can be beneficial
• To show participants the resources that their group members have to offer

Number of Participants: Any number

Time Frame: 30 minutes

Materials:

1. One yellow Post-it note per participant.
2. Three white Post-it notes per participant.
3. One empty wall, hallway, or chalkboard for each group.

Procedure:

1. Divide participants into groups with about 10–15 people in each group.
2. Provide each group a large space, such as a blank wall, chalkboard, or stretch of hallway.
3. Have participants write down on their yellow Post-it one thing that they would like to get more information about. For example, a participant may want to know how to get a discount plane ticket to New York City.

4. When everyone has finished, have the members of each group place their Post-it on the blank wall.
5. Have each participant read the Post-it notes that their group members have placed on the wall. After reading these, each of them should use his or her three white Post-it notes to write down a suggested answer/solution to one of the inquiries. (e.g., if someone wanted information on how to get discount plane tickets to New York City, a participant may write on one of the Post-it notes that www.priceline.com offers cheap plane tickets.)
6. Have the members go around and verbally ask their group the question they wrote on the yellow Post-it. The members who addressed that question on a white Post-it should give the information they have to the person who asked the question and place the white Post-it under the respective yellow Post-it on the wall.
7. After everyone's question/inquiry has been addressed within the group, have each participant pick up their yellow Post-it and the white Post-it notes underneath that answer their question.
8. Lead a discussion with participants about this exercise, asking the following questions:
   • Did everyone get at least one answer/solution to their inquiry (even the outrageous ones)?
   • Were group members more or less resourceful than what each participant expected?

Exercise 6   Networking

Category: Icebreaker

Objectives:

- To help participants meet one another
- To add energy to a workshop

Uses: The activity is especially useful after lunch, after a break, or near the end of a day to perk up a group.

Number of Participants: Any number

Time Frame: 15–20 minutes

Materials:

1. A watch.
2. Large Post-it notes (one per person).

Procedure:

1. As participants arrive, have them pick up one Post-it.
2. Tell participants to write two things on their Post-it about themselves. One thing should be true and the other should be false.
3. Once participants have finished writing the two things on their Post-it, have someone volunteer to go first. That participant should read both items on the Post-it to the other participants. Have the group vote on which item is true and which item is false.

Exercise 7   Who Am I?

Category: Icebreaker

Objectives:

- To help participants meet one another
- To add energy to a workshop

Uses: The activity is especially useful after lunch, after a break, or near the end of a day to perk up a group.

Number of Participants: Any number

Time Frame: 15–20 minutes

Materials:

1. One writing utensil per participant.
2. Index cards.

Procedure:

1. Choose one person to be the facilitator.
2. Have each participant write down one interesting, embarrassing, or outrageous fact about themselves on an index card and hand it to the facilitator.
3. Have the facilitator read each fact aloud and let the group come to a consensus about who they feel the fact belongs to.
4. Have the facilitator read each fact and announce the fact's true owner.

CLOSERS

It is good to end a teaching/training session in an "up" way, something that will have the participants laughing and feeling good about themselves and the sessions or session. A closer should not be just about having fun, it should also relate to the session, and would optimally extract learnings from the training. Providing feedback is one way to close a group session, while finishing the session with humor, energy, and creativity is another.

Exercises

Exercise 1   Positive Folks

Category: Closer

Objective: To conclude the group process through positive feedback

Number of Participants: 3–30.

Time Frame: About two minutes per participant

Materials: None.

Procedure:

- Move the chairs around and form a circle.
- Someone volunteers to be the first to receive feedback. He or she sits in the chair that has been placed by the facilitator in the middle of the circle. Three people should give behavioral feedback to the participant. An example of behavioral feedback is: "When I worked on _____ exercise with you, I found that you did _____ and _____. Your actions were beneficial because _____."

The participant leaves the seat after the three participants have given them positive feedback, after which the next person will sit and receive feedback.

Exercise 2   The Web

Category: Closer

Objective:

- To bring closure to a training session
- To congratulate, compliment, and recognize individual team members for their contributions

Special Requirements:

1. Training group must have 15 or more participants.
2. Activity is best used after a multiple-day training session.

Time Frame: Approximately 30 minutes

Material: One large ball of yarn.

Procedure:

1. Organize the individuals in the group to stand in a circle. Give one member the ball of yarn.
2. Tell the group member with the yarn to pick someone else out of the group that has really had a positive effect on him or her during the training session. The person with the yarn should say one reason why the chosen individual has had a positive effect on him or her. Once the person with the yarn is finished with his or her comment, the ball of yarn should be thrown to the chosen person. Whoever is throwing the yarn must remember to hold on to a piece of the string when he or she throws it.
3. The person receiving the ball of yarn repeats the process until everyone in the group gets the ball of yarn. Once an individual group member has had the yarn thrown to him or her, he or she may not have it thrown to them again.
4. After a while, a web of yarn will form in the middle of the group. After everyone has the ball thrown to him or her, the facilitator can comment on the team-building and bonding that occurred throughout the training session(s), comparing the bond that was created to the web that is connecting every group member.

Exercise 3   Commercial

Category: Closer

Objective: To reflect on the key lessons in an enjoyable format

Number of Participants: Up to 5 per group.

Time Frame: 15 minutes preparation, up to 3 minutes for each group's presentation

Materials: Props and materials in a classroom.

Procedure:

1. Divide participants into four groups.
2. Each group goes to a corner of the room and develops a commercial that portrays some of the concepts learned throughout the seminar/lecture.
3. The commercial should not exceed three minutes.
4. Participants may sing, dance, and use props.
5. The groups take turns acting out their commercial. Everyone must participate.
6. When a group is presenting their commercial, the other participants should take notes about the lessons that they have learned.

Exercise 4   I Have Grown!

Category: Closer

Objective: To acknowledge and encourage participants who demonstrated a positive attitude throughout the course

Number of Participants: Up to 40

Time Frame: Three minutes preparation; one minute per pair to share

Materials: None

Procedure:

1. Have participants break into pairs.
2. Each person spends three minutes describing how he or she developed during the session to his or her partner.
3. Each participant share with the rest of the class how their partner developed.

INDEX